FREE THE MARKET!

FREE

the

MARKET!

WHY ONLY GOVERNMENT CAN KEEP
THE MARKETPLACE COMPETITIVE

Gary L. Reback

PORTFOLIO

Portfolio
Published by the Penguin Group
Penguin Group (USA) Inc., 375 Hudson Street, New York, New York 10014, U.S.A. • Penguin Group
(Canada), 90 Eglinton Avenue East, Suite 700, Toronto, Ontario, Canada M4P 2Y3 (a division of Pearson Penguin Canada Inc.) • Penguin Books Ltd, 80 Strand, London WC2R 0RL, England • Penguin
Ireland, 25 St Stephen's Green, Dublin 2, Ireland (a division of Penguin Books Ltd) • Penguin Books
Australia Ltd, 250 Camberwell Road, Camberwell, Victoria 3124, Australia (a division of Pearson Australia Group Pty Ltd) • Penguin Books India Pvt Ltd, 11 Community Centre, Panschsheel Park, New
Delhi - 110 017, India • Penguin Group (NZ), 67 Apollo Drive, Rosedale, North Shore 0632, New Zealand (a division of Pearson New Zealand Ltd) • Penguin Books (South Africa) (Pty) Ltd, 24 Sturdee
Avenue, Rosebank, Johannesburg 2196, South Africa

Penguin Books Ltd, Registered Offices:
80 Strand, London WC2R 0RL, England

First published in 2009 by Portfolio,
a member of Penguin Group (USA) Inc.

1   3   5   7   9   10   8   6   4   2

Library of Congress Cataloging-in-Publication Data
Reback, Gary L.
Free the market! : why only government can keep the marketplace competitive / Gary L. Reback.
p.   cm.
Includes index.
ISBN 978-1-59184-246-0
1. Trade regulation—United States. 2. Competition—United States. I. Title.
HD3616.U47R136 2009
381.30973—dc22   2008046689

Printed in the United States of America
Set in Adobe Garamond Pro
Designed by Daniel Lagin

For Kathy

It will remind everyone—some conservatives painfully—that a mature capitalist economy is a government project. A properly functioning free market system does not spring spontaneously from society's soil as dandelions spring from suburban lawns. Rather, it is a complex creation of laws and mores.

—George Will, on the collapse of Enron

Contents

FREE THE MARKET!

Introduction

With the stock market in turmoil, the credit markets disintegrating, and the nation's economy headed toward apocalypse, a grim-faced President George W. Bush stood before reporters in the Rose Garden, trying to avert disaster. Flanked by the Treasury secretary, the Federal Reserve chairman, and the head of the Securities and Exchange Commission, Bush said he would deal with the crisis by asking Congress to approve the federal government's purchase of privately held bad debt at a price widely estimated to exceed $1 trillion. The root of the crisis, according to experts, lay in the misuse of complicated financial instruments—credit-default swaps, subprime investments, and mortgage-backed securities—producing vast financial portfolios of "toxic assets."

"Toxic assets" didn't fell the nation's economy. A toxic philosophy did. Thousands of people lost their homes, tens of thousands their jobs, and even more their retirement savings because of a stupefyingly naive belief in markets that self-regulate with minimal government supervision.

For more than a decade, Federal Reserve Chairman Alan Greenspan resisted increased government rule making, instead glorifying "private market discipline" as the "most effective form of regulation." "Lenders are now able to quite efficiently judge the risk posed by individual [loan] applicants," he claimed, "and to price that risk appropriately." He said the market would correct any errors without government intrusion by "counterparty supervision," the notion that financial institutions would monitor and restrain their trading partners out of self-interest. None of it worked.

Greenspan "overdosed on Ayn Rand," observed Charles Munger, Warren Buffett's longtime partner.

The financial sector's meltdown could hardly have come as a surprise. By September 2008, the pervasive policy of blind faith in market self-regulation had already engendered multiple catastrophes. After food contamination problems produced fatal salmonella outbreaks in the spring of 2007, official records revealed that the Food and Drug Administration, overwhelmed by industry growth, had relied on food producers to police themselves. Even more widespread salmonella outbreaks the following year showed that the agency still lacked the money and resources to properly monitor the industry.

When traffic congestion brought the nation's air transport system to the brink of collapse in the fall of 2007, the Federal Aviation Administration chief advised air carriers to address the problem voluntarily. Two weeks later, with no voluntary solution in sight, President Bush directed his deputies to devise a plan for reducing airline delays. "We understand there's a problem," Bush said. "And we're going to address the problem." The administration never really had to. The brutal economic conditions caused by inattention to financial regulation rendered the administration's passing attention to air traffic congestion far less pressing.

Even when facing the nation's imminent financial demise, Bush found it difficult to acknowledge a role for the government. "Our system of free enterprise rests on the conviction that the federal government should interfere in the marketplace only when necessary," he said. He then proposed the largest government bailout since the Great Depression. More timely and more measured intervention—before it became "necessary"—would surely have prevented the extinction of venerable financial institutions, the loss of countless jobs, and the destruction of public confidence.

While protecting the public interest in some industries requires powerful oversight commissions and close scrutiny of commercial activity, most markets neither require nor profit from extensive government regulation. Free and open competition often protects the public far better, producing higher quality products at lower prices. But the benefits of free market competition do not come free. Competition must be nurtured and protected by the government, as Americans first discovered more than a century ago, in a turbulent time driven by technological change, an era not unlike our own.

Starting in the late nineteenth century, in response to the rise of the financiers and oil companies, Congress enacted by overwhelming majorities a series of statutes—called antitrust laws—intended to govern the interactions between a business, on one hand, and its competitors and customers, on the other. The seminal notion of antitrust policy was that the national government had a role to play in the relationship between business and the rest of society. The government was to safeguard the free enterprise system from unfettered corporate power. Over many decades, antitrust enforcement rather than outright regulation emerged as the preferred approach to government oversight.

The relatively few heavily regulated markets aside, antitrust law sets the rules of competition in a free market economy. These rules affect just about every aspect of modern life, from the price of clothing to the availability of airline seats, from the selection of books at the local bookstore to the variety of music on the radio. Antitrust policy fosters the development of new computer products, telecommunication services, Internet technologies, and lifesaving pharmaceuticals.

The developed world eventually came to embrace the uniquely American legal commitment to free market competition. The countries of the European Union now use their own antitrust laws to make their industries more competitive in world markets. The Japanese and the Koreans enforce their antitrust laws to prevent dominant companies from excluding competitors. Last year, the People's Republic of China, a Communist country with a centrally planned economy on the road to liberalization, adopted a comprehensive set of antitrust laws to hasten the transition to capitalism. But in the United States, the same misplaced reliance on self-policing, self-correcting markets that gutted effective regulation also undermined antitrust enforcement.

Today's antitrust policies can be traced to a group of conservative law professors and economists who argued that interference with the unfettered operation of the free market usually ends up hurting consumers and damaging the competitive process. Proponents of the Chicago School (named for the university at which many leading economists of the 1960s did their research) claimed that more limited antitrust rules based on sound economic reasoning encourage the free market to produce the most goods and services from available resources.

President Reagan appointed William F. Baxter to head the Antitrust Division in 1981. Through a series of bold initiatives, Baxter imposed the will of the Chicago School on government policy makers, curtailing antitrust enforcement and adopting more business-friendly procedures. The Chicago School notion that the free market works best when the government leaves it alone has dominated antitrust doctrine and enforcement ever since.

That philosophy might have been valid, to some extent, in the old smokestack industries that were important in the mid-twentieth century. Many of Baxter's early reforms were both welcome and productive. But the high tech industries that are important to the new economy manifest a very different set of economic characteristics. Dominant firms can more easily manipulate these markets. And natural forces make the strong even stronger.

As the economy grew more complex and economic analysis became more sophisticated, Chicago School adherents continued to rely heavily on laissez-faire doctrine from the earlier time of simpler economies. Chicago School enforcement strategy focused increasingly on what the government should not do rather than what it should. Reticence gave way to retrenchment. Antitrust enforcement withered in both rust bowl industries and high technology markets.

In our modern economy, Chicago School policies only serve to damage free market capitalism (and consumers specifically) by entrenching incumbents, retarding innovation, and making life miserable for entrepreneurs. Yet the Chicago School has been difficult to dislodge, notwithstanding its questionable record of protecting consumer welfare, because it is much more than just an enforcement policy. It is what one conservative economist called a "system of belief." The influence of the Chicago School is felt on both liberals and conservatives and can be seen in *New Yorker* articles as well as *Wall Street Journal* editorials. The Chicago School approach is what antitrust law professors teach their students at the nation's leading law schools. Chicago School thinking factors prominently into the scholarship of industrial organization professors in university economics departments. The federal judiciary has fallen deeply in thrall to the Chicago School.

All the while, unremedied anticompetitive conduct forestalls innovation, raises prices to the American public, and limits consumer choice for all kinds of vital goods and services. Mergers were rarely investigated during the Bush administration, much less opposed by the government. During the last two years of the administration, the government raised no substantial objection to the merger of the two leading suppliers of home appliances, or to the combination of the nation's two largest hog producers. Nor did it object to the consolidation into two companies of five of the nation's leading telecommunication providers, or to the acquisition that combined the nation's two largest financial exchanges for futures and options. In each case, protests by consumer groups, competitors, and even customers of the merging companies were dismissed out of hand.

Other types of anticompetitive conduct run no greater risk of government rebuke. Consumer groups and the Federal Trade Commission brought suit under the antitrust laws to prevent brand name drug producers from maintaining high prices by paying generic manufacturers not to compete. But the Bush Justice Department persuaded the Supreme Court not to review lower court decisions that threw the cases out. The Justice Department even called on the Supreme Court to adopt legal rules that shelter dominant firms from monopolization claims.

The disastrous effects of Chicago School antitrust policy may be somewhat less visible to the public than the spectacular calamities from regulatory inattention, but they are no less toxic. Our nation has only recently come to grips with the occasional yet pressing need for regulation. Now our policy makers must reject the outmoded Chicago regime in favor of more modern and beneficial policies or risk even more pervasive damage to the nation's economy.

PART ONE

PROTECTING COMPETITION

CHAPTER 1

Beyond the Robber Barons

Antitrust was born of the excesses of the robber barons. The American economy grew at an unprecedented, almost alarming rate in the decades after the Civil War. Power-driven machinery and new production techniques spurred rapid industrialization. Employment opportunities attracted more of the nation's population to cities that were connected to each other by new rail and communications networks. Capital markets formed, permitting the growth of large corporations. These companies built enormous manufacturing and distribution operations to capture scale economies. Between 1850 and 1910, the average manufacturing plant increased its payroll by a multiple of seven and the dollar value of its output more than nineteenfold.

The lure of high profits and the easy availability of capital attracted swarms of entrepreneurs into nascent industries. Few of the newly minted industrialists had business experience of any kind, much less experience in the management of high growth companies. As markets matured and growth rates declined, chronic overcapacity and relentless competition forced prices lower and lower. Supply did not adjust easily to demand. Sunk costs from initial investments were usually financed by bank loans. Entrepreneurs found that they could pay the interest on their debt by operating at a loss. They continued production, more or less unabated, driving prices even lower. Business insolvencies multiplied. Workers lost their jobs. By 1877, 18 percent of all railroad track was in the hands of receivers, and an even larger percentage of railroad bonds were in default.

Oil was first commercially pumped from a well in Titusville, Pennsylvania, in 1859. Oil fueled the growth of the industrial economy. It could be refined into kerosene, a cheap and safe luminant for people's homes. Oil could also be used for heating and cooking and was a better lubricant than lard for greasing the gears of most engines.

John D. Rockefeller, the son of a confidence man, invested in his first Cleveland refinery in 1863. Cleveland was a rail hub with a port on Lake Erie located close to the oil fields of western Pennsylvania. Using borrowed capital, Rockefeller merged five refineries into a single company, which he subsequently reorganized as Standard Oil of Ohio. Standard's refining capacity was larger than the next three refineries combined, permitting Rockefeller to secure concessions from railroads by providing a steady volume of freight. Rockefeller intended to protect his business from what he saw as "destructive price cutting" and "ruinous competition."

In 1871, Rockefeller struck a deal with the railroads that transported his oil. He agreed not to ship oil on other railroads. In return, the railroads agreed to raise shipping rates for oil, and to rebate to Rockefeller not only a percentage of his own freight costs, but a percentage of the freight fees paid by his competitors who were not members of the cartel. In addition, the railroads agreed to provide Rockefeller with information about the prices charged by other refiners, so he could undersell them without leaving money on the table. Rockefeller used the threat of the railroad cartel's increased freight rates to force his Cleveland refinery competitors to sell out to him at prices equivalent to roughly a quarter of their original construction costs. By March 1872, Rockefeller had taken over twenty-two of the twenty-six refineries in Cleveland.

Rockefeller then began to replicate the techniques he used in Cleveland to force competitors in other refining centers to sell out to him. He bullied railroads into aiding his scheme by threatening to delay the shipment of lubricating oil they needed to run their trains. When higher transportation charges were insufficient to make refinery competitors succumb, Rockefeller blocked the competitors' access to customers by forcing petroleum distributors and even local grocers and hardware merchants to sell only Standard's products. If merchants refused, Standard threatened to open its own general stores or even to sell petroleum door to door. By 1877, Rockefeller controlled the oil markets of Cleveland, Philadelphia, Pittsburgh, Baltimore, and West Virginia.

Most Americans knew little of Rockefeller's power over them until Henry Demarest Lloyd, the chief editorial writer of the *Chicago Tribune*, published a sixteen-page article, "The Story of a Great Monopoly," in the March 1881 issue of the *Atlantic Monthly*. "We use more kerosene lamps than Bibles," Lloyd explained. Yet "very few of the forty millions of people in the United States who burn kerosene know that its production, manufacture, and export, its price at home and abroad, have been controlled for years by a single corporation—the Standard Oil Company."

Lloyd brought home to *Atlantic*'s readers the costs of monopolization. "People who burn kerosene are paying the Standard Oil Company a tax on every gallon amounting to several times its original cost to that concern," he wrote. Lloyd backed up his arguments with detailed calculations. Starting with the price of crude oil at the well, Lloyd meticulously added the costs of transportation, refining, and barreling to calculate a total cost to Standard of 11 cents a gallon for kerosene, as delivered to Chicago. Standard charged 19¾ cents a gallon. "There is a tax on the public of eight and three-fourths cents," Lloyd concluded. "A family that uses a gallon of kerosene a day pays a yearly tribute to Standard of $32," an enormous amount in those days.

Lloyd's account captured the public's attention. The *Atlantic* published seven editions of its March issue. Lloyd's article was reprinted extensively, both in the United States and abroad.

Rockefeller ignored the rising tide of public indignation. When he could not get outright ownership of the entire market, he tried to eliminate overproduction by organizing an industry-wide cartel. His initiative failed. Some producers refused to restrict their own production. Others joined the cartel but cheated on quotas. Cartels in other industries also failed as new competitors entered the market and poorer cartel members found ways to avoid restrictive agreements. Even when Rockefeller was able to buy controlling interests in competitors, Standard Oil remained a federation of companies with many autonomous managers. Coordination to maintain high price levels was difficult.

A lawyer in Standard Oil's legal department came up with a solution.

He set up a "trust," the common legal structure giving one person, a "trustee," the power to make decisions for others. In 1882, the principal shareholders of the key companies in the oil industry assigned their stock to a board of nine trustees, selected by Rockefeller. The trustees could vote the stock as they wished. They controlled all the properties of the various Standard Oil affiliates and could make price and output decisions for all of the constituent companies. The profits of all the companies were sent to the trustees, who distributed dividends to the companies that had handed over their stock.

The trust arrangement enabled competitors in an industry to operate as a highly disciplined monopoly. The trustees could order a constituent company to shut down a plant if ample market supply threatened to erode high price levels. The shareholders of the company would still receive their proportional percentage of industry profits. The Standard Oil Trust was an enormous financial success for its members. The Distillers and Cattle Feeders' Trust (more commonly known as the Whiskey Trust) and the Sugar Trust copied Standard's form. Other industries followed, including steel, copper, rubber, and tobacco. Sometimes the combinations adopted other legal forms, such as holding companies, companies that controlled other companies by holding their stock. The effects were always the same— restricted production and higher consumer prices.

Lloyd wrote a second article, "The Lords of Industry," to explain how collusion among competitors hurt consumers the same way monopoly did. Lloyd claimed that in just about every market in the country, competitors had organized into combinations of one form or another, dedicated to raising prices by reducing output—"a war against plenty."

Lloyd gave many examples: the National Burial Case Association, which took secret action to keep prices up and keep the number of coffins down, "lest mortality should be discouraged"; the Western Anthracite Coal Association, dedicated to preventing production of "too much of the raw material of warmth"; the Pulp Handle Association, which set the price of milk by agreement; the pool of thirteen companies that united to "prevent the calamity of too much iron pipe." The price of redwood, Lloyd revealed, was fixed by the Redwood Manufacturers' Association, just as the price of pine was fixed by the Pine Manufacturers' Association. "Lords of industry are acquiring the power to pool the profits of scarcity and to decree famine," he wrote.

Faced with business combinations that controlled the supply and set the prices of most basic agricultural inputs—from fertilizer to financing—farmers began to organize politically. They campaigned for state laws to regulate railroads and grain elevator operators.

The journalists and politicians who championed the interests of ordinary American consumers, on the other hand, looked directly to the free market for a capitalist solution to capitalism's shortcomings. They sought to guarantee better products at reasonable prices by demanding that companies compete against each other. Competition, they believed, would check the power of a few dominant corporations without curbing overall economic growth. Competition would provide opportunity to entrepreneurs and usher new inventions to market.

Americans conscripted their government in the movement to guarantee free market competition. Competition produced an abundant supply of products at low prices. Big businesses choked off competition by running competitors out of the market or by conspiring with them. So, Americans demanded laws to prohibit monopoly and conspiracies to restrain trade. People called the new program to harness the productive power of free market competition "anti-trust," a reference to Rockefeller's scheme.

Politicians responded to the public outcry. Bills against the trusts were introduced in the House and Senate in early 1898. Seven parties campaigned in the presidential election later that year. All seven incorporated antimonopoly positions into their political platforms. The Republicans, the Democrats, and the two other leading parties expressly declared against the trust form of business organization. The summer following publication of the party platforms, Senator John Sherman of Ohio introduced an antitrust bill, one of many proposed in Congress. Sherman's bill was amended extensively and debated in the Senate in January and February 1889.

In his first message to Congress in December 1889, President Benjamin Harrison urged "earnest attention" to "the restraint of those combinations of capital commonly called 'trusts.' . . . They are dangerous conspiracies against the public good and should be made the subject of prohibitory and even penal legislation." The following day, Senator

Sherman introduced his antitrust legislation for a second time. As before, his proposal was amended repeatedly and debated exhaustively over a four-month period. During the debates, Standard Oil was frequently invoked to justify the need for national legislation. Senator Sherman's proposal passed both Houses with only a single dissenting vote, and was signed into law on July 2, 1890.

The Sherman Act reflected the public's concern with restraints of trade and monopolies, but stated only the general legislative intent, leaving for the courts the precise balancing of benefits and costs from restrictive business practices in specific situations:

Section 1. Every contract, combination in the form of trust or otherwise, or conspiracy, in restraint of trade or commerce among the several States, or with foreign nations, is declared to be illegal.

Section 2. Every person who shall monopolize, or attempt to monopolize, or combine or conspire with any other person or persons, to monopolize any part of the trade or commerce among the several States, or with foreign nations, shall be deemed guilty of a felony.

Once enacted, the Sherman Act was all but ignored. The few court decisions construing the act focused on whether the statutes should be read literally to prohibit all restraints on trade, or to prohibit only those that were unreasonable in light of circumstances. Early Supreme Court decisions held that the Sherman Act flatly prohibited cartel price-fixing, without regard to whether the fixed prices were reasonable. Overall, Sherman Act enforcement was inconsequential. "For many years," wrote Rockefeller biographer Ron Chernow, "the Sherman Act was a dead letter, and big business went on as usual."

Did it ever. In 1898, there were twenty multimillion-dollar trusts. By 1901, there were 185. In 1902 alone, sixty-three new trusts were capitalized. An astounding 65 percent of the national wealth was attributable to the trusts, even before the formation by J. P. Morgan of U.S. Steel, the first billion-dollar corporation in America. The Sherman Act by itself accomplished nothing. Someone would have to enforce the law in order to change business behavior.

Before blogs and nationally syndicated talk radio, the print media shaped public opinion. In 1902, *McClure's*, the nation's most influential magazine, published an exposé of Standard Oil's business practices written by Ida Tarbell, who had already produced acclaimed biographies of Lincoln and Napoleon for the magazine. Originally intended as a three-part series, Tarbell's account grew to nineteen installments. Standard, by that time, was no longer a trust, having been compelled to dissolve by the Supreme Court of Ohio earlier in the year. The company reorganized in New Jersey as a holding company that marketed 84 percent of all petroleum products sold in the United States.

Tarbell grew up in the oil region of northwestern Pennsylvania, the daughter of one of the independent refiners ruined by Rockefeller in the 1870s. She spent almost two years exhaustively researching government records, court testimony, and news reports to prepare her series. She delivered her account in a tone of disgust, chronicling Rockefeller's unethical tactics—the "hard dealing," the "sly tricks," the "special privileges"—with unmistakable sympathy for the independent oil producers.

Tarbell's articles described events she had personally witnessed. She explained how Rockefeller would "crush men who are pursuing legitimate trade," reducing them, their families and the entire region to "hopelessness." When she wrote of the "injustice of restraint of trade" and the "dangers of monopoly," she meant the effect of Rockefeller's conduct on his smaller competitors and on the nation's moral conscience.

Tarbell compiled all of the installments into a book, *The History of the Standard Oil Company*, that she had published in 1904. Almost a hundred years later, the *New York Times* listed the book as number five among the top hundred works of twentieth-century journalism. Historian Daniel Yergin called it the "most important business book ever written."

While the public sympathy Tarbell generated for the plight of Rockefeller's smaller competitors invigorated antitrust enforcement, it also highlighted an underlying tension in antitrust doctrine that had gone unresolved since the agitation that originally produced the Sherman Act. What does it mean for the antitrust law to protect "competition"? Rockefeller claimed that Standard Oil's conduct during the first twenty years of the company's operations actually made the price of kerosene cheaper for consumers by lowering the costs of production and distribution. The very same tactics ran smaller, arguably less efficient competitors out of business. When interests conflict, does the antitrust law protect competitors or does it protect consumers? Can antitrust fulfill a mission of protecting the process of competition without protecting small competitors?

Among *McClure's* three hundred thousand readers was Theodore Roosevelt, the president of the United States. Roosevelt was elected vice president in 1900 on the Republican ticket headed by William McKinley, a man widely perceived as an advocate for the trusts. Roosevelt succeeded to the presidency on McKinley's assassination in 1901. Roosevelt's reputation as a reformer worried the business community, and Roosevelt evidenced in private correspondence and public speech a personal revulsion to the excesses of the new industrial class. But he was a pragmatist, not a radical. He recognized the modern corporation as a vehicle for increased productivity and prosperity, and he accepted industrial concentration to exploit economies of scale.

Roosevelt wanted to secure the cost savings of more efficient operations, so he distinguished among large corporations based on conduct, not size. Trusts that offered consumers fair prices would be tolerated. Those that gouged consumers would be brought to heel. Roosevelt preferred cooperation with the business community over confrontation, but the industrialists needed to understand who was boss. Big business would have to submit to the national government. The public demanded at least that much.

In the 1890s, the Justice Department had only eighteen lawyers in Washington. Roosevelt quickly realized that the national government would need far more resources to take on industrial giants. By manipulating the public's disdain for John D. Rockefeller (who was, by then, retired), Roosevelt secured congressional approval for the creation of a Bureau of Corporations to investigate the trusts. The bureau began to gather information on Standard Oil's business practices. Whatever Rockefeller's early pricing practices, it was clear that John D. Archbold, Rockefeller's combative successor, had raised and maintained high domestic oil prices (in part to subsidize the low foreign prices he charged when he faced competition). Standard's profits soared between 1900 and 1906.

Archbold openly opposed Roosevelt's antitrust initiative. Standard refused to cooperate in the government investigation. The company's management publicly mocked the government's efforts. It was time for the big stick. Following a meeting with Roosevelt, the attorney general announced the preliminary investigation of an antitrust suit against Standard. There was more to come. On November 15, 1906, the federal government filed suit under the Sherman Act to dissolve Standard Oil. The complaint charged Standard and the sixty-five companies under its control with conspiring to restrain trade through industrial espionage, secret ownership of competitors, illegal rebates, and pricing that "leaves the Standard little or no profit," among other anticompetitive practices, and with monopolizing the oil industry.

Roosevelt spoke frequently about the need to channel corporate power in ways that helped the public. He brought high-profile cases against powerful adversaries. He established antitrust enforcement as an important function of government and affirmed the sovereignty of Washington over Wall Street. Congress responded in 1903 by appropriating half a million dollars for the prosecution of antitrust offenses and by authorizing the creation of what would become the Antitrust Division of the Department of Justice.

Yet over nearly two full terms in office, Roosevelt's administration brought just forty-four antitrust cases, leaving hundreds of trusts to operate more or less unchecked. Roosevelt's actions addressed the public perception of growing corporate power and influence. But Roosevelt never really affirmed the Sherman Act's commitment to economic competition through legislation. He usually preferred regulation to antitrust enforcement and saw no pressing need to reverse market concentration.

During the campaign of 1908, Roosevelt's handpicked successor, William Howard Taft, vowed to continue the Standard Oil case. Taft's opponent, Democrat William Jennings Bryan, vowed to send Rockefeller to prison. Taft won the election with the blessing of the business community but his Justice Department stepped up the pace of prosecution, initiating sixty-five antitrust cases over a four-year period. Private parties also filed antitrust suits.

The Standard Oil case finally reached the Supreme Court in 1910. In the months leading up to the Court's decision, the financial markets "virtually stood still," *Harper's* magazine observed. Standard executives predicted a nationwide economic disaster unless a lower court's decision dissolving the company was reversed. The case had to be argued twice in the Supreme Court because of the death of one of the justices, adding to the drawn-out drama. Chief Justice Edward White, writing for an 8–1 majority, upheld the decision to break Standard into thirty-four companies, each with its own board of directors. The Court gave Standard six months to comply and forbade its officers from reestablishing the monopoly.

Antitrust scholars recognize the Supreme Court's *Standard Oil* decision as a milestone in antitrust enforcement. The opinion associated monopoly with the power to set market price and limit production, often reducing product quality. The monopoly was dissolved, at least on paper, and the Court's opinion took Standard's 90 percent market share as proof of monopoly, providing a basis for future courts to infer market power from large market share.

Nevertheless, reformers were dismayed. The Court's opinion held that the Sherman Act's language did not mean what it said. Despite the act's express prohibition, "every" contract, combination, and conspiracy and restraint of trade was not illegal, according to the Court. The statute must be interpreted "by the light of reason" and "public policy." The Court ruled some of Standard's practices, such as below-cost pricing and secret competitor buyouts, "unreasonable" and therefore illegal. Conduct that almost always raises prices, like collusion among competitors to restrain production and cartel price-fixing, was deemed illegal per se—illegal without the need for detailed analysis. But overall, antitrust law was to be made by judges on a case-by-case basis, applying a "rule of reason."

On the political front, Taft proved unsteady at handling Roosevelt's legacy. Taft's tariff and conservation policies alienated more progressive Republicans, and he frequently aligned himself with the conservative faction in his party. Taft's personal relationship with Roosevelt eventually unraveled over the issue of antitrust enforcement. The complaint in the Justice Department's October 1911 antitrust lawsuit against U.S. Steel implied that Roosevelt had unwittingly aided the corporation in achieving a monopoly position by approving one of its acquisitions. An irate Roosevelt replied to the accusation in a magazine article that assailed as "hopeless" the Taft administration's policy of addressing the trust issue through "a succession of lawsuits."

Roosevelt ran for the presidency in 1912 on a third-party ticket after his efforts to unseat Taft as the Republican nominee failed. Taft, for his part, remained committed to enforcement of the Sherman Act through judicial interpretation of the rule of reason. The more telling debate in the campaign pitted Democrat Woodrow Wilson's vague notions of economic freedom for small businessmen and dreams of restoring small-scale competitive units by limited government action against Roosevelt's plan "to regulate big corporations in a thoroughgoing and effective fashion." None of the three candidates advocated laissez-faire. Roosevelt dismissed Wilson's vision as "foolish" and "foredoomed to failure," but the Republican schism permitted Wilson to win a landslide in the Electoral College with 42 percent of the popular vote.

The antitrust movement originally started with two competing philosophies for government's role in controlling private economic power. The campaign became just one more round in the long-standing contest between antitrust enforcement and regulation. Proponents of the antitrust approach wanted to rely on competition among market participants to produce broad-based economic benefits, limiting the government's role to guaranteeing the conditions of a competitive marketplace—usually by prohibiting private impediments to competition. Antitrust sets the rules of the road, so to speak, but does not tell people where to drive. Advocates of regulation wanted continuing governmental oversight and rule making to produce what would be the beneficial results of a free market, low prices as an example, regardless of the actual market structure.

Neither approach works all the time, and deciding between them remains difficult. Antitrust enforcement produces greater efficiency, a better allocation of resources, and increased innovation, if a market can support competition. Some markets can't, especially where the scale of production or distribution favors a single supplier. A strategy of breaking up the municipal water utility to produce lower rates through competition among smaller units will likely fail. After a period of instability in which most of the smaller units get run out of business, a single company will end up dominating the market. Nor will free market competition provide an adequate substitute for effective government regulation of the financial markets or the consumer market for pharmaceuticals, where the needs of purchasers and the difficulty of obtaining timely and accurate information necessitate greater government involvement. As a law professor before his appointment to the Supreme Court, Stephen Breyer wrote a detailed academic evaluation of markets best suited for regulation, rather than antitrust enforcement.

Regulation presents its own difficulties, even where economically indicated. Frequently, regulators fall sway to the influence of those they are supposed to regulate—"regulatory capture," as some call it. In other cases, regulators prove incompetent. They are slow to act, a significant drawback for dynamic markets. "See the helplessness of the [Interstate Commerce] Commission," Ida Tarbell wrote in her Standard Oil exposé. "It takes full testimony in 1889, digests it carefully, gives its orders in 1892, and they are not obeyed. More hearings follow."

In Wilson's time, the correct approach was even less obvious than it is today. A majority of those in Wilson's party sought an amendment of the Sherman Act to enumerate prohibited restraints of trade, outlaw interlocking directorates, and clarify if not abolish altogether the rule of reason promulgated in the Standard Oil case. The progressive Republicans and a minority of the Democrats thought it impossible to define by statute every offending restraint of trade and instead called for the creation of a government commission to deal with unfair competition. The national debate evidenced little sentiment for letting the problems fester until the market worked them out without getting the government involved.

Wilson's first antitrust proposal was embodied in a bill authored by Congressman Henry D. Clayton that prohibited specified unfair business practices, including exclusive dealing. Meanwhile, Wilson's key adviser,

Louis D. Brandeis, pushed for a bill to establish a strong trade commission intended to oversee business activity. When the Clayton bill bogged down in Congress, Wilson threw his support to the commission bill. Both pieces of legislation were eventually enacted, but the Clayton Act was watered down in the Senate by the addition of the qualification "where the effect may be to substantially lessen competition or tend to create a monopoly in any line of commerce," after each of the enumerated prohibitions. The Federal Trade Commission, created by the legislation Brandeis pressed for, also proved ineffective after Wilson appointed cautious administrators to key positions.

In any case, by the end of Wilson's second year in office, the most important federal antitrust laws were on the books, more or less in their current form. The statutes addressed anticompetitive business conduct, by prohibiting "restraints of trade" and "attempts to monopolize," as well as anticompetitive industry structure, by prohibiting "monopolization," and mergers that may "substantially lessen competition." Under the statutes, courts are empowered to enjoin individual firms acting alone or groups of firms acting together. Courts may block mergers in order to preserve competition and dissolve monopolies into smaller firms in order to restore competition.

Little came of all the legislative activity. Confronted by a severe economic depression in late 1913, Wilson redirected his efforts to easing tension between the administration and the business community. The attorney general, with Wilson's approval, announced that the Justice Department would provide advice to any large corporation that sought the government's aid in complying with the law. AT&T (American Telephone and Telegraph), among other combinations, reached an accommodation with the administration.

Wilson returned to his progressive platform in 1916. He appointed Brandeis to the Supreme Court and supported legislation that addressed farm credits, child labor, and workmen's compensation. But he also championed tariff, antidumping, and export legislation favored by the business community. Wilson's business-friendly policies ushered in a twenty-year period of collaboration between big business and government. Support for competition waned. Supreme Court decisions of the era reflected Wilson's approach. Cooperation (and even collusion) among firms was treated more tolerantly. Antitrust controls over dominant firm behavior were loosened by court decisions. The courts also narrowed the Federal Trade Commission's powers.

The benign view of big business continued through the First World War, the Roaring Twenties, and into the Great Depression. When President Franklin Roosevelt first struggled to turn the country's economy around, business leaders proposed suspending the antitrust laws to permit trade associations to engage in industry-wide planning. Labor leaders agreed, and the proposal was incorporated into the National Industrial Recovery Act in 1933. Many industries were cartelized with the government's blessing. Big business abandoned the Roosevelt coalition in an about-face a year later. The U.S. Chamber of Commerce denounced the New Deal. Roosevelt responded in kind. He openly endorsed the breakup of holding companies through which business interests controlled the markets for electric power.

Liberals within the administration called for even greater government action, arguing that monopoly pricing impeded economic recovery. In December 1937, the assistant attorney general for antitrust delivered a radio address in which he blamed the economic downturn on monopolists. The president's message to Congress the following year took the same position. In March 1938, as a part of a series of staff changes, Roosevelt appointed a new Antitrust Division head, Thurman Arnold. The economy continued to plummet.

Arnold faced unprecedented challenges. The government had abandoned enforcement of competition law during the first phase of the New Deal. The Antitrust Division, formed as a separate group within the Justice Department in 1933, devoted most of its resources to policing the enforcement of industry price-fixing codes against discounting. When central planning failed as a strategy for economic recovery, no one knew what to do next.

Arnold turned the Antitrust Division's lawyers into prosecutors. Using a case-by-case approach in the federal courts, they recommitted the nation to a program of economic competition enforced by the antitrust laws. Arnold attacked abuses of power by monopolies and cartels, what he called "bottlenecks" on production and distribution that produced higher prices and artificial shortages. He resolved many of the cases he brought by consent settlements that proscribed anticompetitive conduct and reinvigorated competition without costly market restructuring.

Over Arnold's five-year tenure, the Justice Department filed almost as many antitrust lawsuits as it had since the Sherman Act was adopted in 1890. With the support of Congress, Arnold increased the Antitrust Division's head count from eighteen to almost five hundred. And he set up division offices across the country to uncover and prosecute antitrust violations. He recruited the best students from the top law schools to work for him, making antitrust an elite specialty.

Arnold brought criminal indictments against the dairy industry for artificially increasing the price of milk. He secured criminal convictions against the American Medical Association and the District of Columbia Medical Society for illegally boycotting a neighborhood clinic that used a prepaid medical plan for patients. He won a price-fixing case against the big oil companies in the Supreme Court, reaffirming judicial endorsement for per se treatment of price-fixing by competitors. He successfully challenged patent licensing schemes that reinforced monopolies and set resale prices. Arnold's accomplishments validated antitrust enforcement as a vehicle to correct business misconduct and open markets to competition, a preferable alternative to ongoing and largely ineffective regulatory supervision.

Arnold's most famous win came in a case decided in 1945, after he left the Antitrust Division for the federal bench. Learned Hand, one of America's most famous judges, upheld the government's charges of monopolization against the Aluminum Company of America. Hand's opinion looked at market concentration—the size of Alcoa's market share—rather than just the company's overall size in terms of assets or capitalization. Hand concluded that a 90 percent market share would support a charge of monopolization, a share of 33 percent would not, and 60 percent would be "doubtful." Today's judges still use these rough standards.

The government proved Alcoa's monopoly position by showing its large market share. But, in Hand's view of the statute, proof of a monopoly share alone was not enough to support the government's charges. After all, a monopoly might be secured through "superior skill, foresight and industry." To support liability, there must be evidence of anticompetitive conduct—"some exclusion of competitors." The government proved this as well. By building new capacity in anticipation of future increases in demand, Alcoa deterred competitors from entering the market.

The *Alcoa* decision launched a postwar period of intense antitrust activity. Congress amended the Clayton Act in 1950 to tighten merger standards. Big business was once again viewed with suspicion. Antitrust's new vitality drew upon advancements in economic research. Economists investigated the relationship between market concentration and competitive performance, measured by pricing margin and cost, as well as by other indicia. Markets with few sellers—known as oligopolies—were thought to manifest limited competition and to produce higher than competitive prices, just as monopolies did.

A wave of consolidation in the 1950s and 1960s triggered the academic interest in oligopolies. By the end of 1968, the two hundred largest industrial corporations controlled over 60 percent of the total assets held by all manufacturing companies in the United States. A 1968 task force appointed by President Johnson recommended legislation that would subject any firm with at least a 15 percent share in a concentrated market to involuntary divestitures, requiring the sale of assets to smaller competitors.

Early in his first term, President Dwight D. Eisenhower named Earl Warren, the governor of California, Chief Justice of the United States. Warren turned out to be far more liberal on a number of issues than Eisenhower anticipated. During Warren's tenure of more than fifteen years, the Supreme Court encouraged aggressive antitrust enforcement by the executive branch and sanctioned private antitrust lawsuits against big businesses. With little explanation, the Court extended the per se rule against price-fixing by competitors to sales and marketing activities by individual manufacturers. Setting exclusive territories for distributors or conditioning the sale of one product on the purchase of another risked per se condemnation.

Reprising Ida Tarbell's theme, the Court opinions emphasized the welfare of small business owners and equated a desirable level of competition with the preservation of small, locally owned businesses in fragmented markets. In one case, price cutting by a national bakery to challenge small but well-established local producers was condemned. Mergers among competitors, even those with small market shares, were invariably barred. "Vertical" mergers between a company and its suppliers or distributors fared little better in court challenges. The government's antitrust enforcement policies echoed these judicial concerns. During the decade of the 1970s and into the early 1980s, the federal antitrust authorities brought monopolization cases against the leading companies in the computer industry, the telecommunications industry, the oil industry, and the breakfast cereal market.

The economic foundation of antitrust's new populism was never all that firm. The notion that higher prices invariably flow from industry concentration came under attack by academics. A 1964 article by University of Chicago economist George Stigler argued that it is difficult for sellers, even in industries with few competitors, to raise prices above competitive levels. Over the next decade, empirical research by conservative scholars further undermined the notion of a correlation between market concentration and monopoly profits. A particularly influential article by conservative economist Harold Demsetz pointed out the challenge a firm faces in maintaining a monopoly. If the firm charges a monopoly price, competitors will enter the market, output will increase, and prices will fall. Only by assuming a barrier of some kind to entry by other firms, Demsetz wrote, is it possible to justify a concern about industry concentration. Demsetz argued that barriers to market entry created by government, such as patents or industry regulations, were far more likely to prevent competition through market entry than free market forces.

The most unsettling research came from an unlikely source, the Democrats in control of the Antitrust Division. In 1965, President Johnson appointed a Harvard law professor, Donald Turner, to head the division. Turner held a doctorate in economics in addition to his law degree. He reorganized the economic staff of the division and began to solicit the opinions of staff economists before filing cases. Turner also created a "Special Economic Assistant" position that a young economics instructor from the University of Pennsylvania, Oliver Williamson, filled in 1966.

Turner asked Williamson to prepare an economic evaluation of the merger of two daily newspapers in a small community. The merger would certainly eliminate competition, but the single resulting business might consume fewer resources than the two newspapers operating separately. Balancing the loss to consumers from the elimination of competition against the potential savings to consumers from more efficient business operations had never been attempted in a formal way. Antitrust enforcers usually assumed that any increase in market power by a merged company would more than offset the benefits from whatever cost savings the merger achieved.

Williamson used economic "models" in his analysis. Economists frequently gain their insights about human behavior and industry phenomena by representing the actions of producers and consumers as mathematical functions generated from assumptions that are intended to approximate real-world conditions. By manipulating these mathematical functions, economists can study relationships that would be difficult to observe accurately in the real world.

Studying real-world situations by reducing them to a set of equations is not unique to economics. This approach has long been the staple of hard sciences like physics and biology. Of course, the conclusions drawn from mathematical models are only as accurate as the assumptions about the real world used to generate the mathematical functions. Reliance on flawed models helped to bring down the financial markets in 2008.

The two most straightforward economic models that Williamson had to work with described perfect competition and complete monopoly. Generally speaking, suppliers in a competitive market produce more goods for sale at lower prices than in a monopolized market. In a perfectly competitive market, the production of wheat by thousands of family farms, for example, each producer sells his output at the market price, which he takes as a given. He cannot raise price. If he raises his price, consumers will buy from other producers. If he tries to raise price by reducing his output and creating artificial scarcity, another farmer will simply increase production to satisfy market demand. In a perfect competition scenario, it makes sense for each farmer to produce another unit of wheat so long as the price at which he can sell it (his "marginal revenue") exceeds his incremental cost of growing it (his "marginal cost"). Since the farmer just accepts the market price as a given, the farmer's marginal revenue is the market price for the wheat. So he will grow more wheat until the cost of growing the next increment exceeds the market price.

Most competitive markets show a direct relationship between price and supply. Economists call this the law of supply. As market price increases, producers will make more of a product. Price and demand are related inversely (the law of demand). As the market price for a product increases, fewer and fewer consumers are willing to pay for it.

For many common products, increasing industry-wide production lowers price. If there is greater supply than demand in the market as a whole, the market price will fall and inefficient producers (those with high costs) will get squeezed out of the market because they can't make any profit. So, competition from other producers forces each producer to become more efficient. In theory at least, this weeding-out process will occur in all the industries throughout a perfectly competitive economy with the result that resources will be moved from the production of oversupplied goods (where the industry production exceeds consumer demand) to the production of undersupplied goods.

By contrast to the farmer in a perfectly competitive market, the monopolist sets rather than accepts the market price. It controls the entire industry output for the product. The market price changes as the monopolist produces more or less. If it produces less of its product, the price for each unit will go up as consumers who value the now-scarce product outbid those who value it less. Conversely, if the monopolist produces more, the market price will go down. The monopolist will not increase production and drive down prices until the price level gets to what would be charged in a competitive market. That's not how a monopolist makes the most money. Instead, like the farmer in a competitive market, the monopolist will only increase output so long as the incremental revenue it gets from each additional unit exceeds its own marginal cost of production.

At the production level where the monopolist's marginal revenue equals his marginal cost, the monopolist is making fewer units than a perfectly competitive industry would produce, and it can charge more for each unit because its lower production has made the product somewhat scarce. This is one of the big economic differences between a monopolized market and a competitive one. There are many consumers who would be willing to buy the product at the lower perfect competition price. But the monopolist doesn't want to produce enough to satisfy these consumers who would buy the product at a lower price. Assuming the monopolist has to charge each customer the same price, the increased production to satisfy these additional consumers would drive down the price the monopolist is able to charge on all the other units it produces.

Some consumers who want the product and would buy it at competitive prices will not buy it at all at the higher monopoly price. They will substitute alternatives less desirable to themselves and they will suffer harm because they did not make the purchases they would have made at competitive prices. Overall, society's resources are misallocated. Goods that would have been made and sold in a competitive market were not made at all. Instead, less desirable substitutes are made and sold. This misallocation is known as deadweight loss. Antitrust economists identify this deadweight loss as one of the undesirable effects of monopoly.

In a monopoly market, there are also some consumers who will continue to purchase the product they desire, albeit at a higher price than they would have been charged in a competitive market. The monopolist is richer as a result of these sales and the consumers are poorer as their wealth is transferred to the monopolist. As odd as it may seem, antitrust economists, looking at the big picture, care a lot less about these "transfers" than they do about deadweight loss. Transfers do not affect the efficient allocation of resources. The overpriced goods would have been made and sold under perfect competition, so that portion of the monopolized market is operating efficiently from an economic point of view even if consumers are paying more than they would have, had the market been competitive. By contrast to the economic viewpoint, antitrust legislation emerged from dissatisfaction over the transfer of wealth from ordinary consumers to those producers who dominated markets.

Williamson started his analysis with these two well-established models, complete monopoly and perfect competition. Merging the two newspapers would certainly produce the familiar deadweight loss of monopoly. At the same time, the newspapers would avoid duplicative expenses by merging. They would operate more efficiently and their costs as a combined operation would be lower per unit for just about every level of consumer demand. To his amazement, Williamson found that even if prices went up after the merger, small reductions in costs produce savings for society that easily offset the misallocation of resources created by large increases of market power. A reduction in costs more than offsets a tenfold increase in market power, Williamson found.

Williamson showed his results to Turner, who was also surprised. Williamson published the results in a prestigious economics journal, and subsequently prepared a less technical version, which he published in a law journal. The implication for antitrust policy was enormous: promoting efficiency appeared to be far more important than preventing monopoly, at least in terms of correctly allocating society's resources.

Williamson's research played a part in transforming antitrust doctrine. In the 1960s and '70s, a group of lawyers and economists associated with the University of Chicago challenged the populist, egalitarian antitrust regime of the Warren Court, thought by those in the Chicago School to be illogical in its methodology and ideological in its results. The prevailing populist approach to antitrust enforcement usually harmed consumer interests and produced misallocation of resources, Chicagoans argued, by protecting small, inefficient competitors. A more economic approach to antitrust enforcement would produce more defensible and more productive policies, they claimed.

Robert Bork's 1978 book, *The Antitrust Paradox*, laid out the Chicago School's case. Drawing on the legislative debates over the antitrust statutes, Bork, a Yale law professor, rejected the notion that antitrust is intended to benefit those who produce goods and services, arguing instead that the only legitimate goal of antitrust is to benefit consumers.

Consumers benefit, according to Bork, if society's resources are allocated to maximize the ability of consumers to satisfy their desires. Resources must be allocated optimally from industry to industry, and employed productively within each company. Courts can decide in a reasoned way if business conduct and industry structure enhances the welfare of consumers only by looking to economics. But not to the entirety of economics, Bork was quick to point out. Although a common form of market structure in the economy is oligopoly—competition among a few sellers—Bork dismissed the academic attempts to predict the behavior of firms in such markets—what economists call oligopoly theory—as a "frame of mind, a mood" that is unworthy of real-world application. In formulating the Chicago School approach to antitrust doctrine, Bork relied on the familiar monopoly and perfect competition models. "Microeconomics is a field in which the simple ideas are the most powerful ideas," Bork explained.

Bork's economic argument was deceptively simple. It started by looking at industry output. Business conduct or industry structure that artificially reduces output produces a deadweight loss, raising prices in the process. Conversely, at least in Bork's view, unless the conduct or industry structure limits output, it does not harm consumers. The precise methodology for evaluating individual cases had already been provided by Oliver Williamson. Balancing the deadweight loss of reduced output from the exercise of increased market power against the efficiency benefits of lower cost is the appropriate way to determine whether a monopoly should be dissolved, a merger prohibited, or a distribution agreement restrained by a court.

Citing Williamson's analysis again and again, Bork argued that many antitrust cases are easy to resolve. Sometimes there will not be a deadweight loss, as in a merger between small industry participants, because the companies involved do not have the power to restrict output (and raise price), and, hence, no government intervention would be warranted. A conspiracy to fix prices among market suppliers, on the other hand, produces a deadweight loss from the lower level of output at artificially high prices, but the conspiracy does not lower costs because each conspirator continues to maintain its own operations. Conspiracies among competitors fixing product prices present compelling cases for government action.

Most cases are somewhere in between. The conduct at issue increases consumer prices but decreases producer costs. Bork claimed that evaluating the trade-off between the economic loss of reduced competition and the benefit of greater competitive efficiency flowing from a merger or business practice in any given lawsuit is not only well beyond the competence of judges, but is simply impossible for anyone, even the most talented economist. Invoking Williamson's findings, Bork argued that even small cost reductions more than offset large price increases in terms of overall efficiency. The need for competitive efficiency is so compelling and the prospect of accurate empirical analysis so remote that claims of competitive efficiency should trump all other considerations, Bork argued, rejecting the approach of basing antitrust liability on case-specific empirical analysis.

Bork reinforced his position by arguing that market entry by new competitors will invariably erode market dominance that is not based on efficiency. Bork derided the notion that companies or market conditions could create barriers to prevent new entry. If a monopoly endures, in Bork's view of self-correcting markets, it will likely be the result of superior efficiency. And a monopoly based on efficiency benefits consumers and should be left alone. One of Bork's conservative contemporaries made the point more explicit: "There is the strongest presumption that the existing structure is the efficient structure."

Overall, the likely prospect of net efficiency gains, coupled with ease of market entry, should preclude government intervention in business conduct except where economic theory unequivocally indicates harm will result—which is hardly ever in the case of mergers, and virtually never in the case of actions by a single company.

Bork wrapped his economic analysis in powerful conservative rhetoric. The "reckless and primitive egalitarianism" of the Warren Court, wrote Bork, did not merely deny consumers the benefits of free market resource allocation by protecting small, weak, poorly managed, inefficient, and inadequately funded businesses. Rather, Bork saw in the antitrust policies of the day a looming "social policy" with "sweeping implications" that affected and infected all aspects of political life. Equality of outcome cannot be achieved, Bork explained, "by making the slow faster, that being beyond the power of legal compulsion, but only by holding the faster back." These ideas at work in antitrust, he concluded, are "merely special forms of larger ideas contending for domination of society at large."

Starting with Bork's broad pronouncements, the antitrust policies of the succeeding decades were shaped less by changes in economics than by the outspoken advocacy of those demanding retrenchment of antitrust enforcement programs for political and social reasons. Bork himself vastly overstated what economics had to say about industrial organization. Williamson's model assumed a market going from perfect competition to complete monopoly through a single transaction. But perfectly competitive markets exist only in economic textbooks and a complete monopoly is as rare as a Bigfoot sighting. When other economists applied Williamson's approach to normal markets in the real world, it took big efficiency gains to offset substantial price increases, even on paper. Williamson readily admitted the limitations of his model. He called his initial proposal "the naive model." Sophisticated case studies of actual transactions eventually showed merger-specific efficiencies not all that common.

Nor, as critics later explained, do the efficiencies Bork was talking about necessarily benefit consumers. His commentary notwithstanding, Bork counted as consumer benefits in his efficiency analysis the cost savings achieved by producers whether the savings are passed on to consumers through lower prices or simply retained by the producers as profit. "If consumers lose but producers win more than consumers lose," wrote two of Bork's critics, "'consumer welfare' has been increased" under Bork's analysis.

Bork not only counted all efficiency improvements as gains to consumers. Like many economists, he also ignored the transfer of wealth in his calculation of consumer benefit. In effect, Bork wasn't just proposing to abandon antitrust's misdirected efforts to protect small, inefficient producers. Bork wanted to move antitrust away from its traditional role of guaranteeing to consumers the benefits of free market competition, like lower prices, in favor of promoting efficiency throughout the economy.

There was much to criticize in Bork's work. But none of the shortcomings and limitations of Bork's analysis ended up mattering one whit, as the Reagan Revolution engulfed the country.

CHAPTER 2

Chicago Comes to Washington

In 1980, Ronald Reagan was elected president, and in 1981 he appointed William F. Baxter to head the Antitrust Division. Baxter had been my antitrust professor in law school. He was a slight-of-build, mild-mannered man whose sharply chiseled features bespoke what one journalist later called a "frostily cerebral" demeanor. His personality was hardly warm and engaging, but he wasn't the intimidator type of law professor, either. In personal conversation, he often seemed remote and philosophical.

Baxter moved to California as a boy when his father went (unsuccessfully) into the gold dredging business. He attended Stanford as an undergraduate, served in the military, and returned to complete his legal education. A remarkable student, Baxter was invited to join the faculty upon graduation from law school. After a brief stint as a junior faculty member, he spent two years in private practice at the largest firm in Washington, D.C. His participation in a major Federal Trade Commission antitrust proceeding kindled an interest in economics, although he did not have a formal degree in the discipline. Returning to Stanford in 1960, he brought economic analysis to bear in published articles on legal issues as disparate as aircraft noise, environmental pollution, and electronic banking. In 1968, he was appointed a member of the White House Task Force on Antitrust Policy and coauthored its report, urging forced divestiture to reduce the market concentration of American industries. When economic research undermined that approach, Baxter changed his position, and by the time I took his course, he was clearly in the Chicago School camp.

The first several weeks of Baxter's antitrust course consisted of a review of microeconomics, or an introduction for those unfamiliar with the field. Then Baxter used an economic approach, sometimes including complex mathematics, to critique the leading Supreme Court antitrust cases. Baxter was not an animated speaker. He did not have a commanding voice. But most of the best students in the law school took Baxter's class whether they intended to become antitrust lawyers or not. Just about everyone praised the academic rigor of Baxter's course.

By the time I enrolled in Baxter's class in the spring of 1974, I had already completed two antitrust courses in law school. Few subjects were as relevant and exciting to me. Antitrust doctrine, I thought, touched the heart of a free market system and seemed to implicate many of society's hotly contested issues. The rational, deductive Chicago School approach to legal decision-making was particularly alluring. Nevertheless, some of Baxter's arguments sounded unrealistically academic, not in keeping with how decisions are made in the real world. I frequently challenged Baxter in class, but I also asked his help on an important paper I wrote in my third year. From time to time when I faced complex antitrust issues throughout my career, I went back to Baxter for counsel, knowing full well I might not accept his advice. It was reassuring just to work through problems with him.

At the time of Baxter's nomination, he was virtually unknown outside antitrust's small academic community. His confirmation hearing passed without challenge or incident. The senators on the Judiciary Committee had little idea of what lay ahead. Better informed of the looming sea change, big law firms offered $1,100 (in 1981 dollars) to any former student who could produce a complete set of notes from Baxter's antitrust class.

Baxter brought with him to Washington an abiding faith in economics. Describing his approach to antitrust enforcement in *Fortune* magazine, he said, "If it doesn't make economic sense, it doesn't happen." Like Bork, Baxter espoused the notion that economic efficiency is the "sole goal of antitrust," but there were important differences in philosophy between Baxter and Bork. Bork's rules were largely based on presumptions. The essence of Baxter's economic approach was a detailed factual analysis of each situation and an empirical examination of each theoretical proposition.

Baxter did not even teach the Williamson trade-off in the antitrust class I took. Bork's economics were simple. Baxter's economics were complicated. And Baxter implied that his approach would change as economic research advanced. "Antitrust policy should be based on whatever it is we know at any particular moment about the economics of industrial organization," he later explained.

The Antitrust Division head and his immediate subordinates—known to the bar as the division's "front office"—change with each administration and sometimes more frequently. The front office controls, at least for the duration of the administration, the hundreds of lawyers and economists with career civil service appointments who comprise the division staff.

Once confirmed, Baxter directed the Antitrust Division lawyers to review all outstanding cases in order to ensure that every request for court relief would actually produce beneficial economic results. He elevated the stature of economists in the division by making their office chief a full deputy assistant attorney general, on a par with the attorneys who headed the merger enforcement and litigation sections. Baxter even organized elementary and advanced economic courses for the division's career attorneys.

Baxter's changes produced tension in the division, especially among older attorneys who openly called the economists "case killers" because of their insistence on an economic rationale for every case filing. These organizational changes were just the preliminaries. "We're really going to shake some people up," one of the new division deputies told the *Wall Street Journal* a few weeks after Baxter's confirmation. Baxter would begin his tenure by shaking up some of the people in Ronald Reagan's cabinet.

———

For most of Baxter's first year in office, the Antitrust Division agenda was dominated by two enormous monopolization cases, both of which had been filed by predecessor administrations. The government's lawsuit against IBM (International Business Machines) for monopolization of the computer industry was already eleven years old, prompting one appellate judge to quip that the case had "lasted longer than World War II and probably cost as much."

The lawsuit against AT&T for monopolization of the telecommunications industry had an even more storied and more troubled history. From the late 1870s, when telephone service effectively began, through the first part of the Progressive era, AT&T consolidated ownership of dozens of phone companies with the government's blessing. Eventually, AT&T's unwillingness to let competitors tie into its system created public pressure, leading to an agreement with the Wilson administration under which the phone company divested Western Union. During the Second New Deal, Franklin Roosevelt's administration issued a report critical of AT&T procurement and rate-setting practices, and after the war the Justice Department filed suit against the company. AT&T settled with the government in 1956 under an agreement that restricted the company to the telephone business.

Eighteen years later, the Justice Department under Gerald Ford's Republican administration filed a second lawsuit against AT&T, seeking to break up the company. The case went to trial in January 1981, weeks before Baxter took control of the Antitrust Division. Anxious to resolve the case, the administration of Democrat Jimmy Carter negotiated a settlement with AT&T that required only a few divestitures, mostly in the company's equipment manufacturing subsidiary.

Stephen Breyer's book on regulation, written just before Baxter came to town, laid out over pages and pages the hand-wringing equivocation of Democratic policy makers. Before taking the bench, Breyer served in the front office of the Antitrust Division during the Johnson administration, and on the staff of the Senate Judiciary Committee, chaired by Senator Edward Kennedy.

The FCC, set up to regulate the telephone industry, "inadvertently created a competitive long-distance communications market," Breyer observed, almost as a lament. Now what? On one hand, permitting competition in the long-distance market might make it difficult for AT&T to achieve the most effective scale economies. On the other hand, denying competitors entry into the market slowed down the advancement of new technology. Oh, what problems! Breyer concluded by identifying the sale of telephone equipment as a separate business that could be divested, but he otherwise called for "detailed analysis" of the problem.

When Baxter took control of the division's front office, he rejected the Democrats' plan as inadequate before it could be formalized. The proposed agreement "did not do the one thing that should be done—separate all the regulated components of the enterprise from all the unregulated," Baxter explained to the *Washington Post*. "I was not going to sign that settlement," he said emphatically.

Baxter did not share Breyer's concern with the prospect of competition or the Democrats' paralyzing indecision in the face of uncertainty. But, like Bork, Baxter was generally skeptical of government efforts to end monopolies. Divestiture is appropriate, Baxter taught in his antitrust classes, only if it will produce relief more quickly than the erosion of monopoly power that naturally occurs as competitors enter a market.

AT&T did not look like a garden-variety monopoly to Baxter. AT&T used the profits, set by government regulation, from its local telephone monopolies to subsidize its long-distance rates, to the disadvantage of long-distance competitors who had to sell against artificially low prices. AT&T wanted relief from its 1956 consent decree so that it could deploy new technologies and enter the burgeoning field of computing. Baxter was afraid that AT&T would use the profits from its government-sanctioned local phone monopolies to damage competitors and retard innovation in all of these new markets. "Divestiture would be necessary to deprive the regulated monopolies of the opportunity to engage in that kind of cross-subsidization. Experience indicates that nothing else will accomplish that," Baxter told an American Bar Association audience in 1977. Baxter wanted nothing less than a spin-off of all of AT&T's local operating subsidiaries into separate, independently owned companies.

The Commerce Department and the Department of Defense privately opposed the Antitrust Division's lawsuit against AT&T from the day it was filed by the Ford administration. Baxter had barely found his desk in the Justice Department when Reagan's secretary of defense, Caspar Weinberger, sent a classified letter to the attorney general, Baxter's boss, urging the Justice Department to drop the suit on grounds of national security. The letter pointedly cautioned against divestitures and disruptions of AT&T networks "that are essential to defense command and control." When the letter was leaked to the press, Weinberger acknowledged the

Defense Department's opposition to the suit. News stories emphasized that any divestiture of regional telephone operating units would affect "critical elements of the nation's nuclear attack force."

Baxter responded the following day with his first news conference. He pledged to "litigate to the eyeballs" the Justice Department's lawsuit. "I don't intend to fold up my tent and go away because the Department of Defense has expressed concern," Baxter told reporters.

AT&T's support extended far beyond the Defense Department. An administration task force set up without Justice Department participation to study the telecommunications industry recommended dismissing the AT&T suit. Then Commerce Secretary Malcolm Baldrige released draft Senate committee testimony in favor of legislation that would have permitted AT&T to enter unregulated markets through a wholly owned subsidiary. Baxter sent a letter of his own to the Office of Management and Budget opposing the legislation. An embarrassed Reagan administration canceled Baldrige's testimony, and Baxter was sharply criticized in the press by conservative Republican senator Barry Goldwater and moderate Republican senator Bob Packwood, the cosponsors of the bill.

The Commerce and Defense secretaries took their efforts to restrain Baxter to a cabinet-level council. Reagan and his close adviser Ed Meese, along with Baxter, were invited to one of the cabinet council's meetings. Baldrige presented the report of the task force he had chaired. The report identified the AT&T litigation as an obstacle to maintaining the U.S. worldwide lead in telecommunications. A separate Defense Department report, also presented at the meeting, read, "DoD can unequivocally state that divestiture as currently proposed by Justice would cause substantial harm to national defense and security and emergency preparedness and telecommunications capability."

Then it was Baxter's turn to talk. He looked at the president and in his almost laconic manner presented the Justice Department's position. Competition would do a lot more for the country than merely relying on AT&T, Baxter explained. He talked about how the government had tried regulating AT&T without success. He explained that the Justice Department had also tried to modify the company's behavior through consent settlements and litigation, again without success. Nothing had worked, Baxter explained, so unless the president directed him not to, he was going to break up the company.

All eyes turned to the president of the United States, awaiting his fateful decision. Over the course of his lifetime, Reagan remarked, the cost of making a cross-country phone call had declined significantly. Whatever the president intended to imply, no countermanding instructions were forthcoming. The council asked Baxter to suggest a legislative plan that would satisfy the Justice Department. Baxter later responded by announcing that he would drop the lawsuit if Congress passed legislation that would prevent AT&T from subsidizing its unregulated operations and would require AT&T to guarantee access by long-distance competitors to AT&T local networks.

When the Telecommunications Bill, as amended by the administration, passed the Senate in October 1981, Baxter astounded administration officials and Senate leaders by announcing he would still not dismiss the lawsuit because the bill did not meet his goals. The government lawyers "continue to seek an approach no one else in government seems interested in trying to do and that is to break up AT&T," said a company spokesperson to the press. AT&T's chairman called the government "a three-ring circus" and referred to the Justice Department as "lawyers without any client." He attacked Baxter personally in a subsequent interview. "I imagine the Reagan administration is embarrassed at the pronouncements of Mr. Baxter," he said.

In an attempt to discredit the Justice Department, AT&T's lawyers tried to introduce into evidence in the antitrust trial the Defense Department's report to the cabinet council opposing divestiture. The trial judge, Harold Greene, held a special hearing on the issue during which it was revealed that the Defense Department had prepared the report in collaboration with AT&T and had sent the company a draft copy more than a week before giving it to the Justice Department. "The position of the United States in this lawsuit is being stated by the lawyers for the United States, and not by people making statements in other forums," the trial judge ruled.

The judge's decision was a small victory for a man who was besieged from all sides. Notwithstanding the 1956 court order, the Federal Communications Commission ruled that AT&T could enter unregulated markets through a wholly owned subsidiary, in effect supporting the Senate bill. The FCC was created in 1934 as part of the New Deal efforts to regulate big business. Its members are appointed by the president but the agency reports to Congress. The FCC's jurisdiction in the telecommunications industry relative to that of the Justice Department has never been all that clear. Baxter, like most conservatives, had little but disdain for government regulation of business. He considered it a poor substitute for free market competition.

Baxter taught a course in law school on regulated industries that examined how government regulatory agencies invariably work for the benefit of the regulated companies rather than consumers. Even before his appointment, Baxter wrote a paper supporting the Antitrust Division's efforts to eliminate fixed commissions at the New York Stock Exchange. As assistant attorney general, he pressed for deregulation of the trucking and gas pipeline industries, repeatedly warning the newly deregulated companies that they would be subject to antitrust restrictions on anticompetitive behavior. In the AT&T case, Baxter's court papers argued that governmental regulation had been and would continue to be ineffective.

Baxter viewed the FCC decision to permit AT&T participation in unregulated markets as a direct challenge to his reliance on free market competition. In response, Baxter personally signed a stinging brief asking the federal appeals court to set aside the FCC decision, which the brief derided as "irrational." The FCC had itself admitted an historic inability even to monitor AT&T's records, the brief explained.

Today, antitrust doctrine has turned timid, obsessed with the possibility of error by overzealous enforcement. Academics insist upon detailed economic theory and unambiguous facts to justify government intervention. "The basic rule should be nonintervention," teaches a contemporary antitrust professor, absent "a high degree of confidence" that the challenged conduct is anticompetitive and can be remedied effectively.

Baxter could provide no such assurances. AT&T boasted an impressive record of innovation. Its scientists invented the transistor in 1947 and the company launched the first international telecommunications satellite in 1963. There was no indication that whatever came after dissolution could produce anything comparable. Nor did dissolution guarantee increased competition or lower prices. After Baxter's remedy was applied, local Bell operating companies would still be monopolies. Telephone charges for local service were likely to rise.

The uncertainty did not end Baxter's analysis. Unlike some of today's antitrust experts, Baxter considered the payoff from government intervention to open technology markets, not just the uncertain likelihood of success. Baxter believed that once freed from the Bell system, the local phone companies would have no reason to prefer AT&T equipment or long-distance service over that of competitors. Competition and innovation might blossom in the unregulated markets. However, this conjecture was offset by what even Baxter acknowledged as a sacrifice of "substantial economies" in dissolving the existing industry structure. Discretion, not to mention the Williamson trade-off, cut against Baxter's plan. Many conservatives were critical of Baxter's approach.

Early in January 1982, Baxter made a startling announcement. AT&T agreed to a settlement. The company would spin off its twenty-two local phone companies in exchange for permission to enter the computer industry. The *Wall Street Journal* characterized the settlement as a "surrender by AT&T, largely on the government's lawyers' terms."

"It's exactly what they wanted," conceded AT&T's chairman, the man who had called Baxter an embarrassment not two months earlier. Wall Street railed against the deal. In sworn testimony before a congressional committee, industry analysts predicted "havoc" and industry-wide financial instability.

The dire predictions went unfulfilled. Although more complex than initially thought, the restructuring, administered by a single federal judge, was completed in 1984 without serious problems. Almost six hundred thousand workers changed employers. Residential and business customers served by eighty-six million telephone lines changed suppliers. The changes were "largely invisible" to the public, reported the *Washington Post*.

Even most conservatives eventually conceded that the AT&T settlement set the stage for the country's enormous growth in telecommunications. The proliferation of cellular telephones, pagers, the Internet, voice mail, and microwave transmissions followed AT&T's dissolution. With the benefit of hindsight and notwithstanding the frenetic opposition of the defense establishment, the Commerce Department, the financial community, much of the government regulatory bureaucracy, and even, according to some, the president of the United States, Baxter properly sacrificed the "substantial economies" of monopoly for the benefits of competition.

In mid-1982, lawyers from a huge Japanese multinational corporation called me, exasperated by a document demand they had received from the Justice Department. Earlier in the year Commerce Secretary Baldrige publicly warned the Japanese government about price competition from Japan's manufacturers of dynamic memory chips, important components of computers. The Japanese government in turn warned their companies about offering low U.S. prices, and Baldrige reported to the press that the Japanese manufacturers had agreed to restrain imports so that U.S. manufacturers could benefit by charging customers more for memory chips.

A few weeks later, a polite but thoroughly exasperated Japanese executive demanded some kind of coherent explanation from me. Why, after following the explicit directive of the commerce secretary, was his company being investigated for price-fixing and market allocation by the Justice Department? I advised him to cooperate with the investigation. I assured him that nothing would come of the inquiry, so long as his company did not participate in any future price or production discussions with its competitors, regardless of what the commerce secretary demanded. "Only in the land of the free and the home of the Sherman Act," I thought.

My client produced some documents and one of its executives submitted to interrogation under oath. Five other Japanese chip manufacturers went through the same process. I assured my client that the Justice Department would let the matter drop. It did. Baxter had made his point. In the United States, we believe in free market competition.

A couple of years later, the unrelenting competitive pressure from the more efficient Japanese manufacturers drove Intel Corporation from the memory chip market it pioneered. After considerable soul searching, the company decided to bank on its more innovative technology development expertise. It shifted its resources to the development and production of general-purpose chips, known as microprocessors, that could be programmed to carry out computational functions. Through successive rounds of innovation, Intel grew to dominate the microprocessor market.

In February 1983, Baxter made his point about competition again, in a more celebrated case. The president of American Airlines suggested a 20 percent airfare price increase in a phone call to the president of Braniff, a rival airline. For reasons that were never revealed, Braniff recorded its chief executive officer's phone call and turned the tape over to the Justice Department. The Justice Department's complaint recounted the conversation in detail:

> BRANIFF PRESIDENT: Do you have a suggestion for me?
> AMERICAN PRESIDENT: Yes, I have a suggestion for you. Raise your goddamn fares 20%. I'll raise mine the next morning.
> BRANIFF: Robert, we . . .
> AMERICAN: You'll make more money and I will, too.
> BRANIFF: We can't talk about pricing.
> AMERICAN: Oh bullshit, Howard. We can talk about any goddamn thing we want to talk about.

The remedy the government demanded, even more than the salty language, made the case interesting to lawyers. The government sought to bar American's president from serving in any position with authority over prices for two years. When news of the complaint became public, Baxter publicly suggested that telephone conversations between chief executives should be banned unless tape-recorded. CEOs from across the country complained bitterly in a story on the front page of the *Wall Street Journal*. "Ridiculous," said one. "The knee-jerk reaction of someone who isn't very thoughtful," opined another. "It's lonely being a CEO," said a third, who explained he just wanted to discuss personal matters with his colleagues. "They need to talk about charity work," read the article's lead, only half in jest. A Justice Department spokesman made it clear that Baxter's proposal had no support in the administration.

American Airlines' lawyers decided to fight the suit because of what they saw as a flaw in Baxter's legal theory. American's president made an offer to fix prices, but the complaint acknowledged that the Braniff executive refused the offer, ruling out an agreement to fix prices. Unable to bring charges for price-fixing and unwilling to prosecute Braniff after its cooperation, Baxter accused American of attempted monopolization of air rights out of Dallas, requiring the government to prove both anticompetitive conduct and a "dangerous probability" that the attempt to monopolize would be successful.

American and Braniff together accounted for more than 75 percent of the passenger traffic in the Dallas area, exceeding the 30 to 50 percent courts usually require for attempted monopolization cases. American's CEO would have monopolized the market and raised prices had he secured Braniff's agreement. Nevertheless, Baxter's approach to charging a would-be price fixer struck many as unconventional.

"This is a novel legal proposition," a leading antitrust expert explained to the press. In his confirmation hearings, Baxter had promised to shun "novel theories" of antitrust enforcement. On the other hand, he consistently stated his support for attempted monopolization lawsuits if the behavior at issue "is sufficiently reprehensible." Baxter personally supervised the handling of the American Airlines case, but in a blow to his prestige, a federal judge in Dallas dismissed the complaint. American hailed the decision, claiming that it "fully vindicated" its president. The following year, a court of appeals reinstated the government's case. American quickly settled, agreeing to require its president to consult a lawyer before talking with officials of other airlines and to keep notes of all such discussions.

Baxter's prosecutions were impressive enough, but he became notorious among Democrats far more for the cases he didn't bring than for those he did. On the same day Baxter announced the settlement with AT&T, he dropped the government's thirteen-year-old case against IBM, calling the company "a good corporate citizen." Government lawyers who had spent years working on the case, and even the trial judge, assailed Baxter's decision in the press. Critics charged that IBM "smothered" potential competition by altering the design and lowering the prices of its new products. Among the illegal practices alleged by the government were premature announcements of new products to prevent competitors from taking away IBM's customers.

Baxter acknowledged that a few of IBM's actions appeared predatory, but concluded that these were both insignificant and outside the market covered by the lawsuit. At bottom, the theory of the government's case seemed to shift aimlessly over the years. The charge of monopolizing the market for general-purpose computers became difficult to prove, given the advent of personal computers in the early 1980s and IBM's late entry into that segment.

Baxter also dropped cases against Mack Trucks, Mercedes-Benz, General Electric, a group of hotels in Hawaii, and two manufacturers of facing brick. And he directed one of his deputies to review the hundreds of outstanding antitrust judgments that restrained company behavior, with an eye toward eliminating a substantial number of them. Court orders against can manufacturers and the Safeway grocery store chain, among other companies, were abandoned.

These decisions generated little criticism. More contentious was Baxter's set of new merger guidelines that permitted somewhat higher levels of industry concentration without government challenge. Baxter saw little problem with mergers between companies in different industries, regardless of the company size, and believed that mergers between companies and their suppliers or customers—"vertical" mergers—improved industry efficiency, except in unusual circumstances. Baxter publicly praised big businesses as "very valuable things" because they tended, in his view, to be more efficient than their smaller competitors. But Baxter's new guidelines strongly indicated that even small mergers between competitors in concentrated industries—two equally sized companies with sales as small as 5 percent of a market—were subject to challenge.

Baxter's merger enforcement reflected this view. Baxter blocked the merger of the fourth-largest brewery with the sixth-largest, notwithstanding the two companies together accounted for only about 16 percent of the national market. And Baxter pointedly rejected the argument advanced by Robert Bork and other conservatives that merger policy could be adequately stated in short, simple guidelines that addressed little more than market share. Baxter's approach required detailed economic analysis of each proposed merger. Nevertheless, Democrats blasted the administration's "benign indifference" to the wave of mergers that had engulfed the economy.

All of these changes might well have passed with only the normal political bickering had it not been for Baxter's position on distribution practices. More than 70 percent of the private antitrust cases in the federal courts at the time Baxter took office were filed by dealers and distributors, challenging manufacturers' rules that restrained resellers from competing with each other in the sale of the same manufacturer's product. These cases didn't usually involve competitive restraints among different manufacturers. Instead, the cases focused entirely on how a manufacturer gets its product to market—the "vertical" relationships between the manufacturer and other companies to which the manufacturer sells its product for resale.

Baxter believed that agreements imposed by manufacturers on their resellers were usually intended to lower operating costs and seldom suppressed competition with rival brands. There were many court decisions to the contrary, holding manufacturers' attempts to restrain dealer discounting illegal per se. Baxter ridiculed these opinions as "wacko" and "ludicrous." He said the courts were trying "to penalize [big companies] for their large size." Baxter was determined to change the law in this area, but he could not change distribution law by fiat, not even by altering the government's enforcement policy. More than 95 percent of all antitrust cases were filed and controlled by private litigants.

Baxter took a novel tack. "The answer," Baxter said, "is that we should participate in some way in those private cases, intrude ourselves into those private cases, and urge the courts to abandon the doctrines that have long ago been discarded by sensible and knowledgeable professionals." In particular, Baxter later explained, participation in private cases was intended to persuade the courts "to abandon the rule of per se illegality altogether in the vertical practices area."

Democrats were incensed by Baxter's refusal to honor Supreme Court product-distribution decisions, as well as by Baxter's attempt to change the law through the courts rather than through Congress. "I honestly believe you're a person who violates the law and does it with a kind of presumptuousness and arrogance that is almost unbelievable for an official of the government," Democratic senator Howard Metzenbaum said to Baxter at a congressional hearing.

"I understand that's what you believe," Baxter replied, not bothering to respond further.

Even moderate Republicans began to complain about what Senator John Danforth called "a singular lack of interest in the enforcement of the antitrust laws" by the Reagan administration. Baxter and his opponents were just warming up for the main event.

PART TWO

PRODUCT DISTRIBUTION

CHAPTER 3

Thinking Different

On a slow news day during the late summer of 1982, an otherwise unoccupied *Washington Post* intern named David Vise interviewed Bill Baxter. Vise wasn't expecting much from the interview. He was, after all, only an intern. But what Baxter revealed made the front page of the next day's newspaper and fueled decades of controversy over the nation's competition policy.

At first, the interview hardly seemed newsworthy. A few minutes into the conversation, Vise had to stifle a yawn. It was the combination of Baxter's soft voice and the mind-numbing complexity of competition law. Baxter began by explaining some basic legal concepts. Manufacturers that dictate the retail prices stores can charge for their products are in violation of federal law, Baxter told Vise. Vise already knew the ban on retail price-setting applied to all types of consumer goods. It was familiar to anyone who ever walked through a store. "Manufacturer's suggested retail price" meant that manufacturers could do no more than suggest what customers should pay. Dictating minimum retail prices may result in higher prices to consumers, Baxter continued, unremarkably. Then Baxter delivered the punch line. Without even a hint of drama, Baxter said he would prosecute retail price-fixing only in "special cases" because the law against it did not make good economic sense.

Vise knew he had heard something extraordinary. He raced back to his desk to file a story about a government prosecutor who refused to enforce the law. "Justice Allows Illegal Pricing—Antitrust Chief Sees No Evil," read a front-page headline in the next day's *Post*. In most cases, Vise reported, manufacturers would be free to violate the law with Baxter's "blessing."

Urgent proclamations of outrage and disbelief shattered the usual torpor of Washington in August. Al Gore Jr., the Democratic senator from Tennessee, excoriated Baxter in the *Congressional Record*. Baxter "should either faithfully execute the law or resign immediately," Gore demanded. Republicans joined in the criticism. "This is a most unusual and extreme situation," Arlen Specter, the Republican senator from Pennsylvania, observed gravely.

Within days, two Senate committees scheduled a joint hearing and summoned Baxter to Capitol Hill. Republican senators from New Hampshire, Connecticut, and Washington and Democratic senators from Georgia and Ohio took turns pummeling Baxter with criticism. In his soft-spoken way, Baxter was almost contemptuous. He acknowledged that all retail price-fixing was flatly illegal. But, giving no ground, he argued that minimum retail prices can benefit consumers if used by manufacturers of technically complex products to compensate store owners for point-of-sale instruction and subsequent repair services.

Baxter ignored the senators' calls for his resignation. He would not agree to change his approach. He referred repeatedly to a widely publicized lawsuit recently filed against a young technology company, Apple Computer.

Apple was founded on April Fools' Day, 1976, by two college dropouts, Steve Jobs and Steve Wozniak. Wozniak was the more technical of the two. After his junior year as an engineering student at the University of California, he took a job in Hewlett-Packard's calculator division. In his free time, he designed a home computer terminal to connect to the midsize computers that a local company made available to the public on a time-share basis. A friend at HP told Wozniak about a club for people interested in computer terminals that met in one of the members' garages. At the Homebrew Computer Club's meetings, Wozniak developed plans to convert his terminal to a stand-alone computer by incorporating a microprocessor into his design.

A microprocessor is the fundamental electronic component of a modern computer. It can be programmed to perform basic logic and arithmetic functions on a single integrated circuit, permitting a smaller and more cost-effective design than the discrete switches that formed the central processing units of earlier computers. Intel Corporation, a company located in the Santa Clara Valley of northern California, developed the first commercializable microprocessor in 1971. At the time, the area was known as the "Valley of Heart's Delight" because of the lush plum and apricot orchards that dominated the landscape. Intel was one of many companies in the Valley engaged in manufacturing tiny electronic circuits on wafers of silicon, leading a journalist in the electronics industry to refer to the region as "Silicon Valley USA" in a series of articles.

"If I have seen further, it is by standing on ye shoulders of Giants," Sir Isaac Newton wrote in a letter to one of his contemporaries. The great visionaries of Silicon Valley see further by planting their feet firmly on the backs of American taxpayers. Most people know that the Internet started as a government-sponsored research project. Few people understand just how much the nation's leadership position in computing owes to pervasive federal funding.

The Valley's economy started with the discovery of cinnabar, a mixture of mercury and sulfur that the Ohlone Indians used for trading. In 1845, a group of Ohlone showed a Mexican military officer their source of cinnabar. He filed a mineral claim with the Mexican government and began small-scale mining operations. Subsequent owners expanded the mines. The abundant local supply of mercury, a mineraloid known as quicksilver for its use in extracting silver and gold from crushed ore, helped to make the California Gold Rush possible.

When the demand for quicksilver petered out, the area was converted to fruit trees. Tourists from San Francisco came to see the blossoms every spring. Once ripe, the fruit was transported to the Monterey Peninsula for packing and shipment, a less than glamorous process memorialized by John Steinbeck in *Cannery Row*.

AT&T agreed in 1956 to license some of its technology as part of the settlement of a government antitrust suit. Companies lined up to pay nominal amounts—as the settlement specified—for the privilege of commercializing AT&T's research. William Shockley, a former Bell Labs employee, set up his own business in the Santa Clara Valley to develop and produce transistors, the tiny switching devices he coinvented at Bell Laboratories, winning himself a share of the Nobel Prize.

Disenchanted by Shockley's demanding management style, a group of key employees, celebrated in local lore as the "traitorous eight," bolted from Shockley's firm to form their own company only a year later. With the help of the representative of an East Coast investment company, the group raised money from the Fairchild Camera and Instrument Co. to concentrate on opportunities for producing silicon transistors. Fairchild Semiconductor, in turn, spawned dozens of new companies, among them Intel, and bequeathed the region its new name, Silicon Valley.

The label evokes a powerful metaphor. By itself, silicon is worthless. It is a common element found in nature most often as sand. Human ingenuity and hard work can infuse silicon with great economic value. "Silicon Valley is not really a place," a friend once explained. "It's a state of mind." The name became synonymous with individual initiative and personal achievement, particularly in the field of electronics. Libertarians seized upon the image of Silicon Valley to describe a mythical world in which rugged individualism begets productivity and economic success. On closer examination, the Valley looks like one big public welfare project.

Silicon Valley grew from a symbiotic relationship with the federal government. The Valley's electronics industry began in the early twentieth century as radio communication technology funded by U.S. Navy contracts. In 1933 the navy established a base near Sunnyvale, California, now known as Moffett Field, following a public fund-raising campaign that collected almost $500,000 to buy the site from its private owner and sell it to the government for one dollar. Moffett Field became a magnet for aerospace firms servicing the navy. A few years later the forerunner of NASA, the federal government's space agency, built its West Coast laboratories adjacent to the site.

The Valley's subsequent growth owes much to the federal funding of computer research at Stanford University and other nearby institutions. Beginning in the 1930s, Frederick Terman, an electrical engineering professor, encouraged his students to commercialize the technology they developed in Stanford's laboratories. Two of Terman's students, Sigurd and Russell Varian, pioneered the microwave technology upon which government radar detection and guidance systems were built. Later applications of the same technology include the microwave oven. Terman also invested his own money in a fledgling oscillator business formed by two of his students, William Hewlett and David Packard. Hewlett-Packard grew to become one of the largest electronics companies in the world.

An important study presented to President Harry Truman in 1945 called for the government funding of research to meet national needs in defense, health, and the general economy. Private industry, the study argued, could be counted on only to pursue research for developing specific new products and services. The initiative led to the creation of the government research system, including the National Science Foundation. Many government agencies, from the National Security Agency to the National Institutes of Health, participated in the funding of research into specialized computing technologies. The government also provided direct funding for general computing research and for university computer science departments. Roughly 70 percent of the total university research funding in computer science and electrical engineering since 1976 has come from the federal government, according to a 2003 study.

Starting in the 1960s, the government moved to a policy of permitting universities and private contractors to retain exclusive rights to the results of government-financed research and development as a way to stimulate the commercialization of industrial innovation. Stanford students and faculty used government grants to pioneer and exploit successive generations of technology. A single Stanford laboratory, funded in part by government grants, spawned Sun Microsystems, Silicon Graphics, and MIPS, the industry leaders in a wave of powerful computers called workstations. In succeeding decades, government-funded research at Stanford produced the technical framework for the Internet, as well as Google and Yahoo!, two of the leading companies on the World Wide Web.

Jobs and Wozniak were not the first entrepreneurs to form a personal computer company. Many companies preceded theirs; even more were formed at about the same time. Virtually all failed, usually because they lacked management and investment capital. Experienced executives who could command large salaries from established companies shied away from risky ventures. Traditional investors like banks were scared away by the absence of market validation from established firms. IBM, the industry leader, did not even make a microcomputer. When Wozniak showed his plans to his managers at Hewlett-Packard, his employer, they told him that the Apple computer was not a valuable product and gave him a release that permitted him to build the device on his own.

Jobs and Wozniak solved some of their business problems by turning to the Valley's venture capital community. For many generations, wealthy individuals were the primary source of investment for new business opportunities. After World War II, the process of funding new businesses became more institutionalized. Professional investors, known as venture capitalists, raised funds from financial institutions, university endowments, and, in more recent times, pension funds, to invest in new enterprises, usually at an early stage of a company's development. Venture capital was "born in New York and nurtured in Boston," explained the most thorough study of the phenomenon, "but did not really come of age until it moved to California and joined forces with the brash young technologists."

One venture capitalist introduced Jobs and Wozniak to a retired chip company executive, Mike Markkula. Markkula pitched in with the young entrepreneurs and recruited many seasoned executives to the company. Other Valley venture capitalists provided funding.

The start-ups in which VCs invest could not easily qualify for bank loans. The companies have no track record of business operations. Frequently they do not even have a product to sell. Venture capitalists trade operating capital for a negotiated percentage of the company's stock. The stock ownership guarantees the venture capitalists voting rights on the company's board of directors. Development of the company's product can take years, during which time the company's employees draw modest salaries from the invested capital.

The personal success of each venture capitalist is tied closely to the financial success of the companies in which he invests. The venture fund makes most of its money when the stock of its portfolio companies becomes liquid, either through a stock offering or through a sale to another company for cash or publicly traded stock. The venture capitalists on a young company's board can therefore be expected to press the company for achievements sufficient to produce such results.

In publicly traded companies, board members are frequently chosen by the chief executive officer. While they are obligated by law to represent the interests of shareholders, they are more beholden to the chief executive for compensation, stock option grants, and the other benefits they receive, making board pressure on management unlikely.

The pressure for competitive efficiency that Chicago School advocates tout can be obscured and rationalized in a large public company. The very personal financial accountability of venture capitalists for company performance makes the board dynamics of a venture-backed, privately held company far different. Everyone is out to make money and will do so only if the company succeeds. As a consequence, venture capitalists stand ready to fire underperforming company executives, including company founders, largely without regard to the sentimentality and collegiality of personal relationships.

Like much else in Silicon Valley, the venture capital community owes its being to government largesse. In 1958, Senate majority leader Lyndon Johnson decided to enlist support for his presidential campaign by promoting a financing vehicle for small businesses. Johnson's efforts produced a law that empowered the Small Business Administration to establish and regulate private equity funds, known as Small Business Investment Companies. SBICs are privately managed but funded largely by the sale of SBA-guaranteed securities. Government rules specify that the SBA must be repaid with interest before private investors can participate in profits from SBIC investments.

The SBIC program midwived the Valley's venture capital industry. Many of the Valley's most prominent venture capital funds began as SBICs. The federal government was a "limited partner" in these venture capital funds. SBICs have participated in over 60 percent of small business venture financings and at one time were the largest source of risk capital for small companies.

The venture capitalists behind Apple invested some of the taxpayers' money in the young company, just as they had done a few years earlier when they funded Intel. Over the years, SBA money helped to seed many Silicon Valley companies, including the start-ups that produced voice mail, disk drive technology, data storage, Ethernet networking, novel silicon wafer fabrication techniques, and gate array chip technology.

The combination of government facilities, military contracts, unrestricted government research grants to local universities, and government underwriting of high-risk investment provided a foundation on which a dynamic, self-reinforcing industrial model developed. The definitive academic study of the Silicon Valley mind-set, written by AnnaLee Saxenian before she was named dean of UC Berkeley's School of Information, credits the Valley's success to a unique culture of innovation and risk taking, marked by frequent job-hopping and the flow of ideas across company lines. The individuals and firms of the Valley's ecosystem do not regard their fortunes as tied to any one particular company. "People say that when they wake up, they think, 'I work for Silicon Valley,' rather than for a particular company," Saxenian once explained to *Salon*, the online magazine.

From time to time, an arrogant young entrepreneur or investor, imbued with the confidence that a billion dollars can bring, attributes his success wholly to his own abilities. More experienced Silicon Valley hands know the role that luck plays in success—not the luck of the winning lottery ticket, but the good fortune of landing in a place so brimming with opportunities that success can be found through working hard, taking risks, applying intelligence, and catching a few breaks from market forces beyond anyone's control.

The Valley's entrepreneurs and investors enriched themselves from an infrastructure financed by Uncle Sam. Their personal good fortune inures to all of us. Government funding contributed to almost every computer technology in commercial use today, including the graphical elements of the screen displays used by Macintosh and Windows computers, the mouse device, e-mail, messaging, secure online credit card transactions, search engines, speech recognition, databases, video games, flight simulation, and engineering design.

The technologies created and commercialized in Silicon Valley have produced jobs, improved the quality of countless lives, and contributed to the financial well-being of people throughout the country. Those apprehensive about a modest government role in using the antitrust laws to preserve the technology sector's vitality should note the Valley's pedigree. The government's presence in the technology sector has served us well.

Wozniak's first Apple computer consisted of a single circuit board without a case, keyboard, or power supply. A transformer had to be connected just to make the device work. While only a hobbyist would consider buying Wozniak's creation, Jobs saw the potential for a larger market of less technical individuals who would use their own computer—a personal computer—for school and office projects. Jobs worked with Wozniak to produce a fully assembled machine and sold two hundred through the first computer retailers. Jobs designed a more attractive case and an improved keyboard for the next version of the computer Wozniak worked on. The machine was to be ready to run straight out of the box.

The venture capitalists who funded Apple bought into Jobs's vision, as did Mike Markkula. Markkula signed up nationwide distributors in 1977 and began to exhibit Apple's computer at trade shows that featured stereos, calculators, and other electronics products intended for general consumers, rather than technophiles. In August 1977, Apple hired its first professional sales executive, Gene Carter, previously a marketing manager at one of the local chip companies.

As the market for personal computers grew, Apple struggled with distribution challenges. Hundreds of independent retail dealers sold the company's products to end users throughout the country. The dealers bought computers from five authorized distributors. Hardly sophisticated operations themselves, the distributors were nevertheless responsible for selecting, training, and supervising the retail dealers.

After a couple of years of mounting frustration, Carter concluded that reliance on the five independent distributors was hindering Apple's retail market penetration and limiting the company's growth. Carter wanted Apple to participate directly in training retail dealers and he wanted better access to information about end user customers, so he terminated the contracts with the five distributors in February 1980 and began selling computers directly to retailers.

Carter signed up retail dealers at a brisk pace. By the end of the year, he had roughly eight hundred independent retail outlets. Apple launched a public stock offering in December 1980 that generated more money than any initial public stock offering since Ford Motor Company first sold its shares to the public in 1956. As with all Silicon Valley venture-backed companies, most employees, including the company secretaries, owned stock. The public offering instantly created almost three hundred million-aires, bringing notoriety and more growth to the young company. By May 1981, Apple had almost one thousand retail dealers around the country selling its products.

If Apple was really going to succeed over the long haul, Carter knew he had to implement Jobs's vision—people who never even thought of operating a computer were going to have to be convinced to buy one. Early personal computers were difficult to use. Jobs did not introduce the Macintosh, with its more intuitive graphical user interface, until 1984. And personal computers were expensive. A typical Apple computer by itself cost about $1,200 at retail, up to $5,000 with peripheral devices and software packages, far more than the typical consumer product. Some of Apple's early competitors relied on national advertising to generate consumer demand and offered little more than product literature to provide assembly and operating instructions. Jobs and Carter believed that getting the consumer educated was the key to Apple's success. The more the consumer knew about computers, the more likely he was to make a purchase. The more he knew about Apple's computers, the more likely he was to choose them over the competition. In economic terms, Apple needed to "differentiate" its product offerings from those of competitors.

Carter instructed his staff to select retail dealers who could identify and educate Apple's target customers. A retailer needed an enticing storefront in a high-rent neighborhood to lure just the right prospect in. Dealer sales personnel had to provide demonstrations, classes, and other customer services sufficient to give potential buyers confidence that ordinary people could use computers productively. Even extensive point-of-sale service was not sufficient to guarantee market acceptance for such a revolutionary and expensive product. Many potential buyers knew they would have postsale questions and also wanted some assurance that handholding and education would be forthcoming from dealers after a purchase.

All of this cost money. Apple's executives struggled to find the best mechanism to compensate dealers for providing the costly customer services the company demanded. Paying dealers directly for demonstrations and other services that did not result in sales invited misdirected efforts and waste, perhaps even outright dealer fraud.

Dealer self-interest worked against providing customer services. Dealers could make more money most easily by cutting costs. So long as other dealers created a pool of ready buyers by providing presale education and postsale support, the quickest dealer pathway to higher profit was to increase sales volume and decrease customer service. Not surprisingly, a few opportunistic Apple dealers began to advertise low prices nationally, to sell by phone order and mail delivery, and to shortchange storefront activities.

The balance of Apple's dealers grew increasingly annoyed. They bore the expenses of high-rent storefronts and sales training for their personnel who spent time educating potential buyers, only to lose the sales to low-price, mail order solicitations. When dealer sales personnel were asked for instruction by customers who bought their computers from low-priced mail order operations, emotions boiled over.

Dealer complaints to Apple about competition from mail order sales quickly swelled to a torrent. Dealers threatened to stop spending money on expensive storefronts, sales staff, and consumer education. Some even threatened to drop Apple's line entirely. In early 1981, Apple began telling its dealers that it would find a way to address their concerns.

The threats to drop Apple's line took on a new urgency later in the year when IBM introduced its own brand of personal computers. Compared to Apple, IBM had a powerful brand and limitless resources. IBM started selling its computers through independent dealers, including those who sold Apple's products. The dealers had to bear fewer costs on sales of IBM's machines because IBM already had product centers in most metropolitan areas dedicated to promoting its products and dispensing information about them. Another important Apple competitor, Radio Shack, could guarantee customer support and service because it sold its computers through a nationwide chain of company-owned retail stores.

Apple could not afford to ignore the market activities of its closest competitors. If the company was going to prosper, it had to find a way to guarantee better service and support than either IBM or Radio Shack. Apple lacked both the expertise and resources to open its own nationwide chain of retail stores. Even if capital could be found, it was well beyond the capability of a start-up company with a new technology product to enter the market on two levels, manufacturing and retail, simultaneously. Nor was there time to execute such a strategy. For better or worse, Apple's future depended entirely on the goodwill and hard work of hundreds of independent small business operators. The company had to stop the opportunistic dealers from destroying its entire dealer network.

The dealers who were making hundreds of thousands of dollars each month drop-shipping Apple computers all over the country at cut-rate prices had other ideas. They were not going to stop making easy money just because Apple told them to, and they would certainly file a lawsuit if Apple tried to stop them. Their leader was a voluble French expatriate named Francis Ravel, who ran a thriving mail order business from a small storefront in Los Angeles. Ravel sued Toshiba Corp. of Japan in 1973, winning what he described as a "substantial" cash settlement. Apple "can't tell us not to ship from our store," Ravel declared in the *Wall Street Journal*. "Hewlett-Packard wouldn't dare do that."

As word of Apple's intentions spread, Ravel sent a letter to Mike Markkula that he copied to each one of Apple's board members. The letter accused the company of "succumbing to the pressure of small Apple dealers," and recounted many meetings in which angry dealers complained to Apple about retail price-cutting by other dealers. Apple's concern with the mail order sale of its products, Ravel's letter concluded, was intended to "eliminate price cutters" and "discounters" and fix "the retail price of Apple products so the dealers could make more money and at the same time protect their territory."

If Apple tried to stop Ravel's mail order sales, he vowed to file a "substantial size class action" against Apple for antitrust violations. Ravel's threats did not stop with a lawsuit. "I will make it my business to go to Washington and make direct contact with Mr. William French Smith," Reagan's attorney general and Baxter's boss, Ravel declared, and "I will request from all the U.S. senators to push for an investigation with the Justice Department of Apple Computer."

Ravel's letter mockingly suggested to Markkula that he "hire the services of a super anti-trust lawyer." The Silicon Valley law firm that had incorporated Apple and successfully represented the company in its litigation with distributors decided that it needed additional antitrust expertise for its bevy of increasingly sophisticated technology clients, so the firm recruited me from Washington, D.C., where I had been practicing law for five years—hardly sufficient experience to qualify as a "super antitrust lawyer."

The firm made the same pitch to me that had already enticed countless technologists and business executives to the Valley and that would be used in the future to lure many more. "If you stay in the East," they said, "you'll be carrying somebody's briefcase until you're forty. Out here, all that matters is how good you are."

Although I had never even seen a personal computer, I felt well prepared for the challenge. I worked my way through college programming mainframe computers for the school's economics department. In law school, I took three antitrust courses. I understood the Chicago School approach. After law school, I spent five years working in the largest law firm in Washington, D.C., doing some of the most sophisticated antitrust work around for clients like Exxon, Nabisco, Scott Paper Company, and American Can Company. I had key roles in some of the biggest and most storied antitrust trials of the era. But none of that prepared me for Silicon Valley.

On my first day in my new office, I got called into a meeting with a group of corporate lawyers. Hewlett-Packard was threatening to sue two young entrepreneurs, clients of my new firm, who had abruptly resigned from the company. A few months later, they began to market a product very similar to what they had been getting paid by HP to produce. Hewlett-Packard claimed that the two had improperly used the company's confidential information in their new venture. The entrepreneurs swore otherwise. I was incredulous at their denials. No way they could have possibly gotten their own product to market so quickly without using HP's trade secrets, I thought.

"What do you want me to tell the judge?" I sarcastically asked the partner in charge. "Do you really want me to argue that these two guys started from scratch, and working in somebody's basement with second-hand equipment for nine months, produced a complex product that a full-fledged development team at HP couldn't perfect, despite three years of effort?"

The other lawyers in the room stared at me in disbelief. "Well, of course," one of them finally said, shaking his head at my naïveté. After a bit of posturing, HP went away, not even bothering to file suit. The experience taught me that bigger companies are not necessarily the most innovative or the most productive. Bigger is not necessarily better.

I had not distinguished myself on my first Silicon Valley assignment. I hoped to do better with Apple's problem. It looked to me like a question straight out of one of Baxter's antitrust exams. The business strategy to remedy the problem was clear enough. Apple simply needed to require its dealers to resell computers at sufficiently high prices to produce margins adequate to fund the various services the company demanded. But the law was not at all sympathetic.

A 1911 Supreme Court decision made it per se illegal for a manufacturer to require its retailers to charge specified prices. The per se rule meant that if a dealer proved that Apple employed resale price maintenance, the company would not even be given the opportunity to explain, much less prove, that its policy helped rather than hurt consumers. No weight would be given to the argument that Apple was trying to make sure that consumers were adequately educated so that they would be satisfied with their purchases. Evidence that consumers could buy any of more than a dozen different brands of computers, produced by manufacturers that did not control their dealers' prices, was beside the point. If Apple fixed retail prices, it violated the antitrust law, notwithstanding any other factors. Dealers terminated by Apple for refusing to sell at the designated prices could sue the company for damages, which under the law would be automatically trebled.

The per se prohibition against setting dealers' resale prices did not extend to "vertical nonprice restraints"—restrictions not specifically directed to price (exclusive sales territories, for example) set up by a manufacturer to curb competition among its dealers. When vertical nonprice restraints first came before the Supreme Court in 1963, even liberals on the Court refused to invoke a per se ban. "We know too little of the actual impact of [such restrictions] to reach a conclusion on the bare bones of the documentary evidence before us," the Court ruled. Vertical nonprice restrictions were to be judged for reasonableness in light of the circumstances of the particular case, the usual rule of reason test. Only four years later, the Supreme Court did an about-face, holding illegal per se territorial and customer account limitations imposed by a manufacturer to limit dealer competition.

Ten years after that, the Supreme Court made another U-turn, reestablishing rule of reason treatment for vertical nonprice restraints like exclusive dealer territories, but maintaining the per se rule against a manufacturer setting its dealers' resale prices. In a case involving the retail distribution of television sets, the Court recognized that a manufacturer's nonprice restriction on its dealers might injure consumers by limiting each dealer's competition with the manufacturer's other dealers. The restriction might at the same time help consumers by improving the manufacturer's ability to upgrade its dealer network and compete against other manufacturers, producing more consumer choices and better product quality in the market as a whole.

The distinction between resale price maintenance and vertical nonprice restraints gave me a hook on which to hang Apple's policy. I advised the company to rewrite all of its dealer contracts to prohibit the mail order resale of Apple computers, expressly leaving to each dealer the price he charged. But simply enunciating what looked like a nonprice restraint did not solve the company's legal problems.

The distinction between resale price maintenance and vertical nonprice restraints often proved fuzzy in court. Both types of restrictions reduce competition among a manufacturer's dealers. Logically, both price and nonprice restraints on dealers raise consumer prices for the manufacturer's product above where they would have been if the manufacturer's dealers competed in a less fettered way with each other. On the other hand, both types of restraints improve a manufacturer's ability to compete against other manufacturers, at least in theory. Conservatives saw no basis for treating vertical price restrictions differently from nonprice restraints, and Baxter was looking for a case in which he could intervene to make the point that all restrictions imposed by a manufacturer, price and nonprice alike, should be evaluated under the rule of reason.

Apple was facing enough difficulties without becoming the test case to challenge the per se rule against resale price maintenance. Better to avoid conduct in the per se category altogether. To avoid per se treatment, I would first have to prove that Apple's mail order prohibition did not amount to vertical resale price-setting. Then I would have to tackle a more complicated issue.

Many agreements among competitors to restrict competition are also illegal per se. Baxter and other conservatives strongly supported this position. Apple did not conspire with any of its own competitors to prohibit mail order sales, but what about a conspiracy among Apple's dealers? They all competed with each other. If the mail order prohibition was the result of an agreement among dealers that was forced on Apple, rather than a ban initiated and imposed by Apple in its own interests, the prohibition would be judged a per se illegal agreement in restraint of trade among competitors, even if it did not amount to vertical price-fixing.

I quickly set about making a factual record to defend the mail order prohibition in court, assuming Ravel would carry out his threats. To rebut claims of resale price maintenance, I hired professional shoppers to buy computers from mail order dealers who resold Apple products at the full retail price suggested by the company. Apple's new prohibition would ban these sales even though they were made at high prices. I also had shoppers buy Apple computers from storefront dealers in fully supported sales at prices well below Apple's suggested price. These sales would be permitted under the mail order prohibition, notwithstanding the low prices the dealers charged. The purchases put me in a position to show that the mail order prohibition did not amount to resale price maintenance. The dealers retained full pricing discretion once the ban went into effect.

Preparing to rebut charges of a dealer conspiracy was more difficult. There was no easy way to separate a ban put forward by the dealers from one initiated by Apple in its own interest. Dealers complained to Apple about mail order virtually every day. Barring mail order sales would help full service Apple dealers as well as Apple itself. Making a legal record to prove that the mail order ban was initiated by Apple in its own interest, rather than created as an artifice to further a dealer conspiracy, was like trying to prove the chicken came before the egg.

I tried to insulate the company's new policy from dealer complaints by making Apple's board of directors the decision maker for the company's mail order prohibition. Most of the board members had not talked to dealers and had never received complaints personally. I had independent industry experts consult with the board about the costs borne by full support dealers. The experts advised the board that, unless prohibited, mail order sales would destroy Apple's dealer network.

I also prepared a rule of reason defense, on the assumption I could get the company's mail order policy past claims of per se illegality. When the Supreme Court approved rule of reason treatment for vertical nonprice restraints, it gave little guidance as to how lower courts, in making reasonableness determinations, were to balance the consumer harm from less competition among the dealers of the manufacturer enforcing the restraint against the potential consumer benefit of more vigorous competition among manufacturers themselves. Earlier Supreme Court decisions that applied rule of reason analysis merely listed a hodgepodge of factors the Court deemed worthy of consideration: how the business at issue operates, the effect of the restraint, the intent of the manufacturer, and on and on.

The Supreme Court's opinion in the television set case called out two factors for significant comment. First, in assessing the effect of the restraint on the overall level of competition in the market, the Court worried more about competition among manufacturers than competition among the dealers in any one manufacturer's distribution chain. Lower courts applied this guidance by trying to determine whether a manufacturer had enough clout in the overall market to hurt consumers when the manufacturer curbed competition among its own dealers.

In antitrust parlance, these cases required plaintiff-dealers to prove Apple's "market power" to win a rule of reason case. Despite its importance in antitrust analysis, courts have had a difficult time defining "market power" precisely. The *Standard Oil* decision mentioned the company's ability to raise prices and limit output. Robert Bork emphasized the "output" part in his discussion. A later Supreme Court decision talked about the power to "control prices or exclude competition." Economists quibbled with this formulation. One offered "the ability to raise price while excluding competition." Another pointed to the ability to maintain prices rather than to raise prices above competitive levels. A Supreme Court decision from the 1980s even injected the notion of reducing consumer choices as a cognizable characteristic of monopoly power.

Whatever the exact words, antitrust enforcers worry about a company's ability to hurt consumers by keeping its prices above the levels predicted in perfect competition models. "Market power" means some of this power, but less than a complete monopolist has. Of course, all companies have a little market power. Consumer preferences or transitory advantages often permit companies to charge more than their own marginal costs without losing too many sales. But if a company has a lot of market power, it can raise prices to the point of creating a significant deadweight loss.

Measuring market power directly is difficult. Instead, antitrust enforcers usually look for market conditions that could support the exercise of power. Lower courts frequently use the manufacturer's market share as a proxy for its market power. The explosive growth of the personal computer industry made Apple's market share a matter of some debate—it could have been as high as 30 percent, depending on when and where you looked. Whatever the company's exact share, I could easily show that Apple had no real power over price or competition. Formidable new competitors entered the business literally every week. If the mail order prohibition hurt Apple's potential customers, they would flock to other brands, punishing Apple for its distribution restraint.

The Supreme Court's television distribution opinion also suggested that a manufacturer might have a good reason for restraining competition among its dealers—a "legitimate business justification." A manufacturer could use vertical nonprice restraints to make dealers provide promotional activities, customer service, and repair facilities. Because of what the Supreme Court called the "free-rider effect," retailers were unlikely to provide these beneficial customer services unless the manufacturer required them to.

A University of Chicago economist, Lester Telser, first explained the free-rider effect in a 1960 academic article. Providing costly consumer services usually increases sales, helping both the manufacturer and its dealers. Telser argued that customers would take these valuable services from the dealer that provided them but would then buy the product at the lowest available price, even from another dealer—permitting the second dealer to "free ride" on the money spent by the first dealer to provide the services. Unless the manufacturer stopped free riding by imposing a vertical restraint of some kind, no dealer would provide desirable customer services and the sales of the manufacturer's product would suffer.

Telser made a theoretical argument about free riding. The Supreme Court credited the free-rider rationale as a legitimate business justification for a vertical nonprice restraint. To win a court challenge against the mail order ban, I had to translate these theoretical suggestions into something a judge could rely on. I had to make a record proving Apple's desire to provide customer services and the company's inability to prevent free riding without the mail order prohibition. The "free-rider justification" could carry the day in a rule of reason analysis if the question of market power was difficult to resolve. Proving the bona fides of a free-rider justification would also cut the guts out of any claim that Apple imposed the mail order prohibition in response to a dealer conspiracy. Proving a free-rider problem showed that the mail order ban actually helped Apple, not just its dealers.

Even after making all of these preparations, I wanted to be able to show a judge that Apple gave all of its dealers every opportunity to cooperate with the company's plan. Apple's written agreement with its dealers permitted the company to stop selling to them for any reason at all on thirty days' notice, but we did not immediately terminate any dealers, even those who had been selling Apple computers mail order. Instead, dealers were all given the opportunity to sign a new agreement stating that they would not engage in mail order sales. All of Apple's dealers signed the new agreements and they were all permitted to continue to sell Apple's products.

I had done everything I could think of to improve Apple's chances in court. "What we're doing is the state of the art in antitrust law," a young

Steve Jobs told the *Wall Street Journal*, referring to the ban on mail order sales. "We could go all the way to the Supreme Court."

A few days later, Francis Ravel and five other dealers, all of whom signed the new agreements, brought suit in federal court in Los Angeles. The dealers asked for an injunction preventing Apple from implementing its new policy. The motion was scheduled for argument a few days before Christmas in 1981 in front of a judge who had been appointed by the Democrats. Both sides filed stacks of papers and affidavits. We grew anxious as the date for the argument approached. Democratic judges generally side with plaintiffs' trial lawyers. If the judge stopped Apple from barring mail order sales, the company's entire distribution network would be thrown into chaos, and the company's stock price would likely crater.

On December 21, the two sides argued back and forth for almost two hours. The dealers' lawyer claimed that the mail order prohibition was nothing more than a price-fixing conspiracy orchestrated by Apple at the behest of disgruntled dealers. He predicted that prices for Apple's computers would rise 25 percent if mail order sales were prohibited. He said that the six dealers would suffer $20 million in damages.

We argued that consumers had plenty of other computer choices, with new companies entering the market every day. And we pointed out how many of Apple's larger competitors had company-owned facilities that they could use to provide support.

Eventually, it all came down to whether the judge would believe what we said about the need for dealer support, our free-rider justification. She directed my partner Bill Fenwick "to show why support is necessary" if he wanted to defeat the dealers' motion. Fenwick walked from the lawyer's lectern, carrying an Apple IIc computer further into the well of the court, until he was standing only a few feet from the judge's elevated desk.

Apple's sleek case included both the central processing unit and the keyboard. The user could put a program into the computer only through a disk drive and the drive had to be properly connected to the case. In most early computers, this was not just a matter of plugging in a cord. A circuit card from the hard drive had to be inserted manually into a specific slot inside the case. To get results out of the computer, a printer or monitor had to be connected, again by going into the case, finding the right slot, and making the installation manually.

Fenwick popped off the top of the computer case, exposing a maze of printed circuits, sockets, and unmarked slots. To make the computer "do anything," Fenwick explained, "you have got to have other peripherals." The judge leaned over her bench, staring down into what must have looked like a hospital patient with his brain exposed, prepped for neurosurgery. Her eyes were wide, more in terror than amazement.

"For instance," Fenwick continued, "to make the disk drive work, the interface card has to be inserted. If it is inserted wrong, it will destroy the card and can destroy the system." The judge sucked in a sharp breath.

"If you don't take the precaution of discharging the electricity out of your body before you handle the card, you will find that you have destroyed the circuit," Fenwick instructed solemnly. The judge rolled her eyes. Of course, to "discharge the electricity out of your body," you just had to touch some grounded object, but the judge didn't seem to know that.

Fenwick never came right out and said it, but his point was clear to everyone in the courtroom. In untrained hands, a personal computer was an instrument of death. Doubtless the judge could see in her mind's eye the front-page picture in the *Los Angeles Times* of some poor soul electrocuted while trying to balance his family budget, the charred body splayed across the kitchen table, gnarled fingers still on the keyboard. "Unsupported Computer Sale Kills San Fernando Man," the headline would read. "Federal Judge to Blame."

The judge started in her chair, but Fenwick didn't notice. He was on a roll. "What happens is the vast majority of consumers go to a retailer in their town. They see it demonstrated. They have it presented. They get the information, and then they buy from a mail order dealer. That means the local dealer doesn't get any revenue out of that. He has had the expense and gets no revenue."

The judge had stopped listening back at "discharge the electricity out of your body." She cut Fenwick off. "I do have more I would like to say," he entreated.

"I don't think that it's necessary," she said excitedly. "The court does not feel . . . there is a sufficient showing of the likelihood of success by the plaintiffs," she announced, pounding her gavel on the desk. There would be no injunction. Apple could prohibit the mail order sale of its products for the time being. But the judge's ruling was not a final decision. There would still be a full trial to a lay jury down the road. If the plaintiffs won, Apple would owe damages to every one of its dealers who lost sales from the mail order ban.

Jurors might side with dealers selling at low prices, regardless of the need for customer support. We could get the judge to toss out the case without ever giving it to a jury, but only by making a record so overwhelming that no reasonable person could find against Apple. It would not be easy. Asking a judge appointed by the Democrats to take a case away from a plaintiff's trial lawyer is asking quite a lot.

CHAPTER 4

The Price Is Not Right

Over the years, Francis Ravel made some well-placed connections to Republican congressmen. A couple of months after the preliminary injunction hearing, one of them arranged for Ravel to meet with Bill Baxter. Ravel demanded that Baxter put a stop to Apple's conduct. Baxter listened carefully as Ravel explained what Apple was doing. Just the kind of case Baxter was looking for. He was likely to intervene in the case, he said, but on Apple's side, not Ravel's. Baxter instructed one of his deputies to call me and get a copy of our court papers.

Ravel was beside himself. He was not going down without a fight. He complained to his congressional contacts about Baxter's intentions. David Vise's front-page article in the *Post* was the last straw. The congressional oversight committees summoned Baxter to Capitol Hill.

The hearing began with a lengthy statement from Senator Metzenbaum. For almost twenty minutes, Metzenbaum attacked Baxter's policies, integrity, and candor. "For the sake of American consumers," Metzenbaum concluded, "I very strongly feel that the only decent thing, the only right thing for Mr. Baxter to do would be to resign his position."

The committee turned to Baxter. Senator Slade Gorton of Washington questioned whether the distribution scheme a manufacturer chose for itself would automatically "be in the consumers' or the general public's interest." Isn't the goal of restrictive distribution agreements to raise the manufacturer's profits, while reducing the output of its product, Gorton wanted to know? Baxter explained that a manufacturer would always try to increase its own profits. That may or may not help the public, depending on how much market power the manufacturer has.

New Hampshire senator Warren Rudman confronted Baxter more directly. The Apple case "is familiar to most of us," Rudman said. "Isn't it pretty likely that that is such a significant case involving the antitrust law that you will probably get involved in it?"

"It seems to me quite a good example of the kind of instance in which the existing per se rule can be harmful," Baxter replied.

Rudman sympathized far more with the mail order dealers than with Apple. "That is kind of a tough battle," Rudman said. "Apple and the U.S. Department of the Justice—against some little distributor out there."

Then Rudman attacked Baxter's economic rationale. Rudman saw no untoward economic effects "if in fact consumers are able to buy Apple equipment through their mail order distributors at a lower cost than they are at their local computer store." Rudman threatened Baxter with "legislative action" if he did not change his policies.

Chicago School proponents, following Robert Bork's lead, usually looked at the antitrust laws as a mechanism to promote efficiency, measured only by output and price. Baxter recognized that in an age of high technology, antitrust policy must broaden its goals in order to promote economic progress. Baxter told the senators that "in the short run" it may be "good for consumers" if they can buy Apple computers at low prices through discount stores. "The problem is that the incentive to invent, to innovate, and develop complex products such as Apple computers is strongly affected over the course of time by the rules that apply to the process of distribution.

"The real question is whether we are going to continue to have Apple computers," Baxter said. He explained that he was using Apple's product to represent the whole new world of complex high tech products. "The rules of distribution that we now have are strongly punitive with respect to technologically complex computer products," Baxter said. Baxter wanted to change the counterproductive antitrust policies. More than that, he wanted to change the discipline's focus. Sometimes, particularly for high technology, antitrust doctrine needs to emphasize innovation over price or output.

The committee's questions moved to other subjects. Although Baxter told the senators that he had not yet decided about intervening, the Apple case remained very much on his mind. Over the next year and a half, whenever Baxter had the opportunity, he used Apple as the poster child for distribution reform.

I cared a lot less about the proper development of antitrust law than about winning Apple's case. All I really wanted to know was whether Baxter would file a court paper supporting a motion to throw out the dealers' lawsuit. I called his office weekly. His deputies always assured me that he was close to making a decision, but it was apparent that the political opposition had slowed things down.

At the preliminary injunction hearing, we convinced the judge that most potential computer purchasers needed the support Apple was trying to get its dealers to supply. Our position relied more on argument than proof. Apple required its dealers to provide hands-on, face-to-face presale support to each potential customer. A mail order dealer, by the very nature of its business, could not possibly give the same personalized service. Mail order dealers *must* be free riding on the investments made by full service dealers in training salesmen, giving product demonstrations, and underwriting attractive storefronts with repair facilities. It all made perfect sense, but we had no real proof of free riding.

Some Chicago School opponents argued that the free-riding justification was just a pretext used by manufacturers to raise retail prices. Free riding doesn't really occur that much in the real world, they said. Other critics claimed that discounting dealers actually perform desired customer services and can charge less because they sell more efficiently than full-price dealers. When manufacturers impose vertical restraints, they punish discounters for being efficient, the critics asserted. Either way, to get the case against Apple thrown out without a trial, I would need more than a logical argument. I would need to show by uncontested evidence that in-store sales activities cost more than mail order sales and that mail order dealers were trying to free ride on that investment.

I pounded the dealers with waves of discovery, demanding documents and deposition interrogations under oath. The documents produced by one dealer showed that he charged less for mail order sales than for in-store sales of the very same Apple computers. By his own conduct, that plaintiff admitted that customer support costs a lot of money. I still needed uncontested evidence to show that free riding was more than just a theoretical phenomenon, so I scheduled Francis Ravel for two weeks of depositions. On the sixth day away from his store, Ravel got irritated. He was tired and just wanted the ordeal to end.

I asked question after question, trying to wear him down. "Do you know what happens, sir, if a potential customer calls [your store] over the telephone and says, 'I don't know much about computers, but I think I might be able to use one.' What happens then?" I asked, for about the fiftieth time.

Ravel had enough. "If I was the salesman, I would tell him, 'Why don't you go to a Computerland store or Macy's; try it and buy it from us cheaper.' That's what I would do if I was a salesman. He's in New York, how can I tell him anything? I cannot send him one for a demo."

Ravel's lawyer was tugging at the witness's sleeve, but there was no stopping him. "I would say, 'Go to Macy's or Sears and Roebuck. Try one. Call me back. We'll give you a better deal and I'll ship it to you.'"

"Got you," I said.

"Okay," Ravel replied. Ravel's lawyer sank his face into his hands.

In late 1982, after months of waiting fruitlessly for Baxter to intervene, I filed my motion to throw out the dealers' case. The motion sat in the judge's chambers for weeks, stretching to months. I feared the worst—a Democratic appointee was not going to take away a case from a plaintiff's trial lawyer. I started calling Baxter's office, begging for help. Finally, at the beginning of March 1983, the government's brief arrived, signed by Baxter himself. It supported our motion in all respects. The judge admitted Baxter's brief into the record over the dealers' objections. But the judge still did not rule on our motion.

In May, a new judge was appointed to the federal bench in Los Angeles. Her docket was drawn at random from the cases pending before the other judges in the district. By chance, not to mention divine grace, the Apple case was assigned to Pamela Ann Rymer. Prior to her appointment by President Reagan, Rymer was one of the most widely respected defendants' antitrust lawyers in the Los Angeles area. She described herself as "a lifelong

Republican." She was one of four women in her graduating class from Stanford Law School where she studied antitrust under Bill Baxter. Her first job after graduation was in the campaign of presidential candidate Barry Goldwater. Our prospects were looking up.

At the oral argument on Apple's motion the week after Thanksgiving, my role consisted largely of watching Rymer pound the dealers' lawyer into the ground like a stake. The judge had read the entire file, including thousands of pages of deposition testimony. She reprimanded the plaintiffs' lawyer whenever he misstated the record. She was familiar with every case either side cited. She even corrected the plaintiffs' lawyer when he misconstrued a footnote in one of the opinions he relied on.

The dealers' lawyer spent most of his time arguing that Apple's conduct amounted to a per se violation of the antitrust laws. We were prepared to present facts showing that the company's mail order policy actually helped most consumers by eliminating free riding in order to guarantee point of sale services. But the dealers' lawyer argued that Apple should pay damages under the inflexible per se rule that assumed competitive injury, even when investigation revealed there was none.

The lawyer's position was not as odd as it sounded. The per se rule is not intended to prohibit only those practices that *always* hurt competition. The courts adopt per se rules more for convenience than anything else. Per se illegality applies to the kind of conduct that *almost always* hurts competition. It's just not worth spending the time and trouble in any particular case trying to see if the per se conduct in that case is the infrequent exception to the usual anticompetitive injury. Conspiring competitors usually try to fix prices at high monopoly levels. Of course, conspirators might occasionally set a lower price that helps consumers by achieving the best allocation of resources. Letting conspiring competitors make the argument that their usually anticompetitive conduct turned out for the best would subject antitrust trials to endless economic explanations and justifications. So courts made price-fixing by competitors illegal all the time, regardless of the specific circumstances.

Injudicious extension of the per se rule to new and not well-understood business practices risks banning by court fiat conduct that, on balance, helps consumers. So courts limit per se condemnation to conduct with a "limited potential for procompetitive benefit" that produces "predictable and pernicious anticompetitive effect." The description hardly fits the mail order ban, so the plaintiffs' lawyer tried to fit Apple's conduct into a category more worthy of per se condemnation.

First, he argued that Apple's mail order prohibition was a "cover-up" to conceal a conspiracy among Apple's dealers for the purpose of limiting competition at the retail level. Plaintiffs' lawyer pointed to dealer complaints about mail order and price cutting as evidence of conspiracy, but Rymer disagreed. "A distributor who complains about free-riding . . . is encouraging, and quite properly, a more efficient system of distribution," she said. She would not infer a conspiracy just from dealer complaints, particularly in light of the dealer admission about free riding.

Then, the lawyer claimed that Apple made price-fixing agreements with the dealers. Again, the judge saw things differently. She held "the allusions to agreements" by the dealers in the evidentiary record to be "just absolute speculation."

The dealers' per se case failed. Apple won hands down when the judge turned to a rule of reason analysis. In the year since the preliminary injunction hearing, even more manufacturers entered the personal computer market, bringing the total number of Apple's competitors to fifty-seven. Apple faced competition from the world's largest and second-largest computer companies, the largest manufacturers of consumer electronics, and the largest office equipment and word processing companies. Even with the mail order prohibition and the hundreds of new dealers Apple added, the company's market share dropped, hovering at about 6 percent in late 1982. All of the competition forced Apple to cut its prices to dealers as well as its suggested retail prices, belying the plaintiffs' prediction of double-digit increases. Apple's sales increased, just as management had hoped, and published comparisons by industry analysts as well as consumer surveys praised the support Apple dealers provided.

"You are out of luck under the rule of reason," Rymer told the dealers' lawyer. The judge granted our motion to throw out all the dealers' claims. Because Apple's mail order ban produced no significant competitive injury, the judge didn't have to further evaluate the bona fides of our free-rider defense or decide when the need to foster innovation trumps other competitive concerns—the more pressing question Bill Baxter worried about. Had the market facts presented a closer case, the balance of policy considerations should still have favored Apple. After all, we want a Steve Jobs, not a small-time electronics dealer in Los Angeles, deciding how to deliver a new technology to consumers.

One aspect of the Apple case remains anomalous, at least by today's standards. The litigation centered on the economic effect of Apple's mail order prohibition, yet we put on our case without submitting an expert opinion from an economist. The dealers didn't rely on an economist either. Nor did the trial judge voice any need for an economist to help her decide which side should win. Despite the vagueness of the rule of reason standard, earlier court opinions gave Judge Rymer sufficient guidance to decide, within the framework of a fully formed evidentiary record, whether the mail order prohibition hurt competition.

A more complicated case might well call for expert testimony from economists. But the resolution of a properly framed antitrust case turns on what the late Harvard antitrust professor Phillip Areeda called "estimates and judgments about reality" and the application of "matters of policy." Judges, not economists, are most qualified to make these decisions. Economics played its proper role in the Apple mail order case. Policy factors were identified using the insights provided by economists. The trial judge made factual determinations. Economics illuminated the analysis. It did not dictate the result.

In Washington, things were not going as well for Bill Baxter. With the delays in resolving Apple's motion, Baxter's attention turned to another distribution case that was moving more briskly through the courts. A manufacturer of pesticides had terminated one of its distributors in northern Illinois after receiving complaints about price cutting from other distributors. The terminated distributor claimed its low prices and its competitors' complaints were the reasons for the manufacturer's action. A jury agreed and awarded the distributor more than $10 million after mandatory trebling. When a court of appeals affirmed the verdict, the Supreme Court agreed to hear the case.

Under the terms of Baxter's sabbatical agreement with Stanford, he was required to return to the university by the end of 1983. The pesticide case was going to be Baxter's best, and likely only, opportunity to change the antitrust rules for product distribution. Baxter filed a brief urging the Supreme Court to abandon the per se rule for resale price maintenance and instead to judge vertical price-fixing under the rule of reason standard used to evaluate other types of dealer restraints imposed by manufacturers. He received the Supreme Court's permission to press his point in oral argument, scheduled for the first week in December.

Robert Bork and other Chicago School adherents argued for a legal rule making all vertical restraints unilaterally imposed by a manufacturer, including resale price maintenance, completely lawful all the time. A manufacturer would never use vertical restraints to raise price or restrict output, Bork contended. Getting dealers involved in reducing output required a manufacturer with market power to share its monopoly profits with the dealers. If a manufacturer had enough market power to raise prices by limiting output, it would execute that strategy by itself, without using dealer restraints on competition to reduce output, so that the manufacturer could keep the entire monopoly profit. Since a manufacturer would not logically use vertical restraints to restrict output, there must be some other explanation for the use of such restraints. By eliminating the output-reducing explanation, Bork concluded that vertical restraints were used to increase the efficiency of the manufacturer's distribution network.

More careful analysis by Harvard economist F. M. Scherer proved Bork's conclusion incorrect. Bork's analysis looked only at a single manufacturer, failing to consider the effect on the overall level of efficiency in the market if many manufacturers employed vertical restrictions at the same time. If most manufacturers imposed vertical restraints, prices for all of their products would go up. Many consumers would be charged for services they neither need nor want, so the overall level of efficiency would decline. A legal rule that always holds vertical restraints lawful actually hurts consumers. The better approach is a situation-specific determination of market power and consumer benefits under a rule of reason analysis.

Baxter took this approach. He even testified against a bill that would have permitted exclusive territories for beer distributors. "The malt beverage industry is a good example of those very special circumstances in which widespread use of [exclusive territories] might have anticompetitive effects," he said.

Baxter knew the Supreme Court's vague and uncertain approach to rule of reason analysis needed improvement. He called for a "structured judicial inquiry" that is "as short and efficient as it can be" to determine whether vertical restraints are "potentially harmful" in a specific situation. The precise steps of the analysis were less important to Baxter than the notion of a limited but structured investigation into the facts of each particular case.

Baxter argued that high tech consumer products, what he called "information impacted goods," present the clearest justification for vertical restrictions. Most consumers need and want pre- and postsale services with these products. To increase consumer sales, manufacturers need a mechanism to ensure consumer education and to prevent free riding.

At the other end of the spectrum were commodities, particularly those produced by only a few sellers in a concentrated market. Baxter used the example of aspirin. He feared that manufacturers would employ dealer restraints as a mechanism to raise consumer prices.

The consumer effect of vertical restraints on a third set of goods was more difficult for Baxter to evaluate. He called these "brand-image goods" and used logo-bearing golf shirts as an example. Price-discounting dealers would discourage manufacturer investment in image-building advertising for these products. Although Baxter conceded that "the case is nowhere near as compelling in economic terms as it is for information-impacted goods," he would, in general, have permitted resale price maintenance to encourage product diversity.

Examining the key facts in an orderly and systematic way will resolve the easy cases in which one side or the other can't prove something important. But, even the best rule of reason analysis, Baxter acknowledged, will not always provide a clear empirical answer to the question of whether consumers are injured by a vertical restraint.

Baxter explained the point using the example (before electronic banking and ATMs) of a second bank setting up business in a growing town with a single bank at its commercial center. If the second bank sets up operations across the street from the first one, the two banks would engage in head-to-head competition, lowering prices for banking services more than if the second bank located in a suburb across town. But the suburban location would be more convenient and therefore preferable for consumers in the suburb, even if the second bank's prices were higher. The suburban location differentiates the second bank's offering, making it less desirable for some consumers and more desirable for others. Deciding whether the overall level of consumer welfare declines if the second bank locates in the suburbs requires calculating the trade-off between price and convenience for each consumer individually—what economists called a utility function— and then adding all the individual trade-offs together.

The calculation is just too complicated for real-world application. Whether consumers benefit more from a higher price differentiated product, such as a closer bank, a knit shirt with a logo, or a full service retailer, is more a series of approximations than a precise calculation. If there are many competitive offerings in the marketplace, including low-priced products, the availability of higher price differentiated products will logically increase consumer welfare by providing more choices, with little effect on the overall price level for the product.

Chicago School opponents grudgingly accepted this explanation to justify rule of reason treatment for vertical nonprice restraints, like assigned dealer territories. But the opponents drew the line at resale price maintenance, which they wanted to keep illegal per se. Empirical studies showed that consumer prices rise when manufacturers successfully implement resale price maintenance programs. Economic models indicated that resale price maintenance prevents high-volume dealers from passing cost savings along to consumers by lowering retail prices.

There was also a greater dimension to the dispute. Chicago School opponents believed that the economic arguments used to justify resale price-fixing were just smoke screens to allow manufacturers to increase their profits. Manufacturers make more money by charging dealers more. But manufacturers can't very well raise their prices to dealers unless the dealers can pass on the price increases to consumers. Price competition among dealers stops the "pass-on" from happening, so manufacturers can't raise prices in the first place. Resale price maintenance helps the manufacturers by curbing the retail competition that stops manufacturers from being able to raise their prices.

"Occasionally," wrote antitrust scholar Robert Pitofsky in 1983, "issues of law of modest importance in themselves become symbolic of a broader difference of view between contending schools or ideologies." Resale price maintenance was one of those issues, pitting common sense and empirical studies showing higher consumer prices against complicated economic explanations.

Congressional opposition to Baxter's position intensified as the date of the Supreme Court argument approached. Senator Rudman attached a rider to an appropriations bill passed by both houses of Congress that prohibited the use of government funds to "alter the per se prohibition on resale price maintenance." Congress also cut off funds for Baxter's participation in private cases.

"Court observers could not recall a similar situation or similar rider so broadly restricting the power of the Justice Department to litigate issues," reported the *Washington Post*. A reluctant President Reagan signed the appropriations bill and Baxter was forced to stand down. He took a charged day of personal leave to participate in the Supreme Court argument over dealer complaints, but he made it clear to the Justices that he could not advocate the rule of reason for resale price maintenance.

A few days later, Baxter resigned. It had been a tumultuous two and a half years. Supporters and critics paused, ever so briefly, to consider Baxter's tenure. "If controversy were the measure, clearly Mr. Baxter's performance would be a striking success," suggested Professor Ernest Gellhorn. "Dispute and contention seemed his most enduring mark."

"John D. Rockefeller would have liked a trust-buster like Baxter," observed *The Economist*, intending a compliment.

Baxter raised the fortunes of big business. Economists were also the beneficiaries of Baxter's policies. Those in the Antitrust Division were given more prominent roles. Outside the division, economists became a permanent fixture in antitrust consulting and litigation. No lawyer worth his salt would consider going to an important meeting at the division without at least one economist in tow. Every antitrust trial required extensive economic testimony. The testimonial expert invariably needed a whole team of consulting economists to gather and analyze data. Economists started organizing themselves into lucrative consulting firms and charged high hourly rates. The Chicago School became synonymous with the transfer of wealth from lawyers to economists. Thanks largely to Bill Baxter, those in the dismal science acquired the Midas touch.

Whether for good or ill, few doubted that Baxter's legacy would endure. "The Baxter effect will continue long after the man has gone," *The Economist* predicted, because the new way of thinking about antitrust "has established itself in American law schools and courts. . . . The Chicago School took 20 years to come to the top. It will probably be that long before it is ousted."

Baxter ended up winning the pesticide case, although not on the grounds he would have preferred. The Supreme Court refused to abandon the rule of per se illegality for agreements between manufacturers and dealers to fix resale prices. But the Court made it far more difficult for plaintiffs to prove such agreements in litigation. The Court established as a national rule what Judge Rymer decided in the Apple case. Dealer complaints, even about price-cutters, would no longer be sufficient to establish an agreement between a manufacturer and its dealers to fix prices.

Four years later, the Court made it even more difficult for antitrust plaintiffs, ruling that a manufacturer's agreement with a full-price dealer to terminate a discounter did not by itself establish per se illegal resale price maintenance. To prove a per se case, the terminated dealer had to show an agreement with the manufacturer on a specific price or a price level the terminated dealer was required to charge customers. The Court's opinion justified its ruling by assuming the manufacturer had a free-rider rationale for terminating the discounter, even though no such proof was offered in the case. Merely because the elimination of free riding is a "quite plausible" explanation for terminating discount dealers, the Court reasoned, resale price maintenance claims should be discouraged.

The Supreme Court decisions signaled to the lower courts an attitude of permissiveness to manufacturer-imposed distribution restraints, making it far easier for manufacturers to restrict competition among their dealers without fear of antitrust liability. Plaintiffs' lawyers filed fewer cases, intimidated by the stringent requirements for establishing a per se violation.

The elaborate record to justify limiting dealer competition that we prepared for Apple was no longer necessary to win even a rule of reason case. So long as manufacturers steered clear of actually setting specific resale prices, they could impose restraints that differentiated their products, even if those restraints raised dealer prices. The urgency that animated Baxter's crusade to change distribution law subsided; the issue was resolved sufficiently for most business purposes.

After Baxter returned to Stanford at the end of 1983, his prominence faded. He died in 1998. His work in Washington implicated all five of the most important areas of antitrust practice—collusive conduct, product distribution, intellectual property restrictions on competition, dominant firm behavior, and merger enforcement. He renewed antitrust's commitment to competition among competitors. He forged a workable solution to distribution issues that threatened the efficient marketing of consumer products. And he transformed the discipline's approach to the other three practice areas.

Notwithstanding Baxter's many achievements, two antitrust questions, both vitally important for the emerging high tech economy, remained largely untouched. How was the discipline to integrate advances in economic research that permitted more realistic analysis of market behavior? How should the need to foster innovation affect antitrust enforcement?

To represent Apple effectively, I had to do a lot more than just advise the company to adopt a mail order prohibition. And I certainly couldn't stop with telling the company what the relevant court opinions said. Apple hired me to use my knowledge of the case law and the legal process to formulate a strategy to solve a business problem. My strategy had to take account of how both adversaries and more neutral parties to the conflict might behave. I had to anticipate what the mail order dealers would do when Apple changed its policy and plan for their actions. Then, I had to consider how a judge would view each side's moves and counters.

Every good lawyer thinks strategically about the best way to represent his client. Many occupations require a similar kind of strategic planning. A good football coach doesn't just send his players out onto the field; he creates a winning game plan. Diplomats think strategically about how to get other countries to agree to treaties. Generals plan out strategies to defeat their enemies. Politicians think about how to "work the system" to get what they want. Ordinary people devise strategies to solve everyday problems—how to bargain for a better price, how to get children to behave, how to negotiate a raise. In each case, devising a strategy requires considering interdependencies—how the choices of others interact with your own.

The branch of social science that studies strategic decision-making is known as game theory. The French mathematician Antoine Augustin Cournot first proposed a model for interdependent duopoly behavior in 1838, but John von Neumann, the mathematical genius who also pioneered computer science, usually gets most of the credit for the early insights in the field. Nobel laureate John Nash, the Princeton mathematician profiled in Sylvia Nasar's Pulitzer Prize–winning book, *A Beautiful Mind*, broadened the application of game theory. In 2005, two economists shared a Nobel Prize for additional contributions to the field.

The simple Chicago School models of perfect competition and complete monopoly ignore strategic decision-making. The models present stylized markets in which consumers base their purchasing decisions solely on a product's price and companies act without considering what other companies will do. The small company in a perfectly competitive market accepts the market price as a given. The perfect monopolist sets its production levels and prices by looking only at its own marginal cost and marginal revenue.

In the real world, even if a monopolist currently faces no competition, it still has to worry that some other company, drawn by the allure of high prices, might enter the market. A rational monopolist plans for this contingency by spending some of its monopoly profits to protect its monopoly from competitors. The monopolist might build plants it doesn't need (the government's claim against Alcoa) to make market entry by competitors less profitable (because the potential competitor has to consider that building its own plants further increases the industry output and drags down prices). There is no end of tactics a rational monopolist could employ to protect its monopoly by raising its rivals' costs.

If Apple had more market power in 1981, it could have developed a strategy to make IBM's entry into the personal computer market costly and difficult. For example, Apple might have demanded its dealers sign exclusive contracts. If Apple signed up all the best dealers to exclusives, IBM would have had to create its own dealer network from scratch, something it took Apple years to accomplish.

Of course, that strategy would not have worked. Given IBM's powerful brand, enormous resources, and prospects for success, most independent dealers who could get IBM authorization would have refused an exclusive relationship with Apple. So Steve Jobs developed a better strategy. Applying the old Silicon Valley adage, "If you can't fix it, feature it," Jobs ran a full-page ad in the *Wall Street Journal* welcoming IBM to the personal computer market. "Welcome, IBM. Seriously," the headline read. Observers interpreted the ad as Apple's attempt to position itself as the high-profile alternative in a burgeoning market—the "Pepsi" to IBM's "Coke."

Not every company would roll out the red carpet for a powerful competitor, but every successful business considers its competitors' actions, one way or another, in planning strategy. Sometimes established firms with market power use their positions to impede their competitors. Strategic behavior by dominant companies may hurt competitors without helping consumers at all. Other actions by a dominant firm, like lowering prices or building plants, might help consumers in the short run, but so badly damage competitors that, in the long run, consumers are worse off.

Antitrust enforcers sometimes call strategic conduct directed against competitors predation. The term is more a label for something undesirable than an explanation, or even a definition. Disagreements abound about what redeeming characteristics the conduct that hurts competitors must have to escape the "predatory" category. Must the conduct be profitable to the dominant firm? Must the conduct help consumers, at least in the short run? Must the conduct make the dominant firm more efficient?

Chicago School advocates resisted the consideration of interdependencies. Interdependencies undermine straightforward Chicago School predictions about corporate behavior from simple perfect competition and monopoly models. And, interdependencies threaten the fundamental notion of self-correcting markets.

During Bill Baxter's last year in Washington, he appeared in a panel discussion with Oliver Williamson. Williamson spoke about the growing need to incorporate game theory into antitrust analysis. He criticized the Chicago School's refusal to even recognize strategic behavior. He gave one example after another of how corporations use anticompetitive conduct to gain business advantages.

Baxter's response foretold the next quarter-century of antitrust enforcement. The study of strategic behavior "will call for a more intrusive form of antitrust," a prospect he characterized as "ominous." "I do not want [economists] back in the courts talking about new and not well-understood justifications for intervention," Baxter continued. Strategic behavior is likely so "infrequently realized in the real world" and so difficult to identify, Baxter argued, that incorporating the concept into antitrust enforcement invites an overwhelming number of errors.

Shortly after Baxter returned to Stanford, University of Chicago law professor Frank Easterbrook gave new voice to the Chicago School's platform calling for the retrenchment of antitrust enforcement. In a 1984 lecture (called "The Limits of Antitrust") memorable for its breathtaking simplicity, Easterbrook didn't respond to academic concerns about strategic behavior as much as he ignored them.

Government intervention in the free market invariably produces harm by condemning beneficial business practices that are not well understood, he claimed. The free market, on the other hand, will correct its own imbalances. "Monopoly is self-destructive" because it attracts competition, reducing the power of dominant firms in favor of "those offering customers a better deal." If a firm raises prices, it will sell less. If it improves quality without raising price, it will sell more. The law of demand writ large. No need to consider anything beyond the firm and the market. No sense worrying about strategic behavior.

The intoxicating simplicity of Chicago School thinking swept through all of antitrust jurisprudence. The Supreme Court made it easier for lower court judges to throw out antitrust claims that make "no economic sense," at least from the Chicago School perspective. One populist-era doctrine after another was deconstructed and transformed, but more in Bork's image than Baxter's. Baxter's willingness to weigh the long-term costs to competition against short-term consumer benefits was rejected. Baxter's confidence in case-by-case economic analysis yielded to the notion that judges, juries, and even antitrust enforcement officials lack the ability to parse complicated cases. Better to leave questionable business practices alone in the name of economic efficiency. The presumption of self-correcting markets became more important in antitrust analyses than the proven facts in an evidentiary record.

The Chicago School held antitrust enforcement to an impossible standard. Intervention in the free market is not justified, a leading scholar recently wrote, unless "relatively unambiguous facts" suggest a "fairly robust" economic theory that the challenged behavior is anticompetitive. "Unambiguous facts" exist only in fairy tales and economic models. Judges routinely decide other types of cases on far less than "relatively unambiguous facts."

Among academics and jurists, Chicago School thinking captured antitrust doctrine because it carried the right economic message for the manufacturing economy of the mid-twentieth century. At that time, bigger really was better. Larger companies could produce more cheaply than small-scale enterprises. The nationwide decline in transportation costs after the mid-century enabled large manufacturers to deliver their products efficiently to what were previously insular local markets. Protecting small businessmen from larger, more efficient national competitors in the name of economic pluralism cost most consumers a lot of money for little tangible benefit.

The Chicago School mantra of efficiency hit home for another reason, as well. In the 1970s, Japanese manufacturers began to challenge American economic hegemony by making higher-quality products at lower prices. Domestic manufacturers needed to become more efficient to compete in world markets. Antitrust law could hardly stand in the way. Targeting efficiency as the principal goal of antitrust enforcement made so much sense that it attracted bipartisan support.

Optimal resource allocation and each firm's productive efficiency will always be important goals for antitrust policy. But as the nation evolved to a high tech economy, the Chicago School's obsession with efficiency as the only legitimate goal of antitrust enforcement made less and less sense. Economic efficiency was the right message for its day. It is not even the most important message for our day.

In high tech markets, consumers benefit more from technological innovation than from efficiency-driven increases in output or decreases in product prices. The development of the microprocessor did more to enhance consumer welfare than the previous intermittent efficiency advances in more primitive processing technology. To produce growth in a high tech economy, competition policy needs to focus on innovation more than on the modest efficiencies of price and output.

Joseph Schumpeter, a Nazi-era refugee who taught at Harvard in the 1930s and '40s, was among the first economists to emphasize innovation and technological change. Schumpeter ridiculed the notion of looking at price and output to explain corporate behavior or to understand economic growth. Instead, he focused on the importance of "quality competition"— new ideas and groundbreaking technologies that command such decisive cost or quality advantages that they "revolutionize" markets.

Baxter and some of his contemporaries embraced the same priorities. Baxter told his congressional interrogators about how he weighed promoting Apple's "incentive to invent" over lowering consumer prices for the company's computers. Harvard's Phillip Areeda also cautioned against relying too heavily on simple models of price and output. "The most 'competitive' answer in the short-run unchanging world of standard microanalysis is not necessarily the best answer in the long-run dynamic world where strategic considerations abound and where entrepreneurship and innovation may be our greatest salvation," Areeda explained.

Misdirection rather than precise navigation would mark the road to antitrust's "greatest salvation."

PART THREE

PATENT AND COPYRIGHT
LIMITATIONS
ON COMPETITION

CHAPTER 5

The Eagle Dared

E agle Computer's founders naively thought they could get rich by making a better product. The company spun off from a New Jersey audiovisual equipment manufacturer in 1981, relocated to Silicon Valley in the spring of 1982, and started manufacturing sophisticated personal computers for small businesses. Technical reviews in the computer magazines lauded Eagle's machines—attractive case, well-designed keyboard, easy to upgrade, even easier to use. But Eagle's sales lagged while IBM's took off.

IBM got to market more than six months before Eagle, but the head start in time didn't fully account for the difference in fortunes. IBM's reputation for big, general-purpose computers gave it an advantage in the fledgling personal computer industry, whatever the actual quality of its product. IBM stood for "confidence and security in a field known for instability and uncertainty," *Time* magazine reported. Consumers demanded the imprimatur of IBM before paying thousands of dollars for what was a new type of device. "The name is magic," a computer retailer once told me during the break in a deposition.

By the end of 1981, IBM shipped thirteen thousand machines. Dealers pleaded for more inventory. IBM revved its production line. As IBM personal computers sold in increasing numbers, makers of application programs—products like spreadsheets, word processors, and video games—devoted more and more of their resources to producing programs that would run on the IBM PC. The cycles reinforced each other. New software applications attracted more users. More users created a demand for even more software applications. The spring of 1982 was already too late for Eagle.

Eagle brought a better, more powerful product to market. Eagle's machine, already priced more attractively than IBM's, came bundled with a word-processing program and a financial software package at no additional cost. A better product at a lower price. Yet Eagle couldn't even get market traction, much less make a dent in IBM's sizzling sales trajectory. At the time, it was all so bewildering. Offering a better product for less got Eagle next to nothing. What happened to the law of demand, the most fundamental postulate in all of economics? Interdependencies, that's what happened.

Economists applied early game theory research to interdependencies among sellers in order to investigate strategic behavior. In some markets, interdependencies among buyers turned out to be even more important. New purchasers wanted computers that ran all the most important application programs. Third-party application vendors devoted their resources to making programs for the largest-selling computers because that's how they made the most money. So, the more consumers bought of a computer brand, the more desirable that brand became to other consumers.

Once economists started to study the phenomenon, they saw similarities to other markets. In the early days of the telephone industry, when rival networks didn't interconnect with each other, new subscribers favored the carrier that would connect them to as many other parties as possible. Each new subscriber made a network more valuable to all the other existing subscribers and more desirable to potential new subscribers.

The early telephone networks physically connected their subscribers over wires. But physical connections did not always turn out to be necessary for consumer interdependencies to form. Craigslist (and its predecessors, the classified advertising sections of local newspapers) became more valuable to each individual consumer as others used the service. More people advertising cars for sale will attract more potential buyers. More potential buyers mean more sellers will post listings. A powerful network effect characterized the market for classified advertising despite the absence of physical connections.

In a 1985 journal article, Stanford economist Paul David explained the most famous modern example of a network effect, the layout of the common keyboard, known as the QWERTY configuration because of the order of the keys in the first row of letters. Primitive typewriters were unreliable mechanical devices, David wrote. So the QWERTY keyboard was deliberately designed for dysfunction—to slow typists down and keep them from striking the keys so rapidly that the device would jam.

Years later, the innovative "touch" typing system was adapted from its inception to the QWERTY format. Better typewriter design had already eliminated most of the jamming problems, and more efficient keyboard formats proliferated in the market. Nevertheless, QWERTY's early association with touch typing gave it an advantage, which market forces magnified as time passed. Companies wanted to buy typewriters with the keyboard layout most familiar to typists. Typists wanted to learn the touch typing system for the keyboard layout most prevalent in business. The market dynamics drove QWERTY to complete dominance, all but eliminating more efficient alternatives from the market.

Though directed more to the past than the future, David's speculation about "the many more QWERTY worlds lying out there" pointed like a dagger to the heart of Chicago School doctrine. David's QWERTY example implied that the free market does not invariably favor efficiency. Network effects reinforce whatever alternative gets a lead, driving that alternative, even if less efficient, to market domination. Market forces, David wrote of QWERTY, "drove the industry prematurely into standardization *on the wrong system.*"

The implications of David's research bode ill for the Chicago School. Policy makers could no longer count on market forces to correct monopoly or even lesser competitive imbalances. In many markets, market forces are more likely to exacerbate market power issues than to relieve them. Natural forces drive the market to a single outcome—an industry standard. Once widely adopted, a standard becomes entrenched, almost impossible to dislodge. The QWERTY standard remains so entrenched that we go right on teaching it in elementary schools notwithstanding the lawsuits alleging that the design physically harms those who use it.

Economists at Stanford and the University of California saw much in the performance of Silicon Valley's high tech markets similar to the phenomenon David described. These economists formalized the intuition about self-reinforcing markets into mathematical models.

Many in the Chicago School refused to accept the new learning. Two conservative economists attacked the historical accuracy of David's account, attempting to discredit the challenges to market infallibility. David's critics suggested that consumers can be expected to examine alternative standard offerings and select the best. Lengthy entrenchment of inferior standards is rare, they argued.

Eagle's management had to make important decisions well before any of these economic theories had been proposed. The market at the time revealed little to support any kind of technical evaluation of competing personal computer standards by either consumers or software developers. Purchasing and development decisions were based on market factors, not technical performance. Consumers wanted to know the computer they purchased would run all the leading computer programs.

Three hundred different companies made personal computers at one time or another, Eagle among them. Despite the quality of Eagle's product, the company could do little to convince software developers to spend resources creating products for its machine. It fell further behind in the market. IBM surged further ahead. "Many buyers would rather wait for months for an IBM computer than walk out the door with an Eagle," the *New York Times* reported. For Eagle to survive, its management reasoned, the company's computers needed "IBM compatibility"—the ability to run without modification the vast number of application programs written for the IBM PC.

The IBM PC architecture gave Eagle an opening. IBM was late to the personal computer market but still wanted its brand to become the industry leader quickly. The head of IBM's personal computer development project owned an Apple computer and attributed much of that company's success to its "open" architecture. Apple published technical specifications about its computer and encouraged third parties to make software programs and hardware devices that would work easily with Apple's machine.

Although usually a secretive company, IBM decided to make it as easy as possible for other companies to make complementary products. Going Apple one better, IBM produced its personal computer largely from off-the-shelf components made by third-party suppliers. Intel made the computer's main processor chip. Matsushita manufactured the company's monitor. And the software program that made the computer work, known as the operating system, was written by Microsoft, a start-up located in Bellevue, Washington.

An operating system controls basic computer operations like storing files and provides a set of fundamental functions used for running application programs. Although computer people referred to the IBM PC as the industry standard, in reality the industry standardized on the specifications in the operating software that application writers used for their programs. Eagle's engineers therefore reasoned that they had to adopt the same operating system IBM employed in order to run applications written for the IBM PC. In early 1983, Eagle launched a new line of personal computer products using the same Microsoft operating system as IBM. The Eagle computer ended up running a few of the programs written for the IBM PC, but not all of them. Customers were confused; the investment community withheld endorsement.

Microsoft's operating system, it turned out, was necessary to run programs written for the IBM machine, but the operating system program alone was not sufficient. The off-the-shelf Microsoft program did not contain a few crucial operating system functions, like recognizing keystrokes from the keyboard or displaying characters on the monitor. IBM wrote its own program, known as a BIOS (basic input-output system), for these functions. Searching for a solution to the compatibility problem, Eagle's engineers discovered that IBM published every line of the BIOS program in its technical reference manual to make it easier for programmers to write application programs. The IBM BIOS was a simple program, only about eleven hundred lines of code, short enough that it could be copied easily into Eagle's machine.

In the late spring of 1983, Eagle introduced the third generation of its personal computer. It could run just about any program written for the

IBM PC. Computer retailers, unable to secure adequate inventory from IBM, eagerly turned to the Eagle PC. "It's got hot buttons for easier computing, it's cheaper and it looks nicer," one securities analyst told the *New York Times*. After more than a year of trial and error, Eagle finally had a business plan that investors were excited about. Really excited. In May, Eagle filed a proposed stock offering with the Securities and Exchange Commission. The shares that had been doled out to entice employees to join the risky start-up would actually be worth a lot of money in the public market.

The offering became effective on June 9, 1983. Eager investors snapped up the company's shares, priced at $13 each. The share price rose to $17. The company raised $37 million. The mood was jubilant at Eagle's headquarters in Los Gatos, California. It was your typical Silicon Valley success story—work hard for a year or so, then make millions.

Dennis Barnhart, Eagle's forty-year-old president, celebrated by taking his yacht broker to a late lunch. It was never clear which man was at the wheel of Barnhart's $70,000 red Ferrari on the way back. A block from Eagle's headquarters, the driver lost control. The car "had to be flying," a police officer told the press. Literally. The car tore through twenty feet of guardrail, sailed through the air, and crashed into a ravine. Barnhart died at the scene. His Eagle shares were worth $9 million. The SEC halted trading in the stock.

A personal tragedy to be sure. But a corporate tragedy? Not in Silicon Valley. That night, the underwriters huddled with the company's board of directors and newly named officers. The stock offering was rescinded. Anyone who bought Eagle shares got his money back. The stock would be offered again after the registration documents were revised to account for Barnhart's death and the company's management changes.

A week later, Eagle, with a new president and CEO, went public for a second time. The stock sold out within five minutes. The share price closed at more than $17. Over the next few days, it rose to about $25. Jubilation returned to Eagle's headquarters. "Eagle seems to be doing quite well so far," an industry analyst told the *Times* four months later. "We have more IBM-compatible products than IBM does," Eagle's new president, Ron Mickwee, bragged to *Time* magazine a month after that. Sales rose from about $6 million a quarter to nearly $19 million. The company was expecting $25 million in the next quarter. Then a real disaster struck.

Near the end of February 1984, three lawyers from IBM showed up at Ron Mickwee's office. They carried two documents. One was a complaint for copyright infringement ready to be filed in federal court. The other was an agreement that Eagle would pull all of its computers from the market immediately. The copyright statute that made it illegal to copy books and music without permission had been amended by Congress in 1980 to cover computer programs. There were only a few cases under the new amendments. No one knew exactly how copyright protection applied to computer programs. "Which document would you like?" IBM's lawyers snickered as they presented the choices to Mickwee. "You have until tomorrow morning to let us know."

The congressional decision to put computer programs under copyright law was a difficult one, long in coming. Policy makers wanted to do whatever they could to encourage the growth and development of computer technology, which became an important component of the nation's economy by the mid-century. Progress required designing new machines ("hardware") and writing instructions for the machines to execute ("software"). People in the industry sometimes call the instructions "code." A set of instructions written to solve a particular problem or produce a particular result is a "program" in computer parlance. A computer's instructions are often long and complicated, sometimes expensive to create and always easy to copy once put in a form that machines can process.

A free market economy generally relies on vigorous competition to spur innovation. Business competitors invest in research and development to get ahead. Joseph Schumpeter, the famous Harvard economist of the 1940s, argued that the constant threat of innovation by actual and even potential competitors forces every company to produce better products and sell them on better terms, or else risk losing its market position to rivals.

In practice, though, too much of the wrong kind of competition can actually stifle innovation. If rivals can compete legally against a software developer by making copies of the developer's work, the rivals can always charge less for the software than the original developer because the rivals bear none of the developer's costs. Developers would get little out of their hard work. Few would go to the trouble of creating software in the first place. To get more computer programs written, policy makers reasoned that developers need a financial incentive. There has to be a guaranteed reward that rivals can't appropriate for creating a product people want.

Usually, a company needs to make better products more cheaply to succeed. But, as an incentive to innovate, economically advanced countries frequently give innovators the power to exclude competition for a specified period of time. The benefit to the innovator from the exclusion is secondary and incidental to the goal of creating more artistic and useful works, goods and services for the benefit of society.

Precisely honing the fine balance between promoting competition to maximize the creation of goods and services and suppressing competition to foster innovation presents a daunting challenge. Congress could have adopted a whole new set of laws to encourage the creation of computer programs, but there were already two well-developed legal doctrines on the books to foster innovation, patent law and copyright law. The patent law was drafted to promote "useful arts" like technology, while copyright law was directed toward protecting "writings," including music and movies, as a way to encourage culture, the arts, and the development of general knowledge. Both patent and copyright law limit competition in order to promote innovation, but they each reflect a different calculus because of the subject matter to which they are directed.

Machines, useful processes, and other technologies improve incrementally, sometimes in very small steps. Almost every invention is based, to one degree or another, on the earlier inventions of others. Blocking incremental improvement is very costly to society, so the law makes it difficult to get a patent, at least in theory. An applicant must demonstrate to a trained examiner that his invention is "novel," "nonobvious," and "useful"—meaning that it is a substantial improvement over whatever existed before. If applicants meet these requirements, they get the right to stop others from making and using their inventions for twenty years.

Adopting a scheme to exclude competition and retard the free exchange of ideas did not come easily to America. Thomas Jefferson, the nation's first patent commissioner, reluctantly defended the "public embarrassment of an exclusive patent" because sometimes these "monopolies of invention" serve the "benefit of society" by encouraging "men to pursue ideas which may produce utility."

Incremental improvements in books, music, and the like are less valuable to society. Ten alternative endings for *Gone with the Wind*, for example, create little additional value, so there is no point in encouraging someone to write them. Society would be better off if each of those trying to improve the original work instead wrote his own book on the same subject matter.

Copyright protection takes this approach. It is easy to get (more or less automatic) and it lasts for a very long time (approximately a hundred years), but under the rules courts and government officials propounded, little of importance to society is put off-limits to competition. Copyright holders can prohibit others from making copies and derivative works, but rivals can use the same general themes and concepts in their own writings. And independent creation of a work, even if the work ends up similar to the original, constitutes a complete defense to claims of copyright infringement.

Copyright laws, like patent protection, grew from the nation's early experiences with commercial practices. Hannah Adams, the first professional woman writer in America, successfully lobbied for the nation's first copyright law after her agent kept the proceeds from the sale of her book.

In the early 1960s, the head of the Copyright Office published a report describing the revisions needed to bring the existing 1909 copyright statute up to date. After a long series of public meetings, legislation was introduced in both houses of Congress, updating the statute to account for a number of technological advances. The proposals were debated for years and modified from time to time. In 1974, Congress created a commission to study the issue of whether computer programs should be protected under copyright law. To government policy makers, computer software was a strange animal. Programs are most assuredly "writings." They are written as a series of English-like statements consisting of word snippets, mnemonics, and other symbols. But a program is also a "useful" article. Unlike a book or a movie, it is a "writing" that makes a machine work.

A new copyright statute was enacted in 1976, before the commission completed its study. More precise than the earlier law, the new statute specifically excluded ideas, processes, procedures, systems, and methods of operation from copyright protection. The commission appointed by Congress issued its report in 1978. The commission recommended adding a definition of "computer program" to the 1976 statute—a "set of statements or instructions" used in a computer "to bring about a certain result." The commission concluded that the text of a computer program and the processes embodied in that text are sufficiently distinct to permit the former to be protected by copyright without automatically protecting the latter, in violation of the proscription against protecting methods and processes. Congress attached the proposed definition to the statute that was officially amended in 1980, but Congress did not otherwise change the 1976 law.

Eagle's general counsel summoned me to his office as soon as IBM's lawyers left. I explained the basis of copyright law to the company's management while one of my colleagues compared Eagle's BIOS program to what was in an IBM machine. To no one's surprise, the two sets of instructions were identical.

"We'll take the agreement," I told IBM's lawyers the next day. Eagle agreed to stop filling orders and to pull all its computers off dealers' shelves until it could offer a noninfringing BIOS. The IBM lawyers agreed to go back to Armonk, New York, the company's headquarters, without filing suit.

Eagle was already taking delivery of supplies in anticipation of a glowing future. Circuit boards, monitors, and disk drives gorged Eagle's southern California manufacturing plant. Eagle had copious quantities of all the components necessary to make personal computers, but unless Eagle's computer could run the software written for the IBM PC, there was no point in even trying to sell it. Mickwee stopped the assembly line; nothing went out the door. Eagle had to find an IBM-compatible BIOS that would pass legal muster.

Two vendors offered to license BIOS programs to Eagle, guaranteeing IBM compatibility. Mickwee brought in the first company's BIOS for compatibility testing. Eagle's technicians tried to run one of the best-selling programs written for the IBM PC, a video game that featured an animated frog. "The little frog just died on the screen," Mickwee told me. On to the second vendor, a huge multinational corporation headquartered in France. Its BIOS worked flawlessly, principally because the French company's program was an identical copy of IBM's code.

Lacking market alternatives, Eagle had to write its own noninfringing BIOS. Eagle's engineers bought a copy of the IBM reference manual that set out the BIOS code. The BIOS program comprised a collection of smaller subprograms known as routines, each of which performed a particular function. One of the routines displayed images on the video screen. Another recognized characters typed on the keyboard. IBM gave each routine an arbitrary number. For example, "10" identified the video routine, and "16" the keyboard routine. When a third-party application needed to display something on the monitor, it transferred execution to the appropriate routine in the BIOS for video merely by listing that routine's number—10—in the application program's code. A compatible BIOS had to recognize the numbers listed by the third-party application program and perform the function called for. But the exact code in the compatible BIOS—the actual instructions written to perform each function—did not have to be identical to IBM's code. There were a lot of ways to write code to perform each function.

As long as IBM did not claim copyright protection over the number it assigned to each function, a competent programmer could create a compatible BIOS. The programmer could use the IBM numbers to identify each function but write his own original code to execute those functions. Copyright law was vague on the legality of copying letters or numbers used to specify tasks. Claiming copyright protection over an arbitrary numbering system seemed like a stretch to me. If IBM could stop rivals from using the numbers, it could dramatically curtail the overall level of competition in a self-reinforcing market, denying rivals the programs needed to be competitive, and, at the same time, limiting the sales of application programs written by third-party developers. The third-party developers had invested the time and money to create application programs. They should be able to decide which computers they wanted their programs to run on.

I made the argument to IBM's lawyers. They assured me they were not trying to stop the use of their numbering system. They just wanted competitors to stop copying their code. IBM's position struck the right balance between too much competition and too much protection, I thought, wholly in keeping with what copyright was supposed to do. Each competitor had to write his own original BIOS program, producing more works for the benefit of the public. At the same time, every manufacturer's IBM-compatible computer could run the programs written by third parties so there would be plenty of competition in the market, based around a common standard.

The legal rules were clear enough, but Eagle died a slow and agonizing death trying to execute them. Under the supervision of my legal team, Eagle's engineers (who had already worked with IBM's code) started writing their own BIOS code. Lawyers checked every line of code the programmers wrote for illegal similarity to IBM's code, sometimes sitting next to the programmers as they typed on their keyboards, a tedious process that took a couple of months to complete. Shipments to dealers resumed in May, but by then Eagle's marketing window had closed. The quarter that was projected for $25 million in sales netted a $10 million loss. The company laid off personnel and failed to meet debt obligations. Directors and executives resigned. Mickwee left the company in early 1985. By 1986, the company was gone.

Phoenix Technologies, a small software firm headquartered in Norwood, Massachusetts, saw a market opportunity in Eagle's failure. Phoenix hired me to give legal help for the design of an IBM-compatible BIOS, which the company licensed throughout the computer industry. The IBM-compatible computer business thrived. By the mid-1980s, every significant computer manufacturer except Apple concluded it could compete effectively only if its computers ran the vast number of application programs written for IBM's personal computer. IBM-compatible machines came to dominate the personal computer market. Consumers could buy any of a large number of competing brands without losing their investment in application programs they had previously purchased. Manufacturers competed fiercely, driving prices down and improving product functionality. IBM and its compatible rivals brought out new and more powerful computers. The manufacturers always took care to run the programs written for previous hardware releases.

Later in the decade, Compaq beat IBM to market with a new generation of powerful computers that ran all of the old compatible software. IBM gradually lost control of the standard it promulgated and left the market. "Good-bye, IBM. Seriously," read the headline in the *Washington Post*. Faced with tough competition, IBM couldn't cut it. But if the company had asserted copyright protection over its arbitrary numbering scheme and sustained that position in court, it might still dominate the personal computer market. And consumers would be stuck with whatever IBM sold them in terms of price and quality.

In the spring of 1985, Hitachi Ltd., one of the largest industrial corporations in the world, called me seeking legal advice. Hitachi wanted to invest $400 million in a new line of powerful data-crunching computers known as super minicomputers. Hitachi's new computer was designed to accept instructions using a set of about eighty commands published by Motorola, a U.S. company.

Hitachi did not intend to incorporate any Motorola technology into its new machines at all, other than a simple listing of Motorola's commands, which Hitachi proposed to use without even getting permission from Motorola, much less paying a licensing fee. Before committing hundreds of millions of dollars to the project, Hitachi wanted to know if its plan would run afoul of U.S. copyright law. Hitachi's engineers told me that they could easily make a minicomputer better than any of the others on the market and profitably sell the new minicomputer at a much lower price than charged by other manufacturers. But few customers would buy the new computer, regardless of price or quality, unless it flawlessly executed the same commands that other comparable minicomputers accepted, namely, the set of commands published by Motorola.

By 1985, this had become familiar to me. Many software markets revolve around standards of one kind or another—labels, formats, and specifications, all adopted as common conventions to facilitate product development. It was the same in some other industries. Retrofitting early, incompatible rail lines to a standard track width ("gauge") permitted the growth of a national rail network with trains running across the common standard. The specifications in Microsoft's operating system and IBM's BIOS together comprised the personal computer industry's standard.

Software developers adopted through industry practice a set of competitive principles. Reputable companies did not copy each other's code without permission, but the labels used to designate particular computer functions were not considered copyrightable. IBM used arbitrary numbers to designate functions in its BIOS. Motorola's labels were not quite so arbitrary. The Motorola labels were a set of about eighty abbreviations, like CLR for "clear." Each label told the computer to perform a specific rudimentary task. Hitachi asked to send a team of engineers to my office from Japan. They would stay as long as I wished and would answer every question I asked. The size of my legal bill was of no consequence. However, within a month of the day I dismissed them, I was to provide Hitachi with a detailed legal report.

My report explained that U.S. copyright law incorporated a large number of limiting restrictions and exceptions so that authors could not harm the public by curbing legitimate competition too severely. These doctrines grew largely from copyright's traditional subject matter—books, music, and art. Although the general policy was clear enough, there was no specific limiting doctrine that squarely fit Hitachi's situation, or Eagle's for that matter. The result of a lawsuit against Hitachi was difficult to handicap.

Hitachi showed the report to Motorola. The two companies quietly reached agreement in private discussion. Productive competition in the marketplace continued. How long would the ground rules last? Sooner or later, I said to myself, a company is going to get greedy and try to use copyright to exclude legitimate competitors from the market.

CHAPTER 6

The Allure of the Lotus

After three long and painfully frustrating years of litigation in Boston's federal court, I was finally set for a big win. I stood before Judge Robert E. Keeton in the waning days of the summer of 1993, asking that he enjoin the sale of Borland's software program Quattro Pro.

Boston's best-known software company, Lotus Development Corporation, claimed in a 1990 lawsuit that Borland copied the menus from Lotus's spreadsheet program, 1-2-3, costing Lotus tens of millions of dollars in lost sales. Anyone looking at the two programs on a computer screen could see that Lotus was right. Borland copied all of Lotus's 469 menu commands in the exact order they appeared in the Lotus program. Borland did not even contest the charge. Yet it took Judge Keeton two years to issue an opinion stating the obvious. "Lotus has sued," the judge wrote in 1992, "and Borland is liable." Proceedings dragged on for another year after that. A resolution of the case was long overdue. I wanted the judge to issue an order stopping the sale of Borland's product.

"An unusual legal step," said the *Boston Globe*. "An unusual twist," echoed the *Wall Street Journal*.

Lawyers ask courts for injunctions against copyright infringers all the time, but never in circumstances like this. Borland was my client. I was asking the court to enjoin the sale of my own client's leading product. Bizarre, to be sure, but everything about this case was unusual.

The first commercial spreadsheet product was developed by a Harvard MBA candidate, Dan Bricklin. Bricklin called the program VisiCalc, for "visible calculator." VisiCalc automated the familiar spreadsheet form by interconnecting each data entry so that a change in one spreadsheet cell would automatically change related data entries. A patent lawyer was consulted but advised that computer programs were not eligible for patent protection.

Bricklin made a deal to distribute his product through a small marketing company set up by a young Harvard Business School graduate, Dan Fylstra. Fylstra moved his company to California, negotiated venture capital funding, and released VisiCalc in 1979. The program proved a powerful tool for business planning because it permitted valuation of alternative business scenarios and sales forecasts quickly and easily. Business executives bought the program without even thinking about the computer it ran on which, initially, was only the Apple II. VisiCalc's success helped to propel Apple into an early lead in the nascent market for personal computers.

Mitch Kapor, a Yale graduate turned transcendental meditation instructor, developed programs to plot and analyze VisiCalc's data. He sold the programs to Fylstra's company in 1981 for $1.2 million, but retained the right to create an integrated software package including spreadsheet, graphics, and other capabilities.

Working with professional programmer Jonathan Sachs, Kapor launched Lotus Development Corp., a reference to Kapor's days as a transcendental meditation instructor, in 1982. Lotus released its first product, a combination spreadsheet and graphics program called 1-2-3, in January 1983. The program was designed specifically to take advantage of the IBM PC's technical capabilities. Not coincidentally, the vast majority of PC users quickly adopted the Lotus product as their spreadsheet. The IBM PC standard surged to market dominance, carrying 1-2-3 right along with it. In keeping with the practices of the time, Lotus did not secure any patent protection over its product. Neither Kapor nor his investors needed government assurances of exclusivity to induce their entrepreneurial activity.

Users operated the 1-2-3 program through a set of 469 commands—ordinary words like "copy," "print," or "quit"—organized hierarchically into fifty menus and submenus. Kapor selected words for his program that conveyed the purpose of the commands. He grouped them according to predictive frequency and other loose guidelines he established. 1-2-3 users could select a command by highlighting it on the screen or by typing its first letter. Those who used the program frequently became so familiar with the order of the commands that they could type command sequences from memory, much as a touch typist uses a keyboard without looking at it.

The instructions that came with 1-2-3 explained that users could employ the product more efficiently by using the menu commands to write their own programs. These programs—called macros—automated a series of designated commands through a single keystroke. Some macros were simple, a sequence of just a few commands, but other macros, including some written and sold by third-party developers, involved hundreds of 1-2-3 command combinations.

Mitch Kapor was not the only software developer to recognize that IBM's new computer provided an opportunity to market a successful spreadsheet. James Stephenson, a West Coast developer, began to work on his own spreadsheet program in early 1982. By the fall of 1984, as he continued to improve his prototype, he realized that just about everyone who wanted a spreadsheet had already purchased an early version of 1-2-3. Users had already invested time to learn the 1-2-3 keystrokes. Many large corporations had already set up their financial records in 1-2-3 spreadsheets. Individuals and companies had written macros incorporating 1-2-3 commands. The user base was "locked into" 1-2-3. Switching to a new spreadsheet meant losing substantial investments of time and money. Even new spreadsheet purchasers would need to share files with established 1-2-3 users.

Unless Stephenson's spreadsheet could be used just like 1-2-3 and could fit easily into a business already dependent on 1-2-3, there would be little demand for his product, regardless of its other features. So he wrote his own original code, but he adopted 1-2-3's commands and copied them into his program. In July 1993, Stephenson started selling his product for $99. 1-2-3 sold for about $300.

It was the same story I had seen in the IBM-compatible market, but this time somebody hit the detonator. Lotus brought suit in Boston under the copyright law to enjoin the sale of Stephenson's product. Lotus had to make an example of one of the many Lotus-compatible spreadsheet companies before it lost control of the market. Judge Robert E. Keeton drew Lotus's case. Raised and educated in Texas, Keeton joined the faculty of Harvard Law School in 1953 and became a nationally recognized expert on insurance law, torts, and trial tactics. He was appointed to the federal bench by President Jimmy Carter in 1979.

Keeton was tall, of stately demeanor, smart, and very proud of his intellectual achievements. He was also intensely stubborn. In one case, Keeton ruled that double-bunking inmates at a local jail violated their constitutional rights, even after the jail was approved for safety, health, and suitability by all relevant state and local agencies and certified for double-bunking by the American Corrections Association. The Supreme Court ordered Keeton to reconsider his ruling, but Keeton dug in his heels, requiring the local sheriff each night to transfer inmates to an out-of-county facility where they were double-bunked.

The *Boston Herald* inveighed against Keeton in a lead editorial. "His ruling is insufferably dense," said the *Herald*. The Supreme Court ordered Keeton "to be less narrow-minded," the editorial continued, "but true to form, Keeton either doesn't get the message or chooses to ignore it."

Stephenson's small company, Paperback Software, defended Lotus's suit as best it could, given its limited resources. Paperback's lawyers showed that many of 1-2-3's features, including the use of macros and most of the command names, came from VisiCalc or some other software product. Keeton, nevertheless, held for Lotus, in an opinion that was so long it had its own table of contents.

After touching on every subject from basic computer technology to the U.S. Constitution, and citing everything from the letters of Sir Isaac Newton to Ecclesiastes, Keeton held that Paperback infringed Lotus's copyrights by copying every detail of what the Lotus program displayed on the screen. Keeton laid out his own general test for copyrightability, ruling that copyright law protected the Lotus menu commands because there were other words Stephenson could have used to evoke the same functionality. Keeton rejected the argument that the Lotus commands had become an industry standard that Stephenson needed to copy in order to compete. If something is so good that it becomes a standard, Keeton said, it should be protected by copyright.

Mitch Kapor was never all that comfortable with Lotus's lawsuit and even less so with Keeton's opinion. Kapor made his views plain in 1990 congressional testimony. "Over-protection of intellectual property is as pernicious as under-protection in its stifling effects on innovation and consequent loss to society," Kapor told a House committee. Not that Kapor's opinion mattered to Lotus, which by that time was run by professional managers. They wanted a precedent out of the Paperback lawsuit they could use against other competitors. Lotus quickly agreed to settle the Paperback case for a token cash payment so that Stephenson's company would not appeal. Paperback Software went out of business.

Borland International, a Silicon Valley company, was Lotus's real worry. Philippe Kahn founded Borland in 1983. Kahn grew up in France where he worked as a high school teacher after getting a master's degree in mathematics. He played both the flute and saxophone, and rode a motorcycle to work. His father had been a member of the French Foreign Legion, his mother a Nazi death camp survivor. He got interested in computers in the 1970s and wrote a program to run on an early French-made personal computer. Carrying only pocket money, Kahn came to the United States in 1982, at the age of thirty-one, looking for a programming job.

Once in the land of opportunity, Kahn decided to work for himself. Although an illegal immigrant at the time, Kahn and a group of Norwegians set up a company to sell software through the mail at cut-rate prices. Kahn wrote a business plan and solicited investors, but there were no takers. "Worst business plan I'd ever read in my life," one investment banker later told the *Wall Street Journal*. Kahn called his new company Borland, a name he bartered from an Irish customer in exchange for forgiving a $15,000 debt. "Borland" means "Land of the Deep Forest" in the ancient Celtic language, Kahn explained to anyone interested.

With a total payroll of three employees, Borland electrified the computer industry in 1983 by introducing a powerful software development program. Kahn sold the program by mail order at a fraction of the price

IBM and other large companies charged for similar tools. After that, Kahn introduced SideKick, a product that became the industry's most popular personal computer scheduling program.

Working in secret for the next three years, Kahn and a team of engineers he hired developed a new spreadsheet program. The program had its own set of menu commands and an alternate 1-2-3 command set for users who wanted the Lotus keystroke sequences. The product's technical features were so impressive that Lotus adopted some of them. In the fall of 1989, Kahn introduced a fully reengineered version of his spreadsheet, Quattro Pro, one better than 1-2-3. Quattro Pro won every major award for spreadsheet excellence given in the software industry. It invariably ranked substantially higher than 1-2-3 in head-to-head reviews and user comparisons, including those conducted by Lotus.

Quattro Pro had far greater technical capabilities than 1-2-3, but was engineered to run on less powerful, much cheaper computers. Unlike 1-2-3, Quattro Pro was designed to work with a mouse. It displayed icons and other graphical images, in addition to words, so Quattro Pro looked very different from 1-2-3 on a computer screen. Quattro Pro had its own set of menu commands as the default choice, and also a set of menus that included all the keystroke sequences from 1-2-3. The compatible menus ensured Quattro Pro's ability to run 1-2-3 macros and to permit users to type the 1-2-3 keystroke sequences they already knew.

Kahn's price really got people's attention. Lotus charged a new user about $300 for its product. When Lotus introduced a more advanced version, it permitted existing users to upgrade for $150. Kahn targeted these Lotus customers who were in the market to upgrade by offering, for $99, a much better product that could read all the users' old files. He sold 200,000 copies in just a few months.

Kahn's game plan revealed much about Silicon Valley strategy. "We arrived later than the other guys," he told the press, "so we always had to compete against an entrenched rival." Some Silicon Valley start-ups— Apple as an example—pioneer new markets. Many others are created specifically to attack a complacent market incumbent by developing better products for the incumbent's existing customers. Venture capitalists are always on the lookout for these opportunities. If an established company has already identified a viable market, a start-up can avoid the difficult process of creating its own market. The start-up can focus instead on making a better product more cheaply than the established firm. The ensuing competition prevents the established firm from overcharging customers and skimping on product development.

The first business day after the release of the *Paperback* ruling, Lotus sued Borland in Boston. The case was assigned to Judge Keeton because he was already familiar with the subject matter. Lotus's suit ignited a sell-off of Borland shares; the company lost more than 20 percent of its value in a single day. The press began to follow the case closely, highlighting every element of confrontation: the staid East against the freewheeling West, the powerful incumbent against the upstart challenger, the conventional against the unorthodox, yesterday's hero against the champion of tomorrow.

Kahn hired me to stop Judge Keeton from putting Borland out of business. I had plenty of misgivings about representing a Silicon Valley company in Boston. The Boston courts were notoriously inhospitable to companies from other parts of the country. Local favoritism was even more pronounced when Silicon Valley companies were involved in disputes with Boston-based employers. I saw it myself when my firm represented Dan Fylstra's company in a lawsuit over rights to the original VisiCalc spreadsheet. A Boston judge almost threw one of my partners into jail for contempt when the lawyer tried to get into the court record evidence the judge did not want to see the light of day.

The Boston area seemed to have a collective chip on its shoulder when it came to Silicon Valley. Boston's universities were even more prestigious than those of Silicon Valley, at least according to the locals. The regional economy had received far more in the way of government funding for a much longer period of time. Scores of venture capitalists dotted the local landscape, all with money to invest. As recently as the 1970s, the Boston area was the computing capital of the world, with companies like Digital Equipment, Data General, Wang, and many others. The Boston suburbs were called the Massachusetts Miracle. Yet when confronted by technological change and competitive challenge, Silicon Valley flourished while the Boston technology companies faltered.

The study by AnnaLee Saxenian, the Berkeley dean, described how

Silicon Valley pioneers viewed themselves as outsiders to the industrial systems in the East that were organized around individual, vertically integrated firms, each with its own proprietary turf. The first wave of technologists organized the Valley into a regional system based on professional and technical networks with a different set of attitudes. The people of Silicon Valley focus on investment and risk taking. The institutions of Silicon Valley, including universities and large corporations, embrace change and reward flexibility. The past is not something to bind the future. Everything can be improved.

Whenever I went into the federal courthouse in Boston, I felt like I was fighting against something much bigger than an entrenched company. My real adversary was an entrenched culture, a culture that had failed the region's investors and workers. Lotus's star was fading, but the company was still one of the only bright spots in the local economy. Creating sympathy for the company that sought to displace Lotus would not be easy.

Philippe Kahn's personal style made the chore even more difficult. "Kahn cultivated the image of the French roué with little regard for the rules of corporate America," the *New York Times* observed. Despite Lotus's lawsuit, or perhaps because of it, Borland's sales went up 80 percent and its earnings rose almost 200 percent. Lotus's stock dropped almost 50 percent. Philippe celebrated by using $300,000 of Borland's money to cut a CD with a group of renowned jazz musicians. He gave away copies of the recording as Christmas gifts to vendors and customers, in place of the more traditional bottle of wine. "I don't think I have the time for a tour," Philippe told the *Wall Street Journal*.

Borland explained the Lotus lawsuit to the press as the classic struggle between monopoly and creative freedom. "If software developers have to worry about compatibility all the time, being forced to start from scratch with every new product, it's going to kill innovation and constrain competition," a Borland executive told the *Wall Street Journal*. He continued with an analogy for nontechnical readers. "If Lotus invented the Model T, they'd still want you to be driving it today because they would claim a monopoly on cars."

Lotus filed court papers in the lawsuit asking the judge to rule in its favor without conducting a trial. Keeton gave us a couple of months to respond to Lotus's motion, but he made it clear he was going to rule quickly. On September 30, 1991, I filed papers opposing Lotus's motion and asking the judge to rule in Borland's favor. I argued that Borland copied only the Lotus menu commands, which are not protected by copyright. After much coaxing, I got the Justice Department to file a brief on behalf of the Copyright Office. The brief did not officially take sides, but it said that the Copyright Office did not recognize claims for the protection of menu commands.

Borland's stock shot up 3½ points; Lotus's stock dropped. "Borland has a better chance in this lawsuit than many people believed," a New York securities analyst told a *Boston Globe* reporter. But a prominent Boston copyright lawyer told the same reporter that Keeton would likely just ignore the brief.

Three days later, copyright law professors from Harvard, Yale, Duke, Vanderbilt, the University of California, NYU, and other distinguished universities filed a friend-of-the-court brief, marking the first time a group of copyright law professors had ever taken a position in a software case. Professor Pamela Samuelson of the University of Pittsburgh Law School organized the group and wrote most of the brief. Her language was blunt: "We regard the test employed in [the *Paperback* opinion] to be inconsistent with the copyright statute, the copyright case law, and traditional principles of copyright law. . . . It should not be employed in judging the copyright issues in the *Lotus v. Borland* dispute." Six years later, Samuelson was awarded a MacArthur fellowship—more commonly known as a "genius award"—for her work on copyright policy.

The briefs show that Borland has "some friends," an analyst told the *Wall Street Journal*. Lotus's stock price continued its downward spiral, Borland up slightly. Our courthouse sources told us Keeton dispatched one of his assistants to get a copy of the professors' brief the moment he read about it in the newspaper. We heard nothing further from the judge for almost six months.

Near the end of March 1992, Keeton issued a ruling, denying our request to dismiss Lotus's claims. He wrote more than twenty typeset two-column pages, only to conclude that he was going to stand by the analysis he used in *Paperback*. Industry publications and academic journals published highly critical reviews of Keeton's *Paperback* decision and Lotus's subsequent lawsuit against Borland. Academics accused Keeton of distending copyright law. Industry commentators lamented the damage that Keeton's ruling would do to innovation in the software industry. But Keeton was hell-bent on preserving his *Paperback* opinion, whatever the consequences for the software industry.

The ruling revealed that Keeton was no longer in a rush to resolve the case, as he also denied Lotus's motion for judgment. A final decision by Keeton would give Borland the right to appeal, and with all the criticism of Keeton's analysis, a reversal was possible, perhaps even likely. But if proceedings dragged on and Borland lost little by little, the case would become so burdensome that Borland would have to settle it and Keeton's *Paperback* reasoning would never face appellate scrutiny.

Our strategy also changed. Our only hope of winning lay with the court of appeals and we had to get the case there as quickly as we could. We refiled our motion for judgment without a trial. Lotus also refiled its motion.

Kahn, meanwhile, was positioning Borland to take on Microsoft, the company that dominated personal computer software. Kahn started releasing advanced versions of Borland applications and development programs rewritten to run on Microsoft's new Windows operating system. As he went from city to city touting his new products, customers eagerly anticipated the looming showdown between Borland and Microsoft, run by William Henry Gates III. "Philippe," a voice from the crowd in New York shouted, "what about the rich boy?" Borland's investors voiced optimism. The *Wall Street Journal* reported that Borland "more than held its own" in past competition with Microsoft.

Judge Keeton made sure Kahn went into the battle for software supremacy with a ball and chain around his ankle. The judge issued a second long opinion holding Borland liable for copying Lotus's menus. "A very satisfactory spreadsheet menu tree can be constructed using different commands and a different command structure from those of Lotus 1-2-3," the judge said. Lotus's "macros and keystroke sequences are protected," Keeton ruled.

Forbidding the competitive use of Lotus's menus was not going to spur the creation of other software products. Just the opposite. Unless potential competitors could employ the Lotus menus, they would not even try to enter the market, all but eliminating the prospect of meaningful competition. Consumers would lose both the lower prices and the product improvements competition offered. Keeton denied the obvious. In the name of protecting innovation, he gave an entrenched company in a self-reinforcing market a strategic weapon, the legal power to crush a new generation of innovators and deny customers the benefits of competition. Borland pulled the Lotus menus from the shipping versions of its product in response to the ruling, eliminating Lotus keystroke compatibility.

After reading the ruling, I filed papers asking the judge for permission to appeal his decision without waiting for a full trial that would determine how much money Borland owed Lotus for prior infringement. Borland's stock price was beginning to sag. A long damages trial that resulted in a large award for Lotus would only increase pressure on Borland to settle. The real question in the case was whether the menus are protected by copyright, I argued. It was time to let the court of appeals review the lower court's decisions. Two trade groups for software entrepreneurs from Silicon Valley filed friend-of-the-court briefs supporting my motion.

To no one's surprise, Keeton denied my request. Notwithstanding his two long opinions, Keeton said he had not yet fully decided the copyright issue in the case. He set a date for a jury trial and then, at a subsequent hearing, he pushed the date back four months. I asked him to reconsider his ruling and let Borland appeal, and he again refused. My argument that copyright did not cover the menu commands was not even "debatable," he said.

The next year, Keeton held two trials in the case. At issue in the first trial was whether Mitch Kapor's guidelines for developing the menu commands invariably produced the words in the order Kapor used. I never argued that Kapor was constrained originally to use particular words in a particular order, by his own guidelines or anything else, but Keeton forced

Borland through a trial anyway. Two months later, Keeton held a second trial on whether a feature of Quattro Pro known as the Key Reader infringed Lotus's copyrights. The Key Reader let users run their 1-2-3 macros without displaying any Lotus menus on the screen at all.

Three more months passed before Keeton ruled that Kapor's guidelines did not constrain the words and order of the menu commands. A month and a half after that, Keeton issued a bewildering opinion holding that the Key Reader infringed Lotus's copyrights in the menu commands. Keeton acknowledged that Borland copied no Lotus code nor even displayed Lotus menus in the Key Reader, but deemed these facts "not material." The judge held that Borland infringed by employing what he called "phantom menus" not visible to the user or present in the Borland code, to enable Quattro Pro users to run 1-2-3 macros. Keeton no longer maintained the pretense that he was protecting Lotus's writings against illegal copying. Plainly, he was shielding Lotus's customer base from competition. Once again, he explicitly refused to take account of users' investment in the macros they had created.

Lotus's president gleefully welcomed Keeton's decisions. He told the press he was going "to perform a cashectomy" on Borland to collect damages, which he suggested might be "north of $100 million."

The combination of trying to compete against Microsoft and litigate against Judge Keeton was proving deadly to Borland. The company had difficulty getting new product out on time. It was hemorrhaging cash to keep key developers on its payroll. The litany of liability decisions Keeton meted out to Borland, coupled with the likely damages award of unknown dimension, eroded the company's stock price.

Despite all the problems, Borland executives knew they dared not settle the case. Settlement meant the company would have to give up any hope of competing for Lotus's customers and surrender so much of its capital that future software development would be jeopardized.

If only Borland could get to the court of appeals, its fortunes might change, but until proceedings in the trial court were complete, including a damage award, I had no automatic right to appeal. The law recognized an exception for injunctions. If Judge Keeton entered an order enjoining the sale of Borland's product, I had the right to an immediate appeal, even if a determination of damages had not yet been made.

At the next court hearing, I asked the judge for an order to stop Borland from selling any product with the Lotus menus or the Key Reader feature. Lotus's lawyer balked at my request. He wanted to try the damages case, to make it as painful as possible for Borland to avoid settling. I'm sure Keeton was sorely tempted to take that approach, but the public pressure was just too great. Keeton granted my motion. "I have never entered a . . . permanent injunction in favor of the party who didn't want it before," Keeton told Lotus's lawyer. It was the only contested motion I won in more than three years of litigation in Keeton's court.

Although Keeton granted my motion, he was not finished tightening the screws on Borland. He refused to hold up costly document exchange and witness interrogation for the damages phase of the case while the court of appeals reviewed his liability opinions. He said he wanted the damages portion of the case ready for trial as soon as the higher court rejected Borland's appeal. Continuing to prepare for a damages trial was going to cost Borland a great deal of money in legal and expert witness fees—more than a million dollars, as it turned out. Keeton's motivation was transparent. Just in case anyone from Borland missed the point, Keeton said it as clearly as he could. "At some point along the way the parties will probably decide it's more sensible to settle [the case] than to spend enormous resources fighting it to the end."

Keeton was right about the resources. A small company trying to break into the market by charging low prices simply didn't have millions of dollars to spend on lawsuits. Borland was able to defend itself only because the company had insurance against copyright infringement claims. Once Keeton entered the injunction, the insurance carriers sued Borland to avoid any further obligation under their insurance contracts.

Bob Kohn, Borland's general counsel, saved the day by negotiating an agreement under which the insurers would continue to cover legal fees but would not be responsible for any damages award ultimately entered against Borland. It was one of many days that Kohn saved. As firms in the industry chose sides in the dispute, Lotus counted among its backers big entrenched market leaders, including IBM, Digital Equipment, and Xerox, along with their public relations and legal minions. Kohn, one of Borland's only countervailing assets, exploited every contact he had in the developer community and software industry to rally allies to the company's cause.

Kohn's efforts kept the legal defense from crumbling, but there was nothing he could do for Borland's spreadsheet business. Borland was running out of cash. To save the company, Philippe Kahn sold Quattro Pro to another company for $145 million. Liability for the Lotus case remained with Borland. Borland could still pay its engineers and try to develop new products, but its lawyers were now litigating only to avoid disaster. If Borland lost the appeal, there was no insurance safety net to cover a damages award. If Borland won, it would be making the world safe for other companies' compatible products.

CHAPTER 7

Trial by Ordeal

The federal court of appeals in Boston would decide Borland's fate. I pinned my hopes on two judges. One was the chief judge, Stephen Breyer. Breyer graduated from Harvard Law School, worked for a time in the Antitrust Division and in various congressional and policy-making positions, and returned to Harvard in 1967 to teach administrative law and antitrust. He was appointed to the court of appeals in 1980. In a 1970 law journal article, Breyer questioned the economic wisdom of extending copyright protection to computer programs. And in a presentation to a congressional symposium more than a decade later, he explained copyright protection as an economic calculus designed to give an author just enough incentive to produce his work, regardless of how much it came to be worth to others later on.

Mike Boudin was the only appellate judge in Boston that I knew personally, albeit not all that well. I reported briefly to Boudin when I was a summer associate at a D.C. law firm. He was not yet a partner, but he was already regarded as one of the best lawyers in the firm and one of the best brief writers among all the lawyers in Washington. Boudin was a soft-spoken, complex man. He grew up the son of America's most celebrated left-wing civil liberties lawyer but charted his own conservative course. He attended Harvard as an undergraduate, then Harvard's law school, where he led the law review. He clerked for Judge Henry Friendly on the federal court of appeals in New York and Justice John Harlan on the Supreme Court. There were stories of how Boudin moved a cot into Friendly's chambers so that he could work without distraction around the clock. Boudin had a lot of experience with complex antitrust issues in his years of private practice and was widely known for an open-minded approach to new problems.

The appellate court in Boston included only seven active judges. They sat three at a time to hear cases. On a random draw, the odds favored getting either Breyer or Boudin, if not both, for my argument. Finally, there was a reason for Borland to have hope.

My own optimism evaporated quickly. The panel assignment circulated a week before the scheduled date for argument slated neither Breyer nor Boudin for the case. I researched the backgrounds and interests of the judges named to hear Borland's appeal. A former bankruptcy judge, a former real estate lawyer, and a judge whose key issue was statehood for Puerto Rico were to decide the future of the software industry. For a week, I could neither eat nor sleep. I was sure that champagne was flowing at Lotus's company headquarters.

On April 6, 1994, the appellate panel in courtroom number 5 on the fifth floor of the federal building in Boston took a brief recess before hearing arguments in *Lotus v. Borland*. Judges Juan Torruella, Norman Stahl, and Conrad Cyr left the room through a door on the side of the elevated dais. Those in the jammed courtroom gallery stood respectfully. The judges' law clerks sat in the unused jury box. People lined the walls of the courtroom and crowded four deep in the hallway, trying to get a glimpse of the proceedings.

After a few minutes, the court clerk called the gallery back to order. Everyone stood as the judges' door opened. Judge Torruella stood in the doorway, about to enter the room. My partner Michael Barclay noticed something odd. Torruella, as the presiding judge, should have come on to the bench in the center position, the second of the three judges to enter, but he walked into the room first. The lawyers in the gallery stared at the door, transfixed in confusion. Judge Breyer walked in, taking the presiding judge's position. Jaws in the gallery dropped. No one had bothered to check the clerk's postings that showed Judge Cyr, the former bankruptcy magistrate, recusing himself from the case. Stephen Breyer was to hear Borland's appeal after all.

I stood to make my presentation, not quite knowing what to say. The argument I had prepared for judges who knew nothing about either copyright law or computer software was not going to be effective. Before I could say much of anything, Judge Stahl began to ask probing questions, easing my fears about the abilities of the other judges to understand a complex computer case.

After a few minutes, Breyer joined the questioning. Keeton found that Borland could use other words in its menus, Breyer pointed out again and again. I answered Breyer as I had answered Keeton. "We want a spreadsheet that runs those third party application programs that were written for Lotus," I said. Keeton's rulings permitted Borland to make a spreadsheet, "but we can't have a spreadsheet that does the same thing as the Lotus spreadsheet." In the courtroom, Breyer gave no indication how he was leaning, but everyone on Borland's side was optimistic. At last we had a group of judges who would think carefully about the right decision. The panel took the case under advisement.

In big-ticket litigation, you try to plan for every contingency. Sometimes unexpected events defy even the most thorough planning. A month after the argument, President Clinton named Stephen Breyer to the Supreme Court. Borland's case, among others, sat in legal limbo. The clerk's office told us Judge Breyer would not participate any further in resolving the appeals he had heard. If the other two judges on the panel could agree, they would issue an opinion in the case. Otherwise, unresolved cases would be set for reargument. In July, the clerk's office sent formal notification scheduling the case for a rehearing in the fall. Borland's case had become a trial by ordeal.

Market incumbency automatically confers a formidable array of advantages—a well-recognized brand, user familiarity with the incumbent's product, long-standing relationships with corporate customers, an experienced engineering staff, and enormous financial resources. Borland accepted the challenge of competing against a dominant firm on these terms. The greater impediment to Borland's success came from a legal system that worked against market entry. Few challengers could ever muster the resources to weather years of litigation just for the privilege of competing on a playing field that already favored the incumbent.

In October, I returned to Boston to reargue the case. Judge Boudin replaced Judge Breyer on the panel. The other two judges remained the same. In my argument, I emphasized the peculiar economic characteristics of personal computer software, the powerful network effect. The Lotus menus gained value from investments of users and developers. Lotus should not be able to appropriate the value of those investments, I argued.

Lotus's lawyer tried to pooh-pooh the importance of an industry standard. "Before we feel too sorry for Borland," he said, "we should note that Borland sold its spreadsheet business to Novell for $100 million. So, obviously, Novell thinks it's a viable business without compatibility."

"Unless they were betting on the outcome," Judge Boudin retorted. He pressed the economic issue, asking Lotus's lawyer to identify any copyright cases in which a plaintiff was permitted to capture the investment made by others. The absence of any case law support did not dissuade Lotus's lawyer. "Borland may be in a bad position," he said, "but that doesn't make it legal to copy."

The panel once again took the case under advisement. Once again, we were hopeful. "It was even more like shooting fish in a barrel than the last time," a lawyer for one of Borland's allies told me.

While the judges wrote their decision, Borland's finances went from bad to worse. Philippe Kahn issued plans to restructure the company, cutting head count 35 percent. Borland's stock dropped to $8. The new year came without word from the court of appeals. In mid-January, Kahn resigned as president and CEO. His personal life was in shambles. He sold his twenty-one-acre estate, which was still unfinished after $8 million in renovations, for $1 million. His marriage of two decades fractured and his wife returned to France with the couple's young son. "Philippe put all of his energy into the company," she told the *Wall Street Journal*. Borland's stock price sank to $6.

Borland's new CEO went to Lotus, hat in hand, to beg for mercy. Word of the negotiation circulated in the press. Rumors of a corporate sale swirled in the industry. Just to make itself palatable to a potential acquirer, Borland had to accept whatever terms Lotus offered.

Judge Keeton, in the meantime, scheduled trial for Monday, March 13, 1995, to determine exactly how many tens of millions of dollars Borland owed Lotus. Borland's legal team asked Judge Keeton to delay the trial until the court of appeals announced a decision on liability. Keeton refused. He said there was a "growing risk" that Lotus would not be able to "collect a judgment due to the apparent deterioration of the defendant's financial condition."

On March 9, as Borland was finalizing the last details of its capitulation to Lotus, the court of appeals announced its decision—3–0 in Borland's favor. "A stunning decision that deprives Lotus Development Corp. of up to $100 million in damages," reported the *Boston Globe*.

The court of appeals issued two opinions, both of which ruled the menu commands uncopyrightable. The majority opinion written by Judge Stahl relied on language in the copyright statute to hold the menus uncopyrightable as a "method of operation." Judge Boudin based his concurring opinion more on the policy behind copyright law. He compared the Lotus menus to the QWERTY keyboard, citing Paul David's article. Users are locked into the Lotus menus, he explained, just the way touch typists are locked into the QWERTY configuration. "If a better spreadsheet comes along, it is hard to see why customers who have learned the Lotus menu and devised macros for it should remain captives of Lotus because of an investment in learning made by the users and not by Lotus," he wrote. He even suggested that an industry standard, like the Lotus menus, should be off-limits to copyright protection.

The next morning, Judge Keeton summoned the lawyers who were preparing for the damages trial to his chambers. "Does everybody agree that we should cancel the trial that's set for Monday morning?" Keeton asked.

"I wish I could think of an argument otherwise," Lotus's lawyer answered. "But I think we have no choice but to agree."

"Well, I'm sorry I won't be seeing you Monday," said Keeton. "I was looking forward to this trial."

In a just world, Borland's employees and executives would have returned to the work of rehabilitating their company, but that's not how it turned out. Lotus appealed to the Supreme Court, and in July the Court delivered very bad news to Borland by agreeing to hear the case.

Except for a few special kinds of cases, four of the nine justices have to agree to hear a case before it can be presented to the Supreme Court. The four justices who vote to hear a case likely believe there is something wrong with the lower court of appeals' decision. They only have to convince one more of their colleagues in order to reverse the court of appeals. Not surprisingly, the majority of appeals heard by the Supreme Court result in overturning the lower court's decision.

Borland's prospects looked even worse than the usual statistics would indicate. At the beginning of the summer, IBM launched a hostile takeover of Lotus. The deal closed in July. We were officially litigating against IBM, which made no difference to anyone except Supreme Court Justice John Paul Stevens. Stevens started his legal career practicing antitrust law. As a jurist, he was more outspokenly opposed to the extension of patent and copyright protection than any other member of the Supreme Court. We believed he would endorse our position and perhaps even advocate it to other justices. It was not to be. Stevens always recused himself without explanation from any case involving IBM, perhaps for reasons of stock ownership.

The briefing schedule set by the Supreme Court left no time to be depressed. We had only a few months to get all of our papers in order and to do what we could to dissuade other companies from filing briefs supporting Lotus. The latter task fell to Bob Kohn. He went from trade association to trade association explaining how a Lotus victory would damage the interests of just about every computer company, except for a few entrenched incumbents. When explanation was not enough, he berated and cajoled. Once, he joined a trade association just to keep the group from filing a brief. Kohn did his job well. Lotus ended up with only two supporting briefs, one from four big East Coast companies, and the other from a trade association dominated by IBM.

The copyright issues in the Lotus case, combined with the technical complexity of computer software, presented difficult problems for the Court. The Chief Justice, William Rehnquist, once asked journalists what a CD-ROM was. We could not afford to leave the impression that the case was an insignificant private dispute between two companies in an obscure industry. I asked my partner Michael Barclay to coordinate the friend-of-the-court briefs Kohn marshaled to support Borland's position. Over the two months before the filing deadline, Barclay logged more hours than any of the other six hundred lawyers in our firm.

In the end, more than a dozen briefs supported Borland's position. Two trade associations filed briefs arguing that the rules from Judge Keeton's decisions made it difficult for them to make their products work with those of industry leaders. Three trade groups of Silicon Valley entrepreneurs filed briefs challenging Lotus's claims that the Boston company was representing the interests of developers. Sixty computer groups representing fifty-three thousand corporate and individual users in major cities across the country urged the Court to let them run their macros without interference by Lotus. Thirty-four copyright law professors signed on to Professor Samuelson's Supreme Court brief. A dozen distinguished academics filed a brief explaining the economic significance of the case. Eighty computer scientists signed a brief that laid out the ramifications of the case for computer technology.

With Justice Stevens disqualified, Borland needed four votes to win the case. A tie vote automatically affirmed the lower court decision. Although Justice Breyer never telegraphed his viewpoint in the court of appeals' arguments, I believed the Lotus position contravened his deeply held views about copyright policy. I grasped at straws to put the votes of Justices David Souter and Anthony Kennedy on our side of the ledger. Both employed law clerks who previously worked for me. Under the Supreme Court's strict disqualification rules, the clerks could have no input on the case. Nevertheless, I assumed that these two justices would understand the importance of the case and study the briefs carefully. Besides, years earlier, then-Judge Kennedy presided over the appellate panel that affirmed Justice Rymer's decision in the Apple mail order case. At least, I thought, he understood the importance of computer technology to the economy.

So, I could count to three. But not to four. Where would our fourth vote come from? My colleagues and I called around to former law clerks and others more connected to the Court than we were, trying to figure out how to appeal to the predispositions of the other justices. The feedback was not encouraging. Both liberals and conservatives could find reason to support Lotus's position.

Conservatives sometimes looked at copyright and patent issues through a lens tinted by ideology. Lotus created the menus, they might reason, so Lotus should be entitled to the exclusive use of them. Justice Sandra Day O'Connor, for example, grew up in Arizona as the daughter of a pioneer family. "If you clear the land, you own it," one of her former clerks explained, prognosticating about how O'Connor might look at the case. Rehnquist would likely start from the same position, we were told. "He's so conservative," a former law clerk told me, "that had he been alive at the time of the American Revolution, it's not hard to figure out which side he would have been on." And Justice Antonin Scalia was even more conservative than Justice Rehnquist.

The doctrinaire liberal position was no better for us. Liberals often looked at copyright as what they called a "moral right," rather than as an economic calculus intended to benefit the public. In their view, someone who writes something is entitled to all of the value it accrues, even if most of that value is contributed by third parties after the work's creation. Keeton plainly approached the Lotus case this way, and we were told to expect much the same from Justice Ruth Bader Ginsburg.

That left only Justice Clarence Thomas, who always (to that point) cast his vote with Justice Scalia. Nevertheless, our calls yielded a glimmer of hope about Justice Thomas. "He'll want entrepreneurs to be able to do their thing without government interference," one of his former clerks told us. Great, I thought. Now all I had to do was convince Thomas to split from the other conservatives on the Court. In truth, the viewpoint ascribed to Justice Thomas was the traditional conservative position that had somehow gotten lost as competition policy became more business friendly.

The Court scheduled our argument for Monday, January 8, listing *Lotus v. Borland* third on the docket of three cases, meaning that we would be heard after lunch, at 1 p.m. I flew into Washington the Thursday before the argument to try to acclimate myself to the courtroom in which I would argue.

The Supreme Court's courtroom was even more intimidating than I had imagined. White marble lines the walls. The lawyer arguing a case stands at a lectern, directly across from the Chief Justice, who is seated in the center of the nine Court members behind a long, elevated mahogany desk. The lectern is positioned close to the bench, putting the lawyer almost nose to nose with the Chief Justice, but the Chief Justice sits at a higher level, looking down at the advocate. I had read stories about lawyers, in the well of the Supreme Court, fainting as they rose to address the justices. The long bench bows only slightly, meaning that the lawyer arguing the case cannot stand close enough to the lectern to see his notes and at the same time see the justices at one end of the bench without turning his back to the justices at the other end. Most experienced Supreme Court lawyers stand back a bit from the lectern for this reason.

After I finished gaping at the courtroom, I went to my hotel for a quick dinner. Seated at the next table was a large group from Ohio, with no connection to the dispute, who had come to town just to see the oral argument in *Lotus v. Borland* and to be part of the excitement of a big case. I grew nervous thinking about the size of the crowd expected at the Court argument. My brother had already told me that when he called the marshal's office asking what time he should get in line to see the Lotus argument in the afternoon, he was told to arrive by 8 a.m. if he wanted to get in.

The argument about the contour of competition policy fell at a poignant moment in the ongoing tug-of-war between conservatives and liberals over the operations of the federal government. On Saturday, President Clinton signed legislation to reopen the federal government after a twenty-one-day budget standoff between the Republican Congress and the Democratic administration shut everything down. More correctly, almost everything. The air traffic controllers and other "essential" government employees continued to get paid, but unemployment offices, Meals On Wheels, and similar programs for the poor went unfunded, until Clinton agreed to submit a balanced budget.

Early in the day on Saturday, weather officials issued a warning for a storm of historic proportions. Area residents took notice as the warnings increased in urgency during the day. Lines to get into grocery store parking lots stretched for blocks. Store shelves emptied quickly. The governor of Virginia declared a state of emergency early in the afternoon and called out the National Guard. The Weather Channel tracked the storm's progress.

Snow began falling after nightfall. The District of Columbia declared a snow emergency at 8 p.m. Snow fell all day Sunday and into the night, closing down all the major East Coast cities from Washington to Boston. The junior lawyers coming from my office in California to help us prepare for the Monday argument could get only as far as Pittsburgh. My partner Michael Barclay called the Supreme Court clerk's office late in the day on Sunday to confirm that Monday's argument would be postponed. The Supreme Court heard only a few cases each day, Monday through Wednesday, most but not all of the weeks of September through June. The arguments scheduled for Monday could easily be moved later in the week.

"Are you in town?" the deputy clerk asked Barclay. When Barclay responded affirmatively, the deputy clerk said that the Lotus lawyers had also arrived and Chief Justice Rehnquist wanted to proceed with the argument.

I slept not a wink Sunday night. The snow stopped before dawn. Dulles Airport reported more than two feet of accumulation, National Airport more than seventeen inches. Barclay again checked with the clerk's office and was again told the argument would go forward. I rose from a night of tossing and turning and drank far too many cups of coffee.

The street in front of our hotel was not plowed, nor were any of the streets we could see from our room windows. The District had but fifty-five snowplows in service. Another forty trucks that could have been used to plow streets were out of service because of a shortage of parts. Private contractors with snowplows were available, but the District had only enough money to hire a few of them. Miraculously, Barclay found us a cab that got us as far as half a block from the Supreme Court building, but the deep snow prevented it from going farther.

I arrived just in time for a required briefing session from the Supreme Court's clerk, intended to prepare lawyers for the rigors of oral argument. Sleep-deprived and caffeine-hyped, not a lot stuck with me. Don't confuse Justice Ginsburg with Justice O'Connor, the clerk sagely counseled. And always call Rehnquist "Chief Justice," not merely "Justice," and certainly not "Judge." What an insult, I thought.

I sat with my colleagues in the first row of the gallery as everyone's attention was commanded by an intense grating sound, which, I quickly learned, was the Court's call to order. The curtains behind the justices' chairs parted in three places and the justices emerged. Actually, only seven of the nine justices emerged. Stevens was stuck in Florida, where he lived most of the year, and Souter could not navigate through the snow in his Volkswagen. Flushed face and all, Souter joined the hearing midway into the argument. The court police brought him to work in a four-wheel-drive vehicle, the same as they had done for most of the other justices.

My wife and children somehow managed to reach the courthouse. They had arrived at Dulles Airport on Saturday just before the airport closed, but their lost luggage would not be delivered until after the storm subsided. They stayed with my brother in the Washington suburbs, borrowed clothes from his neighbors, and hiked three-quarters of a mile through two feet of snow to the nearest snow emergency road where one of my colleagues picked them up and brought them to the Court.

My wife approached the police officer at the Court's entrance and asked if she and the children could get in to see the argument, explaining the circumstances in some detail. My family's attire hardly conformed to the Court's strict dress code. My six-year-old son was wearing a Disney World shirt and sweat pants. "Sure," said the guard. "Just sit in the back so Rehnquist can't see you."

At the lunch break, the lawyers in my group were escorted to a private seating in the Court's cafeteria. Rehnquist's decision to keep the Court open meant that the food staff had to find a way to get to work through the deep snow. Only a skeleton crew made it, but they graciously served soup and salad.

Lotus's lawyer led off the argument after lunch. The justices seemed to go easy on him with their questions. As I rose to make my argument, I looked around the cavernous courtroom. Only a few observers sat in the gallery. The seats designated by name and seniority for reporters from the leading East Coast newspapers went unclaimed, as did the seats on the other side of the gallery reserved for guests of justices. I could hear a faint echo as I began to speak.

The justices started asking questions almost immediately. Most staked out the hostile positions that Court insiders had warned me about. Justice

Ginsburg would have no part of an economic approach to the scope of copyright protection. My argument would change the "character and understanding" of the copyright statute, she said.

The conservatives were no more hospitable. "Borland made a wholesale copying of a very complex menu command hierarchy," declared Justice O'Connor. "I mean, just wholesale."

Justice Scalia kept claiming that Borland did not really need to copy any of the contested commands to make its spreadsheet operate in the same way as 1-2-3. "You could have an instruction manual that says to do this thing, move the cursor over three spaces to the right and hit enter."

"I can't use the system effectively in any respect by doing that," I protested. But Scalia did not seem moved by my explanation.

Justice Souter questioned me the most intensely, but I could not understand a word he said. Souter grew up in New Hampshire and speaks with a thick, "down east" accent. I knew that lawyers sometimes had a problem understanding Justice Souter, and I listened closely to each word he said, but after my sleepless night, more than a pot of coffee, and a trudge through the snow, he sounded like he was speaking in tongues. I kept resisting Souter's position, mostly because I couldn't understand him. He was getting more and more impatient, continuing to press a point I could not make out. Finally, a bit of the fog lifted. Souter was arguing that the menus' copyrightability turned on the economic cost to society of protecting them, rather than on the traditional labels of copyright analysis.

"That's right," I responded excitedly. Others on the Court resisted Souter's suggestion, even the justices who agreed that protecting menu commands produced untenable results. They wanted to know the specific exception to copyright coverage that excluded the menus. Justice Kennedy called my argument about harming society by putting too much off-limits to competition "sensible," but he had difficulty pigeonholing it into a recognized copyright exception. "I need to know what kind of label I'm supposed to use to reach that result," he said.

"What is it in copyright that stops me from copying those 469 words?" Justice Breyer demanded. "What is the doctrine? How do I phrase it in English?"

I had not anticipated that the justices would take this approach, and my ability to think on my feet was sorely taxed as I tried to deal with eight different people asking me questions more or less at the same time. Most of the justices appeared willing to assume that copyright protection automatically covered the menus unless I could point to a specific exception in the statute or case law.

The Lotus case turned on unusual facts. Mitch Kapor always intended that users should adopt and invest in the menus he created. And, in fact, the menus gained value as users memorized keystroke sequences and wrote their own macro programs. Even under the relentless questioning, I could think of other kinds of more traditional written works that gain value when adopted by others. Computer languages. Natural languages, like English or French. Dance notation used for choreography.

I rolled off the examples in response to a question from Justice Ginsburg, briefly silencing the questioners. Traditional copyright doctrine recognized a difference between a set of commands to be used by others and compositions written from those commands. The compositions are protected from copying; the commands themselves are not. The distinction was intended to make it easy for standards to develop. No one should be required to create a unique language just to write a book. The rule was clear enough, but copyright law had no specific name for the concept, and the justices were not satisfied with my answer.

My time was running out. Almost exasperated, I tried to explain that requiring me to come up with a copyright exception put the burden in the wrong place. Copyright was the tail. The free and open exchange of information in a competitive marketplace was the dog. Lotus had the burden of coming up with a good reason to put its commands off-limits to competition, not the other way around. Just because the command hierarchy took the form of written words should not prevent others from copying it. The memos and reports from the legislative deliberations over the 1976 copyright act clearly stated that Congress did not intend to protect all "writings." A congressional report listed numerous examples of "writings" that the 1976 act did not protect, including "titles" and "similar short expressions."

I argued that all doubts about what is covered by copyright should be resolved against restricting free market competition. "This Court has repeatedly said that if we can't tell whether the extension of copyright in [a] particular case is . . . within the Congressional purpose or not, we shouldn't take that step," I said.

"What is that," Chief Justice Rehnquist interrupted sarcastically, staring almost straight down at me, "some sort of a tie-counts-for-the-runner approach?"

I often used the words Rehnquist chose—"tie counts for the runner"— to explain the concept to other lawyers. "Yes, absolutely," I said.

"What case do you find that in?" Rehnquist surely thought I had made up the concept. I had only a second or two to decide how to respond.

When Sony invented the videocassette recorder, Universal Studios and Walt Disney Co. sued to prevent its sale, arguing that the device would be used to copy movies and television shows illegally. Justice Stevens, writing for a bare 5-4 majority, turned back the studios' challenge to the new technology. Consumers bought the device in great numbers, and the studios still managed to profit through the sale of prerecorded movies.

The *Sony* decision counseled for judicial restraint "where major technological innovations alter the market for copyrighted materials." If Congress has not "plainly marked our course," the opinion stated, the Supreme Court should not limit competition by expanding the scope of copyright protection. In other words, tie counts for the runner. Subsequent Supreme Court opinions cited the key passages from the *Sony* decision with approval, and the Court relied on the *Sony* language in a unanimous decision, authored by Chief Justice Rehnquist, just a year before my argument.

I was about to read the *Sony* language with great flourish and point out the words that Rehnquist himself had approved not a year earlier. But even sleep-deprived, I concluded that showing up the Chief Justice was not a good tactic. I mentioned the name of the case and argued for a sentence or two about the risks of giving too much protection, the risks of putting too much off-limits to competition by others, as my time ended. The Court retired for the day after my frustrating half-hour.

I went back to the hotel bar with the lawyers on the Borland team and spent a couple of hours trying to find a reason to be optimistic. Notwithstanding my inability to identify a specific copyright exception for commands, Justices Souter, Kennedy, and Breyer seemed reluctant to support

TRIAL BY ORDEAL   135

Lotus's position on competition policy grounds, absent an express directive from Congress. "I can find theme after theme that tells us that the copyright law is not to be used so that one company will monopolize the Internet henceforth into world reality," Breyer said during my argument.

We still needed a fourth vote to win. Justices Ginsburg, O'Connor, Rehnquist, and Scalia had expressed varying degrees of skepticism about my argument. Bob Kohn kept insisting that Justice Thomas would vote our way. "I saw Breyer giving Thomas high fives," Kohn claimed. In keeping with his normal practice, Thomas asked no questions, but his body language suggested to me that he was more receptive to my argument than some of the others—or maybe I was just imagining things. A reporter from the *Washington Post* later asked how I felt coming out of the argument. "We could be ushering in the dark ages of the computer industry," I told her.

Most of Borland's lawyers needed two full days to leave Washington. After a twenty-one-day political standoff and five days of a snow emergency, the federal government finally opened back up on Thursday, only to close on Friday as a new storm moved into the area. Fewer than 25 percent of the residential streets were plowed in the District of Columbia by week's end. The mayor of Washington, Marion Barry, posed with a snowplow for the benefit of television crews, then asked President Clinton to declare a state of emergency.

A week later, one of the younger associates in my office fielded an early morning telephone call from the Supreme Court's deputy clerk. Borland won the case on a 4–4 tie vote, the clerk said. Press calls flooded my office. The tie vote meant only that the Court was not ready to take a position on the question raised in the case, not necessarily indicating that four justices voted each way. Because the Court does not publish an opinion in a case decided by a tie vote, there is no way to know for sure exactly what happened. Nevertheless, the Court's announcement exonerated Borland, finally ending the lawsuit. The Supreme Court's ruling affirmed the court of appeals' decision, but that decision would bind only the lower courts in New England and Puerto Rico, the jurisdiction of the Boston-based appeals court.

Court observers debated the meaning of it all. "At the end of this enormous road, there is no answer. That's breathtaking," a Georgetown law professor told the *Post*. Others disagreed. "The Supreme Court spoke quietly but they did speak. It's still a big win," reported the *Wall Street Journal*, quoting a lawyer for one of the Silicon Valley companies that backed Borland in the case. The outcome of the case ended up moving companies in the computer industry away from trying to rely on copyright's easy-to-secure preclusion as a vehicle to hamper competitors in standards markets.

Bob Kohn announced the Supreme Court's decision to a hastily called company meeting, sparking tumultuous celebrating at Borland's headquarters. Then Kohn left the practice of law. In 1997, he founded eMusic, one of the first music-download services, which he sold to Universal Music Group in 2001. After eMusic, he founded RoyaltyShare, a software company that manages royalty payments for music and book publishers as well as motion picture distributors.

Much had changed in the industry after seven years of litigation. Lotus no longer remained an independent company. Borland no longer made compatible application products. Although Judge Keeton ran Philippe Kahn out of the spreadsheet business, Silicon Valley afforded him other opportunities. On his way out as CEO, Philippe made a deal to acquire a small scheduling product from Borland. He improved the technology and, together with a graphics designer whom he would later marry, Kahn built a company, Starfish, around it. Starfish's product enabled wireless devices to synchronize with each other. Kahn sold the company to Motorola in 1998 for $325 million.

While the sale was pending, Kahn's wife had a baby. Philippe juryrigged a cell phone with a digital camera so he could send pictures of the baby to his friends and relatives wirelessly. I remember him telling me about his idea for a new consumer electronics product. "A cell phone that takes pictures?" I asked incredulously. "Who would want a cell phone that takes pictures?" I didn't want one. Neither did the senior managers of Motorola, the new owner of Philippe's company. Motorola passed on Kahn's invention, so Philippe set up another company, LightSurf, to develop the technology that lets cell phones take pictures and send them over the Internet. He partnered with Verizon and Sprint. Sprint deployed a commercial system based on LightSurf's technology in 2002 and Philippe sold Light-

Surf to Verizon in 2005 for $315 million. Last year, hundreds of millions of camera phones were sold worldwide.

―――――――

Two months after the Supreme Court announced its decision, I received a letter from the clerk of the Court. According to the letter, the Court was considering a change in one of its rules about friend-of-the-court briefs to require the disclosure of anyone "who made any contribution, in money or services, to the cost of preparing and submitting the brief." The letter invited me to comment on the proposed change. I had never received a personal invitation to comment on proposed Supreme Court rule changes before, and I thought I knew what prompted the Court's proposal.

Articles in the legal press confirmed my suspicions. According to anonymous sources in the Supreme Court clerk's office, the proposed rule change came from the justices themselves. "A recent *amicus* [friend-of-the-court] brief indicating that a named party in a high court challenge had paid for the brief may have precipitated the proposal," an unnamed source said. The clerk's office would not identify the case and the press couldn't figure it out. I knew.

As the *Borland* case wound through the lower courts, Bob Kohn noticed opinion pieces in industry publications criticizing Keeton's decisions. Many were written by prominent computer scientists. Kohn urged one of the authors to organize a brief for the Supreme Court. The computer scientist stood willing to write the brief and circulate it to his colleagues, but he didn't want to pay hundreds of dollars out of his own pocket for printing costs. Borland offered to pay the printing costs, after I checked the Supreme Court rules to make sure it was permissible. We extended the same offer to other ad hoc groups of academics and financially strapped entrepreneur support organizations that wanted to file briefs on our side. In each case, we told them to state in the brief that Borland had paid for printing, while the group retained control of the contents of the brief. Apparently, when the justices read the statements, some of them got bent out of shape, or at least curious.

Ultimately, I decided to throw the clerk's invitation away. The whole process of trying to defend Borland through seven years of litigation soured me on the court process. Keeton's rulings limiting free market competition would have wrecked the software industry. It didn't take two trials, four district court opinions, two appellate court hearings, and a tortuous gauntlet run through the Supreme Court to figure that out. How were market challengers to come up with the kind of financing necessary to overcome such overwhelming legal obstacles?

Even without my comments, the proposed rule change caused a stir in the Supreme Court bar that I had not anticipated. The justices' reaction to the statements in Borland's supporting briefs opened to public view, ever so slightly at first, a complicated strategy by the U.S. Chamber of Commerce to move the Court to a posture more friendly to big business. The National Chamber Litigation Center, organized in 1977 by the Chamber of Commerce to file briefs on behalf of business interests, vocally opposed the Court's proposed rule change. "We find it a little disturbing," the vice president of the center told the *National Law Journal*. "A lot of companies join organizations for the anonymity." The Court ultimately adopted its own proposal, after clarifying that the rule change did not require the disclosure of trade association membership lists. Ten years later, the Court proposed additional rule changes to require the disclosure of whether a party to a case before it belongs to a trade association that submitted a supporting brief or contributed monetarily to the preparation of the brief. Once again, the National Chamber Litigation Center's opposition got the proposal amended to drop the requirement of trade association membership disclosure.

According to a cover story in the *New York Times Magazine* in March 2008, the center began in the 1980s to help prepare and coordinate the strategy of lawyers hired to argue the most important business cases. The *Times* feature enumerated the center's successes in persuading the Court to favor big business in antitrust, environmental, securities, and product liability cases. The rules change precipitated by Borland's tiny shoestring effort ended up shedding light on a far more significant undertaking that all but closed the Court to both consumers and entrepreneurs.

CHAPTER 8

The Shakedown

A *Wall Street Journal* article reporting the 1995 court of appeals' decision suggested that Borland's victory would "lead more software developers to look to patent protection." On the day of Borland's Supreme Court argument, almost a year later, the *New York Times* confirmed the accuracy of the prediction. "The big companies are filing [patents] like mad," a lawyer told the *Times*.

The publicity our arguments received throughout the seven-year drama pushed the industry toward greater use of the patent system. Developers might reasonably rely on easy-to-secure copyright to prevent piracy of their code, we argued, because protection of code rarely produces significant economic consequences. Other developers can create their own code to produce the same results.

But technological advances in software of real competitive significance that, like the Lotus menus, permit better operation of computer applications should meet the more exacting requirements of the patent system to avoid copying by competitors. The patent system extracts the appropriate quid pro quo for the privilege of temporarily excluding competitors—a "novel" and "nonobvious" invention that benefits society. Judge Keeton, we explained, gave Lotus one hundred years of competitive exclusion for an invention that never satisfied the requirements to secure the twenty-year patent term.

We grounded our argument more in the theoretical operation of an optimal patent system than in the reality of actual practice. By the mid-1990s, the American patent system had spun out of control. The careful examination and precisely balanced quid pro quo we attributed to the Patent and Trademark Office existed only in policy discussions.

My own introduction to the realities of the patent system came in the 1980s, when my client, Sun Microsystems—then a small company—was accused by IBM of patent infringement. IBM took a hard line enforcing patents after its more benevolent view of copyright cost the company control of the personal computer market. Threatening a massive lawsuit, IBM demanded a meeting to present its claims. Fourteen IBM lawyers and their assistants, all clad in the requisite dark blue suits, crowded into the largest conference room at Sun headquarters.

The chief blue suit orchestrated the presentation of the seven patents IBM claimed were infringed, the most prominent of which was IBM's notorious "fat lines" patent: To turn a thin line on a computer screen into a broad line, go up and down an equal distance from the ends of the thin line and then connect the four points. Like everyone else, I learned this technique for turning a line into a rectangle in seventh-grade geometry, and I assumed it was created by Euclid or some such three-thousand-year-old thinker. Not according to the examiners of the Patent and Trademark Office, who awarded IBM a patent on the process.

After IBM's presentation, our turn came. As the Big Blue crew looked on (without a flicker of emotion), my colleagues—all of whom had both engineering and law degrees—took to the whiteboard with markers, methodically illustrating, dissecting, and demolishing IBM's claims. We used phrases like: "You must be kidding" and "You ought to be ashamed." But the IBM team showed no emotion, save outright indifference. Confidently, we proclaimed our conclusion: Only one of the seven IBM patents would be deemed valid by a court, and no rational court would find that Sun's technology infringed even that one.

An awkward silence ensued. The blue suits did not even confer among themselves. They just sat there, stonelike. Finally, the chief suit responded. "Okay," he said, "maybe you don't infringe these seven patents. But we have ten thousand U.S. patents. Do you really want us to go back to Armonk [IBM headquarters in New York] and find seven patents you do infringe? Or do you want to make this easy and just pay us $20 million?"

After a modest bit of negotiation, Sun cut IBM a check, and the blue suits went to the next company on their hit list.

In corporate America, this type of shakedown occurs weekly. The patent as stimulant to invention has long since given way to the patent as blunt instrument for establishing an innovative stranglehold. Sometimes the antagonist is a large corporation, short on revenue-generating products but long on royalty-generating patents. On other occasions, an opportunistic "entrepreneur" who only produces patent applications uses the system's overly broad and undisciplined patent grant to shake down a productive company.

The American patent system emerged from the identification of a severe market deficiency. Innovation requires the investment of time, effort, and money. Unfettered competition quickly defuses the productive results of innovation throughout society as new inventions are disclosed, used, and copied, sometimes yielding a far less than optimum amount of innovative activity by failing to compensate innovators adequately for their contributions. So, a free market economy has to offer some kind of subsidy to induce the right amount of innovation.

On paper, at least, a direct reward system is the most straightforward and efficient way to subsidize innovation. The government compensates each successful inventor out of the federal treasury in an amount corresponding to the value of the invention. Competitors freely copy and distribute the invention, driving its price to marginal cost and accelerating its market penetration, producing the optimal consumption of the new product. A number of the colonies actually employed direct subsidy schemes to encourage innovation, and the Senate in 1790 passed a bill that would have given Supreme Court justices the "power to determine the compensation which persons shall receive for their inventions."

Such comically ingenuous schemes would surely have proven inadministrable by modern government. Even assuming good faith in the granting of cash awards, the exact monetary value to society of an invention defies accurate determination by a government institution.

Congress instead adopted a patent system in the British model, premised on the exclusion of competition to spur innovation. Rather than trying to ascertain the societal value of an invention, the government grants a worthy applicant a monopoly of sorts over his innovation. The market determines the exact amount of the subsidy, calculated by adding together the payments the patent holder extracts from others (either purchasers of his product or licensees of his technology) in exchange for the waiver of the exclusion granted by the government.

The market power of each patent varies according to the significance of the invention covered, but the draconian character of the preclusion always remains the same. Unlike copyright, the patent law makes no allowances for independent creation. Copying need not be shown to prove infringement. Years of hard work and millions of dollars of investment can be wiped out if a competitor makes the patentable invention first. Companies can unknowingly infringe vague patent claims, yet still subject their own products to injunction and their profits to appropriation by a patent holder.

Although far easier to administer than a direct subsidy program, the patent approach brought its own shortcomings. Like all monopolies, patent grants tend to increase prices and decrease output, producing suboptimal consumption of the patented good, as well as wealth transfer from consumers to the patent holder. Patents diminish the incentives of other inventors in the field covered by the patent, who must stay clear of the patentee's exclusionary privileges, if they wish to create their own innovations. They can't even improve the patented article or process without permission (and, likely, without payment). Patent awards make the creation of complex devices and technological processes that read on multiple patent grants particularly difficult, as permissions must be secured from a number of patent holders, each of which can hold out for more than the market value of his patent standing alone. And a government-administered procedure for granting exclusions from competition is particularly susceptible to manipulation and abuse, producing private benefits at public expense in ways far less visible to the public than excessive direct cash subsidies.

A patent is little more than a federal excise tax, as Bill Baxter explained in a 1966 law journal article that first gained him notice in academic circles. Purchasers of a patented item—collectively, all users of recent innovations—pay an officially authorized charge that is appropriated by the patent holder. Most people (including many policy makers) think about the patent system by looking only at its purported benefit (inducing innovation) without considering its cost. They conclude that more patents will costlessly produce the public benefit of more innovation.

When Japanese companies began to challenge U.S. corporations for technological leadership in the 1970s, just as U.S. productivity—output per hour of labor input—slowed, congressional hearings suggested that changes in patent policy might help restore the country's technological leadership. Some Chicago School scholars, already working to refocus antitrust on the pursuit of economic efficiency, pressed for abandoning the populist-era hostility toward patents. Bill Baxter, among others, argued for greater use of rule of reason review in place of per se condemnation when evaluating patent licensing practices—requiring a licensee to pay royalties on multiple patents in order to use just one, for example—challenged under the antitrust laws as anticompetitive restraints.

The Supreme Court in 1980 broadened the scope of what is patentable by directing the Patent Office to grant patents on human-made, genetically engineered bacteria. In explaining its 5–4 decision, the Court quoted from a thirty-year-old congressional committee report for the proposition that "anything under the sun that is made by man" qualifies for patent protection. That decision (and several others like it) signaled to the Patent Office an about-face in the decades-long reluctance to expand patent protection. The Patent Office interpreted these new decisions very broadly and began to issue patents on computer software—previously considered unpatentable as mathematical algorithms, since they are not really human inventions.

In 1982, patent advocates convinced Congress to create a special court of appeals (the Court of Appeals for the Federal Circuit, the CAFC) for all patent cases. The new court, staffed in large part by patent lawyers, proved to be far more willing to accept the validity of patents challenged for insufficient novelty than the preexisting appellate courts. The CAFC capped off the trend toward broader patent protection by ruling in 1998 that methods of doing business are patentable.

Patent claims for computer software and methods of doing business inundated the Patent Office, and there were few records of prior inventions in these two areas against which to check new claims for novelty. Specious patents were awarded in droves.

Even a patent of questionable validity can be quite valuable to its owner. Because infringement lawsuits usually cost many millions of dollars to defend, software and electronics patents vulnerable to challenge on grounds of insufficient novelty still represent powerful bargaining chips. Sound business judgment counsels in favor of making substantial royalty payments over contesting a patent's validity in court. And, conversely, an undisciplined patent system makes the stockpiling of patents a profit-maximizing strategy.

Each year, since at least 1993, IBM has led the Patent Office's published list of top ten U.S. patent recipients. The company receives about three thousand patents annually. Most of the other patent recipients on the list, year after year, are foreign companies—Hitachi, Samsung, Canon, Sony, Toshiba, Matsushita. Four U.S. companies made the top ten list in 2001, an event so unusual that the Patent Office highlighted it in a press release. The following year only two U.S. companies made the list. "I am proud that American corporations are leaders among U.S. patent holders," the head of the Patent Office said in the 2002 press release, not quite accounting for the companies actually named in the list.

Patents "stimulate economic growth and investment in commerce, creating jobs for millions of Americans," read the Patent Office's 2003 release. Patents help to "nurture industries that create jobs for Americans," said the 2004 release. In both years, foreign corporations dominated the list.

Critics of the patent system raised questions about the wisdom of a government program that operates to fill the coffers of a few big companies, most of them headquartered abroad. The Patent and Trademark Office stopped publishing its annual top ten list in 2007, a move its press release characterized as "emphasizing quality over quantity by discouraging any perception that we believe more is better." Trade associations continued to compile and publish a list of the top U.S. patent recipients by reviewing public records each year. IBM still heads the list, followed for the most part by foreign companies.

The cost to consumers of trying to encourage innovation through patent grants staggers the imagination. Many reputable publications report the patent licensing income of IBM alone—just one company—at over $1 billion annually. IBM royalty payments are passed on as price increases to consumers of its licensees' products. Whatever inflated prices IBM can charge for its own products from the receipt of patent grants are not included in the $1 billion figure, nor are the costs society bears when potential competitors simply quit the field rather than pay the toll.

Worse yet, economic studies indicate the transfer of vast amounts of wealth from consumers to patentees accomplishes next to nothing in terms of encouraging innovation. The expectation of patent protection has little effect on research and development expenditures among large companies, except perhaps in the pharmaceutical industry. And while the CAFC's policies contributed to the deluge of patents, studies show no acceleration in company-financed research and development in the two decades after the court's formation. The argument that fueled the rush toward stronger patent protection—that innovators will create more if they can keep for themselves more of the monetary benefits their inventions produce—ended up a vast overstatement.

My experience with Silicon Valley start-ups parallels the studies of large companies. Many early Valley technologists rebelled at the whole notion of patent protection. They credited their own success to the work of others who preceded them and they believed that knowledge and information should be free for all to use. The Valley grew to become the world's leader in innovation, they argued, precisely because the flow of information did not stop at company boundaries. In any case, free market forces like network effects rewarded the first entrant into a market by reinforcing its position, diminishing the need for a stimulus from patent privileges.

Bill Baxter once suggested to me, after his return from Washington, that the Valley's entrepreneurs changed their views once they realized that patents were necessary to attract early-round investors. I didn't argue with him, but I knew better. It was the incessant demand for royalty payments from entrenched East Coast companies like IBM that forced Valley entrepreneurs to rethink their rejection of patents. They wanted to have "something to trade"—patents that could be used to make countervailing claims—when IBM came calling, they told me. I assuaged any lingering doubts as to the business ethics of their strategy. "Patents are like nuclear weapons," I explained to the start-ups that came to me for advice. "All your neighbors have some, so you need to have some, too."

The ready supply of competitive weapons could not help but promote conflagration. Many cases highlighted the yawning chasm between the patent system's lofty goals and its true operation. Kodak bought patents from a defunct Massachusetts company, Wang Laboratories, and sued Sun Microsystems over Java, the Internet technology, ultimately receiving about $100 million in settlement. Verizon brought (and won) a crippling patent infringement suit against Vonage, its smaller market challenger. A start-up sued Microsoft over what turned out to be such basic Internet technology that the Patent Office agreed to reexamine the underlying patent. The nationwide BlackBerry network was almost shut down by claims based on patents the Patent Office was about to rule invalid. Although intended as a mechanism to secure for each inventor the revenue stream his inventions generate, the system actually permits crafty manipulators to profit handsomely from the hard work of others.

Like much of corporate America, the legal profession grew rich from the bounty of government privileges. Plaintiffs' lawyers, starved by the dearth of antitrust litigation brought on by Chicago School policies, transferred their skills to contingent fee patent cases. Defendants' lawyers, whose associate armadas had thinned with the withering of private antitrust damage suits, replenished their billing books by repelling patent claims. Patent litigation became a growth industry for lawyers and economists.

Patent lawyers started calling their enterprise "intellectual property law," a fancy and fundamentally misleading moniker intended to convey an aura of respectability. "Exclusionary privileges" more correctly describes patents and copyrights and properly raises a reluctance to oblige demands for what sound like feudal prerogatives. But the "intellectual property" terminology caught on, further clouding rational evaluation of costs and benefits.

The rising tide of overprotection did not escape official notice. The Republican-controlled Federal Trade Commission issued a set of recommendations for changing the patent system to restore a proper balance with competition policy. The commission's report invoked the metaphor of a "patent thicket" first proposed by Carl Shapiro, an economist at the University of California. The report explained that patents of questionable validity issued in droves by the Patent Office contributed to a "dense web of overlapping intellectual property rights that a company must hack its way through in order to actually commercialize new technology." The commission proposed procedures to make it easier to challenge issued patents as well as substantive changes in the legal standards to make it more difficult to secure a patent in the first place.

In the wake of the criticism, the Supreme Court announced several rulings against patent holders, making it harder to get a patent, easier to challenge an existing patent, and more difficult to enjoin the sale of allegedly infringing products. The most important of the opinions tightened the prohibition against patents claiming obvious subject matter. A unanimous Court required "more than ordinary innovation" to obtain a patent on a new product that contains elements of preexisting technology. Without the more stringent legal requirements, the Court held, patents might stifle rather than promote the progress of the useful arts. The decision gave patent examiners greater freedom to deny claims and judges more leeway to toss infringement suits out of court. For its part, the Patent Office began to publicize the number of patent applications it rejected, instead of the number it granted. In 2008, the CAFC issued an important decision rolling back the broad patent protection for business methods which it mandated ten years earlier.

———

In 1983, the CEO of a cash-strapped start-up came to me for copyright advice. Nathan Myhrvold told a fascinating story. He graduated from high school at age fourteen, earned a college degree, then two master's degrees, then a Ph.D. from Princeton. After a year studying the universe as a postdoctoral fellow for British cosmologist Stephen Hawking, Myhrvold quit to commercialize some technology that he started working on in England. He recruited a few friends, most of them physicists, to design software for "multitasking." Myhrvold's product enabled an operating system to work on several things at the same time, and to display the results on the computer screen simultaneously in separate windows.

As Myhrvold was about to release his product, IBM announced something very similar. Myhrvold sought my advice to make his product IBM-compatible without violating the copyright law. Intrigued by the technology,

I even took time off my day job to help make sales for the struggling company. But IBM's product flopped, so there was little interest in an IBM-compatible substitute. Rapidly running out of money, Myhrvold and his team decided to seek sponsorship for a software program designed to make an IBM-compatible computer look like and operate like a Macintosh.

I tried unsuccessfully to interest Apple in Myhrvold's company. Bill Gates leaped at the opportunity, buying the few corporate assets and the services of the company's eight employees for $1.5 million in Microsoft stock. Myhrvold's team went to work on a new operating-system project, first called Presentation Manager and then Windows, the industry's most important software product. A book written by a couple of Microsoft insiders years later described Gates's acquisition of Myhrvold's company as "Microsoft's single most important acquisition, changing the future of the company forever." Myhrvold became Microsoft's director of special projects and, ultimately, the company's chief technology officer.

At the height of the industry's anxiety over Microsoft's power in 1997, Myhrvold distinguished himself by telling the *Wall Street Journal* of the company's plans to get a "vig"—short for "vigorish," the underworld term for a loan shark's or bookie's cut—on every transaction over the Internet using Microsoft's technology. He was even more explicit with John Battelle, the managing editor of *Wired* magazine. Myhrvold slapped his wallet on the table and predicted Microsoft would own anything done with a wallet online. Myhrvold's bravado (or cold candor) helped turn public sentiment against the monopolist.

Myhrvold left Microsoft in 1999 with a fortune in excess of $200 million. When the "dot-com" bubble burst in 2000, he saw a business opportunity. Why fight the government trying for a "vig" on electronic transactions, when you can take a cut from every use of technology anywhere in the world with Uncle Sam's blessing?

The precipitous stock market downturn forced hundreds, perhaps even thousands, of inadequately funded young technology companies into bankruptcy, leaving their patent portfolios unattended, much like the nuclear warhead stockpiles left unguarded at the demise of the Soviet Union. Myhrvold set up a company to buy patents out of bankruptcy, raising tens of millions of dollars from Microsoft, then more, according to the press, from Intel, Sony, Apple, eBay, and Google. He closed his first fund-raising period after bringing in more than $1.5 billion. Myhrvold's team called Silicon Valley patent law firms, left with unpaid legal fees from the incomplete patent prosecutions of companies that ran out of money, offering to take over the accounts, clear all past debts, and fund the applications to completion.

Myhrvold first called his company Patent Defense Fund, explaining his intention to buy up patents that might otherwise be used against his financial backers in shakedown litigation. The Patent Defense Fund quickly changed its name to Intellectual Ventures and started buying patents from universities and even from Fortune 100 companies that wanted to get money for patents from business areas they had abandoned. Myhrvold has amassed twenty thousand patents and patent applications, according to press reports, using a business plan that calls for making money by licensing the acquired patents, under implicit threat of lawsuit, to companies that need them to continue creating products.

In August 2003, Myhrvold started signing up technologists and academics to tender ideas that his organization could patent, all for a share of the proceeds. Intellectual Ventures now files about four hundred of its own applications each year, with thousands in the pipeline. In press interviews, Myhrvold touts this side of his business, portraying the operation as a financial vehicle that invests in ideas that can be used to make productive devices.

Not that Intellectual Ventures actually makes much of anything, other than patent applications and the occasional spinout of technology for use by a venture capitalist in a start-up—for a piece of the action, of course. "We're not going to make products," Myhrvold told the press. Companies that want to make products covered by Intellectual Ventures' patents will have to pay Myhrvold.

"I want to achieve what IBM has achieved. That's my financial model. This is a play where I take portfolio theory and apply it to something illiquid to deliver a return for my investors," Myhrvold explained to *Fortune* magazine. "I don't see that as evil." Others in the Valley suggest that it is only a matter of time before Intellectual Ventures starts suing to collect royalties. One of Hewlett-Packard's lawyers even dismissed Intellectual Ventures' invention plans as a "smoke screen to buy time." Another declined comment to the press because of a confidentiality agreement Intellectual Ventures made him sign.

In 2008 a group of big technology companies set up their own consortium, Allied Security Trust, to buy up patents that might otherwise be asserted in litigation. A month later Myhrvold announced plans to raise more money—$2.5 billion, a preemptive strike of sorts. Companies and venture funds that refuse to pay him do so at their own peril. Those that take licenses protect their market positions—all in all, an offer few can refuse.

"We're concerned that these giant pools of patent rights are going to prevent entrepreneurs from entering markets," one venture capitalist told *Newsweek*. Vast aggregations of patents by investment vehicles leave start-ups defenseless to extortion. Having something to trade—a patent portfolio that can be asserted against a more conventional company—provides no protection. Like a stateless terrorist with a dirty bomb, an investment fund has no manufacturing operations to threaten with countervailing claims.

The pharmaceuticals industry has its own problematic counterpart to the patent acquisition and licensing practices that threaten information technology. In 1984, Congress passed a special law, named for its sponsors—conservative senator Orrin Hatch and liberal congressman Henry Waxman—to accelerate the development of low-cost generic drugs by streamlining the regulatory approval process, while maintaining a sufficient reward for brand name pharmaceutical companies so they would continue to innovate. A key provision of Hatch-Waxman provides an easy mechanism for generic manufacturers to challenge the scope and validity of patents held by brand name manufacturers, so generic competitors could get to market before a brand name company's patent would otherwise expire.

The Hatch-Waxman Act proved highly successful. The generic industry flourished without apparent harm to brand name innovation. Consumers saved many billions of dollars as generic equivalents of widely used drugs such as the antidepressants Prozac and Paxil and the heartburn medicine Prilosec, among other drugs, became available to consumers before patent expiration.

With the waning of antitrust enforcement, brand name drug companies exploited a loophole in Hatch-Waxman. They brought patent infringement actions against the generic manufacturers and then negotiated brazenly anticompetitive settlements. In normal patent infringement cases, the accused infringer frequently agrees to make payments—generally royalty payments—as a condition of settlement. In an "exclusion payment" case, the brand name manufacturer agrees to pay the company it is suing to stop competing further. The generic manufacturer agrees to withdraw its product until the brand name company's patent expires. Consumers continue to pay high brand name prices, and the brand name company, in effect, splits the proceeds with the generic manufacturer, which gets paid a share of inflated consumer prices for doing nothing.

When this practice started in the late 1990s, the FTC challenged "exclusion payment" deals as market-division agreements among competitors, illegal per se under the antitrust laws. The practice stopped for a few years. Then one of the big drug companies found a complicated way to achieve more or less the same result. The Bush administration's FTC brought suit but a federal appellate court sided with the drug company, permitting the payments. The commission, firmly under the control of card-carrying Republicans, filed a brief asking the Supreme Court to review the case. The Bush administration's Justice Department refused to sign the FTC's brief. The Justice Department eventually filed its own brief, urging the Court to refuse to hear the FTC's appeal. The Justice Department made a variety of technical arguments to support its position, but, at bottom, it simply disagreed with the legal standard advocated by the FTC. The Supreme Court declined to hear the appeal, leaving the "exclusion payment" agreement intact.

In a subsequent case, a group of consumers challenged a somewhat less complicated exclusion payment scheme. A different court of appeals threw out the suit without even putting the claims to a trial. The FTC asked the

Supreme Court to hear the consumers' appeal. Once again, the Bush Justice Department took a contrary position and the Supreme Court declined to hear the case.

Word spread around the pharmaceuticals industry. Payments from brand name companies to generic manufacturers, coupled with commitments to delay the market entry of generics, became far more common. Exclusion payments spread to leading sleep disorder drugs, oral contraceptives, blood thinners, and high blood pressure medications. Anticompetitive settlements involved the transfer of many tens of millions of dollars.

The court decisions in exclusion-payment cases are so detailed and complicated that lay people have no chance of understanding them. The bottom line, though, is clear enough: companies avoid competition and share the resulting profits of monopoly pricing based on patents of dubious validity. The CEO of a brand manufacturer recently explained why he settled patent claims his own company brought by paying over $135 million to four generics companies that agreed to stay out of the market until 2011: "We were able to get six more years of patent protection. That's $4 billion in sales that no one expected."

The recent Supreme Court decisions and more stringent Patent Office examination procedures may help to rein in an out-of-control patent system, but only to a limited extent. More substantial reforms remain bogged down in Congress, where beleaguered legislators face conflicting interests. Pharmaceutical companies may legitimately need strong patent protection. Some entrepreneurial interests take the same view. Most of the larger information technology companies demand action to curb the power of patent grants, producing a legislative logjam.

When Thurman Arnold took control of the Antitrust Division during the New Deal, he found some industries gridlocked by enormous patent cross-licensing pools and others choked by the dominant patent portfolios of monopolies. Arnold brought a precedent-setting monopolization case challenging the patent-licensing practices of the glass-container-making industry's leading company. That company and others in league with it were ordered to license all of their patents at reasonable royalty rates. More than one hundred subsequent cases ended in settlements requiring compulsory licensing of as many as fifty thousand patents, including substantial numbers held by monopolists AT&T, IBM, and DuPont.

The *Wall Street Journal* editorial page railed against the Antitrust Division's successes, warning that compulsory licensing "strikes at incentive; new ideas and new inventions may be lost." In fact, the AT&T compulsory licenses created the semiconductor industry, spawning all of Silicon Valley's subsequent innovation. And economic studies revealed that the companies subjected to compulsory licensing actually spent more on research and development relative to their sales after the government actions than comparable companies left alone by the lawsuits.

The antitrust laws permit precisely the kind of case-by-case evaluation necessary to correct the patent abuses that plague today's economy, leaving global issues of patent reform for congressional resolution. The Antitrust Division has jurisdiction under the Sherman Act to attack conspiracies and monopolies that rely on patents to choke competition in ways far removed from the intended scope of the government grants. Bill Baxter's creative invocation of "attempted monopolization" to challenge American Airlines' odious conduct serves as a model for going after those trying to build anticompetitive aggregations of power through patent acquisition. The Federal Trade Commission's mandate to prevent "unfair methods of competition" provides even broader jurisdiction.

Government antitrust enforcement must be met by judicial recognition of the need for change. Too often, judges cling to a romantic myth. They view the patent system as the seedbed of capitalism—the place where ideas and new technologies are nurtured. In reality, patents are enormously powerful competitive weapons that must be carefully monitored for misuse. A free market philosophy favors competition over exclusion to produce innovation.

PART FOUR

MONOPOLIES AND
MARKET EXCLUSION

CHAPTER 9

The Empire Extended

One sunny Saturday morning in July 1994, I turned on the TV in my kitchen, searching for something appropriate for my children to watch while they ate breakfast. Instead, Janet Reno, the attorney general of the United States, appeared on the screen, announcing the settlement of the Justice Department's long-running investigation of Microsoft's business practices.

The settlement of an antitrust case carried live on national television? Over the preceding four years, industry pundits had speculated that the government might break up Microsoft, just as it had dismembered AT&T in a previous generation.

Microsoft had agreed, said Reno, to settle charges with a consent decree "that will prohibit the company from continuing to engage in monopolistic practices in the future." Reno promised the settlement would "save consumers money" and "enable them to have a choice when selecting PC operating systems."

As Reno yielded the microphone to Anne Bingaman, head of the Justice Department's Antitrust Division, I turned up the volume. Bingaman hailed the settlement as "an historic achievement," but, as she spoke, it became increasingly clear that the consent decree stopped Microsoft only from using a few specific licensing practices, like requiring computer manufacturers to sign long-term contracts.

For more than a decade, Microsoft had dominated the market for personal computer operating systems, the essential software that controls basic computer operations. Bingaman claimed that Microsoft used restrictive licensing terms to exclude competitors from the operating systems market, permitting the company to retain its overwhelming market share even as more and more people began to purchase personal computers. Few in the industry would have disputed that contention. Bingaman went on to assert, again and again, that prohibiting further use of the licensing practices Microsoft had already employed to secure its monopoly would be enough to dissipate the company's market power in the future. The settlement will "level the playing field for Microsoft's competitors in the operating system software market," Bingaman claimed. The settlement "has enormous impact for competitors in opening the market," she reiterated. "You may be using a different operating system three years from now because of this," she assured the national television audience.

Not a chance, I thought. Bingaman's claims about the settlement appeared to reflect the philosophy of conservative Chicago School antitrust scholars. All monopolies are short-lived in this view and will naturally erode as monopolists restrict output and raise prices to exploit their market power, forcing consumers to less costly alternatives. From this perspective, Bingaman's tepid remedy would simply enable the free market to do its job more quickly. But high tech markets don't behave the same way as manufacturing economies, or so my own experience told me. In these markets, consumers want the goods and services that other users have already adopted (or are likely to adopt), and are willing to pay more to purchase them. Products that get an early market lead tend to stay ahead.

To avoid production delays when IBM introduced its personal computer back in 1981, the company decided to license an operating system that was already commercially available. After making a canvass of market alternatives, IBM was able to reach licensing terms with Microsoft Corporation, a Seattle start-up, and adopted that company's product, despite the widely held belief that the operating system written by Digital Research, a Pacific Grove, California, start-up, was technically superior. Microsoft had not even written the operating system it licensed to IBM. It bought the software for $100,000 from another start-up, Seattle Computing. Seattle Computing had created its operating system software by copying the functionality of Digital Research's superior product. Nevertheless, merely as a by-product of IBM's ascendancy in the personal computer market, Microsoft's operating system, MS-DOS, became the key ingredient in desktop computing.

If little more than serendipity could confer such enormous power in these markets, a skillful businessman, having gained an initial advantage, might logically seek to assure his continued success by manipulating the market's economic forces, rather than awaiting the vagaries of unforeseen events. Bill Gates, Microsoft's founder and CEO, negotiated a contract with IBM that permitted Microsoft to license MS-DOS to IBM's competitors. Gates understood the opportunity IBM had given him. It was Gates's software, rather than IBM's hardware, that set the specifications for application programs that ran on personal computers. By licensing the operating system software to other manufacturers that could produce better hardware components more cheaply than IBM, Gates, rather than IBM, controlled access to what consumers really wanted, the functionality of the application programs. Gates quickly left IBM in the dust. "IBM-compatible," the ability to run software written for the IBM PC, rather than simply "IBM," became the industry standard that consumers demanded.

Microsoft employed increasingly sophisticated and controversial tactics to maintain its dominant operating system position and to expand into new markets. In 1990, Digital Research introduced an improved version of its own operating system, DR-DOS, that not only offered more advanced technical features than Microsoft's product, but also promised to run all the applications available for MS-DOS. Microsoft responded by offering a "per processor" license—a steep discount on MS-DOS to any computer maker willing to pay Microsoft a royalty on every computer the manufacturer shipped. Market pressure required manufacturers to offer MS-DOS to their customers on at least some, if not most, computers. At best, a manufacturer might experiment by offering a non-Microsoft operating system on a small portion of its line. Refusing Microsoft's per processor offer meant that MS-DOS could be purchased only on a much higher per unit basis. But signing a per processor license meant that a manufacturer had to pay two royalties on any computer it shipped with a non-Microsoft operating system—one royalty to Microsoft's competitor, and a second royalty to Microsoft, even though the computer did not include Microsoft's product. Per processor licensing made it prohibitively expensive for manufacturers to do business with Digital Research or any other operating system competitor.

During the same period, Microsoft introduced a new product it called Windows. By employing animation, graphical icons, and a desktop metaphor, Windows made MS-DOS look and operate like Apple's Macintosh operating system. Microsoft made sure that computer manufacturers shipped Windows by offering significant discounts on Windows to those manufacturers that agreed to accept a per processor license for MS-DOS.

These terms kept Microsoft's challengers out of the operating system market, notwithstanding the surging demand for personal computers. The new operating system features in Windows also required application developers to rewrite completely their existing products that ran directly on MS-DOS. Originally only an operating systems company, Microsoft belatedly entered the applications market. Independent application companies complained that Microsoft gave its own internal application teams secret information—what amounted to a "head start"—on the new operating system specifications, permitting Microsoft's applications for Windows to reach the market far ahead of those made by more established rivals. Microsoft had learned to use its dominant position in one market to give itself an advantage in the next market.

The Federal Trade Commission opened an investigation into Microsoft's tactics in 1990, but the complexity of the technical and legal issues proved daunting to the government. Microsoft took the position that it did not have a monopoly in the operating system market at all. Initially, Microsoft also denied the head start charges, repeatedly claiming that its operating system group dealt with its application group only at arm's length. "There is a very clean separation between our operating system business and our applications business," explained Microsoft executive Steve Ballmer to *BusinessWeek* in 1983. "It's like the separation of church and state."

By 1991, even the computer industry press began to report examples of Microsoft giving its internal application developers a head start over the company's application rivals. Confronted with the obvious contradictions, Microsoft did an about-face. One company executive went so far as to tell an industry publication at the end of 1991 that Microsoft never claimed there was an internal barrier between operating systems and applications.

Proving the elements of an antitrust case against Microsoft required some initiative. Microsoft's share of the operating system market, calculated at between 80 and 90 percent in the early 1990s, easily satisfied one of the requirements for monopolization. But even as late as 1992, Microsoft was far behind its principal competitors in the various application markets, making an attempted monopolization case in these markets problematic. Demonstrating that Microsoft engaged in conduct the law would classify as "anticompetitive" was even more difficult. Courts had some experience with licensing restrictions that excluded competitors. But no court had ever ruled on most of the activities Microsoft's rivals complained about. "Sounds like a food fight in the computer industry," one FTC lawyer confessed to me.

The Microsoft investigation roiled the commission. There were press reports of commissioners yelling at each other, and others not speaking at all. The schisms did not follow party lines. The Republican commission chairman and the one Democratic commissioner favored action against Microsoft, while a second Republican, along with the commission's only independent, refused to continue the investigation. The fifth commissioner, a Republican, recused himself because of a conflict.

The most unusual aspect of the FTC investigation was not the law, or the technology, or even the conduct of the commissioners. It was the openly contemptuous attitude of Microsoft's CEO, Bill Gates. By this time, I had been an antitrust lawyer for almost twenty years. I had represented clients in countless government investigations and had seen, up close, some of the toughest, most venal and ruthless executives in all of corporate America. But I had never seen a chief executive who so openly mocked the processes of his own government. "The worst that could come of this is that I could fall down on the steps of the FTC, hit my head, and kill myself," Gates told *BusinessWeek* magazine. The press was filled with accounts of Gates shouting at commissioners who questioned his conduct. One report claimed that he called Commissioner Dennis Yao a "Communist," and responded to the accusations of the FTC's general counsel by snorting, "You don't know what the hell you're talking about." Nevertheless, in February 1993, the commission deadlocked 2–2 on bringing an action against Microsoft. Later that same year, after a thirty-seven-month investigation, the commissioners again deadlocked 2–2. To all the world, Gates had stared down the U.S. government.

But Gates would not have the last word—at least not yet. Even before the second FTC vote, Senator Orrin G. Hatch, a Republican member of the Senate subcommittee with responsibility for antitrust, announced that if the commission deadlocked again, the case should be handed over to the Department of Justice. Liberal Democrat Howard M. Metzenbaum, chairman of the committee, issued a similar statement. Anne K. Bingaman, the new head of the Antitrust Division, took notice.

Bingaman's appointment at the Justice Department had been controversial. She came to the position with few antitrust credentials and no real credibility in the field. Among Democrats, Bingaman's single most noteworthy political credential was also her single most significant personal liability—she was the wife of Jeff Bingaman, the Democratic senator from New Mexico.

Arriving in Washington after her husband was elected in 1982, she felt lost among the tens of thousands of lawyers in the city. "All anybody knows is that you're some guy's wife," she groused. She worked at the Washington office of an Atlanta-based law firm throughout the 1980s. When she heard about an opening at the top of the Antitrust Division, she launched a personal campaign to secure the job, promising to reinvigorate antitrust enforcement. "I killed myself" was her own description of her self-promotion efforts, inundating the White House's appointments office with letters of support from all of her friends. The inside-the-Beltway Democratic crowd favored Robert Pitofsky, a distinguished antitrust scholar at Georgetown, for the top Antitrust Division position; Bingaman, by contrast, had written no journal articles, nor served on any American Bar Association expert panels or committees. When Bingaman was named to the Justice Department position in April 1993, Janet Reno captured the sentiments of many Democratic insiders. "Hmph," Reno later told the *Wall Street Journal*, "there's the White House trying to push a Senator's wife on me."

Then there was the matter of Bingaman's personal style. She displayed a frenetic kind of exuberance that rubbed a lot of people the wrong way.

"Direct, demonstrative and aggressive" was how a sympathetic journalist once described her. Her red hair "matches her fiery personality," noted another reporter. Bingaman described herself as "sort of a keyed-up, nervous type," and she frequently made jumbled oral presentations that suggested an unsettling lack of gravitas. Worse yet, it was never clear whether her personal energy and salesmanship masked a lack of sincerity. The *New York Times* characterized her as "the most seasoned of pols." Regardless, as of April 1993, she was the Clinton administration's top antitrust official.

Any Democrat willing to take over the Antitrust Division in 1993 was going to face enormous challenges, brought on by years of Republican neglect. Between 1981 and 1988, the number of attorneys in the Antitrust Division fell from 456 to 229. Morale fell even farther than head count. The Antitrust Division's record in litigated court cases was charitably called "lackluster." According to the press, the "hands off" approach of previous Republican administrations had decimated the division, resulting in the "asphyxiation of antitrust."

Bingaman attempted to shore up gaps in her own background by hiring tutors and immersing herself in the study of unfamiliar doctrines and technologies. She brought into the Antitrust Division five deputies who could fairly be characterized as among the best and the brightest of the next generation of Democrats—including a respected antitrust professor from the University of Chicago and one of the leaders of the new generation of economists, Richard Gilbert, from the University of California at Berkeley.

She toured congressional offices as well as the Office of Management and Budget, arguing, with the aid of charts and graphics, that the nation's economy had quadrupled since World War II but the budget of the Antitrust Division had remained the same. Congress responded with a budget increase of nearly $5 million. Bingaman also worked to secure the confidence of Attorney General Reno, who transferred $1 million of her own discretionary funds to Bingaman's account. Bingaman used these new funds to hire litigators—more than a half dozen partner-level attorneys from leading West Coast law firms—to join her crusade in Washington, where the top pay was around $87,000. The partners brought with them young associates, eager to work in big cases. Bingaman sprinkled these top-notch lawyers throughout the Antitrust Division. Whatever her good intentions, she sparked instant resentment among the career Justice Department attorneys.

Bingaman streamlined the Antitrust Division's reporting structure, repudiated some of the business-friendly policies of her Republican predecessors, and opened new investigations at a brisk pace. Within months of her arrival, the Antitrust Division was humming again. The press noted Bingaman's "ambitious" agenda and how she had "fired up" the division's professional staff to examine business practices more closely. The *New York Times* declared her a "trustbuster," observing that she had transformed "a dormant antitrust operation into a fountain of activity." The *Wall Street Journal* cautioned its readers, "Anne Bingaman has a blunt message for corporate America: The antitrust cops are back on the beat."

It was the *Washington Post*, however, that succinctly captured the reality of Capitol Hill: "Bingaman has raised expectations," it reported. But Bingaman's early activity produced little of substance. The *Wall Street Journal* quickly concluded that "few people close to the administration believe the Clinton team will do much to slow a concentration of corporate power." There were persistent rumors of potential conflict between Bingaman's nominally aggressive antitrust agenda and the administration's more general pro-business approach. According to the press, Bingaman needed a "really big" court case before influential people would take her efforts seriously.

Right after the FTC deadlocked for a second time, Bingaman placed a call to each commissioner, asking that the FTC relinquish the Microsoft case to the Department of Justice. Three readily agreed, but Deborah Owen, a conservative Republican, balked. Owen heatedly rejected Bingaman's request, claiming that Bingaman was only taking the case to get publicity. Owen then attempted to persuade her colleagues to resist, but the files were sent to the Justice Department over her objection.

As the Justice Department studied the records over the next few months, conservatives began to criticize openly the notion of restraining Microsoft in any respect. "Nowhere is it written," wrote Brit Hume in the *Washington Post*, "that a company that is skillful or fortunate enough to dominate the operating system market cannot use what it knows to improve its other products." "Microsoft is a major asset for U.S. competitiveness in global markets," asserted another opinion piece a couple of months later. "Most governments would be handing awards to a company like that."

In the late spring of 1994, Bingaman met for days on end with her staff and concluded that the facts available to the government would support only a narrow case against Microsoft. Bingaman then asked the head lawyer at Microsoft whether he was willing to discuss a settlement. After two weeks of negotiation, Bingaman and Reno announced the agreement on that Saturday morning in July. Bingaman could not resist the temptation to proclaim victory, promising consumers that the consent decree would lower prices and provide a greater number of operating system choices. When asked why her remedy did not address the allegations regarding Microsoft's head start in the various application markets, she deflected the question, opining that the consent decree "achieves the really 100 percent results that any lawsuit could have achieved, and possibly more."

Several of the nation's leading newspapers quickly exposed the settlement for what it was. The *San Jose Mercury News* said that the agreement was "a major victory" for Microsoft that would "help increase its control of the world of technology." The *Wall Street Journal* dismissed Bingaman's claims as "political hyperbole," noting "the truth is that the Justice Department failed to successfully attack some of Microsoft's most effective tactics stifling rivals." Anything left of Bingaman's credibility was eviscerated by Bill Gates when he explained a day later in the *Washington Post* the effect the settlement would have on Microsoft's conduct:

> None of the people who run [Microsoft's seven] divisions are going to change what they do or think or forecast. Nothing. There's one guy in charge of [hardware company] licenses. He'll read the agreement.

"Nothing" became the watchword of antitrust enforcement.

Over the succeeding months, events confirmed what everyone in the industry already knew. "The battle for the desktop is over and MS-DOS and Windows have won," the CEO of Novell, the company that purchased

Digital Research, observed in September, when he announced that DR-DOS would be withdrawn from the market. In December, *BusinessWeek* reported that Microsoft had doubled the price of its operating system, while continuing to maintain its dominant share of the market. December also brought the news that Microsoft had taken the lead in every major application category—spreadsheets, databases, word processors, and presentation graphics. Microsoft's sales jumped 31 percent in the last quarter of the year, and its profits rose by a nearly equal percentage. None of this was lost on the stock market, where the price of Microsoft shares soared from $48 to $62 in the four months following the settlement.

Each new development was met with the same stony silence from the Antitrust Division—no new investigations, nor even any comment, save from Anne Bingaman, who challenged her critics to come back in a year and check the Antitrust Division's record. In the fall, Bill Gates famously golfed with President Clinton on Cape Cod. Analysts in the computer press as well as the general financial press increasingly wondered whether antitrust enforcement had any role to play at all in the modern technology economy.

With the government investigations behind him, Gates announced in October 1994 Microsoft's intention to use $1.5 billion of stock to acquire Intuit, Inc., in what was to be the largest transaction in the history of the software industry. Intuit, a quintessential Silicon Valley success story, was started at its founder's kitchen table in 1983 to make personal computer software that would help users balance their checkbooks. At one point, it had seven unpaid employees, $51 in the bank, and hundreds of thousands of dollars of debt. Three of the employees left the company, but the other four agreed to stay, taking their salary payments in stock. By the time the company was ready to sell its own software, there were already thirty different competitive products on the market, but none of them worked all that well.

Intuit distinguished itself from its competitors through meticulous attention to customers' needs and it acquired an almost cultlike following. From a single check register, the product's features expanded to analyze all types of personal financial information including stock transactions and taxes, enabling users to more easily manage their personal expenses and household budgets. Favorable product reviews, judiciously placed advertising, and particularly word-of-mouth endorsements (Intuit users would boast at cocktail parties that they knew their net worth down to the last penny) enabled Intuit to take the lead in the market. More than 50 percent of its sales came by word of mouth.

Microsoft introduced a competitive product called "Money" in 1991. But unlike what had happened in every other desktop software category, Microsoft could not dislodge Intuit from its leadership position. Not that Microsoft didn't try. Microsoft sold its product for one-third the price of Intuit's, and spared no expense on advertising. But Microsoft could garner only a 10 percent market share and by October 1994, Intuit's product was still outselling Microsoft's 15 to 1. Unable to overtake Intuit, Gates decided to buy the company.

Much beloved in Silicon Valley, Intuit was one of the few remaining examples of what had always been the Valley's entrepreneurial prowess—a small company that grew through its own hard work until it could stand up to the industry's bully. Although an industry newsletter likened the transaction to "Luke Skywalker joining his father in the family business," few resented the decision of Intuit's founder to sell out to Microsoft. But there was a deep sense of loss, just the same. Many saw the sale as evidence that the period of Silicon Valley's leadership position in technology development had passed. An emotional pall settled over the Valley—"a feeling of hopelessness," as the general counsel of Apple explained in *Fortune* magazine.

The Antitrust Division was slated to review the transaction under a set of merger guidelines that looked largely, but not entirely, to the market share of the surviving company. The review process was subjective in many respects, and there was no legal requirement that the government take any action to block a merger, however anticompetitive it might appear. Lawyers from application software companies, frustrated by years of fruitless effort at the FTC and Justice Department, called me to grouse about the acquisition and to ask whether anything could be done to stop it.

To my surprise, I also started getting calls from big banks worried that the two companies would combine to offer financial services that bypassed traditional financial institutions. I thought Gates had something more ambitious in mind. He was willing to pay twice as much for Intuit as the stock market said the company was worth, and ten times what Microsoft had ever paid to acquire another company. Gates had apparently concluded that electronic transactions would be the most significant use of home computers in the near future, and he intended to use Intuit's product as the entry point for a new type of private online service in which computer users could buy and sell things, track investments, and investigate new purchases, all without leaving their homes.

In fact, Microsoft's plans for Intuit extended well beyond online services. Even before the commercial Internet, workers needed to share information with each other and access data, as well as documents and graphical images, simultaneously. "Server" software permitted dedicated business computers to facilitate these tasks by delivering information to linked desktop computers in businesses and, increasingly, in homes. Right after the Intuit deal was announced, a server software company called me to complain that Microsoft was using hidden specification information to enable its programs to share information easily with each other and, more important, with the Windows operating system, already the key element of Microsoft's desktop monopoly.

It was easy to see how the Intuit acquisition fit neatly into Microsoft's overall strategy. Intuit's products would help drive adoption of Microsoft's electronic network. All of the Microsoft desktop and online products would connect seamlessly with Microsoft's server software, permitting the company, mostly by withholding crucial specification information, to obtain an advantage in the server software markets no other competitor could match.

In a conference call between the server software company and the Justice Department lawyers heading up the investigation of the Intuit acquisition, I noted, almost in passing, that Microsoft's acquisition of Intuit could easily be challenged on conventional antitrust grounds because the two companies together accounted for more than 90 percent of the market for personal finance software. But there were anticompetitive aspects of the deal that were far more significant. A technologist from the server company explained how Microsoft was attempting to leverage its control of desktop computing to business servers. Because of the larger strategic consequences of the proposed sale, I urged the government to block the deal and also to launch a more comprehensive investigation into Microsoft's business practices in other markets before it was too late.

The Justice Department lawyers were more mystified than intrigued. They asked me to prepare a written analysis of the technical and legal issues, known as a white paper, that they could share with their colleagues throughout the Antitrust Division. My server client, fearful that its complaint might cause Microsoft to cut off even more vital specification information, refused to be named, even in a confidential submission to the government. So the Antitrust Division lawyers suggested that I submit the document in my own name.

The difficulty with my analysis became increasingly evident as I struggled to prepare a draft. Most of the events on which I relied to predict Microsoft's dominance of the computer industry had not yet occurred, and there was no guarantee that anything I prophesied would actually happen. Microsoft was yet to announce a commercial computer network. Its online service had no customers and a zero percent market share. Neither Intuit nor Microsoft even offered electronic banking at the time. And the server software markets were all highly competitive, with Microsoft in minority positions. In effect, I was demanding that the federal government deploy its resources to fix a series of problems that were just beginning to develop. This was not going to sit well among conservatives. The Chicago School loathes this kind of approach. According to Chicago School thinking, most business practices are benign or even beneficial. Interfering with business activities prematurely, without conclusive evidence of anticompetitive effects, frequently denies consumers the benefit of more efficient business operations.

Rich Gilbert, the division's chief economist, listened to my reasoning and acknowledged that academic journals were already publishing articles about the new economics of high technology industries. But, he continued, no one had ever used this research to make the antitrust enforcement arguments I was proposing. "After looking at your paper," Gilbert advised, "we might just reject everything you say as preposterous."

With that, I knew I was going to need the endorsement of an economist that Gilbert respected. Some of my colleagues pointed me to Garth

Saloner, an economist at the Stanford Graduate School of Business. Saloner had written several of the leading papers in the field, including a couple that seemed almost prescient, describing how a company with an early lead could manipulate a high tech market to its advantage through behavior that might actually have appeared benign in the old manufacturing economy.

After reading my working draft, Saloner said that many of my observations had been predicted in theoretical research published in economic journals. Network markets are easily susceptible to "tipping," Saloner explained. Once moved off equilibrium by a small event, whether random or contrived, the market tends quickly toward a single standard. Customers can get "locked in" to whatever product or technology first secures a market advantage.

Tipping explained Microsoft's successful use of its dominant position in one market to give itself an advantage in another more nascent market—by withholding specification information from applications competitors, for example. And, as far as I could tell, "lock in" was a common, if not pervasive, phenomenon in personal computer software. In order to switch operating systems, a user would likely have to purchase an entirely new set of application products. In order to switch word processing products, a user would have to make certain that documents created by the old word processor, especially if it was in widespread use, could be opened and displayed by the new one. Once customers had loaded extensive financial data into Intuit's product, and learned how to use it, they were unlikely to switch to new software, if it meant losing data or having to input it again.

But, overall, Saloner was skeptical, almost dismissive, of my argument. Even to an academic in the field, the notion that a single company would soon dominate a series of markets through products that were not yet even released required a rather substantial leap of faith. I could not even convince my own economist of the grounds for my concern. How would I convince anyone else?

Over the next few days, details of Microsoft's plans began to surface in the press. Microsoft intended to integrate its still unannounced online service deeply into its dominant operating system, so that each new computer user would be able to subscribe and connect to Microsoft's network with a single mouse click. The *New York Times* claimed that Microsoft's online offering targeted home users, initially focusing on electronic mail, news and information, personal finance and entertainment, with an array of other services to be added later. "Visualize a private internet," an industry publication quoted an unnamed source as explaining. "That's what they are trying to build." According to the *Wall Street Journal*, Microsoft planned to act as a toll taker, extracting a percentage of all business revenue generated through online sales.

Several days of revelations in the press convinced Saloner. He worked well into the early morning hours many nights in a row, shoring up logical gaps in my draft and adding citations from leading economics journals to the arguments in my white paper. Saloner's citations revealed an extensive theoretical literature, with direct empirical application to a wide range of industries including telecommunications and computers, that implied the need for a more substantial role for the government in preventing anticompetitive conduct. I was astonished. This vast body of research was rarely even acknowledged in antitrust scholarship or court decisions. The fifty-page white paper I sent to the Antitrust Division in mid-November drew on this new thinking to explain the larger markets implicated by the Intuit deal and Microsoft's strategy for extending its dominance to servers that deliver information to homes and businesses.

Mindful of the outcome of Bingaman's negotiation with Microsoft over the settlement agreement, I sent copies of the white paper to a few leading newspapers, hoping to create public awareness before the government made an enforcement decision about the Intuit acquisition. All ran stories about what the *Wall Street Journal* called "unusual economic theories" that were being used to challenge the Intuit deal. The press had no difficulty finding skeptics to quote. "I've never heard anything so speculative as that argument in an antitrust case," said the editor of a computer law publication in the *New York Times*. She claimed that antitrust analysis has "always been based on current conditions." In the *Wall Street Journal* story, a San Francisco antitrust lawyer expressed doubt that the Justice Department would seriously consider an "economic theory that [hasn't] been accepted by any court."

CHAPTER 10

The Bigger Picture

As the Christmas holidays approached, I learned from a reporter that the settlement negotiated by Bingaman in June required the approval of a federal judge in Washington, D.C., who balked at its very limited terms. The proposed settlement was "so limited, specific and precise," Judge Stanley Sporkin had said sarcastically, "that it will only take effect when we have snow days."

Judge Sporkin repeatedly scheduled and postponed public argument on the settlement's terms, hoping that someone might provide information that could be used to question the Justice Department's position. The proceedings attracted little attention and were not reported in the West Coast press. I sent the transcript of the judge's remarks to a number of Silicon Valley companies. Nearly twenty offered to provide information to respond to the judge's questions, so long as I kept their identities secret. Several offered to pay my legal fees to bring the Valley's concerns about the settlement to the judge's attention. The client that refused to be publicly identified during the Intuit discussions with the Antitrust Division continued to demand anonymity, so I would once again submit papers in my own name, this time in a formal court proceeding. The argument was scheduled for January 20, 1995.

The team of lawyers who had helped on the Intuit white paper worked with me to put together a ninety-six-page brief, supported by an appendix containing forty-five journal articles, press stories, analysts' reports, and documents evidencing Microsoft's anticompetitive behavior. We described how Microsoft had used anticompetitive tactics to gain control of the operating system market. Because Microsoft had already used illegal licensing practices for a number of years, its operating system was ubiquitous and long since "locked in." Preventing the future use of anticompetitive licensing practices by Microsoft would have no effect on competition in the operating systems market.

Microsoft reinforced its operating system monopoly by withholding specification information from competitors in order to "tip" the most significant application markets in its favor. Had Microsoft made Windows' new programming specifications available to its independent application competitors and its internal development teams at the same time, competition between the two groups would surely have benefited consumers. But by giving its internal developers a head start, Microsoft simply substituted itself for each of the former leaders in the major application categories. Microsoft irreparably damaged the healthy group of application vendors that had competed against each other across product categories for years.

Microsoft's anticompetitive conduct toward independent application vendors also harmed competition in the operating systems market. The major vendors of application software for MS-DOS were the same companies that made applications for competing operating systems. Once Microsoft ran these companies out of business, vendors of competing operating systems had nowhere to turn for important applications like word processors and spreadsheets that could create consumer demand for their software. It was beyond irrational for the government to expect to restore competition in the operating systems market without challenging Microsoft's behavior in the applications markets. And, unless Microsoft was restrained, we argued, it would use similar tactics to gain control of a host of new markets.

None of this was lost on those who followed the industry. Writing in the *New York Times* in July two days after Anne Bingaman first announced the settlement with Microsoft, a veteran reporter quoted well-known Silicon Valley technologist Bill Joy, a founder of Sun Microsystems, for a proposition that would continue to elude the Justice Department for several more years: "Microsoft's whole empire is based on the interlocking nature of their operating-system and application software."

The brief I intended to file in Judge Sporkin's court endorsed an important role for the government in guaranteeing consumers the benefits of competition. I knew it would generate considerable controversy. But the brief's strict adherence to traditional antitrust standards, including an appropriately firm grounding in economics, would, I hoped, mollify conservatives.

The general counsel of one of my clients, Apple Computer, was not so sure. To make the approach more palatable to free market types, he asked me to seek the approval of Bill Baxter, who had rejoined the Stanford Law faculty upon returning from Washington. "Just chat him up and he'll join the cause," instructed my client. I called Baxter and arranged for a meeting.

As Baxter read through my brief, he began to look more and more troubled. It was not hard for me to imagine the reasons for Baxter's discomfort. The Chicago School's antitrust enforcement philosophy drew on the study of perfect competition and monopoly to argue that the free market, if left alone, will optimally allocate resources according to consumers' needs and desires. This approach elegantly correlated with and supported conservative notions of maximizing individual liberty and limiting the scope of government.

More modern and sophisticated economic analysis pointed in the opposite direction. Game theory sometimes suggested that government intervention rather than laissez-faire might benefit consumers in network markets, like personal computer software, that dominant companies could manipulate to the detriment of the public. The best economic thinking no longer unequivocally supported the notions of limited government, personal freedom, and laissez-faire.

Finally, Baxter looked up from the draft. "I've read all the economic journal articles you cite, but they're all just game theory," he said disdainfully.

"*Just* game theory?" I couldn't believe he said it, only months after John Nash received a Nobel Prize for his pioneering work in the field.

We talked inconclusively for more than an hour. Baxter was clearly attracted by the prospect of playing the prominent role in what was going to be a public debate over the future of antitrust. But he worried about just how far my support for government intervention would go. For my part, I had little interest in negotiating changes that would diminish the force of my brief, just to accommodate Baxter's desire for consistency with his earlier positions. So, after a time, I gathered up my papers and walked out to my car.

Baxter followed me into the rain and I opened my umbrella so he could stand under it, facing me. "All right," he said, unwilling to let our conversation end, "I admit that game theory is economics. But why should this branch of economics be elevated over all others?"

"Because," I answered, "this branch of economics more correctly explains the forces and predicts the outcomes of high technology markets than your old-school economics does. You just don't like what it means in terms of government policy."

Baxter continued to look at me, making no attempt to answer. I shook his hand, got into my car, and drove away.

A couple of weeks later, I filed the brief, without Baxter's imprimatur, and I released it to the national media in another attempt to galvanize the public's attention. "Microsoft Pact's Challengers Use Theory as a Weapon," read the headline in the *Washington Post*. "Competitors Say Firm's Dominance of One Market Can Affect Others," the subhead continued. The absence of client names added to the filing's notoriety. Industry publication *Computer World* referred to a "secret cabal" of Microsoft's competitors and ran an editorial cartoon depicting my clients as hooded men on horseback, lurking in darkness at the graveside of what a tombstone identified as the government's Microsoft investigation.

Three days before the hearing, both Microsoft and the Antitrust Division filed written responses to our brief. Microsoft dismissed our economic approach as "mumbo jumbo" that was "demonstrably incorrect." The Justice Department took a different tack. Bingaman's team filed a declaration signed by Nobel Prize–winning economist Kenneth Arrow.

Arrow's declaration described the economic analysis in our brief as "a penetrating discussion" with which "I have little disagreement." But he

ignored our complaints about many of Microsoft's anticompetitive practices and instead characterized our argument as simply a demand to remedy the natural forces of network markets, which, he said, "tend toward
monopoly." In language that the Chicago School would come to repeat and
more vigorous antitrust enforcers would come to regret, he suggested that
government "interference to pick the winner" of competition in network
markets "is likely to be counterproductive." Arrow's declaration did not
explain how Bingaman's proposed remedy would undo Microsoft's operating system "lock in," nor did it address in any respect Microsoft's practice
of using its dominant position in one market to gain control of adjacent
markets.

When I arrived at the courthouse to make my arguments, half a dozen
camera crews followed me from my cab to the courthouse doors. On the
way to Judge Sporkin's courtroom, I passed a line of would-be observers,
including journalists, lobbyists, and arbitrageurs, all waiting to get in. The
line snaked all the way down the hall and around the corner. Dozens would
be turned away.

The courtroom was already packed. CNN's sketch artist worked feverishly to prepare a depiction of the proceedings for subsequent broadcast.
Justice Department lawyers crowded around one counsel table and spilled
over into the jury box. Microsoft's lawyers occupied the only other table, so
my colleagues and I had to find places in a row of seats just inside the rail-
ing that separates the well of the court from the gallery.

Before taking my seat, I went over to introduce myself to Anne Bingaman. "You should have called me first," she snarled, without responding
to my effort to shake hands.

"You can still do some good," I responded. "There are a lot of jobs at
stake."

"Don't you think I know it?" Bingaman shot back. "My husband is a
senator."

The court was called to order. Things did not start out well for Bingaman. She began by telling the judge that in reviewing the settlement, he
could not substitute his judgment for her own. He bristled. "Can I use my
own pen to sign the decree or is the government going to supply that? I've
got to have some role here."

Bingaman became more animated, describing how hard her staff had worked on the Microsoft investigation. "Let me tell you the effort we put into this, Your Honor, because we sweated blood, blood, blood." At one point, for emphasis, she pounded her fist on the tripod she was using to display a stack of posters. The tripod collapsed in a clatter.

"Take it easy. Let's not destroy the furniture," counseled the judge.

"If somebody wants to save me from myself . . ." mumbled Bingaman as she tried to reassemble her props.

"I do think you got a lot of good in this decree," said the judge, as he tried to reason with Bingaman. "But I do think that, not only for your sake, but for Microsoft's sake, that if they are engaging in practices that are improper, they ought to stop it."

"Your Honor, I couldn't agree more," Bingaman replied. "Boy, do I take this seriously. Boy, do I kill myself. Boy, are we real about this," she exuberantly declared in front of the assembled throng of national media.

What if, the judge asked, he could persuade Microsoft to accept some additional restrictions beyond those the government had negotiated. "Your Honor," said Bingaman, "you don't have the power to do it."

The judge was incredulous. "You mean you wouldn't agree to it if they agreed to it?"

"No," said Bingaman, "I would not."

The judge could not believe what he was hearing. "I am absolutely shocked," he said. Then he said it again. "I am absolutely shocked."

Bingaman, by now waving her finger, said she would not be "bludgeoned" by a law firm or a federal court "or anyone else" to enter "into agreements on a case we don't think we have."

The judge was exasperated. "You don't know what case you do have," he said.

Microsoft's lawyer fared no better. He was well prepared and his presentation was tight and to the point, but the judge interrupted him when he attempted to argue that complaints about Microsoft's anticompetitive conduct had been shown, through two government investigations, "to be supported by literally no plausible evidence."

"You've given me these assurances before and I can't accept them anymore." The judge referred to unequivocal assurances of lawful behavior made by Microsoft's lawyer in previous hearings, which were now contradicted, in the judge's view, by the documents we submitted.

The lawyer took a step back from the lectern. His knees almost buckled. Having your credibility attacked by a federal judge in front of a packed gallery was just about the most unnerving courtroom situation I could imagine. This must be very different from Microsoft's earlier negotiations with Anne Bingaman, I remember thinking. "I cannot agree with that," the lawyer responded haltingly. "I honor my duty of candor to the Court."

"I just cannot accept your word anymore," the judge continued, even more harshly. "This is a trusting judge [but] you've just lost your credibility. . . . People have got to be forthcoming with this Court. So go on to your next point . . . , but I'm not going to accept your statements."

When Microsoft's lawyer tried to argue that his law firm would monitor the company's compliance with the settlement agreement, the judge interrupted him again. "There's what I call LLFLs, lawyers-looking-for-loopholes," admonished the judge. "You take the most narrow definition that you can take and you're going to police this kind of stuff? Don't give me that."

The judge ordered a break in the proceedings and, after talking briefly to a couple of reporters, I walked down the hall to the men's room. Microsoft's lawyer was already standing in front of a washbasin. He unfolded a half-inch stack of paper towels, drenched them in water, and pressed them to his face. Others in the crowded restroom tried to look away, but he was moaning audibly from beneath the compress that covered everything from his forehead to his chin. Water streamed down his $3,000 suit and dripped onto the floor. After several minutes, he collected himself and made his way back to the courtroom.

When it was my turn to argue, Bingaman objected to the judge's hearing me at all. She claimed that my argument was "a subterfuge," but the judge cut her off. "I want to know whether you have any messages for the Court," he said, staring at me.

I began by explaining that my clients had delivered documents to the Justice Department showing anticompetitive behavior by Microsoft but, so far as we could tell, the documents had been ignored. The judge repeatedly interrupted me, asking questions about why my brief had not been filed earlier, exactly what concerned my unnamed clients, and what kind of re-lief would be necessary to make the operating systems market competitive again. Eventually, he allowed me to explain that it was necessary to look beyond the operating systems market, even if the government was only go-ing to remedy the effects of Microsoft's anticompetitive conduct in that market alone.

"You've been asked to approve . . . the battle plan for D-Day," I said. "But the government says, you can only look at Juno Beach. You can't look at Omaha Beach. You can't look at Utah Beach. You can't look at Sword Beach. Now, how are you going to know whether the battle plan for Juno Beach is any good without knowing what's going on elsewhere? It defies common sense."

After a full day of argument, the judge adjourned, taking the govern-ment's request to approve the settlement under advisement. The scene, as I left the courthouse, took my breath away. Camera crews converged on me. Scores of reporters shouted questions and pushed microphones in my face. The media attention was exciting, but, in truth, I was shaken by what ev-eryone had seen in court that day. The nation's economy needed strong and effective antitrust enforcement. The welfare of Silicon Valley depended on it. After twelve long years, a new administration had promised to restore some measure of vitality to antitrust, only to self-destruct in the most pub-lic of venues. Without a Justice Department that could draw at least grudg-ing respect from the business community, there was no hope of restraining Microsoft or, for that matter, any other aggressive company that believed itself above the law. I had intended to deliver a firm nudge, or, at most, a cold slap in the face to Bingaman's Antitrust Division, but the chain of events I started by filing a brief had spun out of control. Would Bingaman ever try to do something important again?

On Valentine's Day of 1995, the judge issued a forty-five-page decision that rejected the proposed settlement. The press reported the judge's deci-sion as a "blunt ruling," a "humiliation," a "considerable embarrassment for the Justice Department," and a "stinging rebuke to Assistant Attorney General Anne Bingaman." "The picture that emerges from these proceed-ings," read the opinion, "is that the U.S. Government is either incapable or unwilling to deal effectively with a potential threat to this nation's economic well-being." The judge ruled the settlement inadequate. "Simply telling a defendant to go forth and sin no more does little or nothing to address the unfair advantage it has already gained."

Industry analysts predicted in newspapers the following morning that public pressure would force the Antitrust Division to oppose Microsoft's other initiatives, particularly the Intuit acquisition, but Bingaman denied that the judge's decision would influence the government's position on the Intuit deal. A day or two later, one of the Division's lawyers called me to report that Bingaman wanted to come to Silicon Valley on a "goodwill mission." Barely able to contain his laughter, he said that the staff envisioned something like New York governor Nelson Rockefeller's infamous trip to Latin America in the 1960s. "You know, Anne sitting in an open top car rolling down Great America Parkway [one of the main thoroughfares in Silicon Valley] with programmers lined up four deep on either side of the street, pelting her with rotten fruit," he chuckled.

Mercifully, Bingaman abandoned those plans and, after a couple of days, Reno announced the Justice Department's decision. Bingaman would have her appeal, and the Antitrust Division joined Microsoft in seeking reversal of the judge's decision. Bingaman had become Microsoft's defender and ally. Even with the appeal, it was too late to save Bingaman's reputation. "Anne Bingaman thought she'd be one of the toughest trust busters in the last 50 years," reported *California Lawyer* magazine. "Instead, she has found herself mired in defeat and compromise."

Bingaman's career in government was nearing an end. "I don't conceive of myself as leaving any doctrinal or theoretical legacy," Bingaman confessed. Unlike her conservative predecessors, she had taken an important policymaking position without a clear doctrinal view of the policy she intended to implement. The conservatives could crisply identify their policy objectives. Bingaman's doctrinal goals, by contrast, remained elusive, even at the end of her tenure.

A week after Reno announced the Microsoft appeal, Joel Klein, a lawyer in the White House counsel's office, was named one of Bingaman's deputies. The son of a postman, Klein was raised for a time in public housing. He was awarded a scholarship to Columbia, where he studied economics, and graduated from Harvard Law School. He served as a law clerk for Supreme Court Justice Lewis Powell.

In 1993, Klein had been given the job left open at the White House by the suicide of Vince Foster. Over the next sixteen months, Klein handled Whitewater matters, earning a bipartisan reputation for competence and honesty. He had even suggested to Linda Tripp, the woman who secretly taped Monica Lewinsky, that she look for employment elsewhere. Soft-spoken and of mild demeanor, Klein had experience in cleaning up messes. A month after joining Bingaman's staff, he was named her "principal" deputy, and it was clear he would be her successor, more likely sooner than later. Once Klein came on board, Bingaman appeared less frequently in public, and later announced her resignation from the Justice Department, well before the end of Clinton's first term. She eventually returned to private practice, more correctly to lobbying, where she billed millions of dollars of fees in the service of Global Crossing, a name that would become infamous in an era of corporate scandal.

On April 27, 1995, the Justice Department filed suit to block Microsoft's acquisition of Intuit. The *Washington Post* announced the news at the top of its front page. "The suit is the greatest legal challenge to face Microsoft in its 20-year history," the *Post* stated. Microsoft executives maintained that the acquisition would enable the two companies together to bring better, less expensive products to market more quickly. Gates vowed to fight the suit in court.

The government's press release defended the decision to bring suit, claiming, in the conventional way, that the merger would raise prices in the market where the two companies were already competing. But, in a marked change of approach, the government's explanation did not stop there. Control of personal finance software, the press release explained, would give Microsoft "a cornerstone asset that could be used with its existing dominant position in operating systems for personal computers to seize control of markets of the future." Apparently, the white paper submitted to the Justice Department months earlier to explain Microsoft's strategy had found an audience.

After a couple of weeks of pretrial maneuvering, Bill Gates abruptly announced that Microsoft was abandoning plans to acquire Intuit, a move that took the industry by surprise. Gates cited the length of time the case would drag on as the decisive factor in his decision. The Justice Department maintained that the strength of its position had scared him off. "This shows how the antitrust laws benefit the American consumer—by resulting in low prices and better product," an Antitrust Division deputy was quoted as saying. Several analysts claimed that the big banks were the real beneficiaries. "It's still a matter of debate whether consumers ultimately will be better or worse off by having Microsoft and Intuit competing," declared the *Washington Post* on May 21, 1995.

The controversy over the government's Intuit lawsuit highlighted the fundamental tension in antitrust jurisprudence between competing theories of how best to maximize consumer welfare. Traditionally, antitrust enforcement had relied on protecting competition as the principal way to benefit consumers. The Chicago School, on the other hand, argued that many seemingly anticompetitive business activities—mergers and exclusive dealing contracts as examples—actually benefit consumers by making businesses more efficient. Laissez-faire, counseled the Chicago School, is the better way to go.

Most assuredly, the government could not dismiss Gates's arguments about efficiency out of hand. The combination of Microsoft and Intuit might well produce a more robust set of products and services far more quickly than either company could with only its own resources. Absent the combination of the two companies, the market for online financial services might never develop in a coherent way. Nor was there any guarantee that Intuit would continue to remain effective as a stand-alone competitor. But permitting the acquisition would eliminate the most vibrant source for future competition.

The Antitrust Division was forced to make a predictive judgment, a choice between competing philosophies, in circumstances of great uncertainty. Over the next fifteen years, economists would brood over the potential for error associated with such predictive judgments, producing a paralysis in antitrust enforcement and a return to laissez-faire. By blocking Microsoft's acquisition of Intuit, the government opted to protect competition. The immediate consequences of that decision were not encouraging.

Gates made his announcement to abandon the Intuit acquisition on a Saturday. The following Monday, the share price of Intuit plummeted 17 percent. In the fall of 1994, shortly after the deal with Microsoft was announced, Intuit's shares were worth as much as $88 each. But the publicity surrounding the white paper, Judge Sporkin's decision, and the government's lawsuit all chipped away at Intuit's valuation. Microsoft's announcement sent Intuit's share price down to $62.

This was not simply the loss of paper profits by pampered multimillionaires. People who go to work for Silicon Valley start-ups get far lower salaries than they would command in more established companies. Instead of market-level salaries, they receive shares of stock in the start-up, typically over a four- or five-year period. If the company is successful, the employees come out far ahead. But if the company falters, a far more common outcome, they will have subjected their families to years of financial struggle for little material benefit. My efforts to block Microsoft's acquisition might well have cost hardworking employees of Intuit, many of whom were members of my own community, the ability to buy a home or send their kids to college.

"Don't worry, Gary," the general counsel of Intuit assured me in a phone call. "The people here don't hate you." The thought had crossed my mind. In fact, as word of Microsoft's announcement spread by e-mail through Intuit's corporate headquarters, swells of cheering rose from many of the conference rooms in which employees were at work planning for Microsoft's takeover. Industry executives hailed the result as evidence that competition in the emerging area of electronic banking would be fierce.

Less than two months later, Intuit announced that it was working with nineteen financial institutions, including American Express and the brokerage firm Smith Barney. Microsoft announced seventeen banking alliances of its own, launching more than a decade of competition, in which Intuit came under intense pressure. From time to time, the company stumbled. Nevertheless, in August 2008 Intuit announced its best financial results ever, with annual sales exceeding $3 billion. In recent years, the company has frequently been listed among Fortune magazine's "Top 100

Companies to Work For." Microsoft Money remains a formidable market competitor. And consumers can do checking and other types of financial transactions over personal computers with well-nigh every bank in America. Even the most uncompromising libertarians in Silicon Valley will acknowledge Intuit's independence as something the government got right.

Although the growth of the public Internet undermined Microsoft's plan for its privately owned network, blocking the takeover of Intuit nevertheless remains a noteworthy achievement in maintaining competitive online markets. Even with the proliferation of Internet banking sites, the acquisition would have given Microsoft an enormous head start in electronic commerce, heightened its ability to control emerging markets, and denied consumers the benefit of many years of productive competition.

Inside the Beltway, the powers that be were oblivious to the bigger picture. On June 16, 1995, the court of appeals ruled that Judge Sporkin exceeded his authority by challenging several of Microsoft's practices, beyond those addressed in the settlement. The appellate opinion was silent on just how the government's remedies would restore competition in the operating systems market, particularly without redressing Microsoft's conduct in application markets. The appellate court simply said that Judge Sporkin should have accepted without further question the unsupported assertion of the government's expert that the settlement "remedied the anticompetitive effects of the practices alleged in the complaint."

Neither the efficacy of the government's remedy nor the reasoning of the court of appeals' decision has improved with the passage of time. Microsoft still monopolizes the personal computer operating system and major applications markets. In recent years, Microsoft has extended its dominance to the server operating system market, as well.

The court of appeals also disqualified Judge Sporkin from any additional participation in the case, citing questions regarding his impartiality. The appellate court said it was "deeply troubled" because the judge read a book about Microsoft that caused him to ask hard questions of Anne Bingaman. The court of appeals also cited, as a basis for disqualification, Judge Sporkin's willingness to permit me to participate in the hearings without disclosing the identities of my clients, something the statute governing the judge's review seemed to permit expressly. The court of appeals ordered the new judge assigned to the case to approve the settlement agreement.

The court of appeals' decision left me disappointed and disillusioned. Although Intuit would remain an independent company, Microsoft was still dominant in desktop computing and well on its way to control in other markets. The reality of network effects stood Chicago School analysis on its head. Had the FTC acted promptly when Microsoft first began its anti-competitive practices in the early 1990s, the simple remedy of prohibiting per processor licenses would have likely been sufficient to maintain a competitive marketplace. By late 1995, a far more draconian remedy would have been required to pry the desktop computing market open to competition. Contrary to Chicago School dogma, government intervention at an early stage of market development was less intrusive and more beneficial than waiting for a bad problem to get worse.

In any event, there were no legal challenges pending against any of Microsoft's tactics or plans. Without vigorous enforcement of the antitrust laws, no other company could realistically compete against Microsoft in personal computer technology. And given the sorry state of antitrust enforcement, what promising start-up would even try?

Five days later, I had my answer, when my assistant put through an emergency call from Jim Clark. A former Stanford electrical engineering professor, Clark had succeeded to moderate wealth and great acclaim by founding Silicon Graphics, a company that made powerful computers with high resolution video displays. He left that company in a dispute with management and used millions of his own dollars to finance a new start-up, known as Netscape, that made a product called a browser.

Clark said he needed my help. Representatives from Microsoft were in a room down the hall threatening to put his new company out of business.

CHAPTER 11

The Ties That Bind

"Hardscrabble" does not begin to describe Jim Clark's early life. He grew up in Plainview, Texas. His father abandoned the family when Clark was a young child. Clark's mother, who worked at a doctor's office, raised three children on $225 a month. A poor student and a sometimes malevolent prankster, Clark was expelled from high school in his junior year.

At the age of seventeen, Clark persuaded his mother to let him join the navy where, after a hard stint at sea, he astounded everyone by getting a high score on a math test. One of his instructors encouraged him to enroll in night classes at Tulane University. He eventually gravitated toward computer science, which had become a formal discipline in the late 1960s after an obscure government agency funded academic departments at four American universities. In eight years, Clark finished his high school and college education, got a master's degree in physics and a Ph.D. from the computer science department at the University of Utah.

Clark's early career is not well documented. He was fired from a university job in New York, but worked as an assistant professor at the University of California at Santa Cruz before landing at Stanford. There he took on responsibility for a contract the university had with the Department of Defense to develop integrated circuits for computer-aided design. With the help of a Ph.D. student, Clark created a revolutionary computer chip to simulate reality on a computer screen. Clark's chip could process three-dimensional images in real time, the equivalent, journalist Michael Lewis wrote, "of bestowing upon the computer a sense of sight." Clark's work permitted engineers to model their designs without the time and expense of making physical prototypes. Cars, airplanes, and even the dinosaurs from *Jurassic Park* could be constructed, deconstructed, and reconstructed inside a powerful computer.

Clark assembled a talented team of engineers, left academia, and, executing the conventional Silicon Valley game plan, raised financing for his new company, Silicon Graphics. Clark had no difficulty attracting venture capital investors. He quickly raised a seed round of $800,000, which he burned through in less than a year, and a second round of $17 million, which lasted a bit longer. The venture capitalists brought in their own CEO to run the company, an industry veteran from Hewlett-Packard. Silicon Graphics launched its public stock offering in 1986, the same year Microsoft first sold its shares publicly.

Clark was quick to recognize Microsoft as a competitive threat. The personal computer was, in many respects, a poor man's version of Silicon Graphics' powerful workstation. Clark's chip had dramatically reduced the cost of creating high resolution computer graphics. PCs would reduce the cost even further, as they incorporated more powerful processing capabilities. Clark urged his company's management to build a cheaper machine to compete with personal computers. Management ignored him and his relationship with the CEO recruited by the investors deteriorated. In 1994, an embittered Jim Clark left the company he had founded.

Shortly after news of Clark's departure appeared in the media, I found myself in a conference room at Creative Artists Agency, the famous Hollywood talent company headed by Michael Ovitz. One of CAA's top people was telling me in impassioned tones how shameful it was that Jim Clark had been forced out of his own company. What Clark needed, the ten-percenter said, was an agent. Then no one would be able to take advantage of Jim Clark ever again.

I thought for a moment what Silicon Valley would be like if every mercurial technologist had his own Hollywood agent. How would anything ever get done? "Want the result of that bubble sort?" I could imagine a smart-alecky software engineer saying to his boss. "Call my agent."

I explained that entrepreneurs retain equity in their companies, so

Clark left owning Silicon Graphics's stock. In Clark's case, he did not leave with as much as he should have, given Silicon Graphics's phenomenal success, because all of the early venture capital rounds reduced his percentage ownership share of the company. Nevertheless, in concept at least, the Silicon Valley model took care of the creative among us. If Hollywood agents wanted to expand into new markets, perhaps they should think about representing superstar athletes, I advised.

I never heard from the Hollywood agents again. Jim Clark never heard from them at all. So, by my reckoning, he was already in my debt when he called me from Netscape on June 21, 1995. Clark explained that Microsoft executives were in the next room, making his company an offer it had to refuse. Clark wanted to complain to the Department of Justice. He asked me to come to Netscape the next morning to meet the company's new CEO, Jim Barksdale.

I knew little about Netscape. Weeks earlier, a reporter from National Public Radio had called me to ask what I thought of the young enterprise. I bemoaned a future economy controlled by a single computer network, owned entirely by Microsoft. Microsoft might well control the future of online commerce, the reporter said, but not by using a privately owned network. The future was all about the public Internet.

The word "internet" comes from "interlinked network." The "Internet" with a capital "I" is a worldwide network of smaller, constituent computer networks that evolved from a Defense Department project in the late 1960s, intended to make the networks connecting university and government computers more resistant to nuclear attack. Many of the constituent networks were built on spare capacity that telecommunications companies leased out. Rand Corporation engineers, working with government money, developed the basic network technology—packet switching—over the vigorous opposition of AT&T. "They pretty much had a monopoly in all communications," one of the developers explained to *Vanity Fair* decades later. "They tried all sorts of things to stop it."

In the 1970s, two UCLA researchers using a Defense Department grant devised the protocols that allow computers using different programming languages to communicate over telephone lines. The interlinked networks increasingly became a communications medium for academics and other scientists. In 1989, a researcher at the atomic research center in Switzerland created the World Wide Web by producing a system of protocols to allow anyone with a networked computer to easily access text posted for viewing on the other linked networks. The researcher also wrote a small piece of software called a browser to permit the viewing of Web postings. The protocols and standards on which the Internet was built were openly published, making the Internet a public facility.

A couple of years later, Senator Al Gore secured passage of an important bill, known as the Gore Act, to increase funding for maintaining and extending the Internet. Gore's legislative achievement earned him little more than derision. In response to a question from CNN's Wolf Blitzer, Gore said, "I took the initiative in creating the Internet," as part of a longer answer about the whole range of initiatives—economic, environmental, and educational—on which Gore took a leadership role while serving in Congress. Republican politicians ridiculed Gore, claiming that he took credit for "inventing the Internet."

A group of University of Illinois students, led by Marc Andreessen, working in a program Gore's bill helped to fund, rewrote the browser code a couple of years later to incorporate graphics and multimedia capabilities and to run on Windows computers, as well as on the Macintosh. Clark introduced himself to Andreessen by e-mail, brought most of the browser development team to Silicon Valley on his own nickel, and created a company to make money using Web technology.

Clark once again turned to the venture capital community to finance his new company. Clark's investors wanted an experienced CEO and recruited Jim Barksdale to the post. Barksdale brought a stellar executive résumé—chief information officer and then chief operating officer at Federal Express (he was responsible for developing tracing and communications systems), followed by a very successful run as president of McCaw Cellular Communications. After completing the sale of McCaw to AT&T, Barksdale joined Netscape.

Clark met me in one of Netscape's conference rooms and explained the gist of the problem. Like desktop application programs, Netscape's browser ran "on top of" the Microsoft operating system, Windows. Windows 95, the newest version, was scheduled for initial commercial release in August, and Microsoft intended to release the first version of its own browser, Internet Explorer, at the same time. Netscape needed technical information to make its browser operate with Windows 95. Obviously, Microsoft had given this technical information to its own browser developers because they were demonstrating the Internet Explorer at trade shows. Yet Netscape's engineers got nothing helpful back when they asked Microsoft to send them the information.

No point in asking the government for help, I thought. The Justice Department had grown adept at ignoring generations of such complaints. This time, though, there was more to the story. After a couple of months of refusing Netscape's requests, Microsoft dispatched a negotiating team to meet with Jim Barksdale and other Netscape executives. While Marc Andreessen sat at the corner of the conference table taking down on his computer nearly verbatim everything that was said, Microsoft's representatives offered to provide Netscape the information it needed, but only as part of a "special relationship." The "special relationship" meant that Netscape could make its own browser run on non-Microsoft platforms, like the Macintosh, and older versions of Windows. Microsoft promised not to compete with Netscape on these platforms, but Netscape would have to agree not to compete with Microsoft on the new version of Windows and its successors, expected to be the lion's share of the desktop computing market.

"It was like a visit by Don Corleone," Marc Andreessen later told the *Wall Street Journal*. "I expected to find a bloody computer monitor in my bed the next day."

Upon hearing the proposal, Netscape's vice president of marketing stepped out of the meeting to inform Clark. Clark called me. My first reaction was one of amazement. Microsoft was trying to bully Netscape into dividing the browser market, with the start-up relegated to a minuscule portion of the computer world. How many different sections of the Sherman Act can you violate at the same time, I thought.

After a time, Jim Barksdale joined my meeting with Clark. Clark introduced me, made small talk, and left the room. His message was clear. This was Barksdale's show. Netscape intended to sell browsers, servers, and development tools to commercialize the Internet, Barksdale explained. While many of Netscape's early browser sales were for home use, the company's real target was the market for corporate intranets, privately controlled networks built on the Internet but restricted by passwords, firewalls, and other security features. Intranets would be used to disseminate information and facilitate communication within a corporation, and between the corporation, its customers, and its vendors.

That wasn't the half of it. Netscape had devised a plan to challenge Microsoft for control of the personal computer desktop. The browser wasn't just a viewer. It was part of a new platform on which the applications of the future would be built. Application programs in Netscape's vision of the future—exotic multimedia applications (like what became YouTube and Facebook), as well as spreadsheets and word processing programs—would no longer reside in each user's PC. Instead, applications would sit in Web servers, computers dedicated to providing Web content, off somewhere in cyberspace. The browser was going to be the user's gateway to those application programs.

The implications of Netscape's vision quickly came into focus for me: a new generation of electronic services and applications beyond Microsoft's grasp. As traditional desktop applications were transferred to the Internet, Microsoft would lose control of them as well. Application vendors would no longer need technical information from Microsoft. And no one would care about the make and model of a computer's operating system. Since Netscape's browser was written to run over all popular operating systems, the browser and Web server would matter a lot more to consumers than the operating system.

A problem, a real showstopper, interrupted my idyllic daydream. Netscape's business plan assumed that Microsoft would obey, or could be made to obey, the antitrust law. But Bill Gates would never sit by and permit Netscape to seize the future.

I glanced at Marc Andreessen's notes from the previous day. Microsoft was already on to Netscape's plan and proposed a market division scheme to thwart it. If relegated to the small markets that Microsoft identified,

Netscape could never grow to become a substantial company. So Netscape had no business alternative but to decline Microsoft's offer. I knew what would happen when Bill Gates learned that his demand for unconditional surrender had been refused. Hell hath no fury like a monopolist scorned.

That was down the road. More immediately, I needed the government's help to get technical information so that Netscape could bring the new version of its product to market. Barksdale instructed me to keep my dealings with the government outside of the public eye. Netscape had begun to plan for the public sale of its stock. Telling the world that Microsoft stood in Netscape's strategic path would likely terrify investors.

I rushed back to the office and called Joel Klein. Microsoft was withholding technical information about its operating system, the very conduct at issue in my challenge to the 1994 consent decree, I said. Anne Bingaman publicly promised that she would continue to investigate allegations of such behavior. While Microsoft's conduct ultimately raised contentious questions about what a monopolist could do unilaterally to protect its market position from competitors and to extend its power to new markets, the company's offer to split the market with Netscape was beyond any justification. Even Chicago School scholars acknowledged that an agreement between competitors to split a market is a per se illegal restraint of trade.

After telling Klein about the meeting, I asked him to compel the production of Andreessen's notes under an official procedure to maintain the confidentiality of Netscape's communications with the government. An hour or so later, Klein faxed me the document demand, issued as part of an investigation into the "bundling of the Microsoft Network with Windows 95."

The following day, June 23, I faxed a single-spaced, four-page letter to the Antitrust Division with Andreessen's notes attached. Years later, journalists hailed the June 23 letter for its role in starting the process that led to the Microsoft trial. "Reback's letter," reads the dust jacket of a book by two *New York Times* writers, "led to the most watched antitrust trial of the century." Actually, the letter didn't start much of anything, other than an ambling dialogue with the Justice Department. Microsoft deigned to provide Netscape with the technical information only weeks later, after Microsoft's browser was out on the market. The government was of no help. It would be more than two years before the Justice Department took any legal action against the monopolist.

After a month of inconclusive telephone discussions and letters explaining how the Netscape browser was a strategic alternative to Windows as a platform for Internet application programs, I finally succeeded in scheduling a face-to-face meeting in Washington. I brought Jim Clark, Marc Andreessen, and Mike Homer, Netscape's marketing VP. A few low-level attorneys from the Antitrust Division sat across the table from us. I asked about some of the more experienced Justice Department lawyers. They were all unavailable, I was told. The division was in the middle of an investigation of Microsoft's plans to bundle its proprietary network, MSN, into Windows, so that users could reach network content with a single mouse click. AOL (America Online, Inc.), CompuServe, and Prodigy, Microsoft's three network competitors, complained that permitting users to launch MSN directly from Windows put them at an unfair disadvantage.

The Justice Department was spending its time on the wrong issue, I told the division lawyers. Proprietary networks were the wave of the past. The Internet was fifteen times the size of the largest of the private networks and it was not proprietary, meaning that any bank or merchant could put up a site to offer goods and services without paying Microsoft or AOL anything. But there was no way to get to the Internet without a browser, and there was no way (at the time) to launch a browser except through a personal computer. So the pathway to the Internet ran through Microsoft's operating system. Thurman Arnold, the Antitrust Division's famous leader during the New Deal, would have called it a "choke point" or "bottleneck." Microsoft was going to be able to control the Internet by extending its operating system monopoly into the browser market.

Jim Clark tried his best to be patient. He said that the Microsoft network wasn't a threat to anyone. He explained how the Internet would evolve. Even Microsoft saw the light. Microsoft had just released its "golden master," the production disk that computer manufacturers used to install Windows 95 on every personal computer they sold. Microsoft's browser came on the Windows 95 golden master, whether computer manufacturers wanted it or not. That was the issue that the government should focus on, Clark said.

The young lawyers in the room dutifully took notes. After about an hour, Clark abruptly walked out, right in the middle of the discussion. I excused myself and went chasing after him. I caught him halfway down the hall. He said he was going back to the airport. He told me to keep working and do my best, but he couldn't take any more of the inconclusive give-and-take.

Near the end of August, Thomas Penfield Jackson, the judge chosen at random to replace Stanley Sporkin on the Microsoft case, held a twenty-minute hearing to enter the consent decree that Anne Bingaman negotiated. "Got my own pen," the judge said, as he affixed his name to the document. That evening, Bill Gates appeared on CNN's *Larry King Live*.

"Before we continue with calls, Bill," King asked, "can you explain what this agreement today, for the benefit of viewers, means to them, the settlement with the anti-trust and the Justice Department?"

"Basically it means nothing," Gates replied.

The next several months offered more of the same. We talked on the phone, we had meetings, we responded to written requests for information. During one of my many discussions with a shifting cast of Justice Department lawyers, I suggested a legal theory for government action—a well-established legal doctrine called monopoly maintenance. Microsoft's conduct was not intended to secure control of the new browser market as an end in itself. Microsoft was trying to protect the lucrative operating system monopoly it already enjoyed.

After about six months, the Antitrust Division pulled lawyers from the Microsoft investigation and redeployed them to other matters. "The Microsoft case has faded into the background as new Microsoft strategies and fast-moving changes in the on-line computer world have dramatically complicated the government's probe," *Bloomberg News* reported. "What remains of the U.S. Justice Department's investigation of Microsoft might be headed toward deep freeze," the *Seattle Times* opined, noting that Microsoft's lawyers had not heard from the Antitrust Division in months.

Netscape's market position was beginning to erode, but the company still enjoyed a commanding market share among browser users, likely accounting, I thought, for the government's reluctance to act, or even to investigate. By this time, anyone advocating more stringent antitrust enforcement faced a new generation of conservative scholars, with an increasingly strident agenda. Frank Easterbrook, the University of Chicago law professor appointed to the federal bench by Ronald Reagan, followed up on his 1984 essay, "The Limits of Antitrust," with an article at the end of the decade titled "Ignorance and Antitrust."

"Antitrust is a complex body of law requiring exceedingly expensive tools, with great potential to injure the economy by misunderstanding and condemning complex practices," Easterbrook wrote. To curb the evil wrought by this dark cult, Easterbrook offered his own not-so-novel prescription: "Do nothing" when firms complain that anticompetitive practices will drive them out of business and raise prices. "Wait." Get courts "out of the business of prophecy." Take action only after the damaging effect of the anticompetitive conduct is demonstrable. Fine the perpetrator after the damage is done in an amount sufficient to make the conduct unprofitable.

Easterbrook offered an appealing game plan. Waiting came naturally to the Department of Justice. But a policy of fixing after the fact the damage caused by anticompetitive conduct was never going to work in a network market. Clark made the point to me many times as we waited, month after month, for the government to take action. Once competition in one of these markets is extinguished, Clark explained, you can't bring it back. The world goes on. The market matures, but on the monopolist's terms. Consumers get locked in. You can't turn back the clock and start the competitive process over again. Stanford economist Garth Saloner gave me the same explanation. "What are you going to do?" Saloner asked rhetorically. "Put the entrepreneurs back in a room and tell them to start their company over again?"

Perhaps the division lawyers just needed more education to spur them to action. I recommended submitting a white paper. Netscape's management proposed a bolder move. Many of Netscape's executives were Silicon Valley veterans and they knew the Antitrust Division's history with Microsoft. Just educating the Justice Department would not produce government action.

Why not write a paper for the general public, as well as for the Justice Department, Netscape vice president Mike Homer suggested. Make it easy for anyone in business to read. Most people know little about the inner workings of the technology markets. Revealing the truth about Microsoft's business conduct would take the luster off the company's image and might even generate public outrage. Homer wanted to have the white paper printed as a paperback book and sold in airport bookstores.

I asked my partner Susan Creighton to reduce to paper Mike Homer's notion of a best-selling antitrust tome. Although Susan came later in life to the high tech antitrust practice, she brought all the right skills, and a gold-plated résumé to match. After an education at Harvard and Stanford Law School, Susan clerked for Pam Rymer, the judge who decided the Apple mail order lawsuit, and then for Sandra Day O'Connor on the Supreme Court. Susan already had experience in Borland's Supreme Court case and she wrote some of the briefs we filed opposing the settlement Anne Bingaman negotiated.

Microsoft, meanwhile, turned up the heat on Netscape. No longer content with just giving away its browser for free and requiring computer manufacturers (sometimes called OEMs, for original equipment manufacturers) to take it, Microsoft actually started paying manufacturers and Internet service providers to make Netscape's browser less accessible to users. Sometimes the payment took the form of a discount on the license price for Windows. Sometimes Microsoft offered free equipment or even cash to make the Microsoft browser the first choice for customers. Microsoft even gave service providers better placement on the sign-up section of the Windows desktop in exchange for favoring Internet Explorer over Netscape's browser. By giving away its product free, Microsoft cut off the most ready sources of revenue to Netscape. By its various promotions, side payments, barter agreements, and license exclusions, Microsoft made it expensive and difficult for Netscape to get its product into consumers' hands.

At the beginning of July 1996, I wrote a six-page letter to Joel Klein. I argued that Microsoft's conduct violated both Anne Bingaman's consent decree and substantive antitrust law. While the Antitrust Division maintained an open file on Microsoft, I noted not quite politely, the division assigned no staff to the investigation, nor had it sought documents from Microsoft in nearly a year. I suggested that the public interest would be better served if the Antitrust Division returned the Microsoft matter to the Federal Trade Commission.

Klein replied by phone, directing me to the division's San Francisco field office where he set up a new team to investigate Microsoft. An insider later told me that Klein's decision to move the investigation to San Francisco got things rolling, but at the time it seemed more like we were starting cold after a year of letters, phone calls, and meetings. One of the San Francisco lawyers wanted to be talked out of the position that Microsoft should be able to withhold the technical information necessary for Netscape to run on top of the OS. "Browser, schmowser," another one said, in response to my entreaties.

The strategy of keeping our complaints about Microsoft confidential had failed. Netscape needed to go public with its grievances in order to get the government off the dime, but Jim Barksdale thought better of positioning himself as a public complainer. "Your job," Netscape's general counsel instructed me, "is to be the government's worst enemy. Criticize them everywhere—in the press, on television—everywhere, until they sue Microsoft. Then you will be the government's best friend."

My responsibilities increased, but my budget did not. Although a public company, Netscape was in many respects still a start-up. Every dollar spent on legal maneuvering, however vital to the company's future, came at the expense of product development. Netscape allocated $50,000 a month for me to spend—on everything—legal research, economic experts, fomenting anti-Microsoft sentiment in the press. Microsoft, in contrast, earmarked $100 million a year for its public relations budget, or so one of my partners told me. Hardly a fair fight, I thought, but no more one-sided than the 10-to-1 advantage Microsoft enjoyed over Netscape in engineering head count.

Anne Bingaman resigned her position at the beginning of August and Klein was appointed acting antitrust head a couple of weeks later. He would need Senate approval to take over the job on a permanent basis, but he was clearly the administration's designee for the post. I rewrote and updated my earlier letter to Klein and released it to the press. The major newspapers and wire services all ran stories. Television crews showed up at my office demanding interviews. I practiced my sound bites. "Microsoft's enemy is not Netscape," I told the media. "Its enemy is consumer choice."

"Irresponsible allegations," "hysterical response," "wild and untrue" were Microsoft's rejoinders. A few computer manufacturers confirmed our charges, albeit on background. Journalists clamored for more information, but antitrust experts pooh-poohed our efforts. "Analysts Say Netscape's Complaints Will Collect Dust," declared the headline of Silicon Valley's leading newspaper.

Susan Creighton, meanwhile, produced a crisply written 220-page draft of the white paper, better than any of us could have imagined. Not quite a potboiler, the white paper was nevertheless a compelling read for anyone with a business background. Susan's husband, a desktop publishing whiz, even formatted the document to look like a book. "I couldn't wait to read what they did to us next," marveled a Netscape sales executive, summarizing his take on the draft.

The white paper retraced the story of how Microsoft thwarted operating system competitors, ultimately extending its monopoly to desktop application programs, and then to server software products. The paper also explained the new Web technologies, including Java, the Sun Microsystems creation distributed along with Netscape's browser, that permitted an application to run without modification on any operating system.

Drawing on the public statements of Bill Gates and Steve Ballmer, Susan's paper laid out the framework for a monopoly maintenance case against Microsoft. Both Microsoft's executives acknowledged Netscape's strategy as a full-fledged attack on Windows. In Ballmer's view, Netscape attacked Microsoft's operating system monopoly the only way it could be attacked—by building on top of it to "take [Windows's] future away." Netscape intended, as Gates observed, to build the browser into a full-featured operating system "to become a *de facto* platform for software development, ultimately replacing Windows as the mainstream set of software standards." Several thousand developers had already registered to create applications on the new platform.

To combat the threat, Microsoft pummeled Netscape with a fusillade of anticompetitive blows that would have awed the robber barons of the last century. I listed several of those in my letters to Klein. Susan created a more comprehensive list from field sales reports and customer e-mails—withholding technical information, pricing its product below cost, paying to exclude Netscape, and tying its own browser to its operating system. Time and again, computer manufacturers and Internet service providers proclaimed their preference for Netscape. They talked freely about how much their customers wanted Netscape's browser. But Microsoft's licensing restrictions, coupled with payments to make it difficult to feature Netscape's product, invariably meant that users got what Microsoft wanted to give them.

With Garth Saloner's help, Susan applied the work of post–Chicago School economists to Microsoft's behavior. According to the new thinking, dominant companies rarely need to drive competitors out of business in one fell swoop to accomplish anticompetitive goals. Frequently, dominant companies at little expense to themselves can take actions that hurt competitors by raising their costs—Microsoft's withholding of technical information being the best example.

Most of the new economic work was less than ten years old, and, as a result, little of the post-Chicago approach had been incorporated into legal opinions. Susan found a Supreme Court case from the early 1950s, widely cited in the post-Chicago economic literature as a classic example of predation against new technology, on which we could build our case. When a newspaper monopoly in a small town was challenged by a new generation of technology, the opening of a radio station, the newspaper refused to carry the advertisements of any local merchant who also advertised on the radio. Because of the newspaper's nearly complete coverage of households in the town, many merchants concluded (in the Supreme Court's words) that they "could not afford to discontinue their newspaper advertising in order to use the radio" and "withheld their business from the radio station."

The radio station brought suit and the Supreme Court ruled in its favor, holding the newspaper's conduct illegal. Susan even showed me where Robert Bork blessed the holding in his 1978 antitrust book. "The decision seems entirely correct," Bork wrote in the Chicago School's version of the Bible.

A unanimous Supreme Court precedent? That was pretty good. Robert Bork's endorsement? Priceless.

As I read through Susan's draft, I quickly checked off each of the elements necessary for a government lawsuit. We had the necessary facts: evidence of anticompetitive behavior that excluded Netscape and other Web technologies like Java from the market. The government would need to corroborate our secondhand accounts, but the white paper told the government investigators exactly where to look. We had the law: a legal theory, monopoly maintenance, and a Supreme Court precedent suggesting that Microsoft's conduct was illegal. We had the blessing, so to speak, of the Chicago School's leading light. We even had some citations to economics articles that could be used to assess the likely effect of Microsoft's licensing and distribution practices on consumers.

Only one piece was missing, a comprehensive economic model to explain our principal grievance, illegal tying. As Tim Bresnahan, the head of Stanford's Economics Department, later wrote, the arguments about Microsoft's conduct outran received economic theory—not just the Chicago School's archaic price theory, but strategic entry deterrence theory and network effects theory, as well. Why would Microsoft condition the sale of its operating system on taking its browser, so that neither manufacturers nor consumers could get Windows without Microsoft's browser, Internet Explorer? To a lay person, the answer is obvious. Microsoft was trying to extend its monopoly from the operating system to take over the browser market, but that kind of explanation gets rejected out of hand by the Chicago School.

The browser complements the operating system. Consumers use the two products together. Bork's 1978 book explained that a dominant company like Microsoft is already in a position to take full advantage of its power through its existing market position, a monopoly on the operating system in this case. The company is already squeezing (or could squeeze) everything it can out of customers through its operating system monopoly and it can't gain additional monopoly profits from customers by bundling together complementary products because there are simply no other monopoly profits to extract—the dominant company already has them all (or could get them without bundling).

So, Bork reasoned, if a company is tying products together, it must be trying to gain a benefit by increasing its own efficiency rather than its market power. Perhaps Microsoft was merely trying to save the cost of distributing the browser separately. Perhaps Microsoft was just trying to increase the sales of its operating system by offering a new feature that would entice additional users to buy Windows. Chicago School acolytes could think of a thousand justifications for Microsoft's behavior.

Bork's argument about tying persuaded just about everyone, accounting for why antitrust authorities in Europe as well as the United States stopped pursuing IBM. IBM had nothing to gain by making life difficult for manufacturers of add-on products, the argument went, because IBM already had a monopoly in mainframe computers and could not get any more power by extending its control to peripheral devices.

But the browser wasn't just a complementary product. Like the radio station challenging the newspaper, it was a partial substitute, a market competitor. Netscape envisioned the browser as the application platform of the future. Gates and Ballmer confirmed the threat to Microsoft's hegemony. Common sense suggested that Microsoft's conduct must have been directed to thwarting competition rather than securing efficiencies. But, still, we had no economic model—only common sense—to explain Microsoft's conduct. Could we get the government to bring suit without a comprehensive economic explanation? The Chicago School would never have permitted it. "You need a model to know what to look at (and for)," Frank Easterbrook wrote, "without one, the world is cacophony." Of course, Bill Gates himself had told us what to look for—a competitive threat posed by new technology. But in the Chicago School's world, Gates's admissions might not be enough.

After a couple of weeks of editing and client review, we shipped Susan's white paper off to the Antitrust Division. By any measure, she had done a good job—too good, in fact. The paper made a convincing case that without government intervention, Netscape was doomed. Seeing the future in all of its glory proved unnerving to Netscape's management. Jim Barksdale, in particular, worried that the financial markets would abandon the young company.

Barksdale ordered top secret treatment for the white paper. Netscape's general counsel numbered each copy and kept a careful record of where every one of them went. Any government office that wanted to see the white paper had to subpoena it. Aside from government employees, only trusted third parties who signed strict nondisclosure agreements could get copies of the document. The security made it just about impossible to raise public awareness and pressure the Antitrust Division. Even after the government filed a complaint, few journalists, industry analysts, or antitrust experts had any idea just how strong the case against Microsoft actually was. Critics regularly sniped at the government's investigation in the newspapers and on television. There was little public outcry when the government tried to settle with Microsoft before trial, something that occurred a couple of times.

Nevertheless, Barksdale's decision was neither unexpected nor unfounded. Earlier demands for anonymity from clients challenging Microsoft were still fresh in my mind. An accurate and well-documented prediction of Netscape's demise would likely have shattered Wall Street's confidence in the company, mooting any benefit from a government lawsuit. So, relying only on the persuasiveness of our arguments, we packed off a large box of bound copies to the Antitrust Division. And we waited for the government to launch a thousand ships. Instead, the government sent a simple and very limited document demand to Microsoft and one to Netscape. No interviews, no depositions, no follow-up.

An unfettered Microsoft steamed ahead, releasing the third version of its browser, together with updates to Windows 95. Reviewers praised Microsoft for vastly improving its browser's quality though few thought Microsoft's product the equal of Netscape's. Microsoft also intermingled the browser code with that of the operating system to ensure, as Judge Thomas Penfield Jackson later wrote, that any attempt to delete browser code routines would "cripple Windows 95." Microsoft tightened its licensing restrictions on computer manufacturers and increased its promotional payments to service providers, all in an effort to make it difficult for consumers to get Netscape's product.

Then Microsoft took an unprecedented step to ensure that it would never face meaningful competition again. The company called a special meeting of all the Silicon Valley venture capitalists, labeling the event Microsoft-VC Internet Day. At the meeting, company officials gave not-so-subtle directions to VCs about their future technology investments. A company executive emphasized that Microsoft would maintain the dominant position of its platform. He encouraged VCs to create companies that would build on that platform, but only if confined to areas that Microsoft did not intend to pursue aggressively itself.

For those venture capitalists who had difficulty processing verbal instructions, the Microsoft executive put a slide titled "Software Industry Opportunities" up on the screen. There were nine groups of "opportunities," all on the Windows platform. The speaker walked the VCs through Microsoft's plans in each area. Microsoft would be investing heavily in four of the areas. Microsoft would also invest in a fifth area, "Online Content," but others would likely have successful investments in that area as well, the speaker allowed. That left four areas in which Microsoft would not be investing—things like "re-engineered/online services and businesses." The message was not quite explicit, but it was unmistakable. VCs were better off sticking to the last four categories.

At least a hundred venture capitalists sat for three hours to hear Microsoft's presentation. While the Justice Department stood by in Washington, cowed by the prospect of massive litigation or, perhaps, merely befuddled, an entrenched incumbent centrally planned the nation's technology sector. The "best of all monopoly profits is a quiet life," economist John Hicks once remarked. Microsoft intended to impose the quiet life on all of us.

Microsoft started investing heavily in online content, just as it promised. The company launched an online travel service, Expedia, for airline and hotel bookings, and a site to promote local events and entertainment, called Sidewalk, that was intended to siphon classified advertising away from newspapers. Microsoft's strategy backfired. As Microsoft moved into businesses beyond the technology sector, it threatened established companies and created ready allies for our antitrust campaign.

More ominous for the free market than Microsoft's own content sites was the company's initiative to "help" bricks-and-mortar companies move their businesses to the Web. Many established companies struggled with the new Internet technology. They welcomed any help they could get. Microsoft offered enticing packages of heavily discounted Web services and development tools. I watched the eyes of many a gray-haired executive glaze over as I tried to explain how Web sites built with Microsoft's technology would forever be subject to the monopolist's manipulation of proprietary standards.

Fortunately, Nathan Myhrvold, Microsoft's chief technology officer, revealed, in a *Wall Street Journal* interview, the company's plans to charge a "vig" on "every transaction over the Internet that uses Microsoft technology." Even the gray-haired guys who struggled to send an e-mail quickly understood the risk of partnering with Microsoft. I put a presentation together called "From Partners to Prey" and I started booking myself at corporate meetings. If you want to control the future of your business, I warned, build your sites on the open standards and protocols of the public Internet and use technologies, like Sun Microsystems' Java, that are not under Microsoft's control.

ABC came to my office to film a segment for *World News Tonight*. A couple of weeks after that, American Airlines incorporated the segment into its in-flight entertainment, which ran free of charge after the film feature on many American flights. Businesses grew wary of Microsoft even as they embraced the Internet. The Web flourished, built largely on open standards and technologies, beyond the control of a single company. Microsoft maintained a choke hold on Internet access, but only because of its desktop monopoly. If Netscape or some other company could ever develop an alternative pathway to the Web, the rich array of content and services there would be freely accessible.

Notwithstanding the headway we were making with the business community, the Antitrust Division showed no greater interest in our case. A vote to confirm Joel Klein as Bingaman's successor kept getting delayed, as he wrestled with the merger of two huge East Coast phone companies. Radio silence on Microsoft remained the order of the day. I started making inquiries. "Didn't you guys check Klein out?" one of my friends at Intel asked. "He's a dove on Microsoft."

Horrified, I got the client's permission to call several Washington insiders. "He's not going to do anything," a Judiciary Committee staffer told

THE TIES THAT BIND 205

me. The message from a lobbyist for the best-connected Silicon Valley VC firm, delivered to me in Washington-speak, was even more unnerving. "I asked someone in a position to know," the lobbyist reported, "and he said Klein won't do anything."

For a while, it looked like Klein would never even get a chance to do anything. He cleared the $23 billion phone merger without any conditions to safeguard competition. Enraged Democrats filibustered his nomination. "We've got an antitrust fellow who rolls over and plays dead," said Democratic senator Ernest Hollings of South Carolina. A *New York Times* editorial deemed Klein "a weak antitrust nominee" and urged the administration to find a "stronger, more aggressive" choice. The White House said it would continue to support Klein, despite the critics.

Only a parliamentary maneuver by Senate Republicans saved Klein's nomination. The Republicans refused to confirm the popular Democratic nominee for the Justice Department's number two position, deputy attorney general, until the dissident Democrats agreed to bring Klein's nomination to a vote. Klein was approved 88–12. All of the "no" votes came from Democrats.

Six more weeks went by without a word about the Microsoft investigation from the Justice Department. At the end of July, the FTC rejected a request from a group of Republican senators to start its own investigation of Microsoft. Netscape is "pretty much at the end of the rope," reported the *San Jose Mercury News*. In an interview published by *Wired* magazine, I lashed out at the Justice Department. "Is Justice prepared to take action against Microsoft at this stage?" I asked. "And if not, when? After Netscape is out of business?"

Barksdale was justifiably unhappy with my public acknowledgment of reality. "Why did Gary have to go and say that?" he complained to his general counsel. Of course, none of us knew that my sarcastic comment would turn out to be an accurate prediction.

I had only two straws left to grasp at. One was the Senate Judiciary Committee, chaired by conservative Utah Republican Orrin Hatch. The Judiciary Committee provides Senate oversight for the Justice Department, vets its nominees, and approves its budget. Hatch was as technology-savvy as he was politically powerful. Two of the flagship high tech companies from his state, WordPerfect and Novell, were early victims of Microsoft's cunning. Washington hands called me to urge Silicon Valley's enthusiastic embrace of Mike Hirshland, one of Hatch's aides, who wanted to know more about the Microsoft issue. "More interesting than blocking Clinton's judicial nominees," Hirshland told me.

Even with Hatch's interest and Hirshland's help, there was only so much the Senate could do. We needed someone in an executive-branch role to step up. Our prayers were answered by Mark Tobey, the top antitrust lawyer in the Texas attorney general's office, who read about the browser wars in *Time* magazine. Texas was the home to two of the top computer manufacturers, Compaq and Dell. After reviewing the white paper, Tobey issued document demands to Netscape and Microsoft. He called to schedule the depositions of Netscape employees in late August.

CHAPTER 12

Trial of the Century

I imagined Mark Tobey with a handlebar mustache, packing a six-gun, just like the grainy pictures I had seen of the Texas prosecutors who relentlessly pursued Standard Oil. Although disappointed when Tobey showed up in a business suit looking a lot more like an experienced trial lawyer than a Texas Ranger, I was determined to make the most of the opportunity. I wanted to get Antitrust Division lawyers into the room while Tobey made a written record, under oath, of Microsoft's illegal conduct. Then, if the Justice Department lawyers continued to sit on their hands, I would have proof that they were ignoring a terrible problem that was staring them in the face.

Tobey's investigation needed more heft, I reasoned. Dan Lungren, California's attorney general who was already running for governor, was a great place to start. "How's it going to look," I told Lungren's staff, "when the people in Silicon Valley hear that the Texas attorney general is trying to help them, but their own elected officials are just standing around?" Lungren's office issued a subpoena and committed to sending two lawyers to the depositions. They neither took notes nor said anything, but all I really wanted them to do was fill the chairs in the conference room.

I was ready to tell the federal lawyers that a "task force" of state attorneys general was poised to steal their thunder, but I couldn't get anyone at the Antitrust Division, either in Washington or San Francisco, to take my phone calls. So I resorted to leaving voice mails. "What's going to happen when the press finds out that state attorneys general are conducting an investigation of Microsoft," I said to many a voice mailbox, "and you won't even accept an invitation to attend?" After two days of my talking to phone lines with no one on the other end, the Antitrust Division issued a document demand to Netscape, and two of the lawyers in the division's San Francisco office told me they could come to the depositions.

The Antitrust Division lawyers, I was sure, would report back to their supervisors in Washington. I wanted to put on a show that would be impossible to dismiss. I set up meetings in the conference room next to the depositions for Hatch's aide Mike Hirshland and his boss, the staff director of the Senate Judiciary Committee, with Silicon Valley leaders. In the conference room next to that, I scheduled a session for Washington lobbyists to explain the mysteries of the Beltway.

When Tobey set the ground rules for his depositions, he told me he would not press any of Netscape's grievances against Microsoft's pricing strategy. The monopolist charged nothing for its Internet software, making no bones about its intentions to harm its competitor. "We are still selling operating systems," Gates told the *Financial Times*. "What does Netscape's business model look like? Not very good."

Although Microsoft's pricing was clearly intended to run its only competitor out of business, the Chicago School had long since made it impossible to win a case against "predatory" pricing—setting prices low to harm a competitor rather than to make money. In a 1981 article, Frank Easterbrook argued that predatory pricing amounts to irrational business behavior. He put forward various theories why a company would lose its shirt trying to make money in the long run by selling below cost in the short run to drive competitors from the market.

When modern economic analysis showed that predatory pricing can be used very successfully as a strategy against competitors, the Chicago School changed its tack, claiming that predatory pricing never happens. A 1986 Supreme Court decision bought the argument, hook, line, and sinker. "Predatory pricing schemes are rarely tried, and even more rarely successful," wrote the Court, citing Frank Easterbrook and other commentators, as opposed to any real evidence. When empirical case studies confirmed the use of predatory pricing strategies in business, the Chicago School shifted its explanation again, arguing that interfering with price cutting might chill competition that helps consumers.

Trying to deal with the Chicago School's ever-shifting justification for tolerating anticompetitive pricing behavior brought back memories of playing the old arcade game Whac-A-Mole. As soon as economic research shot down one Chicago School theory with facts from the real world, another justification was fabricated.

Predatory pricing inevitably harms consumers by eliminating competition. "Regardless of how good your product is, you can't compete against free," a marketing vice president of a Valley company once told me. Justifying a monopolist's exclusion of its only competitor because of short-term consumer benefit from low, predatory prices makes no more sense than countenancing the sale of stolen goods at a flea market because consumers can get low prices there. But given the state of the law, I had to agree with Tobey. Better to build a strong case around other charges, like exclusionary payments, anticompetitive licenses, and illegal tying.

The depositions started on August 25. Only Monday morning and it was already a great week. *BusinessWeek* magazine hit the newsstands with a special issue about Silicon Valley, part of the growing national recognition from the media. In one breathless article after another, *BusinessWeek* described what surely was Milton Friedman's vision of Paradise. A twenty-four-hour-a-day work culture. Seven-day workweeks. Little time for relationships with family. Deals negotiated over breakfast, lunch, and PTA meetings. Entrepreneurs streaming in from all over the world. "The quintessence of the American dream." The region that "led the U.S. in worker productivity and export growth." Thousands of young companies, some of which had already grown to gargantuan size—with many new ones created each week. "A technology blessed realm." "The epicenter of global technology." All fueled by high-risk venture capital, an unbridled desire for great wealth, and, most of all, "sheer brain power."

In one article called "How It Really Works," Steve Jobs bared what sounded like Silicon Valley's deepest secrets. "Silicon Valley is a meritocracy," he said. "What matters is how smart you are."

The afterglow of all the press infused the deposition room. Susan Huber, one of Tobey's colleagues, questioned a Netscape product manager.

"What is your educational background?" Huber asked for the record.

Undergraduate degree from Berkeley; postgraduate work in Japan; research aide to Laura Tyson, chair of the president's Council of Economic Advisers; MBA from Harvard.

Employment history, Huber wanted to know.

Employed by Harvard to incorporate technology into the university's educational process, then product manager for Apple's notebook computer, before joining Netscape in 1995, the witness responded. Huber's face opened in a broad smile, almost a grin. "Oh, yeah," I could imagine her thinking. "Just like the magazine said—the best and the brightest. What greater calling for a lawyer than to protect the 'epicenter of global technology.' I may get the Nobel Prize for law."

The depositions were going well, until the last witness on the first day. Mark Tobey was asking questions of Mike McCue, Netscape's vice president of technology. From the look on Tobey's face, I knew what he was thinking. Netscape's vice president of technology? This guy must be a rocket scientist who cures cancer in his spare time.

"What is your educational background?" Tobey asked the witness. Let's see, Ph.D. from MIT. No, make that from Caltech. Post-docs at Sloan-Kettering and the Max Planck Institute, then a brief stint as an astronaut before coming to Netscape. Tobey was expecting something like that. Actually, McCue wanted to be an astronaut when he was in high school, but Tobey never got around to that.

"I did not attend college," said the witness. "I mostly have kind of learned on my own through experience."

Silence. I looked up from taking notes. Tobey was staring straight ahead. His mouth was half opened, but no words were coming out. "A high school graduate?" Tobey was surely thinking. I'm about to launch World War 3.0 over some high school graduate? We've got high school graduates in Texas. Tobey composed himself enough to stammer through the next question. "What did you do before you worked at Netscape?"

"I was the CEO and founder of a company called Paper Software," the witness replied.

Tobey's expression said it all. What the hell? This guy's "experience" is some pathetic start-up that nobody ever heard of?

The questioning stopped, the official transcript correctly records, because at that moment someone pulled the fire alarm. I didn't do it, nor did any of my associates—that I know of. As people shuffled out of the building and into the parking lot, I took Tobey aside to calm him down. Sometimes, Silicon Valley is mysterious, even to those trying to help us.

"You're worried about explaining McCue's education to a judge?" I asked Tobey.

"Not to mention my boss the Texas attorney general," he responded. "It kind of threw me for a minute."

"I bet you read about that kid who went straight from high school to the NBA," I said. A year earlier, Kobe Bryant transformed the sports world. For the first time in National Basketball Association history, the league drafted a guard directly out of high school.

"What does that kid need with college?" I asked. "College degrees are for people like you and me, Mark. Some of the people out here don't really need what college offers."

I was about to mention Steve Jobs, Bill Gates, and Larry Ellison, none of whom have college degrees, but Tobey was already back on track. When the depositions resumed, he had McCue talk about his three-and-a-half-year stint at IBM before founding his start-up. Over the course of a week, Tobey took eleven depositions, compiling a written record that was chilling, even to me. As a result of Microsoft's promotional payments, Tobey's record showed, Internet service providers relegated Netscape to a secondary position. Consumers received the Netscape browser only if they asked for it specifically from service providers.

Worse still, Netscape could not get a commitment out of any of the major computer manufacturers to distribute its browser for the coming year. Netscape's senior vice president, Mike Homer, explained that the next version of Microsoft's browser, Internet Explorer 4.0, was going to be even more tightly integrated into Windows, particularly the next version of the operating system, Windows 98. Citing the difficulty of connecting the Netscape browser into Windows 98, computer manufacturers declined to offer Netscape's product at all, Homer said.

After the deposition was over and the reporter had put away her stenographic equipment, Homer made a direct appeal to Tobey. "I know the high tech business is like a knife fight," said Homer, "but Microsoft has guns. And unless someone takes their guns away from them, the fight is going to be over very quickly."

Three Antitrust Division lawyers listened to Homer's account. Microsoft expected to ship the new version of its browser at the beginning of October. Industry observers anticipated that it would be the technical equal of Netscape's product. Once installed with Windows 95, the new Microsoft browser would burrow deep into the operating system files and change the Windows screen display. So, once the new version of Microsoft's browser started shipping, there was little reason for consumers to even try to work with the Netscape browser. Unless the government restrained Microsoft before the release of Internet Explorer 4.0, I figured, the browser wars would be over.

I had already pounded on every door at the Antitrust Division, save one. Over the summer, Joel Klein had hired a new chief economist, Dan Rubinfeld from the University of California. Rubinfeld had no public record on Microsoft, but was a distinguished economist with a strong background in network effects. Garth Saloner knew Rubinfeld and praised him for his practical approach to economic problems.

With nothing to lose and nowhere else to turn, I called Rubinfeld and practically begged him to accept a visit from Saloner. Rubinfeld agreed, but at the meeting he said almost nothing, while the Antitrust Division lawyers took turns grilling Saloner. Saloner fielded every question and backed down not an inch. At the end of the meeting, Rubinfeld walked Saloner to the door and thanked him profusely. "Now I have some more ammunition to use against these lawyers," he said. More heartbreaking silence from the government followed. On October 1, Microsoft released version 4.0 of the Internet Explorer. The government said nothing.

Three weeks later, Attorney General Janet Reno finally announced a lawsuit against Microsoft for violating the consent decree Anne Bingaman negotiated. Microsoft, the government alleged, was forcing manufacturers to install IE as a condition of getting Windows 95. "Microsoft is unlawfully taking advantage of its Windows monopoly to protect and extend that monopoly and undermine consumer choice," Reno said at a press conference. The government asked the court to hold Microsoft in contempt and impose a $1 million per day fine, until Microsoft offered the two products separately.

"I say to heck with Janet Reno" was the reply of Microsoft senior vice president Steve Ballmer to questions from the press. Later in the week, Microsoft held its second meeting with the Silicon Valley venture capital community. This time, a few journalists reported on the event. Microsoft suggested that the VCs "check with Redmond to steer clear of start-ups that might run afoul of Microsoft's trajectory," the *San Jose Mercury News* noted.

By the time the government started gathering evidence for its contempt case in the fall of 1997, it was already too late. Microsoft had doubled its share of the browser market to 40 percent in the most recent nine months; Netscape's share fell 20 points. In network markets, the war is over long before anyone tallies a final body count. "With network markets, especially those in which tipping is a real possibility, allegations of anticompetitive behavior need to be treated quickly and seriously," Dan Rubinfeld wrote in a law review journal a year later. "Once the market has tipped it may be difficult or even undesirable to undo any anticompetitive effects that have arisen," he noted in an obvious reference to the Frank Easterbrooks of the world.

Too bad Rubinfeld wasn't named to his position a year earlier. Or, perhaps it was the holdup in Joel Klein's confirmation that delayed a meaningful investigation of Microsoft's conduct. In any case, the browser wars ended before the government took the field of battle.

In response to the government's complaint, but on his own motion, Judge Jackson issued a restraining order to prevent Microsoft from tying its browser to Windows. After a brief hearing in December, he expanded the restraining order into a preliminary injunction to remain in place until a full trial on the merits. By then, Netscape needed a coroner more than it needed a judge.

Right after the first of the year, Jim Barksdale announced a record loss. Netscape's share price plunged 20 percent, settling far below any previous nadir. Analysts predicted a "huge disaster" if Netscape's market share fell below 50 percent. The *Wall Street Journal* reported that Netscape was trying to sell itself and listed the names of potential acquirers. Microsoft apologists would later argue that the high quality of IE version 4.0 caused Netscape's demise. Rubinfeld debunked the myth by publishing detailed market data. Microsoft's browser share, Rubinfeld showed, jumped dramatically as a result of tying and contractual restrictions, not as a result of the introduction of an improved browser.

Because the government's contempt case addressed only infractions of the 1995 consent decree, it drew a lukewarm response in Silicon Valley. The complaint left for a later date the substantive violations of antitrust law like those detailed in the Netscape white paper. The lawsuit also made no attempt to restrain Microsoft's conduct directed against technologies created by other Silicon Valley companies, like Sun's Java and Apple's QuickTime video technology. More was needed. A lot more. With Netscape teetering on its last leg, Sun Microsystems took charge of pleading the Valley's case.

Sun's general counsel, Mike Morris, put together a secret task force of national antitrust luminaries, mostly top lawyers, to help convince the Justice Department to file a real lawsuit. Morris tasked the group with putting together an outline of a Sherman Act case the Antitrust Division might file, together with proposed remedies. Garth Saloner was part of Morris's group, known by the code name Project Sherman, as was University of Chicago economist Dennis Carlton.

If Frank Easterbrook embodied Chicago School jurisprudence, Dennis Carlton personified the Chicago School economic approach in the antitrust world. Carlton was actually educated at Harvard College (where he graduated with highest honors) and MIT (where he got a Ph.D. in three years). He joined the faculty of the University of Chicago's Economics Department in 1976 and worked his way up the academic ladder, eventually becoming an economics professor in the Graduate School of Business. As the Chicago School's influence spread in the 1970s and 1980s, Carlton made a fortune testifying as an expert witness in antitrust and securities cases. He was president of Lexecon, a lucrative, Chicago-based economic consulting firm. He authored scores of academic articles, as well as a leading graduate-level textbook on industrial organization.

After months of arguing with one another in hotel rooms around the country, the Project Sherman group decided they needed a firsthand look at the problem Silicon Valley was complaining about. Morris asked me to set up a series of meetings with some of the top people in the Valley so that the experts could talk directly to the alleged victims, without relying on the intermediation of lawyers. I made a list of the people I wanted the experts to hear—CEOs, technologists, and financiers. I made sure to cover all the key markets—desktop computing, client-server, Internet technology, and Web content.

On the appointed day, I positioned the antitrust experts around the table in one of my firm's conference rooms and ushered the industry moguls in and out at scheduled time intervals. To keep them from running into one another, I instructed them to enter and leave through different doors. Carlton brought two colleagues from Lexecon with him. Economic consultants, like lawyers from high-price firms, travel mostly in packs. The lawyers and the economists were charging Sun thousands of dollars an hour. Altogether, the project ended up costing $3 million.

There would be no warm-up act for the audience of experts, I decided. If I was going to convey to the East Coast types Microsoft's effect on Silicon Valley innovation, I would start with the headliner, Jim Clark, in the first time slot. The Washington lawyers and Chicago School economists thought they knew about competition and innovation. Several had written journal articles about predation, but more as an abstract concept. They had read about the hard times at Netscape. Time to feel the pain.

The heavy air of gloom settled into the conference room as Clark began to speak. The look on his face and the tone in his voice revealed equal measures of resignation and disgust. "Netscape has no prayer of success unless it mutates out of Microsoft's path," Clark said in somber tones. "That is very unlikely, so I'm leaving the [Netscape] board."

Smiles vanished, along with the lighthearted banter that usually accompanies a business presentation. For most of the next hour, Clark explained how predation actually works in network markets. Clark talked about how Microsoft's contracts prevented computer manufacturers from distributing Netscape's browser and how Microsoft withheld technical information from Netscape in an effort to get a board seat. Clark mentioned "thousands of more subtle violations" by Microsoft.

"What else that Microsoft did really mattered to Netscape?" Saloner wanted an explanation, more for the benefit of others, I thought.

"If you're in a close race and someone puts a ball bearing underfoot and you slip on it, you will lose," Clark continued. "So small things like latent threats and giving marketing dollars to people who [agree not to] use the competitor's product add up to disadvantaging the competitor. The perception that Microsoft is winning is all they need."

I was waiting for someone at the table to tell Clark that he didn't know what he was talking about. Perhaps Frank Easterbrook would have, had he been there. Easterbrook's famous 1984 law journal article ("The Limits of Antitrust") described "those who lose in the competitive struggle" as "sluggish" and "inefficient." "They are probably less knowledgeable than the average business executive about why they failed and others succeeded," Easterbrook wrote. "If they knew what went wrong, they might have improved."

Come again? Jim Clark, "less knowledgeable" than the average business executive? Sluggish? Inefficient? To Easterbrook, losers in the "competitive struggle" are losers, plain and simple. They deserve what they get and society is the better for giving it to them. "It is through the process of weeding out the weakest firms," Easterbrook later wrote, "that the economy as a whole receives the greatest boost."

"Strictly rust bowl," said Saloner when I read him Easterbrook's diatribe. "Silicon Valley's the best of the best. Start-ups don't get beaten because they have higher costs."

None of the antitrust experts challenged Clark. They all asked questions respectfully, accepting their station as students of the free market and conceding the role of teacher to Clark. For the economists in the room, this was a close encounter of the most telling kind—the opportunity to test antitrust theory with a real live high tech investor. Silicon Valley is filled with financiers who put other people's money at risk. Clark trusted his own money to the perils of free market competition. He told the group he invested $5 million, about one-third of his net worth at the time, in Netscape.

"When I invested in Netscape," Clark continued, "I thought Microsoft was going in the wrong direction." Clark was referring to Microsoft's failure to recognize the potential of the Internet. "Had I known Microsoft could get away with [restricting] OEMs to prevent Netscape from getting a market space"—Clark was shaking his head—"I was astonished it took the government two years to act. The damage was done in the first six months."

"What if we stopped all of Microsoft's anticompetitive marketing and contract behavior?" one of the economists asked. "Would that make a difference to you as an investor?"

"No," Clark replied without hesitation. "I've lost faith in the government. They're inept and can't react in an adequate amount of time."

I glanced over at the contingent from Chicago to see how they were taking it. They all stared at the table, too uncomfortable to look Clark in the eye. Clark was willing to consider investing in high tech again, he said, if the government broke up Microsoft, or perhaps if the government imposed a fine of many billions of dollars, equal to the amount Microsoft earned by illegally protecting its monopoly. Such a large fine would have likely bankrupted the company, and, in any case, the antitrust laws do not permit this type of remedy, so the discussion ended quickly.

"Some people think the system is working OK the way it is," Saloner suggested to Clark as he was getting ready to leave.

"Would you invest?" Clark asked. No one bothered to reply.

The Project Sherman group heard from other investors later in the day. They all said the same thing. No one would invest in Microsoft's strategic path. No one would sponsor a Microsoft competitor. Start-up capital was plentiful, and venture capitalists were investing at record levels. But the investments were going into health care, biotechnology, life science, and e-commerce, markets far removed from Microsoft's monopoly power.

I brought into the meetings some of the Valley's top technologists and business executives. They explained how Microsoft had leveraged its control of the operating system into the browser market and how, unless restrained, Microsoft would leverage its market power to control the server market, the market for media players, and perhaps even the wireless device market. Not one of the antitrust experts disputed the claims about Microsoft's use of its operating system domination to gain control of adjacent markets. Nor did anyone object to the conclusion that Microsoft did this as much for the purpose of protecting its existing monopoly as for finding new sources of revenue.

But the Chicago School contingent remained restive. The traditional economic view, countenanced by Robert Bork, among others, held that a monopolist could not gain higher profits or any other anticompetitive benefit by taking control of the next closest market. It would do so only to lower its transaction costs or for some other efficiency-enhancing reason.

One of Carlton's colleagues asked Saloner to collaborate on creating an economic model to explain mathematically how Microsoft could get anticompetitive benefit from its behavior. Saloner demurred. He wanted to spend his time working on the presentation to the Justice Department. Besides, the explanation for Microsoft's behavior was obvious. Microsoft was trying to protect its operating system position. Bill Gates and Steve Ballmer even said so, publicly. Carlton and company did not dispute what they were told by executives and technologists, but the normal kind of evidence judges rely on in trials every day was no longer good enough in an antitrust case. A formal economic model was necessary to make it all true.

At the next opportunity, I passed out to the group several pages from Carlton's industrial organization textbook. The pages explained the circumstances under which a monopolist could increase its profit by taking over a market in the same chain of distribution—a near equivalent to Microsoft's takeover of the browser market. I spent a few minutes working through the equations and proofs to show the group, using the formulas in Carlton's book, just how economically logical Microsoft's behavior was.

"This is your book, Dennis," I said. "Your book explains that our position is economically sound." Carlton studied the pages but said nothing.

A few days after he returned to Chicago, Carlton sent me a brand-new copy of his book. The inscription read: "Someone who has read my book as closely as you have deserves a copy of his own." Then Carlton prepared a more detailed explanation and flew to Washington with the rest of the Project Sherman team, where he urged the Antitrust Division to take action against Microsoft.

Near the end of the year, Carlton published for academic comment the working draft of an economic model to explain Microsoft's behavior. Carlton completed the final version several years later. He also wrote a paper for less technical readers. Whether business practices like those Microsoft employed—preventing third parties from dealing with rivals and bundling separate products together—actually hurts consumers, Carlton found, depends on the specific factual evaluation of each case. But Carlton was able to create an economic model that explained the use of tying and exclusive dealing to achieve anticompetitive ends. Carlton showed, in a formal, mathematical way, that a monopolist can use these practices to preserve its monopoly and even to extend its dominance to new markets by transferring market power from one product to another, from the operating system to browsers, for example.

"Until the Microsoft case," Carlton wrote in 2000, "the importance of this type of behavior was neither understood nor appreciated, despite the existence of other instances where it seems to have occurred, as for example, in some of the IBM cases of about 20 years ago." Perhaps Bill Baxter was a bit too hasty in his decision to drop the government's case against IBM, after all. Not everyone in the Chicago School bought Carlton's analysis. "What the Antitrust Division wanted the court to enjoin [in the IBM case] was progress," Frank Easterbrook declared in 2002.

The Antitrust Division, as it turned out, didn't need formal economic proof from Dennis Carlton or anyone else to explain Microsoft's behavior. Internal e-mail correspondence from Microsoft's executives, unearthed by the government's document demands, explained the reasons for Microsoft's conduct in unambiguous terms. One document after another identified Netscape as a strategic threat to Microsoft's monopoly. One internal analysis after another raised the need to bolt Microsoft's browser to Windows in order to make customers use Microsoft's product. "We will bind the [Windows] shell to the Internet Explorer so that running any other browser is a jolting experience," one Microsoft executive wrote. Tighter integration between the Microsoft browser and the operating system, one Microsoft executive demanded, "even if OEMs suffer."

E-mail after e-mail described Microsoft's power play to make computer manufacturers and service providers give consumers the Microsoft browser they did not want. E-mail after e-mail detailed Microsoft's threats and payments to exclude Netscape from the most efficient distribution channels.

"How much do we need to pay you to screw Netscape?" an AOL executive stated as he recounted Gates's characteristically blunt query. Microsoft's own customers chafed and pushed back against the monopolist's conduct, but to no avail. "From a consumer's perspective," a Hewlett-Packard executive wrote to Microsoft, "[you] are hurting our industry and our customers. . . . [I]f we had another supplier, I guarantee [that] you would not be our supplier of choice."

With all this evidence in hand, and more coming in every day, Joel Klein made an attempt to settle with Microsoft before filing a new complaint. Microsoft gave no quarter, forcing Klein's hand. Bad move by Bill Gates. Klein hired a top Wall Street litigator, David Boies, to lead the government's trial team. Boies cut his antitrust teeth defending IBM in the case Bill Baxter eventually dropped. Klein also hired as the government's economic expert Franklin Fisher, from MIT. Fisher was IBM's economic expert a generation earlier. And Klein personally committed himself to the Microsoft case, staking his own reputation on restoring the government's credibility in antitrust cases.

In May, months before Carlton published even a draft of his model, the Justice Department filed its first monopolization case in decades, charging that Microsoft's conduct against Netscape violated the antitrust laws. The absence of a comprehensive model mattered not a whit to Rubinfeld. "If you wait until you have all the details straight," he later told me, "there will be nothing left to fix."

Over the summer, the government amended its complaint to add anticompetitive conduct against Apple and other Silicon Valley companies. A win in the case would make Klein a "giant in the field" and "a real hero in the casebooks," a Yale professor told the *New York Times*. But a loss would seal Klein's legacy as "a socialist doodler who destroys the firms that do the best and most important work for the economy."

The federal appeals court in Washington reversed Judge Jackson's contempt decision a few weeks later. Microsoft crowed to the press about the decision, but no one cared. The Antitrust Division steamed ahead with its new case.

When the focus of antitrust proceedings shifted to Washington, Netscape hired Robert Bork to lobby the national press corps. On paper, hiring Bork made a lot of sense, as another important step in creating a nonpartisan, apolitical aura around the issue of Microsoft's conduct, so that Joel Klein would feel comfortable doing the right thing. A Ralph Nader conference the preceding fall brought the political left on board. Widely publicized Senate judiciary hearings chaired by conservative Republican Orrin Hatch earlier in the year gave Klein broad political cover. Retaining Bork could be expected to grease the judicial skids, quelling any lingering unease among conservative jurists who dominated the Washington federal bench. But Bork never seemed entirely comfortable in his new role.

"What do you think of what's being called the post–Chicago School?" someone asked Bork at the press conference where he announced his representation of Netscape. "Are you part of it?"

"Well, now," Bork quipped, "the post–Chicago School is noted primarily for its errors." The audience laughed and Bork continued. "I don't think there is anything post-Chicago. . . . I don't think the Chicago outlook, if you want to call it that, has been rejected."

Bork quickly became a lightning rod for right-wing ideologues who accused Netscape of trading on Bork's reputation and Bork of succumbing to the seduction of "fat consulting fees." Criticism rained down on Bork from the libertarian Cato Institute, Stanford's conservative Hoover Institution, and even from some journalists. "Robert Bork wrote the book on antitrust," Michael Kinsley posted in *Slate*, the online magazine. "He seems to have forgotten he ever read it."

Kinsley called the arguments in *The Antitrust Paradox* "Book Bork," and contrasted them with Bork's latter-day defenses of Netscape, which he called "Browser Bork." He found the two positions "*almost* utterly impossible" to reconcile. Book Bork considered tying harmless and the extension of monopoly power from one product to another "metaphysically impossible" in 1978, Kinsley wrote. But Browser Bork saw Microsoft's bundling of browsers and operating systems as an illegal attempt to preserve monopoly. Book Bork claimed that exclusive dealing and requirements contracts had never been shown, in any case, to injure competition. In fact, they "have no purpose or effect other than the creation of efficiency," according to the 1978 book. Browser Bork, by contrast, found Microsoft's restrictive contracts "predatory" agreements in restraint of trade.

Given the opportunity to respond by *Slate*, Bork could scarcely defend himself. He reiterated his view that tying law is "mistaken," but claimed the whole issue of tying irrelevant to the Microsoft case. He reprised the position he laid out in a *Wall Street Journal* op-ed: "This is not a case about 'leveraging' or 'tie-ins' as it is frequently described, even by the government lawyers who understand the case." Presumably, in Bork's view, the government lawyers who were describing the case incorrectly included Joel Klein and David Boies. Kinsley's own rejoinder to Bork was a bemused incredulity at the notion that extending monopoly from one market to another was not part of the government's case.

When Bork tried to explain that his book's dismissal of predatory conduct did not apply to the software industry where the marginal cost of producing the next unit does not increase, Kinsley pointed out that marginal costs in most modern, information-based industries decline, rather than increase. Because of learning curves and the economies of scale, it is usually cheaper to make each additional unit than it was to make the last. The prototype of a jet engine might cost billions, while the cost of each production copy runs into the tens of millions. The cost of developing a new pharmaceutical compound dwarfs the amount spent to stamp out each pill on the production line. Bork was arguing that his seminal analysis "doesn't apply to most real-life situations," Kinsley taunted.

The government's trial against Microsoft started in mid-October, about three weeks after Microsoft officially overtook Netscape in market share. Joel Klein was to become a fixture at the counsel table, but on the second day of trial he had more important business, giving a speech to the annual invitation-only Agenda conference in Phoenix for five hundred computer industry leaders. Klein told the conference that the government's case against Microsoft would be based on facts. "Theory and spin will no longer dominate the discussion," he said. Defending both competition and antitrust enforcement, Klein unapologetically urged the computer industry to support the administration's antitrust initiative. "Competitive markets are good for our economy, and good for America," Klein said, even as he criticized the industry for fearing the government more than the consequences of unchecked corporate power. Electronic polling immediately after Klein spoke showed that 80 percent of the audience agreed with the need for enforcement in the computer industry.

Back in Washington, Klein's trial team was busy doing what it is that trial lawyers do. They made a record. They called witnesses and they introduced documentary evidence. Over weeks, and then over months, representatives from Netscape, Apple, Sun, IBM, AOL, and even Microsoft's onetime acquisition target Intuit, along with technologists and economists, testified about how Microsoft spared neither pain nor expense to keep ordinary customers from getting access to new technologies that might, over time, displace the Windows monopoly.

A few weeks into the trial, Jim Barksdale announced Netscape's sale to AOL for $4.2 billion. Microsoft made much of Netscape's new, big company ownership, but the deal had little effect on the disposition of the case. The memory of Netscape as a vibrant start-up bringing new technology to the market was still strong, as was the record of Microsoft's threats and deeds.

Microsoft's turn to put on evidence came after the first of the year. Lacking what might be called "friends in the industry," Microsoft led off with its economic expert and called mostly its own executives.

Microsoft's economic expert was Richard Schmalensee, the dean of MIT's School of Management. When I appeared with Schmalensee on a panel debate over Microsoft's conduct years earlier at Harvard Law School, he claimed that Microsoft never withheld technical information to the detriment of independent application vendors. By that time, thick books had been written about the operating system information Microsoft withheld from its application competitors. The antitrust trial would later demonstrate that Microsoft withheld technical information from Netscape as an inducement to conspire and as a punishment for competing.

Schmalensee's direct testimony in the Microsoft case, submitted in writing, ran to over 320 pages. He took issue with just about every aspect of the government's case. Microsoft had no monopoly, Schmalensee argued in the lawyer's style of alternative pleading, and even if it did, its actions did not injure consumers.

Schmalensee calculated the monopoly price for Windows, to maximize profits in the short term, at $1,800 per copy. Because Microsoft charged only $60, it must not have monopoly power, he claimed. Furthermore, Microsoft's low prices proved the absence of injury to consumers, the company asserted. Schmalensee simply ignored the government's argument that Microsoft priced its product to maximize long-term profits, taking into account its high margins on applications and its payments to exclude Netscape.

David Boies confronted Schmalensee with his testimony in an earlier case that appeared to contradict what he was saying in Judge Jackson's court. A day later, Boies showed Schmalensee an article he had written in the *Antitrust Law Journal* that seemed inconsistent with another key point he was making. Then there was Schmalensee's article in the *Harvard Law Review*, contradicting yet another aspect of Schmalensee's testimony. "What could I have been thinking?" Schmalensee replied to Boies on the record, the closest he could come to a riposte. "So many contradictory statements," Judge Jackson later confided to journalist Ken Auletta. "Boies rendered him less convincing" than the government's economic expert, the judge concluded.

Microsoft's executives who took the stand after Schmalensee invariably asserted the time-honored efficiency defense: Microsoft bundled the browser with the operating system because it was cheaper to do so; it was easier; it was technically advantageous; and it brought a benefit to customers. Boies pounded the Microsoft witnesses with their own e-mails in which they minced no words. Microsoft bundled the browser to disadvantage Netscape, whatever the consequences to consumers.

Gates appeared in the trial only through his videotaped deposition, in which he repeatedly professed a lack of knowledge or concern about Netscape's threat to Windows. Boies put into evidence hundreds of pages of internal Microsoft correspondence detailing precisely that concern. "So many [of the Microsoft witnesses] were confronted by their own e-mails, and the e-mails were so inconsistent with the testimony they were giving," the judge told Auletta, "that you have a tendency to discount the rationalization that you have been presented on the witness stand."

After the witnesses were heard and the documents submitted, Judge Jackson did what judges do in contested cases. He decided what really happened, and he drew his own conclusions about the consequences of those events. Jackson published his findings of fact, 412 of them, in an eighty-two-page opinion. Just about everything of importance Jackson wrote contradicted one or another of Frank Easterbrook's most basic Chicago School tenets.

Easterbrook ridiculed the very notion that a federal judge could do a careful cost-benefit analysis in a complicated antitrust case. "It is fantastic to suppose," Frank Easterbrook wrote years before Jackson put pen to paper, that a court could "conduct a full inquiry into the economic costs and benefits of a particular business practice in the setting in which it has been used." Instead of letting judges weigh the costs of dominant firm market activities against their benefits, Easterbrook argued for a set of predetermined rules, designed to err on the side of excusing questionable practices.

Easterbrook's fantasy aside, Judge Jackson had no difficulty conducting an inquiry, full enough to evaluate the costs and benefits of Microsoft's conduct. Microsoft's bundling of its Web browser aided consumers by increasing the availability of browsers and reducing their cost, Jackson found. But these benefits were outweighed by the anticompetitive effects of the bundling—frustrating consumer choice, degrading computer performance, and depriving consumers of innovation.

"In a competitive struggle, the firms that use the best practices [those that reduce costs or improve quality] survive," Easterbrook assured his readers. Not so, Jackson found. Microsoft dispatched Netscape and maintained its operating system monopoly by increasing costs, both its own and Netscape's, and by degrading product quality.

"The firms that selected the [successful] practices may or may not know what is special about them," Easterbrook claimed. "They can describe *what* they do, but the *why* is more difficult." According to Jackson, Microsoft had no difficulty describing in internal correspondence the *why* of its restrictive practices. *Why* was simple—to maintain its monopoly.

"Monopoly is self-destructive," Easterbrook baldly proclaimed. "Monopoly prices eventually attract entry." After hearing the testimony and reviewing the evidence, Jackson saw a world of far more complicated economic forces than Easterbrook's simple rules allow. Consumers want an operating system that already supports a myriad of applications, and an operating system for which many new applications will likely be written in the future. The brief filed in opposition to Anne Bingaman's settlement, the Intuit white paper, and Susan Creighton's opus on behalf of Netscape all described this phenomenon. Dan Rubinfeld gave it a snappy new title for the benefit of Judge Jackson, the "applications barrier to entry." Even if Microsoft charged monopoly prices, the applications barrier to entry would prevent competitors from luring away its customers, Jackson decided.

Judicial predictions about "tomorrow's effects of today's practices" are so unreliable that the courts should "[get] out of the business of prophecy," Easterbrook counseled. Judges are no better at making predictive judgments than psychics who advertise on late-night television, he would later write.

Judge Jackson did not deem himself so incapable. As a result of Microsoft's conduct, Jackson held, Netscape would never attract enough developer support to overcome the applications barrier to entry. Jackson was right. Netscape never again posed a competitive threat to the Microsoft empire.

An activist antitrust policy is likely to reduce innovation, Easterbrook asserted. But Judge Jackson saw Microsoft's conduct as the principal impediment to innovation. "U.S. Judge Declares Microsoft Is a Market-Stifling Monopoly," read the *New York Times* headline announcing Jackson's decision.

How could Thomas Penfield Jackson, a conservative Republican whose personal hero is Barry Goldwater, write a decision so at odds with Frank Easterbrook's Chicago School dogma? Jackson drew his conclusions from the real world, while Easterbrook's homilies sprang from a maze of rationalizations concocted to support a preconceived result, a world of make-believe, a world of assumption and deduction, out of touch with the new economy.

After issuing his factual findings, Jackson ordered the parties to compulsory mediation, which proved futile. So the judge applied settled law to the facts and published his final decision in the case. The judge made no new law. He relied on the opinions published by higher courts in other cases. Microsoft violated the second section of the Sherman Act, the judge held, by illegally maintaining its operating system monopoly and by attempting to monopolize the browser market. Microsoft violated the first section of the Sherman Act (contracts in restraint of trade), according to the opinion, by unlawfully tying its browser to the sale of its operating system. Microsoft's stock value plunged $80 billion in a single day.

After Jackson published his opinions, two reporters from the *New York Times* got hold of a copy of Netscape's white paper and compared its contents to the case the government won. "Over all," they concluded, "the legal and economic theory in the Netscape document is remarkably similar to the themes laid out in the government's suit two years later." Of course, there is a huge difference between laying a case out on paper and proving it in court. Joel Klein's leadership, David Boies's deft examination skill, Dan Rubinfeld's economic realism, and the meticulous trial preparation by career Antitrust Division lawyer Phil Malone and his team account for the result.

A few months later, when Klein announced his departure from the Justice Department, the *New York Times* saluted him in an editorial. Klein showed "that mainstream antitrust principles can be effectively applied to modern markets," the editorial stated, recounting the cases Klein brought against abusive tactics by dominant firms and the anticompetitive mergers his team blocked. "He has not forged new antitrust principles or direction. What he has done is take antitrust enforcement seriously. For that alone he warrants the nation's gratitude."

The balance of the business remained unfinished. What to do about Microsoft, now adjudged an abusive, innovation-stifling, consumer-bashing monopolist? What was the appropriate antitrust remedy? Tim Bresnahan, the Stanford economist who took Dan Rubinfeld's place at the Antitrust Division, likened the situation to a dog chasing a fire truck. What happens when the overzealous dog catches its quarry?

In the 1974 antitrust course I took, Bill Baxter talked about the remedy for monopolization in terms of a "great race" approach to competition policy. When a company has achieved a durable monopoly—when it has bested all of its competition and no significant rivals remain, even on the horizon—the president of the United States invites the company's CEO to a celebratory dinner in the White House. White tie and tails. A string quartet. Exquisite cuisine prepared by the White House chef. An evening of toasts by the secretary of commerce, the chairman of the Federal Reserve, and the president himself. The CEO retires to the Lincoln Bedroom and in the morning flies with the president on Air Force One to New York where he rides in an open-top car in a ticker-tape parade down Wall Street. Cheering crowds. Billowing clouds of confetti.

At the end of the parade, the president turns to the CEO and says, "You've won. Congratulations. You've done an amazing job. Now we're going to break your company into a dozen pieces. Which one do you want to lead?" We break up the company, Baxter explained, not because it did anything wrong, but because we care about the process of competition. The process of competition makes products cheaper and better. Or, as we like to say in California, the journey *is* the destination.

On June 7, 2000, on the government's recommendation, Judge Jackson ordered Microsoft divided into two separate companies, one for applications and the other for operating systems. He ordered the operating systems company to publish information to aid third-party developers and he restricted the company's freedom to bundle other functionality into the operating system.

"I cannot imagine a more important verdict for the future of antitrust," Dan Rubinfeld told journalist John Heilemann. "This ranks with one of the great antitrust cases [the Standard Oil case] in the history of the Sherman Act," Yale professor George Priest told *New Yorker* writer Ken Auletta. "The case is likely to set rules that lay out the antitrust limits for the new economy," wrote two *New York Times* reporters. None of the above. What came after the trial turned out to be far more important to antitrust than any part of the trial itself.

CHAPTER 13

The Right Remedy

Judge Jackson wasn't the only one weighing the contorted logic of Chicago School market analysis against the reality of anticompetitive business behavior. On a winter day in 1993, I sat across from Al Verrecchia's desk in the New York offices of Hasbro, the world's second-largest toy company. Hasbro was a long-standing client and Verrecchia was the company's president. Hasbro owned some of the industry's best-selling brands like My Little Pony and Mr. Potato Head, as well as the Monopoly and Chutes and Ladders board games. The epitome of a successful East Coast business executive—tall, clean-cut, and plain spoken—Verrecchia joined Hasbro's finance department straight out of college and worked his way to the top of the company.

Verrecchia knew from his years in the industry just how tough the toy business could be. Until a new line is actually exposed to the consuming public each year, management can never really tell which new toys will become best sellers and which of last year's successful products will fall out of favor. Making too much of a product nobody wants is the shortest route to bankruptcy. So, the big manufacturers hedge their bets by offering a broad line of toys. But getting a sufficient number of different toys in front of customers is also a challenge. No single manufacturer produces enough different types of toys to justify opening its own retail stores, and one toy is usually not a substitute for another, so most consumers want to shop for toys at retail stores that carry a number of different manufacturers' lines.

Toys "R" Us, established in 1954, revolutionized the retail sale of toys by creating a national chain of large discount stores that stock the major manufacturers' full lines of toys throughout the entire year. The chain became the industry's largest retailer and Hasbro's single largest customer, although TRU still faced competition from small retailers, specialty stores, and national discount retailers, like Wal-Mart and Target stores, that stock all types of products, although fewer toy choices.

In the 1980s, "no frills" retail discount stores known as "warehouse clubs" began to sell a very limited assortment of "hot" toys—those with established consumer demand—at rock-bottom prices. The clubs aimed to capture revenue from the industry's top-selling brands without bearing the costs of stocking a full line or spending money on advertising. Toys "R" Us executives saw the clubs as free riders, and believed that carrying a full line of toys year-round and advertising the suppliers' products helped the toy manufacturers as much as it helped TRU.

TRU executives tried to limit competition from the clubs by demanding that manufacturers sell the clubs only unique or specially packaged toys different from those TRU carried. Verrecchia resisted TRU's demands as long as he could but eventually told his staff to follow TRU's instructions. All of the other big toy companies, accounting for about 40 percent of the industry's business, complied. The FTC, controlled by the Democrats as a result of Bill Clinton's election, promptly issued document demands to all of the industry's top companies.

When Hasbro's general counsel called me to talk about the problem, I gave the normal legal advice—acceding to TRU's demands was going to be a big problem that would follow Hasbro around for years. Apprised of my viewpoint, Verrecchia asked to see me in person. Perhaps, he thought, I just didn't understand.

So there I sat, across from Al. He had printed out some of Hasbro's confidential business records. "TRU is 31.5 percent of our business," Verrecchia said, pointing to the printout just in case I didn't believe the company's president. "I haven't talked to any of the other manufacturers about this," he continued, "but TRU says that our biggest competitor has agreed to stop selling hot toys to the clubs. If we don't go along with TRU's demands, TRU will stop buying our toys. You understand what that means?"

With only about 20 percent of the national retail market for toys, TRU accounted for less than a third of Hasbro's business. Wal-Mart was rapidly overtaking TRU as Hasbro's top customer, and, in theory at least, just about any store could stock toys if it wanted to, making barriers to entry negligible. The Chicago School learning on this kind of situation was clear. A company without market power could not hinder competition. TRU's relatively modest market share (usually a good approximation for market power) rendered the retailer incapable of harming anyone. By disciplining manufacturers, TRU could only hurt itself, passing up available revenue and forcing its suppliers to other retailers. Conduct like that would be irrational, or so said the Chicago School, and quickly punished by the free market. In fact, according to Chicago School scholars, a company with such a low share would not even try to bully its suppliers because of the obvious consequences.

"Don't worry, it's not going to happen. I learned that in law school. TRU can't possibly make its plan work. Their executives won't even try. Chicago School experts say it would be irrational." That's what I thought about saying, as a joke, of course. Verrecchia didn't look like he was in the mood for a joke. So I tried another approach. "Can TRU carry out something like that?" I asked.

"Our competitors make something similar to most of our products, except for some of our top brands. TRU doesn't have to stop buying all of our products to really hurt us. Suppose they cut back their purchases 50 percent or even 30 percent? I'd have to lay off thousands of people. Our stock price would fall off a cliff. There's no way I could make up for that kind of loss."

Really? That was another eye-opener. The Chicago School said that getting enough product distribution never constituted a problem. In his book, Robert Bork mocked antitrust enforcement concerns about restricted distribution by sarcastically advising the FTC to host "an industry social mixer" in order to make sure manufacturers met a sufficient number of distributors for their products. Another Chicago School scholar offered an even more creative idea—simply assume competent distributors will magically appear out of the ether. If a manufacturer "had a promising product," Chicago School judge Richard Posner wrote, "other distributors will be delighted to carry it; if there are no other distributors, new ones will appear."

"Assume a distributor." Perhaps that's what I should have said to Verrecchia. But I didn't. Instead, as I considered Verrecchia's real-world business options, I reflected on how the Chicago School had lost touch with market reality.

"Do what you need to do to save the company," I finally said to Verrecchia. "I'll see if I can talk the FTC out of charging Hasbro with anything. But don't talk to your competitors, and don't talk to Toys 'R' Us about your competitors."

"I've already sent the president of TRU a letter complaining about some of Mattel's products that I saw on the shelves at one of the club stores," Verrecchia admitted.

"Don't do that again," I said firmly. "That will turn your agreement with TRU into a conspiracy with your competitors not to sell to the clubs."

"A conspiracy with my competitors not to engage in profitable business? What are you talking about?" Verrecchia was just feigning incredulity. He had come to understand over the years that antitrust analysis did not always make sense. "I'm just trying to make the whole thing fall apart. Then we'll be able to sell whatever we want," he explained.

"Just, please, don't do it again. Complaining to TRU about your competitors will make everything more difficult. The FTC will say you would not have stopped selling to the clubs unless Mattel also agreed."

"Fine, I won't do it again. But you need to understand that if TRU leaned only on Hasbro to stop selling to the clubs, I'd have to stop, regardless of what they got any other manufacturers to do."

After several months of investigation, the commission's staff filed a complaint alleging a number of conspiracies—each manufacturer conspired with TRU individually, and the manufacturers conspired among themselves. TRU orchestrated all of it, according to the complaint. In a concession to reality, the commission charged only Toys "R" Us with an antitrust violation.

In the commission proceedings that followed, TRU said that it was just trying to keep the clubs from free-riding on the inventory services and advertising the company provided, but the commission ruled that TRU didn't have to worry about free riding because the manufacturers paid it directly for those services. The commission saw TRU's conduct as a power play by a dominant buyer to exclude its retail competition, in violation of the FTC Act.

Seeking a more receptive audience, TRU selected the appeals court in Chicago to review the commission's decision. TRU argued that it lacked market power, and, hence, under Chicago School reasoning, its conduct could not produce an anticompetitive effect. Less than two months after Judge Jackson's final decision in the Microsoft case, Judge Diane Wood, writing for the appellate court, refused to exalt abstract theory over market reality. "The Commission found here that, however TRU's market power as a toy retailer was measured, it was clear that its boycott was having an effect in the market," Wood noted, affirming the FTC. "No more elaborate market analysis was necessary."

Antitrust experts wrote article after article trying to reconcile TRU's control over the manufacturers with the conventional Chicago School wisdom about market power. Some scholars argued that because TRU was the only chain retailer willing to stock a full line of toys, it had more power over suppliers than its share of retail sales suggested. Others claimed that because TRU carried the brands of several manufacturers, it could enhance its market power by playing one off against the other. Whatever the explanation, it was difficult to deny the obvious: a company without a substantial market share found it both rational and effective to deny its competitors products by bullying its suppliers. Applying the Chicago School assumptions about market power without looking at facts would have aborted a meritorious antitrust case.

Microsoft, meanwhile, appealed Judge Jackson's decisions to the federal appellate court in Washington, which had earlier thrown out my challenge to Anne Bingaman's consent decree and reversed Jackson's contempt decision against Microsoft. The Antitrust Division tried to get the Supreme

Court to hear a direct appeal from the trial court, but the Supreme Court refused, sending the case back to the appellate court.

On appeal, Microsoft sounded broad, almost ideological themes. It claimed what the court of appeals called "an unfettered right to use its intellectual property"—the copyright on its operating system—as legal justification for its anticompetitive restrictions on OEMs. High tech markets are so dynamic, the company argued, that the old concerns about monopoly no longer apply. Outside the courtroom, Microsoft's backers fleshed out the logical conclusion: there is no reason or role for antitrust enforcement in network markets at all. Inside the courtroom, Microsoft softened its position slightly. The company argued that the dynamic nature of high tech markets makes the existence of monopoly so uncertain and transitory that the government needs to meet a higher standard of proof. The government must show direct proof of monopoly power, like excessively high prices, in order to prevail, Microsoft argued.

In want of legal precedent for its argument, Microsoft drew on the work of Joseph Schumpeter, the Harvard professor from the mid-twentieth century. Schumpeter claimed that capitalist economies grow by a rather unpredictable but inevitable process that he called "the perennial gale of creative destruction." New ideas and groundbreaking technologies "incessantly revolutionize" old business structures and markets by obliterating them, he argued. Writing before the creation of modern capital markets, Schumpeter saw large corporations in concentrated industries as more likely sources of innovation than small competitors in fragmented markets because of higher profit margins and greater resources to spend on research and development. Schumpeter thought monopoly a transient phenomenon. The normal business cycle will carry the economy forward without government intervention, he suggested, in an era that preceded the identification of "lock in," "switching costs," and other elements of game theory analysis.

All beside the point, said the court of appeals. Whatever the wind speed of the "perennial gale" in technologically dynamic markets, traditional antitrust analysis applies. In an opinion largely devoid of either sweeping rhetoric or ideology, the appellate court upheld Judge Jackson's finding of Microsoft's monopoly power, along with his ruling that Microsoft illegally maintained its monopoly in the operating systems market. The court rejected the government's other two claims, in what seemed like a compromise decision.

The court reversed Jackson's ruling against Microsoft for attempted monopolization of the browser market because the government did not observe the technical niceties of defining a specific market and demonstrating that the market is protected by barriers to entry. By the time of the court's decision, Microsoft commanded an 86 percent share of the browser market. Network effects alone could sustain that position against competitors, not to mention Microsoft's physical integration of its browser into its operating system, which further protected the company's browser position from challenge. The appellate court threw the attempted monopolization claim out of the case, long after Microsoft's attempt at monopolization of the browser market succeeded.

The appellate court vacated Judge Jackson's ruling that Microsoft illegally tied its browser to its operating system in violation of the Sherman Act's first section (contracts in restraint of trade), saying that the lower court improperly used the per se rule to determine liability. The opinion preserved the government's ability to retry its tying claim under a rule of reason approach, but strongly implied the government could never meet the exacting standards of proof the court set. The Antitrust Division never made the attempt.

The court of appeals also vacated Jackson's decision to break up Microsoft because the lower court neither held an evidentiary hearing on the remedy nor explained the reasons for its decision. The appellate court sent the case back to the trial court for a remedies hearing, with instructions suggesting great aversion to a structural remedy. The court disqualified Judge Jackson from further participation in the case because he granted press interviews about the case while it was still pending.

Despite the rulings on less significant issues, the appellate court sided with the government on the charge that mattered most, monopoly maintenance. The court rejected Microsoft's sweeping invocation of intellectual property rights as justification for antitrust offenses—the argument "borders upon the frivolous," the court said. Although dominated by conservatives, a unanimous court similarly dismissed Microsoft's broad incantations of Chicago School ideology.

The Sherman Act applies equally to threats against young technologies as to those against well-developed market substitutes, ruled the appellate court, ignoring Judge Frank Easterbrook's counsel to wait until the anticompetitive damage is done before taking stock of the not-yet-fully-formed consequences of anticompetitive conduct.

The appeals court invoked *Standard Oil*'s rule of reason test, scorned by Easterbrook as an "empty formulation," and balanced the costs against the benefits of Microsoft's conduct, an approach Easterbrook specifically denounced. The monopolist, under the court's legal formulation, had the burden of showing a legitimate, procompetitive justification for any conduct that excluded rivals.

Although the court ruled against the government's stand-alone tying claim, it nevertheless held Microsoft's tying and technological integration illegal as monopoly maintenance. Overall, the court refused to agree to diminished antitrust scrutiny, even in dynamic high tech markets, Schumpeter notwithstanding. Apostasy, said an article on the Cato Institute Web site. "Misguided conservatives need to reexamine their premises."

With the change of administration in 2001, Microsoft spun the appellate court's decision as a vindication. The company, citing the government's failure to show a consumer overcharge in the price of operating systems as evidence of its innocence, mounted a public relations campaign and loosed a swarm of lobbyists over Washington to urge a quick settlement. Portraying itself as an aggrieved innovator just trying to bring good products to consumers, Microsoft argued that government intervention in the workings of the free market, even to enforce the antitrust laws, will impede technological progress. "As badly as they blew the trial," one former Netscape executive told me, "Microsoft really nailed the PR issue." The company known in Silicon Valley more for appropriating its competitors' advances than for creating anything new itself artfully made the government into the boogie man.

The Bush administration proved more than pliable, announcing a settlement of the litigation on terms that made Anne Bingaman look good by comparison. Microsoft acceded to conditions less stringent than those to which it assented in settlement talks before it lost in Judge Jackson's court and the court of appeals. The company admitted no liability and retained the right to freely add other software features to its operating system. It agreed to give computer manufacturers greater freedom to install competing browsers and similar technologies and to share information about how its desktop products connect with server programs, precisely the kind of ineffective, after-the-fact remedies Bingaman made famous.

Newspapers, magazines, and antitrust publications printed howls of outrage, not just from predictable sources like Silicon Valley competitors, but even from mainstream business publications. *BusinessWeek*'s editorial, "Slapping Microsoft's Wrist," labeled the settlement a "weak censure" for "serious monopolistic practices" that "sends the wrong message to the marketplace." Monopoly is the enemy of "innovativeness," said the editorial. "In caving in on the issue of monopoly, [the Justice Department] leaves a serious problem that could harm the country's economy for years."

"An unsettling settlement" is what *The Economist* called the deal that "turn[ed] the company's defeat in court into victory." "Anticompetitive features of the settlement will prove to be a scandalous tax on innovation," an exasperated Tim Bresnahan wrote in *Antitrust* magazine.

A group of states refused to endorse the sellout. After a lengthy remedies trial on the states' claims, the judge to whom the Microsoft case was assigned on remand approved the Antitrust Division's settlement with only minor modifications. Robert Bork, representing a group of Microsoft's competitors, challenged the ruling. The settlement permits Microsoft to integrate its browser into its operating system, Bork argued, even though the court of appeals specifically held that conduct illegal. Bork advanced the very un-Chicago notion that Microsoft's illegal tie could be used to capture two different monopoly profits, one from the operating systems market and a second from the browser market. Most eye-popping of all was Bork's citation to the work of post-Chicago economist Garth Saloner for an economic description of Microsoft's predation.

The trial judge refused to let Bork participate in the appeal of the settlement. The appellate court overruled the trial judge, permitting Bork to participate but rejecting all of his challenges to the deal. Microsoft emerged from more than a decade of U.S. government scrutiny with all of its monopolies intact, retaining all of its ill-gotten gains, and without specific legal restraint on its ability to put vulnerable competitors out of business by anticompetitive bundling.

Many in Silicon Valley struggled to understand how it all happened. Regime change was only part of the explanation. Once Netscape was sold, the effort against Microsoft lost its character as a crusade to protect the entrepreneurial process for the creation of companies and technologies, so vital to Silicon Valley and to the nation's economy. Competitors complained about Microsoft from time immemorial, but it was Netscape that really galvanized the issue. More correctly, it was the concept of a Netscape that had appeal—not merely Netscape's distribution of software for access to the Internet, but the notion of a young entrepreneur (Marc Andreessen, in this case) raising money, hiring management, creating technology, and changing the world. Just like Bill Gates did. And it was easy enough to show that Gates was doing his best to make sure the phenomenon never happened again.

With Netscape eliminated, the crusade against Microsoft focused more and more on the technologies of big companies, rather than on the process of innovation. The opponents of the settlement with Microsoft ended up being the phone company (literally SBC, the precursor to today's AT&T), and other monopolist wannabes like AOL. The head of Bush's Antitrust Division derided their efforts as "just another Washington power grab, like a piece of legislation." So in the end, Microsoft lost the case but won the settlement.

By contrast, the Bush administration's Justice Department managed to successfully pursue two other important antitrust cases initiated by Joel Klein's staff. In the first, a conspiracy case, a court enjoined VISA and MasterCard from barring banks that issued their cards from also issuing American Express and Discover cards. The court found market power despite MasterCard's less-than-impressive 26 percent market share, and employed the rule of reason without difficulty, concluding that the harm from the defendants' conduct outweighed whatever procompetitive justifications were offered.

The second case involved exclusionary conduct by a monopolist that controlled 80 percent of the market for prefabricated artificial teeth. The court found illegal monopoly maintenance, citing the court of appeals' *Microsoft* decision, when the dominant supplier required its dealers not to purchase artificial teeth from rival producers. The court concluded that the harm from excluding rivals far outweighed the feeble business justifications advanced by the monopolist.

Despite these impressive successes, the Bush Justice Department brought not a single case of its own to challenge abusive conduct by dominant firms. In fact, the Bush administration intentionally created impediments for private plaintiffs challenging exclusionary conduct by advocating in friend-of-the-court briefs legal presumptions that favor dominant firms—the kind of approach Frank Easterbrook endorses—over a rule of reason balancing test.

Instead of developing legal standards by bringing their own cases, the Bush administration antitrust enforcement agencies convened panel discussions of academics to propose and debate global rules for dominant firm conduct based on theoretical economic models. Lacking adequate grounding in fully developed factual records from actual cases, discussion over antitrust enforcement devolved into the "theory and spin" that Joel Klein warned against.

Frank Easterbrook dipped his oar into the rancorous discourse with a 2003 article on exclusionary conduct. Easterbrook pronounced antitrust enforcement against dominant firms an unbroken litany of failure. "Few people are able to identify even one success in this line of work," he claimed, conceding in a halfhearted gesture only Bill Baxter's successful dismemberment of AT&T ("something that likely was inevitable because of technological change, independent of antitrust"). He stressed, yet again, the incompetence of judges to identify, much less remedy, anticompetitive conduct. The costs of inadvertently banning procompetitive practices (which Easterbrook said "seem very high") so far outweigh the damage from letting anticompetitive conduct go unpunished (which Easterbrook said market entry would take care of all by itself) that empirical proof of actual anticompetitive effects should be required to justify antitrust enforcement.

By 2003, widespread experience with network markets had long since undermined much of Easterbrook's argument. Nevertheless, he attacked with particular relish the post-Chicago economists who used "raising rivals' costs" models to explain anticompetitive strategic behavior. Their "fancy pants theories of exclusionary conduct" should be left "to the academy," Easterbrook suggested, not quite sagaciously.

Then Easterbrook took his shot at the government's Microsoft case. Easterbrook defined his own carefully circumscribed "program" for antitrust, limiting enforcement to preventing firms from raising price over marginal cost by reducing output. Microsoft's conduct produced no diminution in the output of browsers, Easterbrook demonstrated, at least to his own satisfaction, by naming several competitors' browsers he could download from the Web. So he dismissed the government's contention of diminished competition in the browser market. He ignored Microsoft's overwhelming market share.

Easterbrook quoted Joseph Schumpeter in sound bite increments ("the gale of creative destruction") to support his argument, omitting the disdain Schumpeter heaped on those who look only to prices and restrictions on output to explain the effects of corporate behavior. Schumpeter decried their "sacred precincts of theory" and their "textbook picture" of competition, which he distinguished from "capitalist reality." Innovation mattered far more to Schumpeter's analysis than price or output. Doubtless Schumpeter wore even fancier pants than the latter-day post-Chicago economists.

In modern software markets, a monopolist would never attempt to maximize profit by reducing output because it costs almost nothing to make an additional copy of software and distribute it over the Internet or through the sale of new computers. Each additional sale represents more profit, and because of network effects, each additional sale increases the market value of the product for additional sales. Antitrust enforcers who look only for output restrictions will never find any anticompetitive conduct in software markets.

The government's case against Microsoft asked whether an entrenched monopolist should be able to use tactics that reduce consumer choice in order to crush an emerging rival with a better product that might unseat the monopolist if given a fair market trial. The case centered on what really matters to consumers in high tech markets—innovation. What do we know about the effect on innovation from the government's untimely and ineffective settlement of the case? During the period of intense competition between Microsoft and Netscape, consumers could get a new, improved version of a browser roughly every six months. Once Microsoft ran Netscape out of business, it was more than five years before the monopolist offered a new version of its browser. Microsoft bought itself the ultimate benefit of monopoly power—the quiet life.

Microsoft might well have delayed an updated release of its browser even longer had Google not created real competition in the browser market by underwriting the Firefox browser, first released by a nonprofit foundation in 2004. The Firefox browser won top technical reviews and quickly established a double-digit market share. Google covered the salaries of Firefox's lead developers and paid tens of millions of dollars to Firefox for search queries made by users from the Firefox browser.

Startled by Firefox's success, Microsoft accelerated the release of a new version of its own browser. Microsoft put even more new features into the next version of its browser, including privacy protection for users. Microsoft figured out a way to encumber its key competitor and actually help consumers at the same time. Microsoft's features allow consumers to prevent Google and other companies from collecting detailed information about personal computer use.

Google responded by releasing a browser of its own, with advanced stability features and other innovations, but with less in the way of privacy protections. Google's CEO claimed Microsoft's practice of preferring its own Web content necessitated his company's new browser. Analysts identified Microsoft's advanced privacy features as the real threat to Google. Perhaps, in time, Microsoft will bring greater competition to the markets Google dominates.

Consumers can't depend on the good offices or kindly demeanor of any particular company to protect them from exploitation by businesses. Competition is what protects consumers. Competition begets innovation, while monopoly begets sloth. And innovation helps consumers in ways far more important than increasing product output.

———

At just about the time Microsoft was planning its appeal, I sat across the table from a Silicon Valley venture capitalist, trying to get him to invest in my new company. I had already raised a seed round of $3 million that I put together in quarter-million-dollar chunks from angel investors and wealthy CEOs. Now I needed to raise a big round. I was looking for $40 million.

My partners and I were trying to make the telephone into a platform for a new generation of Internet applications. It was a great idea. Years later, Steve Jobs actually made it happen. I even envisioned a venture capital fund set up just to finance phone applications, something that was announced for Jobs's platform in 2008. Unfortunately, being ahead of your time doesn't guarantee success in Silicon Valley.

"Why are you doing this?" the venture capitalist wanted to know. He was going to ask a lot of annoying questions before forking over large sums of money, but this was likely the most important. The VC needed to assure himself of my commitment to the project. In truth, "I'm hell-bent on making a lot of money" is one of the few correct answers to the VC's question, but that would not really suffice for me. As the question implied, I could make a good living practicing law, so why trade that in for the dicey prospects of a high tech start-up?

The first part of my answer was conventional. I'm not looking to run the company past its start-up phase, I said. Once financing is in place and the prototypes are developed, I'll recruit professional management and turn the company over to them, with your blessing. I just want the Silicon Valley experience of creating a company from scratch—raising investment capital, recruiting engineers, hiring salesmen, running a raw start-up, I explained.

"Why is that?" the VC persisted.

I told him the truth. "Chicago School judges are always claiming they know what is best for investment and innovation," I said. Like everyone in Silicon Valley, the VC knew what I was talking about. He had heard all the Beltway arguments from Microsoft's apologists about how government intervention would stifle innovation. "I want the experience of being an entrepreneur myself. Then, when some judge lectures me about what is best for innovation, I can look back at him and say, 'What would you know about that?'"

I got the start-up funded, and, just as predictably, a few years later,

Supreme Court Justice Antonin Scalia turned the object of my whimsical comment, the Chicago School's poorly informed stab at a coherent rationale for its competition policy, into the law of the land. Scalia authored a sweeping Supreme Court decision in 2004 that strictly limited the circumstances under which a monopolist has to work with a competitor so that the competitor's product can reach consumers. Scalia adopted most of Frank Easterbrook's unsupported assertions and added a few of his own. Strictly speaking, Scalia's opinion did not call the *Microsoft* decision into question because the appeals court opinion did not specifically rely on the monopolist's withholding of critical technical information from Netscape. But much of Scalia's rationale runs counter to the court's approach in *Microsoft*.

Without either a favorable or critical reference to the *Microsoft* court's rule of reason balancing approach, Scalia approved a legal test that makes proving anticompetitive behavior by a dominant firm more difficult. And while the *Microsoft* opinion put the burden on the dominant firm to justify conduct that excludes competitors from the market, Scalia seemed to reverse the calculus, apparently requiring challengers to show the dominant firm's exclusionary behavior inefficient.

Scalia's broad rhetoric called into question the value of antitrust enforcement against abusive behavior by dominant firms. Like Easterbrook, Scalia questioned the competence of federal judges to accurately identify anticompetitive behavior and declared them largely unfit to control it. He cited no actual court results to support his pronouncements. It was as if Bill Baxter never successfully sued AT&T, nor Joel Klein Microsoft.

Scalia extolled regulation over antitrust enforcement, describing the telecommunications regulatory regime as "an effective steward of the antitrust function," despite decades of regulatory failure, stretching all the way back to Ida Tarbell. Bill Baxter's long and frustrating experience with ineffective phone company regulation went unmentioned by Scalia, as did more recent examples of the FCC's difficulty in enforcing its policies. The cynic in me believes that Justice Scalia curtailed antitrust enforcement in favor of regulation knowing full well of regulation's inadequacies.

Like Easterbrook, Scalia viewed monopoly, at its worst, as little more than a passing irritant. Going even further, Scalia declared monopoly good for innovation. Better than good, actually. Vital. The "charging of monopoly prices . . . is an important element of the free market system," Scalia wrote, ignoring the role of competition in fostering innovation. "The opportunity to charge monopoly prices—at least for a short period of time—is what attracts 'business acumen' in the first place; it induces risk taking that produces innovation and economic growth." Scalia cited no factual support for his conclusions about monopoly and innovation.

Unbelievable, I said to myself when I read Scalia's opinion. How would he know what produces innovation? Did he talk to any of the Silicon Valley entrepreneurs whose opportunities for innovation were denied by Microsoft's market domination? Did he ask Silicon Valley's investors how they felt about Microsoft's instructions at VC Day? In the real world, monopoly crushes far more innovation than it produces.

Nor is the prospect of monopoly profits remotely necessary to foster real-world innovation. High tech investors always want to make a lot of money, and start-ups intend to charge prices well over their marginal costs, but no one needs the prospect of a monopoly to induce investment. In fact, venture capitalists try to invest in markets that will support multiple successful companies (sometimes competing around the same technical standards) and, even in network markets, the presence of at least one or two early competitors helps a start-up create demand for a new product. "I don't recall a partners' meeting in which we discussed a portfolio company's prospects for monopoly," one longtime venture capitalist noted dryly, after I showed him Scalia's opinion. "If one of my partners told me we should invest in a start-up because it would likely get a monopoly, we would laugh at him."

Although you would never know it from Justice Scalia's opinion, economists have studied carefully the relationship between competition and innovation. The great weight of their findings refutes Scalia's broad brush assertions and cuts against his ill-conceived policies. According to a growing body of empirical evidence, competition generally encourages innovation. Competition among firms seeking to develop new products and processes fosters innovation, as does competition among rivals searching for ways to lower costs and improve quality of existing products. Dominant firms usually press only for innovations that reinforce their market positions. Real technology breakthroughs frequently come from start-ups or established firms working outside their main areas of specialization, as the development of Internet software illustrated.

Extensive case studies of innovative behavior show productive activity from a variety of different industrial structures, leading one economist after another to call for antitrust policies favoring easy market entry and a diversity of firms. Antitrust enforcement should encourage "multiple commercial visions," in the words of one economist.

Antitrust enforcement can be directed with sufficient precision to situations, already identified by economists, in which protecting competition most likely promotes innovation. Network markets, for example, present some of the clearest cases for enforcement to protect competition. Those theoretical scenarios in which enforcement might cut against innovation can be avoided without recourse to Justice Scalia's carte blanche approach to dominant firm behavior. Case-by-case analysis works.

Bill Baxter once described the struggle over antitrust policy in terms of the difference between "people who believe in science—the use of statistics over large sets of observations to establish general tendencies—and people for whom anecdote swapping is the most reliable source of information." He would have never expected to find conservative Supreme Court justices in the latter category.

"Would the Standard Oil Trust still be with us to this day," one practitioner wrote, if Justice Scalia's opinion "had been the law of the land in 1911?" Not to mention the AT&T and IBM monopolies. Even Chicago School stalwart Judge Richard Posner endorsed the view in his opinions that a dominant firm must cooperate with a competitor when cooperation is necessary for effective competition. Policies that denigrate competition and celebrate monopoly damage the American economy by raising prices and retarding innovation. They need to be reversed before the damage becomes irreparable.

While the legal debate over exclusionary conduct raged, the remedy from the Microsoft litigation began to take hold in Silicon Valley. Not the government's remedy. That was laughable. The judge charged with over-sight of Microsoft's settlement after Judge Jackson was disqualified held quarterly hearings and received reports from the Antitrust Division. From time to time, one company or another complained about Microsoft's com-pliance with the settlement agreement, but the complaints never really went anywhere. The judge honored just about every one of Microsoft's long-winded excuses for its conduct. Deadlines were extended even when the company admitted that it failed to honor the settlement agreement's provisions. Eventually, some of the settlement's requirements were extended into the next presidential administration.

The only remedy that really ended up mattering was first suggested by Silicon Valley executives. At the end of the liability trial, Joel Klein came out to the Valley to solicit suggestions about how to remedy the market effects of Microsoft's conduct. "If you can't break them up," Sun Microsys-tems' CEO Scott McNealy told Klein, "just keep on suing them."

"Just keep on suing them" is the time-honored American antitrust strategy of choice for dealing with dominant firms that choke vast sectors of the economy. The magnitude of the potential gain to society from open-ing multiple markets to competition more than offsets the somewhat un-certain likelihood of producing the right results by bold antitrust enforcement. Time and again, the aggressive approach has unblocked mar-ket bottlenecks to innovation and growth, producing enormous benefits for the American economy.

The relentless pursuit of Standard Oil by the Texas attorney general likely did more to reduce the monopoly's market power than the federal government's lawsuit. The Supreme Court's *Standard Oil* decision neither restructured the various affiliated companies into competitive units nor prohibited the companies from doing business with each other, leaving the trust's operations largely intact.

Texas state officials, on the other hand, sued Standard early and often. After oil was discovered at Spindletop in 1901, the state government's stream of lawsuits blocked Standard's attempt to control the Gulf Coast market, permitting local companies like Gulf, the Texas Company (Tex-aco), and Shell (a foreign company with extensive Texas operations) to grow into large corporations and vertically integrate through the construction and acquisition of pipelines.

The Mellon family offered to sell Standard the precursor to Gulf Oil in 1902, but antitrust concerns scuttled the deal. "After the way Mr. Rockefeller has been treated by the state of Texas," said one of Standard's founders, "he'll never put another dime in Texas." The risks of a state antitrust suit similarly derailed efforts to merge Gulf and the Texas Company in 1905. Consequently, both companies built pipelines into the mid-continent oil fields. By 1910, Gulf had sales offices in New York, Philadelphia, and New Orleans, from which it competed against Standard for Gulf Coast and East Coast business; the Texas Company owned a marketing network throughout the United States east of the Rocky Mountains; and American consumers enjoyed a competitive oil industry.

"Just keep on suing them" was also the recipe for economic growth in telecommunications and information technology. The U.S. government first sued over AT&T's patents in 1885, then charged the company with antitrust violations in 1912. A third suit ended in a consent decree in 1956 under which AT&T licensed the transistor to William Shockley, among others, creating both Silicon Valley and much of the American electronics industry. Bill Baxter kept on suing AT&T until the company broke itself up, setting the stage for the growth of the Internet and the mobile telephone market.

Antitrust enforcement spawned Silicon Valley's software industry as well. IBM settled the government's first antitrust lawsuit against it with a consent decree requiring the monopolist to publish technical information so that independent maintenance companies could repair IBM machines. Competition in the computer market intensified when other manufacturers used the specifications to produce compatible computers that would run software and connect with peripheral devices made for IBM machines.

Nevertheless, IBM remained dominant because, competitors alleged, the company provided its software free to keep its hardware customers from switching vendors. IBM's software bundling practices limited the growth of software as a commercial product. The few available software programs not provided free from hardware vendors were usually written by customers. Attempting to preempt a second government antitrust suit, IBM cut the price of its hardware and started charging separately for application software. In a 2002 industry retrospective by the Institute of Electrical and Electronics Engineers (IEEE), a former IBM senior manager of the unbundling project pointed to his company's decision to offer software separately as a "vital condition" for the development of the independent software industry. IBM's unbundling of software changed customer perceptions and purchasing behavior toward software as a commercial product.

The Justice Department brought suit despite IBM's new policies, and the company's management vigorously contested every aspect of the litigation, losing touch with its business in the process. IBM failed to identify, much less capture or eliminate, opportunities for smaller computer devices, leading to highly competitive minicomputer, workstation, and personal computer markets. Industry observers also credit the government's lawsuits with hamstringing IBM and AT&T while the Internet grew to critical mass as a public facility on a platform of open specifications, free of big-firm dominance.

Although the Justice Department's *Microsoft* lawsuit eventually ran out of gas, that company experienced its own no less effective version of "just keep on suing them." A book by *Wall Street Journal* reporter David Bank chronicles the company's internal response to the government's lawsuit "that slowly sapped Microsoft's energy," and tied the company "in knots." "We stalled and became a muddled mess," one executive told Bank.

After the states' vain attempt to secure more effective remedies, consumer class-action lawyers sued Microsoft. Then competitors like Sun, Novell, and AOL (which bought Netscape) sued Microsoft. The total cost of the settlements reached almost $5 billion. A D.C. trade association even agreed to terminate anti-Microsoft activities in exchange for a $20 million payment.

Microsoft's problems overseas ended up costing the company a lot more, and not just in cash. First, the Korean Fair Trading Commission sued Microsoft to force major changes in the company's marketing practices in Korea. Then, in 2004, after a long investigation started by complaints from American companies, Europe's equivalent of the Antitrust Division found that Microsoft abused its market power. The European

Competition Commission imposed a $600 million fine, ordered the company to sell its operating system without a media player bundled into the program, and required the company to make technical information available so that other companies could make their server products operate with Windows. Microsoft appealed the commission's decision to Europe's second-highest court, but lost in what was later reported as a very close vote, triggering another $400 million in fines.

Although the fines set records for antitrust enforcement, the precedent was more significant, blocking Microsoft from bundling additional technologies into its operating system and extending its dominance further into the server market. The commission followed up by opening new investigations against other aspects of Microsoft's conduct.

"Stay vigilant," counseled *The Economist*, applauding the EU's *Microsoft* decision. Sometimes technological change tightens "incumbents' grips," meaning that some firms "warrant close regulatory attention," the magazine said, mentioning Google, Intel, and Qualcomm. Microsoft eventually gave up further appeals on the merits, and agreed to share proprietary information.

During the long entanglement with government investigations and lawsuits, control of the Internet slipped away from Microsoft. Internal company memoranda recommended strategies against the threat to Microsoft, "particularly in server space," from open-source software (OSS), code created and maintained by an informal, worldwide community of hackers and distributed free, for anyone to use. The memoranda outlined steps to control the Internet like those taken against Netscape and Java on the desktop, including establishing proprietary Internet protocols to lock in customers and "deny[ing] OSS products into the market."

None of these steps was taken. Already mired in bet-your-company litigation, Microsoft's top management disclaimed the memoranda when they were leaked in the middle of the trial. "But for the Justice Department scrutiny, might not Microsoft have mounted an all-out attack next on the open source technologies and open protocols of the Web?" one Silicon Valley entrepreneur asked in *Salon*.

Bill Gates chose a business strategy of retrenchment, binding Microsoft more tightly to the Windows desktop, in lieu of a new Internet platform built around the browser. Brad Silverberg, the Microsoft executive originally named by Gates to head the Internet services initiative, left the company. "Microsoft swore they wouldn't let the antitrust case distract them from the market," one former IBM executive told me in the wake of the Microsoft trial. "So did we, but while we were dealing with the lawsuits, we lost control. So did Microsoft."

One of Judge Jackson's opinions mentioned Microsoft's tentative steps to insinuate its own proprietary extensions into open Internet protocols so that it could control the display of Internet content. But the company moved neither quickly nor forcefully enough to stop the wild proliferation of Internet content and services based on open standards. Businesses wary of dependence on Microsoft bought the open-source Apache Web server. A whole generation of programmers adopted Java, Sun's platform-neutral programming language, as the lingua franca of the Internet. Developers created rich, Web-based applications using a new generation of technology. Cell phones and other alternative platforms began to display the new content. Google developed a superior method to search Web content, together with a business plan to make the World Wide Web a successful business proposition. Then Google introduced Web-based application programs and a new browser, bringing a measure of competition to Microsoft's domain.

Competition remains the order of the day on the Internet, at least for the moment, no thanks to Justice Scalia, whose opinion might well have produced a different result, had it been published years earlier. And there is yet the possibility of a return to monopoly. The market share of Microsoft's Web server continues to grow. Industry observers expect the company to use its control of the browser's default settings to disadvantage Google, as well, once the remaining provisions of the consent decree expire.

The personal computer platform is even more problematic. Both the operating systems market and the markets for productivity software (spreadsheets, word processing, etc.) remain under Microsoft's thumb. Consumers complain in the press and on the Web about how Microsoft forces them into expensive, unwanted upgrades, but neither the government nor the private sector offers much prospect for near-term relief.

Google's attempt to offer application programs hosted on the Internet, while successful at forcing some Microsoft price reductions to students and home users, lacks the broad-based support of large corporations, who cite security reasons for their reluctance to embrace the new product offering. Features in Google's browser might hasten the adoption of Web-based applications and marginalize the influence of Microsoft's operating system monopoly. That all lies in the future. Years after the Microsoft trial ended, the one count in the complaint upheld by both the trial and appellate courts, monopoly maintenance, remains unremedied.

The entrepreneurs of Silicon Valley drew their own conclusions from the government's engagement with Microsoft. "Everybody should compete with Microsoft once in their lifetime, so they have stories to tell their grandchildren," Netscape cofounder Marc Andreessen told *BusinessWeek* on learning of the Bush administration's settlement, "and then don't do it anymore."

Andreessen followed his own advice to the letter. For his next start-up, he purposely chose a business outside of Microsoft's strategic path. He built his new company's technology on Microsoft's Windows server and made Microsoft both a "strategic partner" and a customer for the new company. He eventually sold the business to Hewlett-Packard for $1.6 billion. Mike McCue, who testified in the Texas depositions as Netscape's vice president of technology, followed suit. McCue founded a voice recognition company, which he sold to Microsoft in 2007 for $800 million.

Once Jim Clark walked out of the Project Sherman conference room, he just kept on walking. Answering his own rhetorical question ("Would you invest?"), he stopped investing in Silicon Valley and shut down or sold off most of the investments he had. He moved his home and business to Miami, where he tried to rehabilitate his billion-dollar fortune by investing in Florida condominiums. "I've been out of Silicon Valley for five or six years," Jim Clark told *BusinessWeek* in 2003. "I go there for board meetings, then I split." The Chicago School's myopic focus on the incentives of the dominant incumbent company cost consumers of high tech products the benefits of Jim Clark's gift for invention. While Clark's talent will keep him rich, society will want for the new technologies Clark and similar entrepreneurs, the "losers" in Frank Easterbrook's world, could have provided us.

"Astonishing" was the word Oracle founder and CEO Larry Ellison used to describe the government's settlement with Microsoft. "I have to congratulate Steve, Bill and the guys up there [in Redmond]," he said. "They lost the trial, but the government paid them a reward for violating the law."

Two years later, Ellison would show the leaders of the Bush administration's Antitrust Division that the failure to enforce the law has consequences that markets can't correct. "We have to do what . . . Microsoft did before us," Ellison would say. "We have to roll up our industry." Drawing inspiration from the Antitrust Division's indolence, Ellison vowed to "roll up" the market for complex mission-critical business software "into a very, very few companies with one dominant player," namely Oracle. "We will be that dominant player," he promised.

PART FIVE

MERGERS AND ACQUISITIONS

CHAPTER 14

Storytelling for Lawyers

Months of unsuccessfully berating the government to sue Microsoft left me drained. So, in the spring of 1997, I went to Hawaii for a few days of vacation. Microsoft wasn't the only legal problem wearing on me. I had just spent a year of futility, coincident with my Netscape travails, trying to convince the Justice Department to block an anticompetitive merger that would raise the price of hiring a lawyer for just about every consumer of legal services anywhere in America.

Early in 1996 Thomson Corporation announced that it was buying its only significant competitor, West Publishing. The two companies were the largest publishers of court opinions, treatises, and other materials lawyers use to do legal research. No other company was even close in terms of market share or customer usage. West and Thomson published the only two comprehensive legal encyclopedias, the only two prominent legal dictionaries, and the two most important insurance law treatises. They competed for the contracts to publish state court opinions and statutes. And, most significant of all, the two companies offered the only comprehensive systems for legal research. The Thomson system was not quite as good as the West system, but there were no other comprehensive or even effective competitive offerings, except in small niches of the law, like taxation.

News of the deal drew heated protests. Bar associations raised concerns that the takeover would increase the cost of practicing law. Typical was the reaction in the *Recorder*, San Francisco's legal newspaper: "A West-Thomson deal . . . will be like a tax on all lawyers in California. Think of it as a big increase in your State Bar dues—only without the pretense that the money is going to some public purpose." Because lawyers would inevitably pass on the higher costs to their clients, consumer groups complained that the merger would raise the price of legal representation for average Americans. Even law librarians condemned the deal, predicting it would increase the costs of educating law students.

My client, LexisNexis, licensed materials from Thomson that it used to compete against West in the market for computer-based, online legal research. In that market, LexisNexis represented West's only significant competitor. Without Thomson's materials, particularly its well-organized system of editorial enhancements and cross-references, LexisNexis had little to offer lawyers. Once Thomson owned West, my client reasoned, Thomson would use its resources to support the West online service, and LexisNexis would wither. So the company hired me to oppose the deal. "Piece of cake," I thought, given the public outcry.

Yet despite my white paper and court briefs, the deal sailed through the Justice Department. Threats and lawsuits eventually pried enough concessions out of Thomson to keep LexisNexis a viable and even robust competitor. The client was happy enough, but the public got the short end of the deal.

I always recognized that it would be difficult to get the government to sue Microsoft. After all, the economic underpinnings of my position were unknown in the law at the time I started making complaints about Microsoft's conduct. The West-Thomson deal, on the other hand, was a merger between the two largest legal publishers, the only suppliers of comprehensive legal research systems. How could I have failed to convince the Antitrust Division to block the deal?

I kept turning the question over in my mind. Then, early one morning, the phone in my hotel room rang. My office said that a CNN reporter named Brooks Jackson was urgently trying to get in touch with me. I had never talked to Jackson before, but I couldn't resist the urge to return his call.

"We're about to release a story," he said, "that the former owner of West pledged more than $150,000 in campaign contributions to Democrats while the Thomson deal was pending in the Justice Department." The money, he claimed, was delivered after the deal cleared. To avoid detection, the contribution was broken into eight parts and funneled through state campaign organizations. He started naming the states.

I swooned. Glancing at the clock next to my bed, I wondered if the swim-up bar was open yet.

"Do you have any comment?" he demanded.

"None whatsoever," I replied. Law school never really taught me what I needed to know about merger review, I told myself.

***

Section 7 of the Clayton Act, originally passed in 1914, condemns mergers if their effect may be substantially to lessen competition, or to tend to create a monopoly. Challenged by what was seen as a threatening trend toward economic concentration in markets throughout the U.S. economy, Congress amended the statute in 1950 to broaden its reach considerably. Antitrust scholars use the 1950 amendment of the Clayton Act as the starting point for modern merger law in the United States.

Most mergers lack competitive significance. Businesses get bought and sold every day in America and no one except the parties to the transaction even cares. Some mergers even enhance competition by producing stronger competitors or by creating synergies that result in better products. Looking at the numbers alone, Easterbrook-type concerns about the effect of antitrust enforcement might suggest that government lawyers simply throw up their hands and ignore merger review for fear of disrupting beneficial transactions. But merger law never adopted this approach. Instead, in the decades since the amendment of the Clayton Act, courts and antitrust enforcers have tried to develop strategies and methodologies to identify accurately those transactions that are likely to produce anticompetitive effects.

The essence of merger law is prediction. Prediction always involves some degree of uncertainty, and merger enforcement has little choice but to proceed despite that uncertainty. Once a merger or acquisition closes, operations get combined, personnel get laid off, and duplicative facilities get closed down or sold. Courts lack the resources to unscramble a consummated merger easily and would likely harm customers and third parties if they tried. Although the government can attack a consummated merger, the only realistic way to stop what is likely to be an anticompetitive merger from harming consumers is to stop it from happening in the first place.

The Warren Court began to hear cases brought under the amended Clayton Act in the 1960s. In theory, at least, the statute was not thought to concern itself with the absolute size of a company produced by a merger or an acquisition. Instead, the prevailing economic analysis of the time traced market power to underlying industry structure. The more concentrated an industry, meaning fewer participants with each having a larger share, the less likely the industry to produce competitive results like low prices, low margins, and high product quality. If a merger results in a firm that controls too large a market share, the Supreme Court explained in 1963, the increase in market concentration will invariably lead to the kind of decrease in competition the statute condemns.

The Court's methodology not only presumed a merger's anticompetitive effect just from a showing of increased market concentration, it also set the threshold for the increase at such a low level that virtually any merger between rivals was prohibited. In one infamous 1966 decision, the Supreme Court upheld the Justice Department's suit against the merger of two small grocery store chains in Los Angeles that together accounted for less than 8 percent of the market. Combining two small chains may well produce a larger business that can operate more efficiently and charge lower prices, thereby increasing competition, but the Court repeatedly rejected any such analysis. Sometimes, in fact, the Court suggested that achieving efficiency was an unfair advantage worthy of judicial condemnation. If the Justice Department challenged an acquisition during this time frame, the result was predictable: "The Government always wins," Supreme Court Justice Potter Stewart observed. Less predictable was whether the Justice Department would decide to go after a deal in the first place.

In 1968 the Antitrust Division issued a set of Merger Guidelines to relieve some of the business uncertainty. Drawn largely from the structural approach of the case law, the Guidelines explained the way the Antitrust Division intended to analyze the competitive effects of a merger. The Guidelines were not binding on the courts, but later versions came to be very influential in the development of antitrust doctrine, mostly because the Supreme Court rarely took a merger case for review. The 1968 Guidelines included the recognition that efficiencies flowing from a merger might be considered in evaluating its legality, but only in "exceptional circumstances."

Under the 1968 Guidelines, the government's antitrust enforcers used informal, anecdotal sources like corporate documents or trade association memberships to identify companies in the same market. The decision to block a merger depended largely on "concentration ratios," the share of the market held by the four largest and eight largest firms. The actual shares of the parties to the merger mattered far less in the analysis. The potential for market entry by new competitors hardly mattered at all.

Continuing concerns about anticompetitive mergers prompted Congress in 1976 to set up a government procedure for antitrust review of proposed mergers. Known as the Hart-Scott-Rodino Act for its congressional sponsors, the new law required parties in all but the smallest deals to report proposed mergers and acquisitions to the government and to wait a set time period before closing a reported transaction. The waiting period enables the government to secure and review appropriate information and to seek an injunction from a court to block any deal deemed anticompetitive. Under the established procedure, each reported transaction is reviewed by either the FTC or the Antitrust Division of the Department of Justice, but not both. During the review, the merging parties might drop or alter their plans to take account of issues raised by government opposition. If an adequate resolution cannot be negotiated and the government decides to block a deal, the reviewing agency files a complaint in court and tries to convince a judge to issue an injunction. Alternatively, a deal is "cleared" by the government if the "waiting period" expires without legal action.

During the 1970s, the simple market structure approach to antitrust analysis came under attack by Chicago School economists and antitrust scholars. Many believed that even highly concentrated markets could perform competitively. The courts responded to these attacks by permitting merging parties somewhat greater latitude to rebut the presumption of competitive injury from increased concentration.

When Bill Baxter took over the Antitrust Division, he made reformation of merger review one of his highest priorities. Baxter brought one of his former students into the division as a special assistant to spearhead a rewrite of the 1968 Guidelines along the lines of Baxter's law-school lectures. While the 1968 version of the Guidelines drew on the case law, Baxter's rewrite, published in 1982, was based largely on economics. Many of the key economic concepts Baxter incorporated into the Guidelines were unfamiliar to the antitrust bar, making them highly controversial. Neither the Federal Trade Commission nor the states' attorneys general signed on to his draft.

While a merger might produce a firm with enough market power to raise prices by itself, Baxter was also concerned with the potential harm from what today's antitrust enforcers call coordinated effects. Baxter grounded much of his approach in the work of Chicago School economist George Stigler. Stigler focused on the possibility of coordinated behavior in markets with only a few sellers. The sellers might set up an illegal cartel. Even if the sellers in such markets did not explicitly collude, they could monitor each other's public pricing activity and signal to each other through publicly announced price increases or rollbacks. Without direct communication or express agreement, the sellers could still coordinate their actions to produce higher prices.

Section 1 of the Sherman Act requires evidence of an "agreement" between companies to establish a conspiracy in restraint of trade. Absent such an agreement, the law lacks an easy mechanism to compel more vigorous price competition among industry incumbents. In a market with few sellers, each company's independent self-interested behavior might produce price increases much like an overt conspiracy, but self-interest, without more, offers little basis for antitrust prosecution. Baxter wanted to identify and prevent mergers that exacerbate the potential for this kind of activity.

Baxter's Guidelines set up a methodology to determine whether a company can raise prices as a result of a merger—either by itself or through coordination with other firms. Although the procedures in the Guidelines appear convoluted, perhaps unnecessarily complicated, they are intended to answer a straightforward question: If a supplier raises prices after a merger, would customers switch to the offerings of other competitors, thereby defeating the attempt to raise prices, or would customers pay the higher prices? The latter implies a need for antitrust enforcement to block or modify the proposed transaction.

The Guidelines relied on inference. In 1982, economists lacked the tools to measure directly whether the combination of the merging firms was likely to produce price increases. Instead, the Guidelines asked whether the combination of the merging companies leaves an industry structure (insufficient customer alternatives, for example) in which price increases are likely.

To calibrate the market power of the merged firm and identify the products customers might switch to in the event of a price increase, Baxter's Guidelines began by "defining the market" under review, that is, identifying the products and companies in competition with each other. "Defining the market" for merger analysis implies a rigorous, frequently empirical exercise, rather than the abstract, free-form thought experiment political pundits perform on daytime television when they suggest their own market definition is every bit as valid as anyone else's.

Baxter's Guidelines adopted a "hypothetical monopolist" paradigm to define the appropriate market for antitrust analysis. The Guidelines asked how many buyers would shift to other sellers' products if the merging companies raised their prices a small but significant amount, say, 5 percent, after the merger. If large numbers of buyers would shift away, making the price increase unprofitable, the Guidelines started the process again, combining not only the products of the merging companies, but also the next closest substitute made by a competitor.

After successive iterations, the process revealed a group of products from a number of competing companies that customers would not shift away from in response to a small but significant price increase. In other words, if a single company owned all these products, that company could charge higher prices. For purposes of Guideline analysis, those are the products (and competitors) in the relevant market. The relevant market usually includes products from the merging companies, and others, as well. The Guidelines used a similar procedure to identify the relevant geographic market, extending in iterative steps the area in which the merging firms compete, until the area is large enough to sustain a price increase.

Many experts voiced skepticism about the hypothetical monopolist paradigm, painting it as little more than abstract theory. George Stigler himself blasted the approach as "completely non-operational." Stigler faulted Baxter's Guidelines for failing to specify how data could be used to delineate markets empirically. Nevertheless, the Antitrust Division adopted Baxter's approach, including the hypothetical monopolist paradigm. Over the next two decades, antitrust economists developed empirical techniques to implement the paradigm. The FTC eventually embraced the approach. The U.S. courts adopted it, and competition enforcement officials throughout the world now employ it.

Having delineated the relevant market, Baxter's Guidelines next calculated supplier concentration within that market to determine the ability of the merged company to raise prices by itself or through coordination. Instead of measuring concentration by summing the shares of the four (or eight) largest firms in the market, the 1982 Guidelines incorporated a measurement known as the Herfindahl-Hirschman Index—HHI, for short. Compared to the old four-firm concentration ratio, the HHI calculation better predicts both the impact of a merger on market dynamics and the ability of companies in the market to engage in coordinated behavior after the transaction.

A market's HHI is calculated by adding together the square of each firm's market share (i.e., a 6 percent market share equals 36 HHI points). The Guidelines called for the calculation of a market's HHI both before and after a proposed merger and specified that a merger will likely be challenged if the increase in market concentration and the postmerger level of market concentration exceeded specified HHI thresholds. If entry into the market by new competitors was easy, or there were other market factors that make it difficult for firms to collude, the 1982 Guidelines permitted the government to exercise its discretion and allow the merger to proceed. The flexibility in the Guidelines enabled Baxter's Antitrust Division to adopt a far more lenient attitude toward mergers than the case law sanctioned.

The Antitrust Division's experience with the 1982 Guidelines quickly revealed some problems. For example, the HHI thresholds for challenging problematic mergers were set at too low a level. Most markets work competitively at concentration levels considerably above the challenge thresholds in the Guidelines. The division never formally amended the Guidelines to account for the differences, but, in practice, operated as if higher thresholds apply.

The issue of market entry by new competitors also turned out to be a lot more complicated than Baxter's Guidelines contemplated. If new competitors can enter a market easily, harm to competition is unlikely according to the 1982 Guidelines, regardless of the HHI levels at the time of the merger. As economists applied more sophisticated game theory analysis to market entry, additional considerations surfaced. After a merger between firms, a new competitor might be able to enter the market quickly and easily, just by diverting some of its existing output.

In other cases, a new entrant has to make substantial investments in things like plant, equipment, personnel, and product development to enter the market. The new competitor *could* enter the market, but whether it actually *would* or not depends on its evaluation of what happens after it takes the plunge. How will those companies already in the market react to the new market entry? Will the new manufacturing capacity entering the market drive prices down, making the company's market entry unprofitable? If the attempt at entry fails, can the company recover its investments by selling off the newly acquired (or constructed) assets? The difference between what a potential entrant *could* do and what it *would* do turns out to be an important distinction in merger analysis.

In 1992, the Antitrust Division revised the market entry discussion in the Guidelines to explain and apply this more complicated approach. The revisions came after the division lost two highly publicized merger challenges in the federal appellate courts over issues of market entry. In one of the opinions, then-Judge Ruth Bader Ginsburg (generally viewed as a liberal) joined then-Judge Clarence Thomas (universally viewed as a conservative) in roundly criticizing the government's market entry analysis. Some antitrust enforcers attributed the setbacks to a judicial misunderstanding of the government's approach.

After the 1992 clarifications, the government had more success in court overcoming ease of entry arguments by merging firms. The Guidelines explained that new market entry must be "timely, likely and sufficient" to offset the anticompetitive effects of the merger under review. If the

Guidelines' methodology predicts that a merger is likely to produce price increases, entry must be sufficient to roll back prices to competitive levels before the enforcement agencies will permit the merger to proceed. "Timely" market entry must occur within two years of the merger.

The Chicago School's reliance on ease of entry as a cure-all for untoward market power ended up being badly misplaced. Subsequent economic research showed that, even after very large mergers, price increases are frequently insufficient to induce new entry, leaving the injury from anticompetitive mergers unremedied by the free market.

Baxter's approach proved most helpful in identifying when firms can coordinate with each other following a merger in the market. But some mergers harm consumers by permitting a company that acquires a close competitor to raise its prices, without regard to what other companies in the market do. The merged company doesn't have to be a monopolist to raise prices. It might be a dominant company, or even a company with a few competitors in a market with high barriers to entry. The merged company can increase its prices because some customers of the merging companies view their products as next-best substitutes for each other. After the merger, those customers lack good competitive alternatives, so they accept higher prices.

The 1992 revisions added this widely recognized economic concept of "unilateral effects" to the Guidelines as an independent basis for assessing mergers and blocking those likely to produce price increases. Some conservatives claimed that the incorporation of unilateral effects analysis into the Guidelines was pretextual—"political" was the word they used—a move by antitrust activists undertaken without economic validation simply to justify blocking more mergers. Former FTC chief economist Jon Baker replied in a journal article, explaining that antitrust concerns about unilateral effects were well supported in both theoretical and empirical economic research. Most recent merger challenges, particularly during the Clinton administration, were based on unilateral effects analysis.

Finally, the 1992 revisions deleted from earlier versions the requirement of "clear and convincing evidence" to justify efficiency claims by merging companies, a move viewed by the bar as signaling greater receptiveness to efficiency arguments. Late in the Clinton administration, the section of the Guidelines devoted to efficiencies was replaced with a more complete discussion of how the antitrust authorities evaluate efficiency claims. The Guidelines require claimed efficiencies to reverse the merger's potential to harm consumers, by, for example, preventing price increases after the merger. And merging companies claiming efficiencies must demonstrate that the efficiencies cannot be achieved by any practical means (technology licensing, for example) less anticompetitive than the merger at issue.

The changes to the Guidelines made it more difficult to rely on efficiencies to justify problematic mergers. The enforcement agencies grew skeptical of efficiency claims. In the end, the Chicago School's to-do about efficiencies amounted to much ado about very little. Economic research produced little to support widespread claims of efficiencies by merging companies. In fact, optimistic predictions of efficiencies by acquiring companies invariably turn out to be overstated.

The Guidelines deal mostly with the potential for price increases from anticompetitive mergers. None of the various iterations incorporated a methodology for evaluating the effect of a merger on future innovation in a market, mostly because academics could not come up with a precise way to correlate increases in market concentration with innovation. During the Clinton administration, two Antitrust Division officials proposed a procedure to identify "innovation markets" for merger analysis, but conservatives dismissed the approach, arguing that it would lead to a decline in the predictability of enforcement policy.

More recently, economists have explained how to analyze a merger's effect on innovation using a case-by-case approach, but only in a handful of deals has the outcome of a merger review been determined by innovation rather than price effects. Much like the drunk looking for his car keys under the lamppost where the light is better, as opposed to the dark area down the block where he actually lost them, merger review continues to turn on meticulous calculations of future prices, for no reason other than our nominal ability to predict them accurately, even in "Schumpeterian" markets that develop more through innovation than price.

Although successive versions of the Guidelines retained Baxter's complex methodology for defining a market and calculating concentration, by

1992 almost no one associated with merger review actually followed those steps. The 1992 revisions invited a more freewheeling qualitative competitive effects analysis, which one of the Guidelines' authors called "storytelling." In advising clients, lawyers frequently cut to the chase, asking bottom line questions about the merger's effect on prices, the likely customer reaction to the deal, and the true value of the deal to the merging companies in terms of reducing costs or raising prices. Courts continued to honor the presumption of anticompetitive effects from increased concentration, but gave the presumption far less weight. The antitrust enforcement agencies gave industry concentration even less consideration, especially in unilateral effects analysis.

Just about any approach sanctioned by the Guidelines should have condemned the West-Thomson deal. Because West and Thomson were the only providers of comprehensive systems for legal research, a "unilateral effects" analysis would have predicted higher prices for customers of the merged companies. The structure of the legal publishing market, with a few large providers and many small, poorly informed purchasers who buy on standard terms, also suggests a postmerger market conducive to coordination in which almost all suppliers, including those not party to the merger, can raise prices. And, even the old presumption of anticompetitive injury from untoward market concentration should have raised acute concerns.

Had the Antitrust Division lawyers really wanted to know what to expect from a West-Thomson merger, they need only have asked customers or taken note of the universal predictions of price increases. Customers had all the information necessary for a meaningful analysis of the merger— records of how they bought and used legal research, and their ability and willingness to substitute in the event of a price increase. As with many manifestly anticompetitive mergers, convoluted economic analysis obscured the obvious more than it revealed the truth.

The West brothers of Minnesota began publishing legal reports in the 1870s and gradually expanded their offerings into a national system of law reports in which particular opinions can be found by volume number and page number. At the time of the merger, West had a comprehensive retrospective database of court decisions. In fact, West published the only bound volumes of court decisions for the federal trial and appellate courts. In addition, West was the official case law publisher for court decisions in thirty-two states.

Over the years, West developed a detailed legal taxonomy—an index, so to speak, for tens of thousands of legal topics. West editors annotated the court decisions and other legal materials that the company published by preparing summaries with each important legal point keyed to the appropriate index topic. Court decisions in the United States are largely based on opinions in earlier cases with similar facts (what lawyers call precedent), so attorneys must be able to locate, review, and reference prior judicial decisions in order to represent their clients effectively. The West index made legal research easier and much more reliable. Once a lawyer identified a legal point of interest, she could search West's annotated, cross-referenced publications for opinions, statutes, and commentary on the same point.

Among print publishers, only Thomson Corporation provided any significant competition to West. Thomson started as a small Canadian newspaper publisher and grew into a multinational conglomerate. At the time of the merger, Thomson was West's only real challenger for selection as an "official" state publisher of legal opinions, having won that designation for six of the largest states in the country, including New York, California, and Illinois. Thomson also published annotated sets of federal statutes and Supreme Court opinions.

Thomson developed its own legal taxonomy, built around an integrated set of articles—known as American Law Reports, ALRs for short—that gathered and analyzed cases by subject area. A lawyer could use Thomson's publications as an alternative to West's. In fact, Thomson's collection of indexed, annotated, and cross-referenced judicial opinions, statutes, and commentaries represented West's only substantial competitor.

Thomson did not compete against West in the burgeoning market for online legal research. LexisNexis pioneered that market. The predecessor to LexisNexis started in business in Dayton, Ohio, in 1966 as a contractor to the U.S. Air Force. The Ohio State Bar hired the company to provide a text service and retrieval system for Ohio statutes. The business expanded rapidly and, in 1973, the company launched Lexis, the first commercial online legal research service. As the service grew to incorporate more and more court and legislative archives, lawyers could do all of their legal research without using bound volumes. West entered the market with its own online service a couple of years later.

Long before the commercialization of the Internet, my client gave me a tour of the Lexis network control room and computer center in Dayton. It looked like what I imagined the Strategic Air Command headquarters might look like. Control consoles sat on an elevated part of an enormous room. A huge video screen with a map of the United States covered the wall in back of the consoles. Down a couple of steps was a transparent wall that ran the width of the building, with what looked to be a hermetically sealed door, separating the control area from the computer equipment— mainframe computers, superminis, blocks of storage devices, all with lights blinking off and on, as far as my eyes could see.

The whole complex was built underground as a precaution against Midwestern tornadoes. Great, I thought. In the event of a devastating thermonuclear exchange with the Soviet Union, lawyers will still be able to cite-check their briefs.

The online business was purchased by an Anglo-Dutch publishing conglomerate in 1996 and officially named LexisNexis. At the time of the West-Thomson merger, several of the most important legal databases Lexis offered online were actually licensed from Thomson, as was the most vital feature for a successful online legal research service—a citator, the software product that enables a lawyer to quickly determine if a particular reference has been affirmed, overruled, or superseded and to find related points of law. LexisNexis offered a citator licensed from Thomson and based on the annotated set of Thomson legal articles. West offered its own citator.

When lawyers at the Antitrust Division first sat down to evaluate the competitive significance of Thomson's acquisition, they followed the conventional practice of looking for overlaps. They identified the products and services for which the two companies competed. At the behest of the merging parties, the government compared the two businesses, book title by book title. It is less clear whether the government lawyers ever stepped back to assess realistically whether combining the only two legal research systems would leave the industry without a challenger to West-Thomson that could offer a fully integrated set of products.

Instead, the division's antitrust review focused on analysis of the markets for particular books. "A treatise on torts is not a substitute for a treatise on contracts," one of Bingaman's deputies told *The American Lawyer*. Journalist John Morris drew a more telling conclusion: "In its microanalysis of competition, the government appears to have become obsessed with competing seedlings and overlooked how the giants of the forest can block out the light."

The Antitrust Division could not have missed the issue. Legal newspapers wrote editorials about it. Law librarians publicly criticized the deal in bar publications, filed written comments with the government, and demanded a face-to-face meeting with division lawyers. My partner Susan Creighton wrote a lengthy white paper for LexisNexis, explaining in detail the competing legal research systems and predicting the anticompetitive price increases the deal would inevitably produce.

The market dynamics looked so eerily familiar. Legal publishing manifested some of the same network effects found in high tech industries. Law students wanted to learn the research system most acceptable to the established law firms that would hire them upon graduation. Law schools wanted to teach what law firms wanted students to know. Law firms wanted the system in widest distribution with the most titles. Practicing lawyers wanted the security of knowing the system most likely to be accessible in the myriad of law libraries scattered around the country. Once a lawyer learned one system for legal research, she was less likely to want to take time to learn another one. And, once a law firm started buying a set of court decisions or a treatise from West, the firm became dependent on West for updates. In the face of a price increase, the law firm could not switch to another publisher, even if there was a competitor, without losing the value of the investment it had already made. The firm was "locked in."

Economist Brian Arthur argued early on that these interdependent economic conditions are pervasive in the economy, especially in markets with knowledge-based products. My experience with legal publishing seemed to confirm the point. Michael Kinsley's remark, half in jest, that Robert Bork's traditional Chicago School analysis "didn't apply in most real life situations," became less contestable with each passing day.

CHAPTER 15

Monopolizing the Law

In the United Kingdom, to this day and in perpetuity, the Queen's printer owns the copyright to the King James Bible. Owning the exclusive printing rights to the Bible is an easy way to make money. West never had a copyright for the Bible, but in this country it had the next best thing to heaven on earth—ownership of legal citations.

Lawyers identify judicial decisions by the names of the parties in a case, the volume of the official printed reporter (usually published by West) in which the decision is bound, and the page number of the volume on which the opinion starts. In addition to the number of the first page, court rules invariably require lawyers to note the specific page number of the bound volume on which a referenced legal point appears. When West compiled and bound volumes of court decisions for publication, the company decided more or less arbitrarily where to put page breaks within the printed text of each opinion. West permitted other publishers to reproduce the volume number and the starting page numbers of cases in its bound volumes, but West asserted exclusive ownership of all page numbers after the first one in an opinion, claiming copyright protection in the sequence and arrangement of its page breaks. As unbelievable as it may sound, West used the copyright law to charge other publishers a royalty for page numbers.

In 1986, long before the acquisition by Thomson, West convinced a federal trial court and then an appellate court to uphold its copyright claim and to enjoin LexisNexis from using the internal page numbers from the opinions West published. Lexis did not copy the opinions from West. Lexis compiled its own database of opinions, into which it inserted references to the official page numbers from the West bound volumes. Without them, the Lexis service had little value for legal research. After the court rulings, Lexis settled the case by taking a license from West and paying to use West's page breaks.

Publishers, enraged by the outcome of the court decisions upholding West's claims, demanded congressional action to cancel West's copyright. A hearing was convened in 1992 at which a senior Thomson executive testified that West's monopoly position in the legal publishing industry "has forced librarians and others to pay tens of millions in monopoly charges for access to legal texts, and has deprived users of the improved choices, quality and timeliness that competition could have provided." In response, a West executive invoked the specter of "Lord Thomson and his foreign-based conglomerate" trying to profit "at the expense of American jobs and prosperity." In all, the West executive referred to Thomson's "foreign" origin a total of five times and its threat to "American jobs" twice in one short paragraph of testimony. Congress took no action. A Justice Department investigation two years later fizzled after an informal inquiry from the Clinton White House.

Two years after that, during the negotiations between the merging parties and the Department of Justice, Thomson offered what it trumpeted as a key concession. The merged company would not only sell off an agreed list of overlapping publications, it would also license West's page numbers on standard terms at capped rates. With that "sweetener" the Antitrust Division's staff okayed the deal and sent it to Anne Bingaman, who signed off a couple of weeks later, giving ownership of the U.S. "monopolist" to the "foreign-based conglomerate" that was trying to profit "at the expense of American jobs and prosperity."

The concessions turned out to be illusory. None of the small publishers could afford the stated rates offered by West-Thomson for licensing page numbers. And the list of divested titles drew sarcastic remarks in the press. "I was really surprised by how few publications they were forced to divest. . . . I just looked at the list and laughed. . . . I mean, BFD," the librarian at a large New York law firm told *The American Lawyer*. Worst yet, the overlapping titles did not have to be sold to a single publisher, meaning that the market might well be left with only fragmented competition to oppose the West-Thomson juggernaut.

The agreement approving the deal contained a couple of concessions intended to maintain the viability of LexisNexis as a competitor. First, Thomson agreed to sell off the citator LexisNexis used. But the agreement did not specify that the product would be sold to LexisNexis. Nor did Thomson commit to divesting the taxonomy and integrated set of articles on which the citator was based. Thomson also agreed to extend several of its database licenses to LexisNexis for an additional period of five years. After that, LexisNexis would have to find comparable content from other sources to remain competitive.

A Thomson executive candidly described to the press his company's reaction to the settlement: "I wouldn't use the word 'overjoyed.' But 'elated' would be fair," he said. Taking his cue from Bill Gates, he added, "I mean they gave up nothing." Thomson secured the government's permission to raise the cost of legal representation for everyone in America.

In 1971, Richard Nixon's Justice Department agreed to settle a Clayton Act suit filed two years earlier over the acquisition of an insurance company by ITT (International Telephone and Telegraph), an international conglomerate. The settlement, negotiated by Deputy Attorney General Richard Kleindienst, contained far less relief than the complaint in the case originally sought. The settlement required ITT to divest a few of the insurance company's subsidiaries but otherwise permitted ITT to proceed with the acquisition.

During subsequent confirmation hearings of Kleindienst to become attorney general, Brit Hume, then a researcher for muckraker Jack Anderson, broke a news story that linked the settlement of the suit to a $400,000 contribution to help finance the 1972 Republican National Convention. The quid pro quo was never proven, but Kleindienst later pleaded guilty to a misdemeanor for failing to tell the Senate hearing that Nixon told him to settle the ITT case.

The public spectacle surrounding the Kleindienst nomination prompted California senator John Tunney to sponsor a bill to insulate the government settlement process from corporate influence. Legislators' concerns extended well beyond the ITT case. After all, most antitrust complaints initiated by the government never got to trial. Eighty percent were settled by an agreement known as a "consent decree," the legal label for a contract filed in court between the government and the accused parties to specify terms for ending a case.

The negotiated settlement of a government antitrust case prior to a complete adjudication in court may well benefit the public. If the government gets effective relief through settlement more quickly and cheaply than after a full trial, limited enforcement resources can be applied to additional competition problems. But as the consent decree came to be the most prevalent antitrust remedy in federal civil enforcement, few safeguards protected the public against "sweetheart" settlements that left the issues raised by antitrust complaints largely unremedied. Supreme Court precedent actively discouraged trial courts from questioning the terms of government antitrust settlements, absent evidence of bad faith or malfeasance. In passing the Tunney Act, Congress rejected the notion that the courts should defer to the executive branch when evaluating the terms of an antitrust settlement.

The Tunney Act breezed through Congress and was signed into law. It imposes specific rules guaranteeing public notification of antitrust settlements, the opportunity for third parties to comment on those settlements, and judicial review of the agreements themselves. Under the Tunney Act, the court in which the complaint is filed must determine whether the settlement is in the public interest before making it official. According to the legislative debates over the statute, Congress increased scrutiny of settlements to prevent the Department of Justice from "knuckling under" to corporate interests by accepting ineffective settlements, not just to prevent payoffs and other types of outright corruption.

A federal judge cleared Bill Baxter's negotiated breakup of AT&T under Tunney Act procedures, but application of the law was limited until Judge Stanley Sporkin threw out Anne Bingaman's settlement with Microsoft. When the court of appeals reversed Sporkin's decision, the appellate judges not only disqualified Sporkin from the case, they limited the statute so dramatically as to make it almost meaningless.

The opinion by neoconservative judge Laurence Silberman ruled that a trial judge in a Tunney Act proceeding can evaluate the remedy negotiated by the government only by comparing it to the charges filed in the complaint. A court has no business worrying about unremedied competitive injury in a market that the complaint does not address, Silberman held. So, if the government first negotiates a narrow cosmetic remedy for anticompetitive conduct and then files a narrow complaint tailored specifically to that remedy, a Tunney Act court would have little alternative but to approve the settlement.

Just for good measure, Judge Silberman held that the "public interest" language of the statute didn't really mean what it said. As long as the remedy is "within the reaches of the public interest," meaning presumably that if the remedy does anything beneficial at all, it must be upheld.

Even with all the limitations on Tunney Act review imposed by Judge Silberman, the West-Thomson settlement still had to be filed in and approved by a federal court, giving me the opportunity to challenge the deal. By this time, Anne Bingaman had resigned, yet Joel Klein continued to defend the settlement in court as if he had approved it himself.

Mindful of the strictures imposed by Judge Silberman's *Microsoft* opinion, the brief we submitted tied our objections directly to the complaint the government filed against the West-Thomson merger, along with its proposed consent decree. The government's complaint recognized the potential for competitive injury in markets for enhanced legal products—publications annotated with summaries of points of law and cross-referenced to legal taxonomies, relevant court decisions, and secondary sources. Having identified the problem, we argued, the remedy did little to correct it. The settlement required Thomson to sell off some of its minor publications, but Thomson was permitted to keep its principal enhancement, ALR. After the merger, the surviving company would control both major sets of enhancements and the two systems used for legal research. The consent decree also required Thomson to divest the citator on which LexisNexis relied, but, again, Thomson was permitted to retain control of the enhancements that kept the citator current.

At the oral argument over the settlement, the Antitrust Division attorney detailed the government's investigation and gave short shrift to all of our challenges. When he talked about how hard the government worked on the merger investigation, he sounded like he was reading from the notes Anne Bingaman used in front of Judge Sporkin. "We interviewed over the course of this over 100 people. . . . We did 25 depositions. Reviewed about 230 boxes of documents." I kept waiting for him to pound the podium and shout about sweating "blood, blood, blood."

"This is garden variety merger practice," he told the judge. "We negotiated a consent decree and this as well is garden variety merger practice. This decree solves the problems that [were] found in the investigation. . . . The relief contained in the decree is garden variety relief."

The government attorney categorically rejected the potential for unremedied competitive injury from the acquisition. "In particular, we looked at the question of whether there is a case for divesting ALR or a case based on competition between two competing legal systems. We evaluated that question extensively and very carefully and decided not to bring that case. . . . [T]he question of what case the government should bring is a question that's inappropriate in a Tunney Act proceeding," he concluded.

My turn came next. Before the hearing, I spent a lot of time thinking about how to show the judge that, notwithstanding the divestitures, Thomson was getting to keep control of everything that mattered. I carried with me to the podium one of the volumes from a title Thomson was supposed to sell under the consent decree.

"Now the government states that Thomson is making a divestiture of this . . . product," I said, holding up the book, "but in point of fact all these enhancements in the back, the ALR's, the comprehensive legal descriptions described and identified in the complaint, Thomson gets to keep."

With that preamble, I opened the book and in a single dramatic motion tore out one hundred bound pages of annotations and put them on the desk of Thomson's legal team. Then I pointed to and tore out of the bound volume the many pages of cross-references at the beginning of the reported decisions, stacking up the pages neatly in front of Thomson's lawyers.

Actually, fearful of looking like a wimp in open court if I couldn't tear apart a bound book, I had the pages cut out of the binding ahead of time, and placed back into the cover with Velcro. When I pulled the pages out in front of the judge, it made a loud tearing sound. The legal press covering the argument loved the display. The judge smiled, but only slightly.

I pointed to the statement from a Thomson executive printed in *The American Lawyer* about giving up "nothing" in the divestiture negotiations.

The judge interrupted me.

"This isn't evidence in the case, is it? . . . There have been depositions by the Government. Has anybody ever probed with this person what he meant, what the basis of it was, and to what extent should a Court give that sort of anonymous statement any credence?"

I waited for the Antitrust Division's lawyer to answer. He said nothing. Plainly, the government had never asked anyone at Thomson about the statement. Yet the judge showed no frustration with the government, so I moved on to my next point. Under its contract with Lexis, Thomson couldn't sell off its citator piecemeal, without selling all of the associated business and assets to the same purchaser. The contract was intended to ensure that Lexis always had a reliable vendor that would keep the citator current. The consent decree purported to override the contract and permit Thomson to sell off the citator without any of the assets on which it was based.

"It's as if a local government were having a dispute with a landowner, a big landowner that proposed to build a high rise property and the building of the high rise would require the moving of a public roadway," I explained. "If the local government and the high rise owner resolve their differences by simply putting the highway right through the middle of my house without giving me any compensation for that, it's an illegal taking."

Even Judge Silberman's *Microsoft* opinion recognized the importance of third-party rights, I said, putting up a poster with a blowup of the quote from the case. "Here's Judge Silberman's holding: 'Certainly if third parties contend they would be positively injured by the decree, a district judge might well hesitate before assuming the decree is appropriate.'" I paused for emphasis.

"What am I supposed to do after I hesitate?" asked the judge. The article about the argument published in the legal press said that the judge asked the question "with a smirk." That's how it looked to me.

"I think under the holding of United States versus Microsoft you're not supposed to approve the decree unless we're compensated for the taking," I said. The judge said nothing. He wasn't going to take issue with the government's decision.

When the judge published his opinion approving the consent decree, he required only what amounted to a minor modification in the licensing terms for West page numbers. "The Court finds that the government was reasonable in concluding that divestiture of [Thomson's entire system] is unnecessary," the opinion read. "[U]nder *Microsoft*, the Court will not second-guess these reasonable conclusions."

As to our argument that the decree would permit Thomson to break its contractual obligation to sell all the businesses and assets related to the citator together, the judge told us to go peddle our papers to some other court. "If Lexis-Nexis still believes that it has not received the full benefit of its contract, it may pursue a contract remedy in an appropriate court."

So that's what we did. We filed suit for an injunction in Dayton, Ohio, where LexisNexis was headquartered. Thomson tried to get the case dismissed, or at least delayed, but the Dayton judge granted our motion to expedite the proceedings. At that point, we were invited by Thomson and the Department of Justice to negotiate. Thomson agreed to sell all the divested properties together to LexisNexis, which had submitted the highest bid. LexisNexis agreed to drop its suit and release Thomson from antitrust liability for the merger. The government agreed not to object to any of this, provided LexisNexis passed the normal inspection for divestiture buyers. But no matter how hard we tried, we couldn't get the government to require that Thomson sell its ALRs and system of cross-references, along with the citator.

Although the judge thought LexisNexis could do just fine with Thomson owning the business and properties on which the citator was based, LexisNexis's management thought otherwise. No rational business executive would rely on a product that depended for viability on the goodwill of an arch-competitor. "If you let this deal go through the way it is," one LexisNexis senior manager told the lead government lawyer on the case, "we're going to have to buy Shepard's." Shepard's was a citator product owned by an independent company.

"In fact," the Lexis manager continued, "just to stay competitive, we're going to have to buy a lot of companies." He ran through a list of a half-dozen companies, virtually all of the remaining legal publishers of any size still in the market. "And I don't want to hear a peep from the Department of Justice," he said, looking the government lawyer squarely in the eye.

"Okay," said the government lawyer.

Hmm, I thought. Central planning of the legal publishing industry by a Justice Department lawyer. Of course, without the Lexis acquisitions, the merged company would not have faced any real competition.

We all shook hands and the government filed a two-page motion for court approval of the final settlement. The judge was taken by surprise. "One of the things that flows from the decision to sell off everything to Lexis," he said at a subsequent hearing, "is that all of the myriad issues that have been written about [by] other commentators, argued in *amicus* briefs and everything, that there's no one left to challenge either the process that the Justice Department or the Court has gone through or the decisions that have been made with respect to this consent decree because the Justice Department and all the States agree to everything or don't object and you don't even have Mr. Reback around to argue."

I couldn't believe my ears. I was getting chastised by a judge for not appealing a decision in which he ruled against me.

"I lost on those issues here," I said in response, "but I did do what Your Honor suggested in [his] opinion which is that we resorted to self help and we sued Thomson in Dayton." As a consequence of our actions, I said, LexisNexis secured all the divested products, which was a first step toward preventing Thomson from monopolizing the industry. "The States have sought assurances from us that we will support employees, that we will support publications," I explained. "I think the Court will acknowledge that it would be very hard for a small publisher to give the kind of assurance to the State of California that we can give."

The judge still wasn't satisfied. "I may have ruled against you, but you were there raising the banner for what you thought was the public interest and the issues that were important to you. . . . I obviously feel that my opinion is right . . . and I think it's consistent with the Microsoft opinion but I also think it's important for someone to be doing what you did in Microsoft in the Court of Appeals which is to try and persuade the Court of Appeals that maybe there are some points that the Justice Department wasn't aggressive enough on or that the Court wasn't aggressive enough on."

Very flattering, I thought. But my job is to protect my client. The Justice Department and the court are supposed to protect the public. Besides, by keeping a second big competitor in the market, the settlement I engineered helped the public far more than what the court approved. I made the point somewhat more politely. "In my view this settlement is far more in the public interest . . . than what was contemplated in the proposed final judgment."

The judge did not disagree. He stopped criticizing me. "You notice I even took your suggestion . . . from Microsoft," he said.

What in the world was he talking about?

"I hesitated," he said with a slight smile. Or was it a smirk?

"Yes, Your Honor," I replied, finding my seat.

With that, the judge approved the final settlement agreement. No one ever appealed the judge's decision. I withdrew to Hawaii to lick my wounds.

Within a few days of the brief phone conversation from my hotel room, CNN released a story reporting that the owner of West channeled $155,000 in political contributions to eight state parties. *Time* magazine followed ten days later, listing $329,000 in contributions to ten state parties. Even the venerable *ABA Journal* reported the story.

The transcript of Joel Klein's confirmation hearing contains no questions from senators of either party about clearance of the West-Thomson deal.

———

After the merger, the legal publishing industry might well have been left with a single large vendor, but Reed Elsevier, Lexis's parent company, decided to move aggressively. Rather than try to compete with what it had, a weak position in a market dominated by Thomson, LexisNexis bought Shepard's, the citator service, and then invested millions of dollars adding editorial features and expanding coverage to make the product more directly comparable, some would say superior, to the West-Thomson citator. In order to replace the titles Thomson withdrew after the merger, Lexis-Nexis bought other legal publishers, completing its retrospective databases and its offering of treatises and other secondary legal materials. And Lexis-Nexis hired four hundred editors to write annotations and compile cross-references.

Eventually the legal publishing industry got back to two comprehensive systems of annotations and cross-references for legal research. But the competitive dynamic in the industry has changed. Two, rather than three, companies dominate the industry. Most of the smaller publishers have been acquired or eliminated. Although some Chicago School proponents, starting with Robert Bork, argue for less merger enforcement by claiming that markets with only two suppliers nevertheless produce competitive prices, the West-Thomson merger (and the economics literature) teaches otherwise. A market with two dominant suppliers will support tacit price coordination far more easily than a market with three large suppliers and a competitive fringe of many smaller niche players.

By acquiring West, Thomson eliminated its closest competitor. By moving its products from LexisNexis to the West online service, Thomson raised the costs of the only remaining company in the market that could mount a significant competitive challenge. LexisNexis's subsequent acquisitions, editorial growth, and product improvement came at great expense—billions of dollars. Potential acquisition targets understood Lexis's pressing need for high-quality titles and demanded extraordinary premiums, which Lexis had little choice but to pay.

Thomson *could* have exploited the high costs and more general vulnerability of its key competitor by slashing prices in an attempt to run Lexis-Nexis out of the market. But that's not what a rational company in Thomson's position *would* do. Provoking LexisNexis's huge and well-funded parent company in a price war would hardly maximize Thomson's profit. Better to let LexisNexis set its prices at the high level necessary for it to make a profit, leaving Thomson free to price the more widely established products it acquired from West at comparable or even higher price levels without loss of its dominant market share. By raising its rival's costs, Thomson maximized its own profits, injuring consumers in the process, but without really hurting LexisNexis all that much.

Even the successful market expansion by LexisNexis failed to stem dramatic price increases. The West-Thomson merger had precisely the effect that everyone, other than Thomson, the Justice Department, and the judge, predicted it would. Prices for print publications soared. Thomson started putting fewer pages into each West volume of court cases and charging more for the books. Price increases for West publications following the Thomson takeover exceeded both the rate of inflation and the rate of increases for prices in the legal publishing industry more generally. One study documented a price increase of over 70 percent for "value added" legal publications (books with supplements) in the four years following the merger.

Prices for online legal research also climbed astronomically. Thomson raises rates to private firms each year. In each of the recent years, Thomson's charges for online legal research in the West databases have increased roughly 7 percent. To search the comprehensive West database for state and federal decisions now costs more than $17 *per minute*. The federal minimum wage, by contrast, is about $7 an hour. In addition, both Thomson and LexisNexis started charging law schools for online legal research, originally provided free of charge. Last year the annual rate increase to law school librarians was roughly 7 percent, breaking the budget of many university law libraries.

"They are egregious in their approach," one law librarian said of West in the *National Law Journal*, "buying everything in sight and squeezing us, and we are powerless to do anything." Another librarian compared West's conduct to familiar Microsoft competitive strategies. "We buy things and they tie other stuff to it and say there is no way to separate the service you want from the other service you end up paying premium prices for," he complained.

So who cares if lawyers get charged too much for legal research? Lawyers are hardly a sympathetic constituency. Most people would like to see lawyers make less money. But the truth is, the exorbitant overcharges for legal research don't really hurt lawyers. The overcharges hurt everybody else.

At big firms that represent corporations and wealthy individuals, legal research charges are passed through as disbursements (in addition to hourly billing fees) for payment in full by the client. Perhaps at the margin, if the client objects to the total amount of the legal bill, the law firm's partners might feel some pressure on their profits from the excessive legal research charges. In the usual case, the research charges are paid without incident.

Lawyers who represent small businesses and ordinary people with everyday legal problems, on the other hand, face real constraints. Most clients can't afford a lot of research at $17 a minute. As a consequence, many lawyers shortchange their research to avoid bankrupting their clients. Case citations go unchecked. Comprehensive investigation is curtailed. Turning over every stone in search of legal authority gives way to pushing around a few pebbles. People who go to lawyers for problems like contested divorces, unfair employment terminations, insurance disputes, and other kinds of lawsuits pay the price for insufficient competition in the quality of the legal representation they receive.

The Antitrust Division and the federal judge who reviewed the merger could have easily prevented this outcome by blocking the transaction. Fixing the problem now by, for example, dismantling the merged company under Section 2 of the Sherman Act entails costs like those involved in the proposed breakup of Microsoft—restructuring an integrated product offering, reassigning thousands of employees, and licensing software products and legal search systems under compulsory licensing terms. Yet few more attractive alternatives present themselves.

High prices have induced some market entry. A few years ago, a large European publisher bought a small Internet-based supplier of case law, statutes, and other legal information, raising the prospect of greater competition in the online market. That service still lacks a citator and annotations, so its utility is limited and its market share remains small. Bloomberg, a large provider of business and financial news data, also entered the market, but has yet to register appreciable market share. Perhaps Google will extend its databases to legal materials. None of these actual and potential entrants has restrained the ability of the incumbent firms to charge high prices.

The legal publishing merger aside, Joel Klein had some success in restoring a measure of integrity to the Antitrust Division's merger review process. Klein's office blocked a series of high-profile mergers—between Lockheed Martin and Northrup Grumman in the aerospace industry, between WorldCom and Sprint in telecommunications, and between Northwest and Continental in the airline industry. But the lessons Larry Ellison learned from the Microsoft settlement scuttled the Bush administration's intentions for merger enforcement.

CHAPTER 16

A Hostage Taking

On June 2, 2003, PeopleSoft announced that it had reached a definitive agreement to merge with J. D. Edwards, a Colorado company, creating the world's second-largest enterprise application software company, and displacing Oracle from that position. Oracle had suffered through a difficult three years. Oracle's market share for large enterprise applications—complicated software used by the biggest corporations for financial transactions and personnel management—was declining, along with the company's application revenue.

The growing success of PeopleSoft, Oracle's closest competitor in the business application markets, accounted for Oracle's decline. Oracle's own bid data showed that it was losing head-to-head customer sales opportunities against PeopleSoft far more often than it was winning. Oracle's position had deteriorated dangerously over the preceding three quarters. Customers publicly criticized Oracle's applications and support, and even the company itself, while lavishing praise on PeopleSoft and its products. Eighty-five percent of Oracle's customers indicated in a survey in the summer of 2003 that they would pick a different vendor at their next purchasing opportunity.

Oracle could have responded simply by addressing customer complaints. But after reflecting on what he saw as Bill Gates's successful attempts to keep the fruits of illegal predatory conduct, Oracle's CEO, Larry Ellison, decided to use the financial markets and the legal process to achieve competitive success for his company.

Only four days after news of the PeopleSoft-Edwards merger became public, Oracle announced a hostile tender offer for control of PeopleSoft. PeopleSoft was hardly a failing company in need of rescue. Its products were widely adopted by the world's largest automotive companies, the world's largest retailing enterprises, the world's largest pharmaceutical companies, the world's largest financial services companies, the world's largest manufacturing concerns, and many other global enterprises, as well as agencies of the federal and state governments. Its star was in ascent; its market share was increasing, largely at Oracle's expense.

From an antitrust perspective, the tender offer was absurd: the deal would eliminate the industry's most innovative and aggressive competitor, reducing the number of qualified vendors for business software to many large businesses from three to two, and in some cases, to one—Oracle alone. Most at risk were cash-strapped state and local governments and divisions of the federal government, like the Department of Defense, and the nation's leading educational institutions.

None of this mattered to Larry Ellison. He had his prey in the cross-hairs, and he had to know, from his experience in the industry, that putting the perception of PeopleSoft's long-term viability at issue would grievously damage the company. Large businesses would no more install financial management software from a vendor of questionable long-term viability than a heart patient would submit to the insertion of a pacemaker from a company with a clouded future.

Ellison raised issues of PeopleSoft's viability at every turn. PeopleSoft "cannot compete in this business over the long term," the *Daily Deal* quoted Ellison as saying, "with or without us, I don't believe PeopleSoft can survive." PeopleSoft's "business has been deteriorating for some time," Ellison boasted to a securities conference. "Whatever the numbers say, their real business is actually going to deteriorate for some time." Ellison did whatever he could to fulfill his prophecy that PeopleSoft's business was "going to deteriorate." He dispatched his sales minions to destabilize PeopleSoft's customer relationships, apparently to damage the very asset he sought to acquire. "We all recognize a need to target PSFT customers," read one Oracle internal message.

Oracle's vice president of analyst relations took stock of the strategy in an internal e-mail right after the announcement of the tender offer. "We've certainly wounded PSFT," she wrote to other executives. "Even if we don't end up closing the deal, this is going to take PSFT time to recover. . . . I dunno about you guys, but today I was very proud to be an Oracle employee."

"This isn't a takeover," observed one hedge-fund manager. "It's a hostage taking." Before it was over, thousands of employees would lose their jobs. Billions of dollars would change hands. Antitrust enforcement would teeter on the edge of extinction. And the lawyers of the once-proud Antitrust Division would retreat to Washington, exhausted and demoralized, unable to enforce the division's own Merger Guidelines.

I once gave a talk on the perils of cross-examining Larry Ellison. Not that I've ever had the chance. In fact, he was once my client. In the early 1980s, Oracle called me in to help the company solve some sticky software distribution issues in Europe. Ellison's company made software to automate the storage, retrieval, and analysis of data. The technology revolutionized corporate America. By the time I first met Ellison, the government was using his small company's product to pilot the space shuttle.

Born in 1944 to an unwed teenager in New York City, Ellison almost died before his first birthday when he contracted pneumonia. At his mother's request, he was given up for adoption to his grandmother's sister and her husband, Lillian and Louis Ellison, of Chicago's South Shore. Larry Ellison grew up in the family's two-bedroom apartment in a lower-middle-class neighborhood. He told *60 Minutes* that he had "all the disadvantages required for success," including a remote, dismissive, and scornful adoptive father, who assured the boy at every opportunity that he would never amount to anything.

After a year or so at the University of Illinois and a brief stint at the University of Chicago, Ellison moved, sans college degree, to northern California. He worked briefly at Amdahl Corporation, a maker of big IBM-compatible business computers, and then for Ampex, a company in the business of audio and video data storage. At Ampex, Ellison assisted on a data storage project for the CIA, code-named Oracle. He learned to program mostly on the job, although he had some exposure to computers in college.

In 1977, Ellison and two friends formed a small company to do software contracting jobs. Ellison's big break came when he read some technical papers published by an IBM researcher about a new way to organize computer data. IBM dominated the market for big computers, known as mainframes. When the company, to avoid antitrust issues, spawned the software industry by unbundling its programs from its hardware, IBM quickly came to control the lion's share of the market for programs mainframes ran to store and retrieve data, like purchase orders, employee records, and financial documents.

The IBM software programs, called database management systems, or just databases, organized data hierarchically, by headings and subheadings, the way a student might outline a term paper. To a lay person, a database looks more or less like a big file cabinet, with documents organized behind tabs in each drawer. The IBM programs permitted a user to start from the top drawer and look through the tab labels to find records on a particular subject. But there was no easy way to get at information on the records if that information was not specifically referenced in the hierarchy headings.

A hierarchical database could provide a quick answer to questions identified in advance. Once data was organized in a particular hierarchy, answering new questions about the records proved difficult. If a year into a product cycle, for example, a vendor wanted to direct its sales personnel toward customers that used a product feature initially thought unimportant, each record in the database had to be examined, one at a time, in search of the relevant information.

The IBM papers Ellison read described a new computer language (known by its initials SQL, or phonetically, "sequel") to better organize and retrieve information. Despite the technical advances, IBM's business managers believed the new approach ("relational" management) could not be developed commercially because it was too slow and, beyond that, IBM didn't want to push a technology that would undercut the existing market for its hierarchical program. So it back-burnered the breakthrough its own lab produced. Had the monopolist bothered to suppress publication of the research, the business community might still be using obsolete technology.

Ellison seized on the new idea. He saw it as a superior technological design that IBM would in time adopt. Few shared his vision. He couldn't get venture capital to finance the development of a new database product, so for two years his company did contract jobs for computer firms just to support itself. Ellison mortgaged his house to keep the company going. When the lender filed to foreclose, a venture capitalist gave Ellison a loan. Finally, in 1979, with his company close to insolvency, Ellison sold his first relational database. Some accounts say Ellison's first customer was the technology division of an air force base in California. Ellison says the CIA was his first customer.

In any case, Ellison made the right bet. The SQL design performed well. IBM introduced its first SQL product a few years later but it ran only on a limited line of computers. IBM eventually converted its flagship mainframe database to SQL, endorsing the standard and pressing the industry to follow suit. By the time the industry's technical committee of hardware vendors embraced SQL, Ellison was already a multimillionaire. He had beaten IBM to market with its own technology standard.

Ellison's first few customers used different computers made by different vendors. One early government customer wanted the database to run on an IBM mainframe. Another customer preferred newer midsize computers made by IBM's competitors. Known as minicomputers, these new machines represented the first step toward the modern personal computer. Ellison designed a "cross-platform" database as a concession to these customer demands. Oracle's code implementation made sophisticated database technology available on minicomputers, fueling their market penetration. IBM didn't offer its leading database for any computer smaller than a mainframe until 1993, by which time Oracle was already well established in the market. Ellison owned the "killer app" for the new generation of computing.

Although Ellison was one of the first to adopt the SQL standard, the emerging database market attracted many entrants, including Microsoft, which acquired a product originally made by another company. Ellison bested most of his competitors, largely through aggressive and controversial sales techniques. According to even sympathetic accounts of Oracle's growth, the company signed on customers using grandiose promises of product availability and performance that ultimately proved false. Eventually, the market came down to IBM and Oracle for the most sophisticated database deployments, joined by an ever-more-competitive Microsoft for somewhat smaller businesses.

In the mid-range computer market, no single vendor of operating systems had anything like the kind of control Microsoft exerted over the personal computer market. Midsize computers ran many different operating systems, but Oracle's database worked with well-nigh all of them. So the database, rather than the operating system, became the platform on which sophisticated data-intensive applications for business management—so-called back office applications—were based.

Oracle started offering its own back office applications in 1977. The company's suite of products for managing corporate finance, including bookkeeping, payments and receipts, and tax records, quickly came to dominate that sector of the industry. Ellison designed Oracle's back office applications to work only with the Oracle database.

Oracle's success made Larry Ellison one of the richest people on the planet. The company went public in 1986 with $55 million in annual revenues. Two decades later, Oracle's annual revenues push $15 billion. On the twentieth anniversary of the company's public offering, Ellison reminded everyone that a $10,000 investment in the IPO would have grown to be worth more than $4 million.

In 1987, Ellison bought an expensive estate in Atherton, California, and renovated it in the Japanese style, complete with sliding shoji screen doors, a koi pond, and hand-painted wooden cabinets. He decorated the house with Japanese art and rare historical objects, including samurai helmets and armor. Once a year, he threw a party at his house for Oracle executives and their guests. Everyone dutifully assembled in the Japanese gardens, trying to make cheerful conversation. After a time, Ellison, in traditional Japanese attire, emerged from behind the sliding screens to converse with his guests. "Worst night of the year," a former Oracle employee once told me.

Oracle's success prompted Ellison to move his company to a newly constructed corporate campus studded with sparkling emerald-colored glass towers so striking that they were used as the set of a futuristic Robin Williams film. Valley wags called the place "LarryLand." Oracle employees called their CEO "his Larryness," at least behind his back. Ellison's biographer, Mike Wilson, rephrased a well-known Valley punch line for the name of his book—*The Difference Between God and Larry Ellison: God Doesn't Think He's Larry Ellison.*

Ellison always seemed obsessed by Bill Gates and his company. Microsoft and Oracle started at about the same time and went public within days of each other. From the end of Microsoft's first day of public trading, except for one month in 2002, Gates's net worth exceeded Ellison's. Ellison has never gotten over it. In just about every interview, Ellison talks about Microsoft, which he calls "the most important company on Earth."

According to Valley lore, Ellison once showed Gates around Ellison's Japanese-style estate. Gates made it clear that he was building an even bigger home. Not to be outdone, Ellison traded up. He bought a 23-acre site to replace the 3-acre embarrassment. He dismantled and relocated the historic 1913 house on the site that was designed by a famed architect who built a castle near San Simeon for William Randolph Hearst. In its place, Ellison constructed ten separate buildings, including an 8,000-square-foot Japanese-style main residence, a replica of a historic Japanese tearoom, a guesthouse, a moon parlor, 3.2 acres of ponds, two cascading waterfalls, and two bridges, all supported by almost four thousand tons of hand-chiseled Chinese granite. The construction moved enough earth to raise a football field forty-five feet in the air. I was trying to buy a tree to plant in my front yard at the time, but Ellison's landscaper had raided every nursery all the way to the northern border of Oregon, in search of the more than five hundred mature trees needed for the project.

A *New York Times* reporter called the estate "a $40 million conceit." It actually cost about $200 million.

Not without personal virtues, Ellison, by his own account, has given more than half a billion dollars to charity. When his ex-wife's parents fell ill, Ellison bought them a house. Yet he is better known for parsimony and small-mindedness. He challenged the county's high tax assessment for his estate, claiming the property suffered from "significant functional obsolescence," owing to the limited appeal for sixteenth-century Japanese architecture. The tax refund he won cost the county's financially strained public schools almost $1.4 million. Ellison's local school district scrambled to compensate for the loss by cutting six positions from its staff.

Then there was Ellison's dispute with San Jose's airport authority. The airport issued a written reprimand to Ellison for landing one of his private jets in violation of the 11:30 p.m. noise curfew. Ellison kept doing it. The airport authority issued more reprimands, so Ellison sued the airport, claiming a curfew based on airplane weight was "unreasonably discriminatory." A judge agreed. In addition to getting the right to fly late at night, Ellison learned what turned out to be a valuable lesson. By stubborn perseverance, he could outlast the government and get his way.

Ellison's wealth, lifestyle, and ego attracted considerable attention in Silicon Valley. But what really set him apart from his peers was his proclivity for firing associates. Not those who performed poorly. Ellison became famous for firing his most successful lieutenants. The Valley's favorite explanation: Ellison can't bear to share the limelight.

Among the casualties of Ellison's management style was Craig Conway. Conway's résumé earned him major credibility in Silicon Valley's world of self-made men. Conway's family home growing up was a house trailer. His father's occupation: elevator operator. Conway's father started college late in his twenties and wound up as a regional manager in the construction industry, moving the family every two years as projects were completed and new ones started. Conway's mother, an émigré from Sudan, met Conway's father when he was stationed in Africa serving in the military during the Korean War.

Urged on by his parents and despite their modest means, Conway graduated from the State University of New York with a double major in mathematics and computer science. After college, he migrated to northern California and held positions at some of the pioneering firms in the Valley, including Atari and Digital Research. He was recruited to Oracle in 1985.

Conway started in operations and worked his way up to vice president of sales and marketing, before leaving the company. By one account, Ellison's next-in-command fired Conway because Conway was such a demanding, detail-oriented micromanager that he alienated people. Conway says he left of his own accord when his path to Oracle's presidency became clouded.

There is no dispute about Conway's career after Oracle. First he took over an Internet start-up, grew the company, took it public, and sold it to Cisco for more than $100 million. Then he joined a failing interactive broadcast network. He overhauled the company, restored its business, and sold it to Hughes Network Systems, cementing his reputation as a turnaround specialist. Conway was ready to return to the big time and PeopleSoft needed him in the worst way.

Dave Duffield, a serial entrepreneur, founded PeopleSoft. Duffield started his career at IBM but left to form a company that made a payroll system for the University of Rochester. Then he moved to human resources software—programs that help companies recruit, manage, and compensate employees. He started a successful company to make human resources software for mainframe computers. After taking the company public, Duffield tried to redirect the company toward the growing client-server market, computer networks built around personal computers. When the company's board of directors refused to support his plans, Duffield resigned to start PeopleSoft, which he financed with a mortgage on his house.

Duffield scored a bull's-eye. His company grew at 80 to 90 percent a year, taking the leadership position in human resources software for big businesses ("large enterprises," as they are known in the industry). Duffield launched a set of large enterprise software products for financial management in competition with Oracle and several other companies and took PeopleSoft public in 1992. Then he expanded into the market for software that helps large enterprises work collaboratively with their suppliers to control spending. PeopleSoft roared through the 1990s. *Fortune* magazine recognized it as one of the fastest-growing companies in America four years running. But by the end of the decade, Duffield's management style caught up with his company.

The polar opposite of many Silicon Valley entrepreneurs, Duffield was kind, considerate, modest, and understated to a fault. He never talked to the press. He set up a $200 million fund in memory of his beloved miniature schnauzer to save unwanted house pets. He coddled his employees and they adored him. They came to work in shorts and Hawaiian shirts, and brought their pets. Twice he invited all of them to spend a weekend at his summerhouse on Lake Tahoe. Duffield signed all of his memoranda with his initials, "DAD."

PeopleSoft, even as a public company, held no patents. Duffield, like many in Silicon Valley's first wave, believed it wrong to claim ownership of intellectual property, which should be free for everyone's use. His company employed no secretaries. He didn't believe in them either. Or in receptionists. As CEO, Duffield answered his own phone and worked from a cubicle.

Customers paid their bills more or less when they wanted to. People-Soft had no collections department, nor did it have a budget. When global economic issues reduced the demand for PeopleSoft's products, profits flattened, the stock price tanked, and employees started getting laid off.

Enter Craig Conway, hired initially as president and quickly promoted to CEO. Conway put rules and procedures into place. He slashed some projects to focus on an Internet implementation of PeopleSoft's product. Conway's demanding, meticulous, hands-on management style was not for everyone. In his first nine months, PeopleSoft lost a quarter of its workforce and two-thirds of its senior managers, but the financial results came almost instantaneously. Within two years PeopleSoft went from a loss of roughly $200 million to a profit of more than $200 million. The company's revenue soared almost 50 percent and *BusinessWeek* named Conway one of the world's top twenty-five managers.

Conway next bought a company that made software to help big businesses support customers. The acquisition enabled Conway to offer a complete line of back office applications (financial, human resources, and customer service) to large enterprises, just like its two biggest competitors, Oracle and SAP. Each of these companies enjoyed dominance in one back office application market for large enterprises. PeopleSoft maintained its top position in human resources software. Oracle led the field in financial software. Overall, drawing strength from its pioneering position in software that manages supplier relationships for businesses, German-based SAP held the largest market share for back office applications.

Conway's acquisition of J. D. Edwards was the icing on the cake. Edwards sold few back office products to large enterprises, even after years of trying. But the company enjoyed considerable success among midsize businesses, despite competition from many other vendors in that market, including Microsoft. The additional revenue from J. D. Edwards moved PeopleSoft into the number two position in the markets for back office software and dropped Oracle to the third position. No business executive ever wants to be in third place, particularly in a market with network effects where the strong get stronger.

When the news of Ellison's hostile tender offer crossed the wire, Conway was driving between customer appointments in Amsterdam. His cell phone kept ringing and ringing. He pulled off the road and checked into a hotel so he could tune in to the financial channel on European television.

Conway's emotions ran from surprise to shock to anger as he watched the news scroll across the screen. Executives in the software industry rarely launched unsolicited offers for acquisition partners, feeling that a rancorous takeover attempt might drive talented engineers out of the target company. Weighing the developments, Conway concluded that Oracle intended its bid only to harm PeopleSoft by scuttling the Edwards acquisition and freezing the pipeline of potential customer deals. Ellison admitted as much. "If they launched on J. D. Edwards," Ellison told the *Wall Street Journal*, "we were going to launch on them." Ellison even told the press that his company wanted only PeopleSoft, not J. D. Edwards. And Ellison offered little more than the public trading price for PeopleSoft stock, depressed by a technology downturn, hardly what the investment community expected from a serious tender offer. PeopleSoft's stock price quickly shot above Oracle's $16-a-share bid.

Many investors agreed with Conway's assessment of Oracle's intentions. One analyst called Oracle's offer a "bullshit bid." Another commentator told the press that Ellison's shrewd move had put PeopleSoft "on hold." "Owning PeopleSoft is the last thing Ellison wants," wrote a *Wall Street Journal* columnist. "Instead he's just messin' with their heads."

Conway released a statement calling Oracle's offer "atrociously bad behavior from a company with a history of bad behavior." He spent the next few days in Europe, trying to calm anxious customers. He met with several face-to-face; he talked to others on the telephone.

PeopleSoft's customers had much on their minds. Back office software implementations sometimes cost hundreds of millions of dollars. The software itself is only a small part of it. The customer's staff has to be trained in the new products. The whole process can take years for complete installation and customization to fit the peculiarities of each business. Once the software is stable, the customer remains dependent on the vendor for critical updates—tax laws change all over the world every year, as do employee benefits rules.

PeopleSoft's existing customers worried about what would happen to maintenance and support if Oracle, famous for software that is bug-ridden and hard to work with, took over. New customers working on deals with PeopleSoft thought twice about a long-term relationship with a company that might not survive the year. Gardner, a leading market research firm, advised its clients to postpone new purchases of software systems from PeopleSoft "until it's clear what's going to happen to them." Three other research firms issued similar guidance. Ellison and his top lieutenants fed the fears by announcing plans to stop actively selling PeopleSoft's existing programs and halt development of additions to the PeopleSoft line. All Oracle really wanted were the PeopleSoft customers, who could be switched over time to the Oracle products, along with a few of PeopleSoft's top programmers, analysts surmised.

Conway told the press Ellison's plans were "like asking me if I could buy your dog so I can go out back and shoot it." Ellison took the joke further: "I think at one point Craig thought I was going to shoot his dog. I love animals. If Craig and [the dog] were standing next to each other [and] I have one bullet—it wouldn't be for the dog."

"Abbey and I decided not to take any chances," said Conway at a user conference a couple of months later, as he and his black Labrador appeared on a stage in front of a packed auditorium wearing matching bulletproof vests.

Oracle launched its hostile tender offer after I had completed the recruitment of professional managers to run the start-up I cofounded. I was ready for another legal battle.

Ellison's gambit looked familiar to me. Most antitrust commentators focused on anticompetitive effects of a proposed combination between two competitors in the back office software markets. Traditional antitrust concerns lean heavily on that kind of "horizontal" analysis. But from a business perspective, Oracle's strategy was more complicated. The company made only a tiny profit from its sale of back office applications, not really enough to justify a multibillion-dollar bid for a back office competitor, even one with better profit margins. Oracle generated operating profits of more than 40 percent on its database, but it faced aggressive competition in that market from IBM and Microsoft, putting Oracle's profit margins under pressure.

PeopleSoft's success exacerbated Oracle's problem in the database market. Oracle's back office software ran only on its own database, but PeopleSoft's applications worked with any of the leading databases. Increasingly, PeopleSoft's customers were deciding to run their applications on the databases of Oracle's competitors. More sales of PeopleSoft's applications programs meant more sales of IBM and Microsoft databases. Eliminating PeopleSoft would make Oracle's database competitors less desirable to customers, who wanted a rich array of software to run on top of the database installations.

I had seen it all before. Just as Microsoft crushed its application competitors, Netscape included, to protect the Windows monopoly, so Ellison intended to take out PeopleSoft in order to shore up Oracle's database position. "Same playbook. Same plays. Different players," I told the *Wall Street Journal*.

Following Conway's lead, the PeopleSoft board of directors rejected Oracle's $16 offer as inadequate. Oracle raised its bid to $19.50 a share.

PeopleSoft's board rejected the new offer, this time citing concerns about antitrust clearance as well as the low offer price. Negotiating with Oracle would only legitimize the fears of potential customers about PeopleSoft's future and more than justify withholding purchases. If the deal was then blocked by the Antitrust Division, PeopleSoft might never regain its market momentum.

Rejecting Oracle's offers put pressure squarely on Conway to produce good financial results for the quarter. Most sales closed during the last few weeks of the reporting period, and Ellison's announcement left little time to assuage the concerns of potential customers. If PeopleSoft announced poor results, some shareholders would likely tender their stock to Oracle. Others might demand that Conway try to negotiate a better price. More potential customers would withhold purchases, producing a downward spiral of expectations and results.

Keeping customers engaged became Conway's key priority. I flew with him on the corporate jet from city to city, crisscrossing the country. In addition to large corporations, universities, state governments, and agencies of the federal government led PeopleSoft's customer list. Whenever we met with customers, Conway would first talk privately with their top executives and purchasing officials. Then we would sit down together with the customers' lawyers to talk about the antitrust situation. They always asked the same question: "What can we do to stop this from happening?"

"Call the Department of Justice," Conway told them. More than 120 of them did, including the Department of Defense. At the end of the month, the Antitrust Division announced an investigation. Oracle's press spokesman attacked Conway in the media, claiming that he was fomenting an antitrust issue to avoid selling the company and losing his job. PeopleSoft directors worried that they would be accused of entrenching management to the detriment of shareholders.

Conway was incredulous at the criticism. The *San Francisco Chronicle* reported that if the PeopleSoft board simply accepted Oracle's offer, Conway would walk away with almost $75 million in stock. "If I wanted to make easy money, I'd just accept the offer," Conway told me as we were flying back to California after yet another week of customer meetings. "I can drive the stock price even higher by competing against Oracle."

"Some people will claim that you're just trying to keep your CEO position," I said.

"I sold my last two companies. If I thought this was a good deal I'd sell this one," he replied in disbelief.

During the first few weeks after the hostile offer, Conway made two tactical moves to stave off Oracle. First, he changed the terms he offered for J. D. Edwards, permitting PeopleSoft to accelerate the purchase and close the deal. Oracle would have to take Edwards, like it or not, if it bought PeopleSoft. Second, Conway offered new PeopleSoft customers a written guarantee that the products they purchased would be maintained and improved for ten years. If Oracle bought PeopleSoft, Oracle would be bound by the contracts. Failure to support the PeopleSoft products would obligate Oracle under the contracts to pay twice—and in some cases up to five times—what the customer paid for the software in the first place. Ellison filed suit to void the guarantee, but he also announced that Oracle would maintain PeopleSoft's products for ten years.

The guarantee satisfied many nervous prospects. Still, Conway cashed nearly every chit he had, trying to make the quarter. He personally called even marginal prospects and turned to strategic partners, like Microsoft and Hewlett-Packard, asking them to place purchase orders. At the beginning of July, Conway announced that PeopleSoft met its second-quarter financial projections, yet the stock price did not respond. Oracle circulated the rumor that PeopleSoft had accelerated every potential transaction in its customer pipeline just to make the second quarter and had nothing left for subsequent reporting periods.

To keep shareholders from losing confidence, Conway and his managerial team would have to do it all again. They did. Early in October, Conway announced that PeopleSoft met its third-quarter projections. The stock price soared past Oracle's $19.50 a share. Undaunted, Oracle vowed to post a slate of nominees to challenge the PeopleSoft directors in a shareholder vote.

PeopleSoft's employees started tying blue ribbons around the trees on the company campus to show their support for management's resistance. They printed up T-shirts with the slogan LARRY, KISS OUR APPS. Right after the first of the year, Conway announced that PeopleSoft met its revenue target for a third successive quarter.

When Oracle announced its hostile bid, the section of the Antitrust Division that specializes in computer and software deals was already straining under the workload of two huge projects. The legal team assigned to analyze the Oracle deal issued document demands to PeopleSoft, Oracle, and other software vendors, as well as to customers and industry consultants. Truckloads of documents poured into Washington from all over the world. Even more data came in electronically. Staff lawyers scrambled to make sense of it all. Few of them had any trial experience. For all its hundreds of lawyers, the Antitrust Division employed only a handful who could put on a big case in court, and most of them were tied up on other matters.

The Antitrust Division had suffered from a shortage of trial lawyers for years, if not decades. Diminished antitrust enforcement meant fewer trials. Fewer trials meant fewer training opportunities. Each trial took on greater public significance. Feeling increased pressure to win, the front office conscripted the same experienced litigators out of the ranks for each trial.

The division also had difficulty retaining its few experienced trial lawyers. The most seasoned government trial lawyers make less in salary than a starting lawyer at the firms the government litigates against, and less than one-tenth of the compensation the lawyer heading the defendant's trial team usually earns. Dedication to the public interest keeps trial lawyers in the division only so long as they can afford to pay for their children's education. As the years passed, it became increasingly difficult for the government to field top-notch trial teams, especially when several cases demanded attention at the same time.

The organizational reforms implemented by Anne Bingaman exacerbated these problems. Bingaman separated the operation of the criminal section, where most young government antitrust lawyers used to get trial experience, from the civil section, which still has to staff big cases like Microsoft and Oracle. After the separation of functions, the top staff position in the division usually went to a lawyer from the criminal group. As the political appointees in the front office turned over every three or four years, no one had the job of worrying about civil litigation capability and morale on a long-term basis.

The shortage of courtroom lawyers made every aspect of trial management more difficult for the division. If a member of a trial team stopped performing adequately, one former division litigator told me, you couldn't replace him with another experienced lawyer because there weren't any other experienced lawyers. You could replace one five-year lawyer with another five-year lawyer, my source said, but the replacement wouldn't be much help.

Jim Tierney, the lawyer in charge of investigating PeopleSoft's side of the hostile takeover, had to make do with what he had. Many times, I called to leave Tierney a voice mail at the end of my day in California, only to find him still at work in Washington. He quickly absorbed the information we sent him and made follow-up demands. We worked feverishly to get him whatever he wanted. Nevertheless, the Oracle matter remained parked behind another division case scheduled for trial. Conway and I flew to Washington to encourage the division to move faster. Sooner or later, Conway pleaded, Oracle's tactics would start hurting PeopleSoft.

Finally, one of the division's big cases settled just before Christmas. The team on the case took a few days off for the holidays before getting detailed to the Oracle matter. Lead trial lawyer Claude Scott complained that he was already tired, having worked weeks on end to prepare the case that settled. Phil Malone, the senior staff attorney on the Microsoft trial team, got assigned to the Oracle case the day he returned to the Justice Department from a two-year fellowship at Harvard.

"You have to go to war with the Army you have, not the Army you want," the Bush administration's secretary of defense once said to justify the absence of necessary resources in far more urgent circumstances. Despite the administration's attitude of ignoring what it takes for effective government, the division did its best to protect the public interest.

CHAPTER 17

The Oracle of Antitrust

As the winter wore on, PeopleSoft started to buckle under the pressure of the Oracle bid. The government's investigation continued, with no end in sight. Conway complained to the division that he was losing key executives. Nine resigned for other jobs over a six-week period, all citing the uncertainty of PeopleSoft's future prospects. The looming proxy battle made it difficult to concentrate on the business. Oracle proffered a well-credentialed set of nominees to challenge for positions on PeopleSoft's board. The longer the investigation continued without government action, the more skittish potential customers became.

I spent much of the winter looking at the bidding and sales data PeopleSoft submitted to the Department of Justice. One of the company's executives raised concerns with me about a bid summary that had been constructed from an incomplete database of potential deals. After searching through PeopleSoft's records and talking to company employees, I told the government that the summary was wrong.

My investigation turned up surprising details. The controversy over Oracle's bid raised cutting-edge antitrust issues. Oracle's scheme to eliminate its closest competitor presented a textbook example of the kind of markets merger enforcement would have to deal with in the coming decades.

Sometimes, products from different suppliers look more or less the same to customers. Purchasers decide which supplier to buy from based largely on price. In other markets, consumers prefer one supplier's product over another's, even though both products are intended to fill the same consumer need. Occasionally, preferences are just a matter of individual idiosyncrasies. Some people like one brand of breakfast cereal, for example, while others prefer a rival's brand. Consumers might also prefer one product over another because they believe it is better suited to their individual needs.

Although PeopleSoft, Oracle, and SAP all made back office software, the vendors incorporated different features and capabilities into their products, making one vendor's product better in some circumstances than in others. Customers recognized important differences among the products. Some companies in the financial sector, like investment banks and brokerage firms, thought the software made by PeopleSoft and Oracle better for their needs than SAP's. Big manufacturing companies, on the other hand, preferred SAP's product. Some big customers in the health care field—hospital chains, for example—felt comfortable using products made by Lawson Software, a small vendor, if PeopleSoft charged too much.

Even within a given market sector, customers had specific requirements that further distinguished them, making one vendor's product a better choice than another's. The location of customer operations made a difference in selecting the right software, for example, because different products had features that made one vendor's software better in some countries than others.

Apple succeeded in "differentiating" its computers by attention to service and support. The suppliers of back office software differentiated their products to an even greater degree. Although differentiated products compete against each other in a general sense, the differences among the products mean that all suppliers are not equally well positioned to fulfill the needs of every customer or group of customers, even within the same general markets. Suppliers of differentiated products can therefore charge prices above the perfectly competitive level, owing to the customers' reluctance to substitute freely one product for another.

Economists worry that when suppliers of differentiated products combine, the merger will increase the ability of the resulting company to raise prices unilaterally (without cooperation of other suppliers) to even higher levels because the merger eliminates many customers' next best alternative selection, leaving only inferior choices. If "a significant share of sales in the market [is] accounted for by customers who regard the products of the merging firms as their first and second choices," say the Guidelines, the merger may result in a significant unilateral price increase.

The Guidelines seemed to mirror the concerns of back office software customers perfectly, assuming that Oracle's acquisition affected "a significant share of sales in the market." Although from an economic perspective unilateral effects do not turn on market definition, the Guidelines' language implied a need to "define the market" for purposes of analysis. Sometimes differentiated products compete with each other across a broad market that is easy to identify. Over-the-counter cold remedies, as one economist explained, illustrate this kind of competition.

Customers of back office software didn't buy standard products off the shelf. When they needed to make a purchase, they each sent out requests asking vendors to submit bids to supply software that could meet a long set of very complicated specifications. The specifications varied from procurement to procurement. For some bidding opportunities, PeopleSoft only competed against Oracle. For other bids, PeopleSoft competed against Oracle and SAP, and sometimes even Lawson or some other small vendor.

After acquiring PeopleSoft, Oracle might not be able to raise prices to every customer of back office software. Some customers had a lot of different choices. But other customers, those that viewed Oracle and PeopleSoft as their first and second best choices, represented prime candidates for post-merger price increases. Under the Guidelines, mergers raise concerns about unilateral effects if the merged company can identify vulnerable customers and target them for price increases, a process known as price discrimination. My investigation left little doubt on that score.

Back office software costs so much that customers spend a great deal of time and money comparing and evaluating the products from different vendors. During the process, vendors learn even more about the prospective customers. Vendors learn what software features customers need the most and which vendor each customer thinks supplies the best mix of key features.

I compiled case studies from a number of different PeopleSoft bidding opportunities. Vendors got so much information, it seemed, that they could charge customers based on what the customer needed and who the competitors for the procurement opportunity were. And vendors could charge different customers different amounts for more or less the same product. PeopleSoft's bidding data showed that the price the company charged varied from deal to deal, depending on how much competition it had. The prices and terms for a software product in one transaction didn't reveal much about the price and terms for the same product sold at the same time to a different customer.

The Guidelines recognized antitrust markets drawn on the basis of price discrimination, but did not clearly indicate how to evaluate People-Soft's records in terms of market definition. Was each customer procurement a separate antitrust market? Or were there broad markets for each type of back office software, within which the merged company could target specific customers for price increases? Did it really matter in terms of the real-world consequences from the takeover whether the market was defined one way or the other?

Working with a team of economists from Dennis Carlton's shop at Lexecon, I pulled together a database of PeopleSoft bidding records. Because the data had not been gathered during PeopleSoft's regular business operations, it could not be used as evidence in a courtroom. But it did illustrate for the government how competition in the market worked. PeopleSoft's bidding records showed that the greater the number of competitors the company faced (up to three) for each deal, the larger the discount it gave the customer on the bid, hardly a surprising result to anyone who has solicited competing bids, even for routine projects like home improvements. A standard type of statistical analysis predicted substantial price increases from the acquisition.

I sent the Antitrust Division a white paper with the results of my study. The paper took no position on the right way to define the "relevant market" in the case because data analysis predicted a substantial price increase for the deal without going through the rigamarole of market definition. "Every method of analysis yields the same result: Oracle's proposed acquisition is manifestly anticompetitive," I wrote in my paper.

After submitting the white paper, Conway and I flew to Washington for a meeting with the Antitrust Division lawyers assigned to the Oracle case. They sat looking distracted and edgy as Conway emphasized yet again the danger to PeopleSoft's business from Oracle's offer. The moment he finished speaking, all the government lawyers in the room scattered, running back to their offices to finish assignments.

I stayed in the conference room to dial into a conference call with a group of state antitrust enforcers. Conway excused himself and went out into the hall to take a more urgent call. Oracle had raised its bid 33 percent, he learned, to $26 for each PeopleSoft share. The new bid valued People-Soft at more than $9 billion. The bid was about 20 percent higher than the trading price for PeopleSoft's stock. "This is our final price," Oracle's chief financial officer announced. Analysts told the press that the pressure on PeopleSoft was increasing, but PeopleSoft's board again rejected Oracle's bid, saying that it undervalued the company.

A few days later, after months of study, the Antitrust Division staff recommended to the front office that the Justice Department sue to block Oracle's takeover. The front office had authority to accept or reject the staff recommendation. Conway and I returned to Washington to meet with Bruce McDonald, the division's second in command. McDonald brought a copy of the white paper with him to the meeting and asked us questions about it. After we returned to California, the *Wall Street Journal* published a story about the staff recommendation. According to the *Journal*, the staff analyzed each purchase as a separate antitrust market. "We were stunned by this unprecedented new theory," an Oracle executive told the *Journal*.

A *Journal* editorial railed against the decision, calling on Hewitt Pate, the head of the Antitrust Division, to clarify the Bush administration's policy by rejecting the staff's recommendation. "The Justice Department antitrust bureaucracy is sorely in need of some adult legal counsel," the *Journal* wrote. The words stung the division's lawyers, who felt they had used neutral enforcement criteria to evaluate the deal's effects on customers. Oracle's "only hope" to overturn the staff recommendation, I told the *Washington Post* for a story that referenced the *Journal*'s editorial, "is to make [the takeover] a political issue and hope to suggest good Republicans would never block a merger, and if you block a merger, you must not be a good Republican."

Hewitt Pate, a good Republican, would make the final decision. Con-

THE ORACLE OF ANTITRUST 307

way and I flew to Washington again, our third trip in three weeks, to make our best and final pitch to Pate. We returned to San Francisco right after the meeting. The next morning, I sat in my office trying to get some work done. The PeopleSoft team at one of the company's investment bankers monitored stock trading activity and news headlines. Every couple of minutes, I got an e-mail update.

11:37: We are monitoring [the trading desk] in real time.
No unusual activity in the stock as of yet.
11:37: Reuters headline just crossed—
Justice Department says to block Oracle bid to buy PeopleSoft on antitrust grounds.

A two-page Bloomberg story followed six minutes later, and then a minute after that, an AP story. Later in the day, Pate held a news conference in which he answered reporters' questions about the lawsuit, the market, and the competitors.

The Antitrust Division filed its suit in federal court in San Francisco, the jurisdiction that covered Silicon Valley, including both Oracle's and PeopleSoft's headquarters. The Division could have filed in Washington, but given the location of the companies, the documents and witnesses, San Francisco made more sense. The San Francisco filing also avoided conservative D.C. judges whose decisions plagued antitrust enforcers for many years, in favor of a jurisdiction thought to be far more liberal. No one counted on what happened next.

The case was assigned, apparently at random, to a federal magistrate—an assistant judge who usually deals with discovery issues. Parties can reject assignment to a magistrate. When an objection was filed, the case was reassigned to Judge Vaughn R. Walker, who was just a few months shy of becoming the district's chief judge. Walker's assignment threw the Division's best-laid plans into disarray. One former Division lawyer told me that the Justice Department would not have filed in San Francisco "under any circumstances" had they known they would draw Walker.

"You guys stand no chance," a prominent plaintiffs' lawyer told me. "Walker will be cordial, but you stand no chance."

"Worst draw for the government in the entire federal judiciary" was the report from someone involved in providing educational courses to federal judges.

Walker cut a colorful swath. Shortly after his appointment to the federal bench by the first President Bush—following a seventeen-year career at a leading San Francisco firm—Walker dismayed Republicans by advocating the decriminalization of drugs. "I certainly have some leanings toward the belief that our political system is founded on the maximum degree of personal liberty," Walker told a reporter. An article in a San Francisco legal newspaper a few years later criticized Walker's "erratic" behavior on the bench, saying that lawyers on both sides of cases "complain of the judge's apparent lack of interest in the court papers they file." In 2001, Walker earned the distinction as the most reversed judge in the district.

Walker made headlines presiding over an antitrust challenge under the Clayton Act to the Hearst Corporation's purchase of the *San Francisco Chronicle* newspaper. The Antitrust Division had threatened to block the deal until Hearst sold its other San Francisco paper, the *Examiner*, on terms that would bolster that paper's continued viability. Hearst unloaded the *Examiner* to a well-connected San Francisco family, rejecting Clint Reilly's competing offer. The Antitrust Division cleared the deal. Reilly, a San Francisco pol, brought suit, claiming the transaction a sham to permit Hearst to monopolize the daily newspaper business in San Francisco.

Walker ultimately rejected Reilly's legal contentions, but took the opportunity to criticize in writing the Antitrust Division's conduct. Walker claimed that "cronyism" behind the transaction "also exerted influence over the DoJ [Department of Justice] investigation." He openly questioned the "impartiality and probity of DoJ's review." The role of judges, Walker later told a reporter, is to "ask questions of the way authority is exercised."

Joel Klein wrote Walker a five-page letter explaining the Division's findings and asking the judge to excise references to political influence from the opinion. Walker released Klein's letter to the public along with his own response, rebuffing Klein. Walker told Klein that since the government had twice declined the judge's invitation to appear during the trial, Walker was unsympathetic to Klein's arguments.

The newspaper case, on top of Walker's long-standing libertarian views, made the government lawyers worry that Walker was hostile to the Antitrust Division, even before taking any testimony in the Oracle case. The government's approach to trial, one Division lawyer told me, was "Don't piss the judge off and try a good case. That's the only hope."

Larry Ellison quickly announced that he would contest the government's case in Walker's court. When asked by a *Wall Street Journal* reporter about merger issues, all Ellison could talk about was Microsoft. "The judge [in the Microsoft case] found that they were breaking the law over and over again. The penalty was not one but several very nasty editorials in the *New York Times*," Ellison joked. "I would look at that kind of severe penalty— which is just dreadful during Thanksgiving dinner—and say, 'Well, I've got $250 billion in cash but I have this terrible article hanging over my head.'" Ellison had learned the lessons of the Microsoft settlement well.

The government built its entire case of competitive injury from Oracle's planned takeover around customer testimony, traditionally the strongest form of proof in an antitrust case. Courts value testimony and documentary evidence from customers about how the products under review are bought and used and about how easily customers can shift to the offerings of other suppliers, given price and availability, without disrupting their businesses. Customers have just the kind of information from which the likelihood of a postmerger price increase can be gauged. Compared to the opinions of paid experts, courts usually consider customer testimony unbiased and reliable. Customers want better products at lower prices, precisely the goal of antitrust enforcement.

Getting third parties, especially customers, to testify at an antitrust trial always represents a big challenge for the Division. Most companies just don't want to get involved. They fear the government will lose, leaving them exposed to an angry supplier with a dominant market position. Even if the government wins, as Silicon Valley companies learned the hard way from the *Microsoft* settlement, the Antitrust Division won't always stick around to make sure they get treated fairly. After the Antitrust Division's vanishing act in the Microsoft case, I thought it unlikely any high tech companies would help investigate Oracle. Only a few of the largest did publicly.

But fearing postmerger dependence on Oracle for software vital to their business operations, large companies in industries other than high tech that bought back office products from Oracle and PeopleSoft came forward in droves to help the government. Vaughn Walker's treatment of customer witnesses proved nearly as controversial as his decision on the merits. Procedural matters in Walker's court, unrelated to the antitrust issues in the lawsuit, nearly sabotaged the government's case.

Walker wasted no time in taking control of the new matter on his docket. He set an early trial date. He ordered Oracle to produce documents the Antitrust Division demanded, and he ordered the Division to give Oracle's lawyers copies of all documents the government had collected from potential witnesses—mostly big corporate customers of Oracle and PeopleSoft—during the eight-month-long investigation of Oracle's takeover bid.

In big cases, the court usually enters an order to control the confidentiality of documents that contain important business information. Seldom is the procedure contentious. Most of the time, only the outside lawyers retained for trial and experts signed up under strict agreements (along with the judge) can see the most confidential documents. Oracle demanded an exception to this procedure. Oracle wanted two of its in-house lawyers, including the Oracle employee who gave the company's marketing group antitrust advice, to see all the confidential information. An opinion of the federal court of appeals supported excluding in-house lawyers from access to the most confidential business information. I argued the case myself. Nevertheless, Walker agreed with Oracle.

When the customers and other witnesses learned of the judge's decision, several, including the Department of Defense, flew their lawyers to San Francisco to address the court. The witnesses knew that they would have to show their confidential records to the courtroom lawyers for both sides, to the judge and to the experts retained during the trial, but they balked at disclosure to Oracle employees. Software customers said they didn't want to give away their negotiating leverage by letting Oracle's employees see how the customers evaluated Oracle's bids against those of other vendors. The customers explained their fears of getting hurt by a court proceeding in which they were only witnesses.

The government backed up the witnesses' objections. Bruce McDonald came out from the Division's front office to tell the judge that the government depended on the goodwill of third parties to conduct investigations. Companies would fight government document demands in future cases, he said, unless their business secrets were protected. Walker listened dutifully to all the arguments. At the next hearing, in the middle of the government's argument in support of the witness objections, Walker equated the companies that were cooperating in the government's case with shady underworld informants.

"In a way, the information you are obtaining from these third-parties is informant information," Walker said, challenging the government lawyer. "One develops some measure of skepticism about the reliability of informant information." It should be exposed to someone from Oracle who will test its accuracy, the judge said.

A bewildered government lawyer explained that he was just trying to keep confidential ordinary business plans and records from well-known companies—"not equivalent to informant information," he said.

Walker asked no other questions. At the end of the arguments, he read, more or less verbatim, a ruling that he had clearly prepared in advance. He denied all of the objections and granted Oracle's in-house lawyers access to all of the other witnesses' confidential information. Several corporate witnesses complained to the Antitrust Division. The Department of Defense dropped out of the case and the Antitrust Division removed the agency from its witness list. One of the other scheduled witnesses filed an extraordinary emergency petition, known as a writ of mandamus, asking the court of appeals to reverse Walker's decision. The Antitrust Division lawyers declined to join in the petition ("Don't piss off the judge," I imagined them thinking) and the appellate court denied the writ.

At the next hearing, a month later, Walker made it even more painful for customers and other corporate witnesses to testify at the trial. Broadly invoking the notion of keeping the trial proceedings open to the public, he ordered detailed data from witnesses, including bids on contracts, pricing details, budgets, and product information, relied upon by either side in the trial placed into the public record. "This is not a national security case," Walker said. He acknowledged the witnesses had "quite legitimate interests in maintaining confidentiality of some of the information that has been developed in this case," but, he held, "any matter that a party submits . . . really needs to be publicly disclosed even if it involves what a party or third party regards as proprietary or highly confidential information."

Flustered witnesses besieged the Division lawyers with calls and e-mails. The penalty for cooperating with the government in Walker's court, the witnesses said, was public disclosure of all of their most proprietary business information. One company went into its local federal court and got a restraining order to prevent the government from compelling its testimony.

Cases involving confidential business information get tried all the time without difficulty. Judges rely on information submitted in confidence, so long as the courtroom lawyers and experts can see it and comment on it. If the judge's decision relies on confidential information, the opinion usually discloses as much of the information as possible, without revealing trade secrets. It is not uncommon for published opinions to contain redactions because of business confidentiality. The federal appellate court that set the rules for Walker's court even recognized explicitly in another case that public access to court records "can be overridden given sufficiently compelling reasons," but the Division took no appeal of Walker's ruling.

Oracle pressed the issue of public disclosure before Walker at every opportunity. Because Oracle made little money on the sale of back office applications, it had little to lose from disclosure of its confidential information. Forcing public disclosure on PeopleSoft, on the other hand, would devastate the company. And witnesses were less likely to testify for the government if it meant exposing confidential business information to their own competitors.

Eventually Walker appointed a widely respected former federal judge, Charles Legge, to evaluate all the claims of confidentiality and to file a report detailing his decision on the public disclosure of each one. Corporate witnesses made thousands of claims. Legge worked with the corporate witnesses for many days and nights. He filed a comprehensive report, then a second report. Walker put them aside after Oracle objected, saying he would address confidentiality issues as they arose. They arose, as it turned out, on just about every day the government tried to put a witness on the stand.

Keeping its important witnesses in tow was not the Antitrust Division's only problem. As the trial approached, Oracle and its sympathizers mounted a campaign in the press to discredit the government's case, starting with the market definition. The government's complaint, as it turned out, did not rely on price discrimination markets drawn around customer bids. Instead, the complaint pled the more conventional type of broad antitrust markets.

The government claimed that only the back office software of Oracle, SAP, and PeopleSoft could satisfy the needs of many large corporations. That was easy enough to prove. But the government started running into trouble when it coined a name for this software, "high function software," the government lawyers called it, and they attempted to define its characteristics—"scalable," "highly configurable," "able to accommodate complex corporate transactions." Trouble was, the term "high function software" was unknown in the industry. Before the trial, no company claimed to make a product in that category.

Straining to accommodate the classic case law approach of market definition, the government defined a market around the made-up product name. What companies sold products in the "high function software" market? The government said there were only three, Oracle, PeopleSoft, and SAP. Whenever any other company won a contract to supply a large enterprise, the press seized on the event as evidence of confusion and ignorance among the antitrust enforcers.

In the weeks before the trial, Oracle trumpeted its market losses to the press, demonstrating, the company claimed, the fallacy in the government's market definition. Microsoft was primed to enter the market, Oracle said. Lawson Software already sold back office products to large health care companies, Oracle's lawyer declared, and would expand to other market sectors if Oracle tried to gouge customers after the takeover. SAP will modify and reposition its products to compete even more directly with the merged company, Oracle's apologists contended.

Right before the trial started, the Justice Department itself selected American Management Systems, a company that specializes in government accounting products, over Oracle and PeopleSoft for its back office financial software, proof positive in the minds of a cynical press corps of an embarrassingly weak government case. The antitrust enforcers didn't even count AMS among Oracle's significant competitors.

The government lawyers recognized the problem with their approach. They believed they were selecting the best trial strategy. Using small markets conformed better to what the customers would say in the trial, but no litigated case had ever relied on small, price discrimination markets drawn around customer opportunities. Taking that approach would open the government to the charge of trying to avoid the market definition requirement of the case law by pleading markets so small, there was automatically a concern about untoward concentration. Besides, given the overall strength of the government's case, market definition amounted to little more than a legal technicality.

A discovery dispute between the government and Oracle a few weeks before the trial went largely unnoticed by the press. During the Antitrust Division's review of the proposed takeover, Oracle claimed that one group of documents the government asked for, "discount approval forms," were too voluminous to produce. Oracle gave the government a sample of the forms along with a promise to produce the rest if that became necessary.

Examining the samples, government economists discovered that the forms documented requests for permission to quote discounts from list prices by Oracle sales personnel in order to respond to competitors' bids. The forms frequently listed reasons for the requested discounts and an identification of competitors for the business. Like the internal e-mails in the Microsoft case, the discount forms showed what was actually going on in the market. They were powerful, almost incontestable evidence. Oracle could not deny the accuracy of the information on the forms without impeaching the integrity of its own business records.

The government lawyers demanded all the forms, but Oracle's counsel resisted. The document demand was too broad, he said. The judge ordered Oracle to produce the forms anyway, giving the Antitrust Division's trial team custody of 188 boxes of documents, more than sixteen thousand discount forms in all.

The forms held the key to the case, especially when coupled with customers' testimony. On one hand, the forms contained just about everything necessary for the government to prove customer-specific price discrimination markets—who Oracle saw as its competitors for each customer opportunity and how much Oracle personnel thought they had to discount the company's price in order to win the deal. More than that, the forms permitted the government to prove likely competitive injury and even to project the level of anticompetitive price increases directly from reliable business records, without going through the excruciating formalism of defining a market to infer competitive injury from concentration.

"Why not make predictions about what *actual* suppliers would do rather than focus on a hypothetical monopolist?" two economists asked in a journal article, criticizing the overly theoretical market definition approach. There was only one problem. Conventional merger analysis always started by defining a market.

Conway did not have the luxury of worrying about the government's trial strategy. After three straight quarters of meeting analysts' predictions, PeopleSoft announced a bad quarter. Analysts attributed the shortfall to potential customers waiting to see the outcome of the Oracle trial, along with the constant management distraction of the lawsuit. On top of all that, SAP and Lawson joined Oracle in trying to capture PeopleSoft's customers. "Without question, the takeover attempt has hurt PeopleSoft," the *Daily Deal* reported, "with no end in sight." Larry Ellison responded to PeopleSoft's financial results, three weeks later, by lowering Oracle's bid to $21 per share. His action convinced many observers that he really didn't want to buy PeopleSoft and was only interested in hurting the company.

Of the fifteen or so lawyers on the trial team the government assembled, only five actually lived in San Francisco. The rest, along with five Division economists from D.C., were housed in three different apartment complexes, each located a short subway ride from the courthouse. The apartments cost the government much less than hotel rooms. Because each rented apartment had a kitchen, the government cut one-third from the per diem allowance each attorney received for meals, transportation, and other personal expenses, on the bureaucratic expectation that the lawyers would cook their own dinners at the end of each trial day.

During the trial, the litigators arrived at their offices at 6 or 6:30 a.m. before going to court at about 9. They worked sixteen or eighteen hours a day. Sometimes, they stayed up all night working. No one had time to go to the grocery store, much less cook dinner. Many evenings, one of the lawyers bought take-out for everyone working on the case. Because of the cut in the per diem allowance, just about everybody on the government trial team ended up reaching into his own pocket for the privilege of representing the United States in court.

The private side of big-time litigation is much different. You travel by cab or chauffeured cars—almost never by subway. You stay in expensive hotel rooms with twenty-four-hour room service. All reasonable personal expenses are approved. You can buy just about anything that will help you spend more time working on the client's business. Just don't order a $300 bottle of wine with dinner.

To exhibit documents during the trial, the government did manage to spring for large, state-of-the-art flat-panel displays, positioned around Walker's courtroom. People in the gallery would be able to see every detail of PeopleSoft's most confidential business information, I told a colleague sarcastically. On the first day of the trial, the *Wall Street Journal* ran a story about the public display of business secrets. "Software Secrets May Be Shared at Oracle-PeopleSoft Trial," read the headline. "Forget paying tens of thousands of dollars for fancy executive courses covering sales and negotiating tactics," *InformationWeek* advised its readers. "Instead, come down to the Oracle antitrust trial."

On June 7, 2004, almost exactly a year from the day Ellison announced his plans to take over PeopleSoft, Claude Scott opened for the Antitrust Division. I could do little more than watch. Although the case would determine the future for PeopleSoft's customers, investors, and employees, PeopleSoft was not technically a "party" to the lawsuit. So I couldn't call witnesses, nor could I make statements to the court about any of the evidence. I couldn't even argue points of antitrust law. I could help prepare PeopleSoft's witnesses for testimony, but that was about it.

Scott got six sentences into his argument before the judge interrupted with a question. Then another. The judge asked him ten questions in two minutes. "Why is the geographic market the United States?" the judge wanted to know. Scott artfully described differentiated products and price discrimination, but twenty minutes later he was still trying to answer the judge's question about the geographic market. Important questions about Oracle's ability to raise prices after the takeover got buried under a pedantic exchange about where exactly to draw a geographic line. For the next month, Walker was not going to let the government skirt the market-drawing issues. Eventually, in his opinion, Walker relied on the traditional approach of market definition to sink the government's case.

Oracle's lawyer made his opening argument with only a few interruptions. He emphasized legal theory rather than evidence, claiming that the Antitrust Division could not prove all the elements of a "unilateral effects" case.

The government then called, as its first witness, the chief information officer of Cox Communications, the big cable company. The Cox witness explained the lengthy process his company went through to buy new software to manage payroll and other financial transactions, once the company outgrew the J. D. Edwards software it had.

The reporters seated around me in the gallery grew drowsy from the detail of the examination. I wanted to nudge a couple of them, if only to point out that the government began its case by putting on an Oracle customer to explain how competition from PeopleSoft made Oracle's product cheaper. The Cox witness explained how Oracle's proposed takeover would hurt Cox, even though Cox was an Oracle customer.

In response to a series of questions from the Justice Department lawyer, the witness explained that Cox would not switch to vendors other than PeopleSoft and Oracle, even if Oracle charged 10 percent more for its products after it acquired PeopleSoft. Other suppliers' products lacked the functionality Cox needed, the witness said.

During the testimony of the Cox witness, a company document was put up on the monitors. The public saw the document with a few confidential sentences marked out. The judge, the lawyers, and the witness all had complete copies without deletions, in accordance with the normal procedure for confidentiality. Judge Legge had approved marking out the sections under the procedure Walker set up, and neither the government nor Oracle objected to Legge's decision.

Judge Walker started talking before the Antitrust Division lawyer could get out even a single question about the document. Walker pointedly asked the witness why portions of the document were marked out. The witness tried to explain, but Walker challenged the witness's assertion that disclosure to competitors of the marked-out information (an internal company assessment of business issues) could harm Cox.

"Aren't these issues of the most generic character, the kinds of issues that any business faces?" demanded the judge.

"These are Cox's specific issues," responded the witness.

"I don't see how you can draw that conclusion," said the judge in even sterner tones. "What specific to Cox is contained on the page?"

The witness started to give an explanation, but the judge kept interrupting him. Color ran from the witness's face. He looked visibly shaken and he started to sweat. Walker kept berating him. Apparently, the lawyer for the witness's company left town before the examination. An inexperienced government attorney who was conducting the direct examination stood stunned and silent. The government lawyer could not fathom why Walker was interrogating the witness so hostilely. If the judge had concerns, he could have raised them before the testimony started with the lawyer who made the confidentiality designations.

Finally Claude Scott jumped up and tried politely to back the judge off. "May I try to get us past this point?" he asked. Scott explained that Cox's in-house lawyer worked out the deletions with Judge Legge. Walker remained adamant. Walker said that he did not see anything confidential about the marked-out information, which he described as "a rather extravagant designation of highly confidential material."

Nothing that Scott could say mollified the judge. The witness's statement that the document contained confidential information "simply cannot be justified," Walker said. The witness "provided no cogent information" why disclosure would be harmful to Cox. Regardless of who negotiated with Legge, "this is the guy who ought to know that information if anybody does," Walker continued to expound on the record.

I kept waiting for the witness to ask for oxygen. He looked like he was going to puke. Finally, Scott got Walker's permission to move on. Lawyers in the courtroom for other third-party witnesses feverishly exchanged messages on their BlackBerrys. No customer witness appeared without his own lawyer after the first day of trial.

The government's second witness, the chief information officer of a $3 billion worldwide engineering company, also turned out to be an Oracle customer. His company wanted to buy new human resources software, he said, and already used Oracle's financial software. After studying the situation, his company narrowed its choices to Oracle and PeopleSoft. No other company had ever tried to make SAP's human resources software work with Oracle's financial software, so the customer eliminated SAP as a potential supplier. One of the consulting firms the customer retained to help with the decision counseled against Lawson, so that vendor was eliminated as well.

At the end of the trial's second day, the judge held a hearing on documents that PeopleSoft wanted kept out of the public record. It was one of the few opportunities I had to address the court. Before I started speaking, Claude Scott announced that the government had cut back the number of documents it intended to use in witness examinations because of the confidentiality problems Walker had. I was going to remember that concession, I told myself, if the judge ended up finding the government's presentation unconvincing. With so much at stake—money, jobs, legal precedent, customer business operations—how could something as insignificant as document confidentiality affect what the judge would consider?

I argued against a rule putting every document the court wanted to rely on into the public record. I tried using a familiar example of cases with confidential business information that get tried all the time. In trade secret cases, I explained, companies sue to keep valuable information out of the hands of competitors. Making the information public just because it is part of a trial would defeat the whole purpose of trade secret protection.

"The public has a right to see what goes on in court," replied the judge. "After all, somebody might want to criticize the judge's opinion."

"You know, your Honor, we have very important rights under the Constitution, but none of those rights is absolute," I said, taking measure of Walker's libertarian viewpoint. "We believe, for example, in the separation of church and state, but if the church catches on fire, we don't expect the fire department to just sit there. We believe in freedom of speech very passionately, but Justice Oliver Wendell Holmes made it very clear that the right does not extend to the ability to shout 'Fire!' in a crowded theater. So there must be a balancing that goes on, that we look to this court to do."

At the end of the argument, Walker agreed to keep Judge Legge's first report about some of the witnesses' confidential documents out of the public record. But Walker refused to accord PeopleSoft even that protection, despite Legge's ruling upholding the confidentiality of PeopleSoft's documents. No matter how much I argued that Oracle was just going to try to make PeopleSoft's documents public to harm the company, Walker saw things differently. Throughout the rest of the trial, whenever the judge denied a request for confidentiality from PeopleSoft or from one of the witnesses, Oracle would post the document at issue on its company Web site to make sure everyone saw it. The public disclosure of PeopleSoft's business information is going to render the company worthless, I thought, regardless of the outcome of the trial.

The next day Walker heard testimony from an executive of IBM's consulting group. The consulting group advises big companies on selecting vendors for financial software, hires out its staff to customize vendor software, and helps to install the software at customer sites. At the conclusion of the witness's testimony, Walker cast aside the entire procedure Judge Legge put in place. Walker announced that any evidence the government relied on, confidential or otherwise, had to be placed in the public record.

Walker interrupted the testimony of the next witness, the senior vice president for technology of Verizon, to challenge the "confidential" designation of a document Judge Legge approved.

"In what way would the public disclosure of this information be injurious to Verizon?" the judge asked. The witness, a no-nonsense executive, pushed back, explaining that the document contained current information on Verizon's labor costs and procedures for reducing computer hardware and staff, but the judge refused to accept the witness's explanation. "This looks like very general information," the judge said.

The following morning, before hearing any additional witnesses, Walker suggested that he would count claims of confidentiality that he found unconvincing against the credibility of the witnesses testifying on the merits. "To what degree can I consider the validity of those claims in assessing the credibility of the witness?" he asked rhetorically.

An appalled Claude Scott tried his best to talk the judge out of it. If a designation of confidentiality has been upheld by Judge Legge, Scott argued, Walker couldn't use the designation to challenge the witness's credibility.

"Let me just say this," Walker concluded after hearing Scott's argument. "I'm going to take a much tougher line on admitting any more redacted documents."

At a break in the testimony, reporters started asking Antitrust Division deputy Tom Barnett if Walker's statement and rulings would keep the government from making its case in court. The *Wall Street Journal* article on the incident referred to "Walker's threats." Barnett put on his game face, claiming that Walker's ruling would not affect the trial of the case. Independent observers disagreed. One industry analyst told *USA Today* that Walker's ruling could have a "chilling effect" on the willingness of corporate witnesses to testify.

Before the next witness's testimony, Walker again criticized Legge's procedure. Then the government put on a senior vice president of Bearing-Point, a competitor of IBM in the business of helping large enterprises select back office software and configure it for their specific needs.

About five minutes into the direct examination, Walker swiveled in his chair, got up, stretched his back, and started to pace. The witness didn't notice him. The witness sat in a small designated area just below and to the right of the judge's bench, but a couple of steps up from the floor of the courtroom. The judge's enormous mahogany-fronted desk sat on a platform several steps above the witness box, so when Walker started to pace, he towered over the courtroom. Walker walked up beside the witness who was looking straight ahead, at the lawyer asking him questions. No more than a foot or two from the witness, Walker stared down at him from the judge's raised floor.

Mid-sentence in his testimony, the witness caught a glimpse of Walker and almost jumped out of his skin. "Scared the hell out of me," said the witness on the record.

"It's good to have that effect on somebody," replied Walker, apparently making a joke.

From time to time, Walker asked the witness questions, which the witness did his best to answer. "I don't want you to stand up and stare at me again," the witness said at one point, making light of the prior encounter.

"All right," said the judge. "I'll stay seated."

But Walker didn't stay seated. Time and again, during the testimony of other government witnesses, Walker would saunter over to the edge of his raised floor, stand beside the witness box, and stare down at the witness while he was testifying. After the incident with the BearingPoint witness, the government briefed every one of its witnesses to make them aware of what Walker would do. One of the PeopleSoft witnesses complained bitterly to me. It was hard enough to deal with the pressure of testifying in court, he said, without somebody standing over your shoulder.

I wanted to object to the judge's demeanor, but I couldn't think of a nice way to demand that the judge sit in his chair. Contrary to what people see on television lawyer shows, attorneys can't walk up to a seated witness in a federal courtroom and try to intimidate him. The lawyer questioning the witness has to stand at the courtroom podium. In fact, the lawyers need to get the judge's permission to approach a seated witness, even to hand him a document to look at. Lawyers from both sides observed this rule during the entire Oracle trial.

CHAPTER 18

The Smackdown

Despite all the problems, the government put on quite a show. Customer after customer took the stand, each for two or three hours. Cox Communications; Verizon; Neiman Marcus; Pepsi-Americas, the soft drink bottling company; Greyhound, the bus company; Daimler-Chrysler, the automotive manufacturer; the state of North Dakota; a worldwide engineering company; a real estate investment trust. They all testified in detail about their months-long projects to decide on software vendors and their years-long, multimillion-dollar software implementations.

Almost all the customers hired industry consultants to aid them in selecting a vendor. Several customers hired more than one consultant. All the customers said that their own studies and their consultants' advice identified only three vendors that could satisfy the customers' needs: Oracle, PeopleSoft, and SAP. A few customers studied Lawson's product and found it inadequate. Another studied Microsoft's product, but, after testing, found it insufficient. Several customers indicated that even SAP's product wasn't a good choice for them.

The customers testified about how PeopleSoft and Oracle bid against each other for business, forcing prices lower. All the customers testified that they would not switch to vendors other than PeopleSoft and Oracle even if those two companies raised their prices 10 percent. Price wasn't the only consideration to these customers. The products of Lawson, Microsoft, and

SAP simply couldn't meet their needs, regardless of how much those vendors lowered their prices.

The government ran out of time to put on every customer witness who
was ready to testify. So the Division lawyers put written deposition testimony and videotapes into the record from Ford, Target, Hallmark, and
two local governments. The government dropped Charles Schwab, the brokerage firm, from its witness list entirely. "Why can't you put more witnesses on the stand?" I asked a government attorney. "The judge is getting
impatient," she said.

In addition to the customers, the government put on three of the four
leading industry consultant companies. The fourth, Accenture, testified
during Oracle's case, but all told the same story. They explained their eval-
uations of competing software products. They each had hundreds of employees assigned to analyze and implement software installations for Oracle,
SAP, and PeopleSoft products, but only a handful of employees dedicated
to Lawson, and none, usually, to Microsoft products. Only PeopleSoft,
Oracle, and SAP could satisfy the needs of the industry's largest customers,
they all said.

The government also put on a witness from J. D. Edwards to explain
how hard it was to enter the market for back office, large enterprise software. Edwards tried for years to leverage its mid-market position into the
large enterprise market, the witness explained, and spent millions of dollars, only to fail. Even SAP testified in the government's case, explaining
why a supplier's success in one industry (Lawson in health care, as an example) would not automatically qualify the company to sell to customers
in other industries.

Despite the overwhelming showing, reporters following the case often
got confused about exactly what the government had to prove in terms of
market definition. During the cross-examination of the government's witness from IBM Consulting, Oracle's lawyer asked about a single human
resources deployment of Lawson software to fulfill a contract with the
state of Arizona. The witness replied that she had not heard about that
engagement.

Out in the hall after the examination, Oracle's lawyers claimed a great
victory, arguing that the Lawson deal with the state of Arizona certainly

fell within the government's market definition, contradicting the government's position that only Oracle, PeopleSoft, and SAP could meet large enterprise needs. Several reporters filed stories with the Oracle spin. No media outlet reports that I saw noted that the Arizona deal represented a single instance of Lawson's participation among the scores, if not hundreds, of deals that were restricted to Oracle, PeopleSoft, and SAP.

After all the fact witnesses testified, the government called the first of its two economic experts, Dr. Kenneth Elzinga, a well-known economics professor at the University of Virginia. At various points in his testimony, Elzinga described himself as a Chicago School adherent. He was there to explain the transaction in traditional antitrust terms. He defined markets limited to the United States for "high function" human resources and financial software using data submitted to the government by various companies. He showed how the merger would produce anticompetitive levels of concentration, from which market power and competitive injury could be inferred.

What attracted the most press attention in Elzinga's testimony was his analysis, displayed as a bar graph, of the "discount approval forms" Oracle fought so hard to keep the government from getting. The forms listed the competitors for each deal in which Oracle sales personnel wanted to quote an off-list price. Everyone in the courtroom could see why Oracle's lawyers never wanted these forms to see the light of day.

On the 222 discount approval forms for large transactions, PeopleSoft or J. D. Edwards was noted as a competitor 152 times, and SAP about 80 times. After that, said Elzinga, "the numbers fell off a ledge." Lawson was noted in about 16 requests and several niche competitors had a few mentions. If Microsoft, Lawson, or others were meaningful competitors of Oracle sufficient to keep that company from gouging customers after the takeover, those companies should have appeared more often in the discount forms, Elzinga explained.

Elzinga's bar chart made his testimony crystal clear. "An antitrust economist testified Friday," read the next day's lead in the *San Francisco Chronicle*, "that Oracle's own sales documents show a merged firm would reduce the incentive to give discounts, causing software prices to rise."

Elzinga used the discount forms to define the markets—to show which firms compete in the markets the government identified. The Antitrust Division's second economist, Preston McAfee, personified the more modern approach to merger analysis. McAfee, a Caltech economist famous for his academic work the government used to set rules for the multibillion-dollar sale of wireless spectrum, didn't define markets at all. Instead, he made three separate studies of the evidence in the case to show, without using market definition, that prices would likely go up after the takeover.

McAfee began with the most traditional type of economic analysis. Using Oracle's discount forms, Oracle's sales representative summaries, PeopleSoft's customer information, the statements of consultants, and other evidence in the case, McAfee explained and analyzed—in narrative rather than mathematics—twenty-five of the procurement transactions from the case record. In economic parlance, he conducted "case studies."

Economic journals used to publish case studies as a favored form of academic analysis. In recent years, case studies have taken a backseat to statistical analysis and modeling in the academic literature, but case studies remain a tried-and-true avenue of economic research. McAfee used the case studies to explain in words how competition in the markets actually worked and to make sure that the pricing data from the companies that he used for statistical analysis accurately reflected real market conditions.

McAfee's testimony connected specific Oracle discount forms to the presentations of customer witnesses who appeared earlier in the case. McAfee showed from the documents how Oracle personnel viewed PeopleSoft's competition for these accounts at the time the competition was actually occurring and how the customers, from their own trial testimony, evaluated the benefits of PeopleSoft's competition in terms of lower prices. Some of the transactions involved additional competitors beyond just PeopleSoft and Oracle, like Lawson. In each study, McAfee used the documents in the record to show how Oracle lowered its prices, taking PeopleSoft into account, regardless of the other competitors. Without using complicated mathematics, the case studies showed how significant losing PeopleSoft would be to competition in the market.

McAfee prepared some summary statistics from his analysis of the discount forms and other transaction data. The summaries showed that Oracle competed most frequently with PeopleSoft and SAP in large deals and that Oracle won bids less often when PeopleSoft was a competitor. This result indicated that Oracle and PeopleSoft were each other's closest competitor for many deals.

Next, McAfee used a standard statistical technique, known as a regression analysis, to show the historical effect of PeopleSoft's competition on Oracle's price level—not just in the twenty-five case studies, but across the board. The regression analysis showed that PeopleSoft's competition for procurement opportunities caused Oracle to offer greater discounts—almost 10 percent greater on average. Oracle charged much lower prices when it bid against PeopleSoft, regardless of whether Oracle was also bidding against SAP or other competitors in the same deal.

Then, McAfee presented the kind of economic model that made him famous—an "auction-based simulation" to predict the price effect of the proposed takeover. What big customers were doing, McAfee explained, is no different from what a homeowner does when he gets multiple bids to reroof his house and uses the lowest bid as leverage to extract an even lower bid from another contractor. Economists call this process an "auction," even though there is no real auctioneer. Using standard mathematical equations that simulate this kind of situation, along with Elzinga's market share data, McAfee predicted price increases from 5 to 11 percent for financial software and from 13 to 28 percent for human resources software, if Oracle took over PeopleSoft.

Then the government rested, leaving Oracle to present its case. At the first pretrial conference months earlier, Oracle's lawyer promised he would meet the government's case, customer witness for customer witness. He laid out a strategy to put on the witness stand a customer supporting Oracle comparable by industry to every customer the government called. As an example, he said that if the government produced Ford as a witness, Oracle might produce General Motors.

The Antitrust Division put on the testimony of both Ford and Chrysler, but no automotive company testified for Oracle. No communications company stepped forward on Oracle's behalf to contradict the testimony of Verizon and Nextel. No consumer products company rebutted Pepsi's presentation. No retailer took issue with Neiman Marcus's conclusions. Oracle called only two live customer witnesses, relying mostly on the testimony of an executive from Emerson Electric in St. Louis.

The Emerson executive testified that his company got a good price from Oracle without involving PeopleSoft in the negotiations at all. But a quick look at the court documents revealed that the Emerson witness had paid more for software than almost any of the other customer witnesses at the trial, simply because he didn't have suppliers bid against each other.

The Emerson witness also minimized the importance of human resources software in large enterprises. Under cross-examination he admitted that he employed software engineers in the Philippines for $8,000 per year to avoid paying U.S. salary levels, and paid $12 per hour to workers in India for software implementation. It was easy for everyone in the courtroom to see why keeping track of employee benefits wasn't a high priority for Emerson.

The bulk of Oracle's case consisted of company executives and paid experts, including an industry consultant who markets his services under the name "Retail.In.Genius." Jerry Hausman, an economist from MIT, took issue with the government's experts. Hausman said the relevant geographic market included Europe, not just the United States. And he argued that competitors in the market should include Microsoft and Lawson. He claimed that although Lawson made software for use only in a couple of industries, it would expand to other industries if Oracle tried to raise prices after acquiring PeopleSoft.

The government lawyer cross-examining Hausman played videotape excerpts from Hausman's deposition in which the witness claimed that even if PeopleSoft, Oracle, and SAP all merged into a single firm, that firm could not raise prices. In fact, even if all the vendors of packaged software joined together, Hausman claimed, they could not raise customer prices. The statements sounded extreme, almost shocking, defying common sense.

Hausman made his own regression studies, but, in a surprising turn of events, Hausman admitted that his studies did not contradict McAfee. Through an elaborate and difficult cross-examination of a hostile witness, the government lawyer got Hausman to confirm that PeopleSoft's participation as a competitor in procurement bids induced Oracle to give a 10 percent greater customer discount than it otherwise would have.

When I heard Hausman's conclusion, I leaned back in my seat, soaking it in. Hausman's studies and McAfee's studies produced just about the same results. The trial is over, I said to myself. Both sides agreed that competition from PeopleSoft forced Oracle's prices lower, regardless of other bidders. Eliminating PeopleSoft would surely raise customers' prices. The judge didn't need to resolve conflicting claims of market definition in light of the takeover's anticompetitive effects.

Hausman went on to argue that he got approximately the same results looking at SAP. SAP also induced Oracle to lower its prices. "So what?" I thought. According to both sides' experts, PeopleSoft's participation in a procurement opportunity made Oracle lower its prices even when SAP was already bidding.

The next day, after the lunch break, Larry Ellison took the stand. For inexplicable reasons, the marshals cleared the courtroom in anticipation of Ellison's testimony. Everyone had to take all materials out into the hall and line up to reenter the courtroom after the break. Journalists who had been covering the trial from the beginning left choice seats and had to get into a new line behind stock arbitrageurs who wandered in off the street just to hear Ellison.

Some reporters from national publications who had left early for lunch came back to find a line so long they would never get back in. One journalist went up and down the queue, offering a hot hamburger for a better shot at getting back into the courtroom.

On direct examination, Ellison claimed he needed to buy PeopleSoft for its customers. With more customers, he could spread research costs over a bigger base, producing better products at lower prices, he argued. Ellison said he had to adopt this strategy in order to compete with Microsoft, which would soon enter the market with very low-priced products. Under Claude Scott's cross-examination questioning, Ellison admitted that Oracle could try to acquire the customers it would get from taking over PeopleSoft simply by competing vigorously in the free market, but the competitive process would take much longer, and, of course, it might not be successful.

Scott also used Ellison's cross-examination to show that Oracle intended to harm PeopleSoft. One internal e-mail quoted an Oracle representative telling an institutional investor that the publicity surrounding the hostile bid would "impact [PeopleSoft's] ability to retain employees and call on customers." A second e-mail described what Oracle's investment banker called a "Twist-in-the-Wind Strategy" to "create doubts in the minds of the market" about PeopleSoft. "Oracle seeks to acquire market share and an ongoing revenue stream without competing for it, while concurrently decimating its chief competitor," read the brief the government filed at the beginning of the trial. Ellison proved the government's main argument.

Scott next offered proof that the three large vendors, PeopleSoft, Oracle, and SAP, all price discriminate. He put into evidence an Oracle document showing an analysis of PeopleSoft's prices for each market segment. The document showed that the same software is sold to customers in different market segments at different prices.

Ellison's most telling admission came when he was jousting with Scott about the importance of innovation to customers. "Absent competition," Scott inquired, "there's no guarantee that [a company is] going to try to innovate?"

The courtroom fell silent. Larry Ellison, one of the great entrepreneurs of our time, was about to opine on the relationship between competition and innovation. Some Chicago School scholars maintain that the relationship is uncertain, and that we should therefore ignore innovation in formulating merger policy.

My white paper, on the other hand, described PeopleSoft's various product innovations and argued that Oracle's takeover would eliminate the most innovative competitor in the market. Industry studies showed that PeopleSoft consistently spent a much higher percentage of revenues on research and development than Oracle. The customer witnesses in the government's case echoed the concern. By reducing competition, they said, the takeover would dampen the remaining suppliers' incentives to innovate.

Throughout the trial, Oracle's legal team countered by claiming that customer demand would drive innovation, even without competition. I looked at the anxious faces of Oracle's lawyers at the counsel table as Ellison considered Scott's question. Apparently, the lawyers had forgotten to brief Ellison on the point. He paused before answering.

"I suppose that's true. . . . I guess if there's no competition, innovation would be wasted effort. Yes."

"Would you agree with me that the less competition there is, the less drive there is for you to have to innovate in order to stay on top of the cutting edge of your industry?" Scott continued.

"Theoretically, sure," Ellison replied.

Reduced competition means less innovation, a concept so obvious to Larry Ellison that all the academic debate hardly seemed worthwhile. "He gave you his answer," Walker later said to Scott. "That's the one you wanted." Pity that Justice Scalia wasn't in the courtroom to get firsthand information about the source of innovation.

After the last Oracle witness, Walker took a three-week break and then called all the lawyers back to the courtroom to present final arguments. Then, Walker took the case under advisement.

A week later, Ellison's predictions of "deteriorating" PeopleSoft business came true. Conway announced a 70 percent drop in quarterly earnings. "The extensive media coverage of the trial was simply too much to overcome," Conway said. "It's clearly the elephant in the room." Some customers adopted a wait-and-see attitude, said PeopleSoft executives. Other potential customers just walked away. The specific examples of customer discounts that came out in the trial had a big impact on pending deals, a top industry analyst told the *San Francisco Chronicle*.

Conway called me after releasing the financial information. If Walker found against the government, Conway wanted me to go with him to a meeting with the top lawyers in the Antitrust Division and convince them not to appeal. Better to sell the company than irretrievably injure it by appealing.

The government lawyers waited for Walker's decision with what one member of the trial team called "guarded optimism." In the minds of most courtroom observers, the government created a strong record. But Walker's viewpoint was the only one that mattered.

Early in September, as I was walking through the lobby of a client's office, my cell phone rang. A reporter from the *New York Times* wanted to know what I thought of Walker's opinion. "Who won?" I asked, my heart racing. "The government," she said.

"Walker enjoined the takeover?" I asked, wanting to make sure I heard the reporter correctly. "No, I mean Oracle won," she answered.

I ended the conversation quickly and called a lawyer at PeopleSoft. "What is it that Walker found the government failed to prove?" I asked. "Everything," he said.

Walker's 164-page opinion started off by listing ten different ways the government failed to meet its burden of proof. Walker found against Oracle on only a couple of small and largely irrelevant points. He credited the testimony of just about all of Oracle's witnesses and rejected as not credible or beside the point the testimony of the government witnesses, including all of the customers. It was like looking at the box score of a basketball game in the newspaper and seeing forty-five personal fouls called on one team and none called on the other. Hard to imagine that so few government witnesses told the unvarnished truth.

One of the government's trial lawyers talked to me about reading Walker's opinion. "I got to the first conclusion," he said, "and I thought, well, it can't get any worse than this. Then I read the next conclusion, and it was worse. It kept getting worse and worse."

The tone of Walker's opinion, even more than its content, stunned the government lawyers, producing what one member of the trial team called a "general sense of disbelief." Walker's opinion read like a tableau of government incompetence and confusion even as to proof of the most basic legal requirements.

Not that the government's presentation mattered all that much to Walker's analysis. In the end, Walker didn't reject just the approach the government relied on at trial to prove competitive injury. He rejected every possible approach the government could have taken to demonstrate an anticompetitive effect from the merger—analyzing broad markets, analyzing narrow markets, ignoring market definition altogether.

Walker imposed a new legal requirement for proof of a merger's anticompetitive unilateral effects. He said the government had to identify a market in which the merging parties after the deal "have essentially a monopoly or dominant position." In other words, the government had to show what Robert Bork and other critics of strong merger enforcement have long agitated for—proof of "merger to monopoly," or at least something close. Under this approach, if the acquisition leaves even a single competitor for the merged firm, the government's case fails.

Because SAP already bid for just about every customer's business and because, in Walker's view, the likely market entry of other companies would thwart Oracle's ability to gouge customers after the takeover, the government failed to satisfy Walker's new requirement. Even the government's direct evidence of competitive injury from data analysis predicting price increases was insufficient, according to Walker.

Economists blasted Walker's ruling. There is no basis in economics for requiring that a merger produce a monopoly before concluding that it harms consumers. Even if SAP offered some competition in bidding situations, the merged company could still raise prices to specific customers who viewed Oracle and PeopleSoft as their top two choices. Beyond that, in the bidding situations the customers described, where they had only a few qualified suppliers, eliminating any one of the bidders through merger would permit the remaining suppliers (usually just SAP and Oracle) to raise their prices. The remaining bidders could charge more because they faced fewer competitors and therefore had less uncertainty about losing the competition. The regression analyses both sides submitted plainly showed the effect of PeopleSoft's competition on Oracle's prices and raised the likelihood of price increases after the merger, even with other suppliers of back office software in the market.

Walker devoted most of his opinion to what he saw as the government's failure to prove a cognizable antitrust market. He hanged the government with its own definition of a "high function software market" limited to PeopleSoft, Oracle, and SAP. According to the judge, PeopleSoft and Oracle customers would have a lot more choices after the merger than even the courtroom testimony of competing suppliers seemed to indicate.

A Microsoft witness explained at trial why his company would not enter the large enterprise software market. Internal Microsoft planning documents backed up the witness's testimony. Yet Walker ruled the testimony "incredible" and said that Microsoft would be "a viable substitute for a significant number of customers" should Oracle try to raise prices. More than four years after the judge wrote his opinion, Microsoft had yet to enter the large enterprise market.

Walker credited the testimony of Lawson's CEO that Lawson competed with Oracle and PeopleSoft on "almost every account." Walker "discounted" (his word) what everyone else saw as a withering government cross-examination that proved the contrary. The Lawson CEO "had a bad day Monday," *InformationWeek* reported, "as he tried to paint his company as more than a mid-market business software vendor, but was confronted with examples of enterprise customers that the Justice Department used as examples of failure."

Lawson was already in difficult financial shape at the time of the trial. The company's sales to large enterprises totaled about one-tenth those of PeopleSoft. Things didn't change much afterward. The company bought a Swedish concern and reorganized its management. The new management produced one quarter of better earnings, then things turned sour again. Lawson still signs up customers in the health care arena, but it generally positions itself as a mid-market vendor. Many back office software industry analysts don't even bother to follow the company.

Walker also said that vendors known as "outsourcers," who contract with business customers to run software services on the vendors' premises, would constrain Oracle's pricing. The outsourcers Oracle presented at trial had few customers and never grew sufficiently in the years after the trial to provide any real competition.

Some new outsourcing companies have started providing services, mostly to mid-market customers. In 2005, Dave Duffield, PeopleSoft's founder, started a new company, Workday, to offer Web-based human resources and financial management functions on an outsourcing model. Workday signed its first customer two years after Walker's opinion was published. In the spring of 2008, almost four years after Walker's decision, Workday signed its first large enterprise customer for human relations management. Other start-ups also offer Web-based human resources services, but few, if any, have secured a customer for financial management. Most large companies still reject outsourcing because they are reluctant to part with control of their financial information.

Just as at the time of the trial, some large customers in today's market can use outsourcing for a few back office functions. Many would not, even at low prices. Some customers find Lawson's software adequate. Most large enterprises do not. Microsoft's back office products and services appeal mainly to mid-market companies, not to large enterprises. SAP continues to have a strong following among manufacturing companies, but less so in the financial services sector. The postmerger choices Walker relied on, sometimes in contravention of sworn testimony, never materialized, especially among customers that viewed Oracle and PeopleSoft as their top two choices.

The government's customer witnesses unequivocally testified about how their choices for back office software were limited to a few qualified vendors, but Walker rejected the customers' trial presentations as "largely unhelpful." He said that customers had stated only their vendor "preferences." To justify blocking the merger, the judge said the customers needed to show him that there was nothing they *could* do to avoid a price increase if the merged company tried to raise its prices. Testifying about what they "would like" or would "prefer" to do was insufficient, Walker ruled. The judge made it sound like customers picked software vendors by whim.

Antitrust has never been about what customers *could* do. You *could* transport dirt with teaspoons, but most people use dump trucks. You *could* walk across the country if airfares get too high. What a customer *could* do doesn't determine whether a merger is anticompetitive. What *would* a customer do if the merged company tried to raise prices? That's always been the question. All the customers answered that question. They would pay the higher price.

Even Oracle's copresident, Chuck Phillips, confirmed the sharp constraints on customer choices. Right before he was hired by Oracle in late 2003 from Morgan Stanley, where he was a respected analyst, Phillips issued a widely circulated report in his own name and that of his employer:

Stepping back a bit, the back-office applications market for global companies is dominated by an oligopoly comprised of SAP, People-Soft and Oracle. The market is down to three viable vendors who will help re-automate back-office business practices for years to come.

The government put the Morgan Stanley newsletter into evidence and questioned Phillips about it in a videotaped deposition. Under oath and on camera, Phillips said the report accurately reflected his opinion at the time.

The government played the Phillips videotaped testimony several times during the trial and yet Walker's opinion never tells the reader what Phillips said or even the general subject of his testimony. The opinion simply states, without explanation, that Phillips's deposition testimony was submitted by the government "for spice." Doubtless the government believed the testimony more probative. An admission against interest by a high executive under circumstances in which the witness could be expected to tell the truth normally constitutes powerful evidence. Walker dismissed it without even permitting the reader to decide its value.

"Was Walker watching the same trial the rest of us were?" an incredulous Antitrust Division lawyer asked me after reading the opinion. He had a point. The customer testimony went far beyond uninformed "preferences." Each customer witness testified for at least a couple of hours about how selecting back office software was as much a matter of functionality and other factors as it was a matter of price. Some vendors didn't have the functionality the customer needed at all, regardless of the price. SAP usually had the necessary functionality but its implementation frequently required expensive training and customization, making it an undesirable choice. Hundreds of customers already had PeopleSoft's human resources software working side by side with Oracle's financial software. Starting over with SAP after the Oracle acquisition would waste enormous amounts of money.

The customers explained why simply accepting an anticompetitive 10 percent overcharge represented a sound business decision. As Emerson Electric, Oracle's live witness, testified, the software itself accounted for only a small part of the total cost of implementing a new back office solution. Raising the product price 10 percent would be unlikely to cause any customer to change its plans.

The most powerful testimony about the likelihood of postmerger price increases came from Verizon. A Verizon vice president testified that when she learned of Oracle's bid for PeopleSoft, she bought software licenses from SAP although Verizon had no current need for them. She expected that SAP would charge more for its software after Oracle bought PeopleSoft, due to lessened competition in each bidding situation.

In effect, the Verizon witness took out an insurance policy expecting higher prices. She hedged to cover her anticipated costs. Preston McAfee, the government's expert, was blown away by the testimony. "A big company like Verizon wouldn't spend its money this way if it expected just a little harm. There has to be a lot of harm." McAfee told me that the Verizon testimony was "unbelievably influential" in his thinking. Walker's opinion doesn't mention the key Verizon testimony at all.

Walker simply refused to credit the testimony of the customers or the industry consultants who appeared for the government. He also rejected Professor Elzinga's market share calculations, calling some of them "sketchy at best." And he dismissed as "inarticulable" Elzinga's description of pervasive price discrimination in the market.

Studies from the government's other economic expert received scant attention from Walker. Through Preston McAfee's testimony, the government submitted direct proof of competitive injury from data analysis, without relying on market concentration. Walker rejected McAfee's results, citing both factual and legal shortcomings.

Walker first faulted McAfee's analysis for relying too heavily on Oracle's discount forms, which Walker refused to credit, despite their authenticity. Walker said he needed additional corroboration from SAP's discount forms. The record contained the corroboration, but the judge chose to ignore the testimony of SAP's vice president, presented as part of Oracle's case, that SAP's discount forms showed relatively little final round bid competition with either Oracle or PeopleSoft, precisely what the government argued throughout the trial.

Then, citing his new legal requirement, Walker rejected McAfee's regression analyses and case studies, saying they failed to demonstrate a postmerger monopoly in any market. Walker compounded the error of his misplaced legal requirement with a misstatement of fact. Walker claimed that McAfee's studies showed only that PeopleSoft competed against Oracle. Perhaps the judge simply misunderstood McAfee's conclusion— corroborated in Hausman's cross-examination—that adding PeopleSoft to bidding opportunities forced Oracle's price lower, even when SAP was already bidding.

The *Wall Street Journal*'s editorial page could scarcely contain its glee at Vaughn Walker's opinion. "An antitrust policy smackdown," the editors called it, and a "much-needed rebuke of the Bush Justice Department," not to mention "an embarrassment for Assistant Attorney General C. Hewitt Pate."

After Walker released his opinion, Conway sent out a letter trying to reassure customers and employees that the opinion did not inevitably mean an Oracle acquisition. PeopleSoft still had defenses under the corporate laws to prevent a takeover, Conway said. PeopleSoft offered key personnel generous compensation packages to stay with the company and sweetened its severance awards for all employees. Nevertheless, according to the *Wall Street Journal*, employees left "in droves."

Walker's ruling was expected to disrupt sales in the crucial final weeks of the quarter, but PeopleSoft unexpectedly announced revenue results that topped analysts' expectations. Conway never got to celebrate. The board fired him on the same day the company released its quarterly results. Board members claimed that the firing resulted from a confluence of circumstances, including tensions with other executives. Most of the rest of the world believed that Conway was fired to pave the way for a sale of PeopleSoft to Oracle.

Hours after Conway was fired, the Antitrust Division conceded defeat, announcing that the Justice Department would not appeal Walker's decision. After holding out for a few weeks, PeopleSoft's board agreed to sell the company for $26.50 per share.

The shock waves from Walker's decision altered both business and law enforcement. Over $10 billion changed hands. The deal made Craig Conway enormously wealthy from his PeopleSoft stock holdings. He still would rather have earned the money by competing in the marketplace.

Just about all of PeopleSoft's senior executives landed highly compensated, high-profile positions after the takeover. Rank-and-file employees weren't so fortunate. Vaughn Walker's opinion put thousands of people out of work, as Ellison slashed payrolls to merge the two companies. Oracle refused to release exact numbers. The press pegged the first purge at five thousand employees, many from Oracle. Some of those retained from PeopleSoft's rolls were placed on "transitional status," to be terminated the following quarter. Oracle's management warned of further job cuts down the line.

When the severance packages of terminated PeopleSoft employees ran out, Dave Duffield set up a fund with his own money to help those facing financial troubles—the equivalent of the soup lines unemployed working men stood in during the Great Depression. Duffield gave away $2 million in a few weeks. Over the program's first six months, 350 ex-employees applied for grants capped at $10,000 each. Duffield closed out the program more than two years after the Oracle takeover. The fund gave out $4 million in total. No one provided for the ex-Oracle employees Ellison fired when he consolidated the two payrolls.

In an advanced postindustrial economy, workers must sometimes lose their jobs to make way for technological progress. One Valley CEO tells the story of how ten thousand organ players went jobless after theaters switched from silent films to talkies. Regrettable, but unavoidable. Sometimes progress requires employee dislocations, but the Oracle case was not one of those times. PeopleSoft's workers were productively employed making products that customers wanted until Vaughn Walker's decision changed their lives.

Before the trial, while I was working with PeopleSoft's publishing office to format, copy, and bind my white paper, the office manager quietly asked me if she should start looking for another job. She wanted a straight answer. Both she and her husband worked at PeopleSoft, like many couples in the area. She didn't want a court decision to leave her family without a source of income.

I've counseled CEOs and corporate boards on the likelihood of adverse legal events more times than I can count. Nevertheless, the question from the office manager brought home to me the cost, in human terms, of losing the takeover battle. Given the customer outcry, I told her, the government would likely win in court. I could not imagine a court inflicting misery on so many households absent the most compelling facts.

PeopleSoft's customers fared better than many of the company's employees. Despite widespread fears, Oracle did not force a conversion to its application software. Instead, to avoid triggering more than $2 billion in contractual guarantees for failing to support PeopleSoft's products, Oracle announced that it would release a new version of PeopleSoft's product suite and would offer "lifetime support" for the software customers already bought. Ellison was motivated less by altruism than by the revenue stream associated with software maintenance. Most PeopleSoft customers stuck with Oracle, if only to avoid the costs of switching back office software, estimated at $10 million for a midsize company.

Oracle's back office software revenues soared once PeopleSoft was absorbed. In mid-2006, Oracle's revenues from back office software applications jumped 83 percent. The following quarter, revenue from the sales of new licenses rose 80 percent. Oracle gained in the database market, as well. Some, but not all, of the growth came from acquisitions.

There is certainly less competition than there used to be, one analyst told me. "How can I prove that?" I asked her, parroting Walker's argument about stronger competition from a variety of sources.

"There used to be three choices for customers and now there are two," she said.

"Does that really mean less competition?" I persisted. "I don't understand why you think there is less competition."

"What is it you don't understand?" she asked, starting to get frustrated with me. "There used to be three choices and now there are two."

The most profound effect from Walker's decision was felt at the Antitrust Division. Morale, already shaky, plummeted. Experienced lawyers left for academia or private practice.

For years, the Republican leadership of the Antitrust Division undermined, by word and deed, important elements of antitrust doctrine. They made no effort to restrain the behavior of monopolists. They promoted, rather than restrained, the patent prerogatives of big companies, even at the expense of innovation. Their message was read as a denigration of the entire antitrust enterprise. Small wonder, when they tried to enforce their own Merger Guidelines, a Republican judge rebuffed them.

In the three years after the PeopleSoft acquisition, Ellison rolled up the back office software markets, just as he promised. "Today, Oracle brazenly acknowledges that it creates innovation and innovative products by buying them from others," observed *CIO* magazine. Ellison integrated the products he bought into a comprehensive customer offering. His strategy restructured the entire industry, forcing customers to choose a single supplier for all components of a back office solution, rather than picking the most desirable products from among different suppliers for each function. The strategy worked, at least for Oracle's shareholders. In mid-2008, the company announced a 38 percent increase in revenue from selling applications and quietly raised its prices for both databases and applications by 15 to 20 percent. Pricing increases "could be viewed as the acquisitive company starting to leverage its growing dominance, as alternative offerings in enterprise software shrink for [technology] buyers due to ongoing market consolidation," reported *Information Week*.

The Antitrust Division brought not a single challenge to any of the almost forty acquisitions Ellison made after taking over PeopleSoft, not even the purchase of Siebel Systems, Oracle's closest competitor in back office customer management software. "You have to ask yourself if you will win before you bring a case," one former Division official said to me.

"Has the Antitrust Division lost its nerve?" shrieked the headline in the *Legal Times*. Larry Ellison wasn't the only beneficiary of the Division's self-doubt. After the *Oracle* decision, years passed before the Bush Justice Department ever challenged another high-profile merger in court.

CHAPTER 19

The Last Mile

"Unthinkable." That's what Reed Hundt, head of the Clinton administration's Federal Communications Commission, said when the chairman of AT&T in 1997 floated the idea of starting to reassemble the national telecommunications monopoly Bill Baxter tore asunder.

AT&T established itself as a competitor in both local and long-distance telephone markets more than a century ago. The company created a national monopoly by enforcing its patent portfolio against some competitors and by acquiring others. Once the company took the lead in long-distance lines, it denied its remaining local competitors connection privileges to its long-distance circuits, depriving the smaller rivals of network advantages.

In 1912 and again in 1949, the Justice Department sued AT&T for antitrust violations (both settled by negotiated agreements). The Interstate Commerce Commission and then the FCC tried to regulate the company. AT&T defended some of the antitrust suits filed against it by claiming that its activities were approved by the FCC. AT&T also asserted the need for a national, integrated network in order to produce innovations, high-quality service, and low prices.

AT&T began to face significant price competition for long-distance services in the 1970s from companies like MCI and Sprint that relied on microwave technology. AT&T responded by making it difficult for the competitors to connect their long-distance lines to AT&T circuits that by

that time controlled access to homes and offices in metropolitan areas. In 1980, MCI won a big damages award against AT&T in an antitrust case over AT&T's denial of connection privileges. Confronted with Bill Baxter's threat to "litigate to the eyeballs" a couple of years later, the monopolist decided to break itself voluntarily into six regional operating companies, sometimes called "Baby Bells," and a long-distance company that continued to use the AT&T name. The long-distance company was to operate without government restraint in a freely competitive market; the divested Bell operating companies were considered "natural monopolies" that the FCC would continue to regulate.

The settlement that broke up AT&T prevented the local Bell operating companies from offering long-distance services. But Sprint and MCI grew, and other competitors also entered the long-distance market, knocking AT&T's share down to 60 percent. Residential long-distance rates fell by half. The new competition also spawned new technology by creating a bigger market for the fiber optic cable that Corning Glass unsuccessfully attempted to sell to AT&T in the early 1970s. Sprint and MCI used fiber optics for long-distance lines.

A couple of new competitors, MFS Communications Company and Teleport Communications Group, started laying fiber cable loops around big cities to connect office buildings to each other and to long-distance carriers more cheaply than the local Bell operating companies would. In most places, though, the Bells continued to carry more than 95 percent of local telephone traffic.

Encouraged by the initial success of the local Bell competitors, a Republican-dominated Congress overhauled the telecommunications laws in 1996 to speed up competition. The new law made it easier for existing long-distance providers and telecom start-ups to enter local markets. Bell operating companies were likewise permitted to enter the long-distance market and sell telecommunications services nationally, once they showed the FCC that they had opened their local markets to competition.

Lawmakers envisioned a competitive free-for-all between AT&T and its former regional subsidiaries. Instead, the new law unleashed an unprecedented wave of mammoth mergers. Less than two months after President Clinton signed the new telecommunications bill into law, AT&T's old

Southwestern Bell operating company, known as SBC, announced that it was acquiring AT&T's old West Coast operating company, Pacific Telesis Group. Critics foresaw an ominous trend. "What you'll see is not a free-for-all, but an oligopoly," said one consumer advocate.

Historically, both the FCC and the Antitrust Division had jurisdiction over telecom mergers. Reed Hundt readily ceded the leadership role for merger review under the new law to the Division. "It's logical to think we'll let the Justice Department have the first crack at this deal," Hundt said. Joel Klein, the Division's acting chief, cleared the $17 billion SBC acquisition of Pacific Telesis. Then Klein cleared the $22 billion merger between the two big East Coast Bell operating companies, Bell Atlantic and NYNEX. Enraged Democrats in the Senate blocked Klein's confirmation.

In June 1997, with Joel Klein's nomination still on hold, the chairman of AT&T proposed the combination of the nation's two largest telecommunications companies. In a widely publicized speech, he laid out the rationale for a merger between AT&T, mostly a long-distance carrier, and SBC, the largest local Bell operating company. AT&T mailed copies of the speech to hundreds of Washington decision makers "in an initial effort to sway opinion in favor of such a deal," according to the *New York Times*.

Hundt didn't wait for a press release announcing the deal. The following week, before what would have been the largest corporate merger in history had even been formally proposed, Hundt made a public statement declaring any merger between AT&T and one of the Bell operating companies "unthinkable" under the antitrust laws. Quoting Theodore Roosevelt ("the true function of the state . . . should be to make the chances of competition more even, not to abolish them"), Hundt described the telecommunications sector as a "monopoly market only just started on the road to recovery." He argued that "billions of dollars in economic growth" and "astounding feats of innovation" could be achieved only through competition.

Hundt left the commission a few weeks later. AT&T abandoned its merger talks with SBC and instead bought Teleport, one of the small companies that competed in metropolitan markets against the regional Bell operating companies. MCI, after combination with another long-distance carrier, took control of MFS, the other local Bell competitor.

The two deals united the extensive long-distance networks owned by AT&T and MCI with the smaller metropolitan fiber networks created by the companies they acquired, MFS and Teleport. These metropolitan networks connected to many urban office buildings, but they did not come close to matching the coverage for homes and office buildings of the Bell operating companies, which connected to virtually every building in their regions. After the new Telecommunications Act became law, other small companies also started laying fiber in built-up urban areas.

None of the smaller local competitors could offer business customers reasonable alternatives to Bell service without connecting to almost every building in major metropolitan areas, but many of the buildings were serviced only by a Bell-owned circuit. To encourage competition, FCC regulations required the Bells to provide smaller "telcos" (telecommunication companies) with access to the Bell circuits and set the rates the Bells could charge for their circuits so that the smaller telcos could provide sufficient market coverage to attract customers.

The smaller telcos, led by AT&T and MCI, pressed for ever-broader access to the Bell networks at lower rates. SBC and the other Baby Bells resisted the moves to open their local networks to competition. Every change in the regulations precipitated a round of litigation, first in the commission, then in the courts. Stephen Williams, a conservative judge on the federal appellate court in D.C., repeatedly thwarted Congress's efforts at reform by rejecting FCC and state telecommunications regulations intended to open the operating companies' local networks to competition.

SBC and Bell Atlantic, meanwhile, continued to expand by acquisition. Bell Atlantic bought GTE, the largest independent telephone company, and changed the merged company's name to Verizon. Verizon dominated local telecommunications markets on the East Coast. Klein cleared the deal after the company agreed to sell some of its wireless businesses. SBC bought the dominant local carrier in Connecticut. A few weeks later, SBC announced a plan to buy Ameritech, the regional Bell operating company headquartered in Chicago, creating the nation's largest telephone company. Even Republicans sounded alarms. "Consolidation without competition can hurt consumers," warned Senator John McCain.

SBC's CEO, Ed Whitacre, publicly offered to sell off cellular telephone lines to competitors in order to get government approval for the Ameritech deal. He also promised increased competition in local markets as a result of the huge acquisition. "There is no doubt in my mind," Whitacre told the *Washington Post*, "that our new [strategy] will cause AT&T, MCI and others to come out from behind and start competing for local telephone business."

Joel Klein approved the deal after SBC agreed to sell off the cellular lines Whitacre had already offered as a concession. The FCC in its review judged the acquisition unlawful but approved the deal after SBC agreed to a set of conditions that the company all but ignored once the deal closed. SBC ended up dominating most of the local telecom markets outside of Verizon's territory. Despite the end of legal restraints, the two companies rarely spent resources competing against each other, even where their operating territories abutted each other.

After the Ameritech acquisition closed, the FCC found that SBC "willfully and repeatedly" violated the merger conditions intended to foster competition and imposed a $6 million fine, barely worth an entry on SBC's rap sheet. A journalist reported in 2004 that over the preceding six years SBC had been fined more than $1 billion by state and federal regulators for anticompetitive conduct. During one stretch, SBC was fined almost every month, receiving multiple Notices of Apparent Liability and Forfeiture Orders as it fought in the FCC, the state agencies, and sometimes even the courts to keep control of local phone markets. A Merrill Lynch analyst explained, "As long as the cost of violating the merger agreements is below the cost of allowing competitors to enter the market, it continues to be cheaper to pay the government for violating certain performance targets versus completely opening up the markets to competitors." How Justice Scalia in his 2004 antitrust opinion could proclaim the telecommunications regulatory regime "effective" is difficult to fathom.

AT&T and MCI did their best to compete vigorously against SBC and Verizon in local markets. The two companies also led regulatory lobbying efforts, continuing to demand access to the Bells' local networks. Consumer groups as well as new market entrants aligned themselves with AT&T. The company "built a reputation for standing up for the little guy," said *USA Today*. "AT&T was the leader in the attempt to create local phone competition," the director of the Consumers Union told a newspaper. Robert Bork frequently represented AT&T in its court cases.

Finally, in the summer of 2004, the FCC ruled in favor of the Bells in the long-running dispute over network access. AT&T and MCI appealed the FCC decision. The federal appellate court, in an opinion written by Stephen Williams, also sided with the Bells. The court decision restricted AT&T's ability to compete against what the company characterized as the "powerful Bell telephone monopolies." Nevertheless, the Bush administration decided not to support AT&T's Supreme Court appeal of Williams's opinion.

Without the backing of the administration, the Supreme Court declined to hear AT&T's appeal, and AT&T sold itself to SBC in January 2005. Verizon acquired its largest competitor, MCI, a couple of weeks later. Everyone associated with the telecommunications industry knew what was happening. "SBC's acquisition of AT&T carries a bit of irony," wrote one analyst, "causing many to believe that the telecom industry appears to be reverting to its pre-1984 state."

On May 10, the head of the Antitrust Division, Hewitt Pate, announced his resignation, leaving the big phone mergers unresolved. The *Wall Street Journal* greeted the event with an editorial that harshly criticized Pate and urged the administration to approve "the recent telecom mergers." Thomas Barnett, the deputy who headed the Oracle case, was named acting assistant attorney general, effective June 25, 2005. He was officially nominated by the administration to take Pate's place a couple of months later.

A group of smaller local and long-distance telecom providers asked me to represent them in opposing the mergers. Companies in the group leased circuits from the larger firms that were merging and combined those leased circuits with their own facilities to offer telecom services tailored to the needs of small and midsize business customers. The smaller telcos sometimes leased circuits from the Bells at rates regulated by the FCC. On routes where AT&T, MCI, or some other Bell competitor offered alternative circuits in competition with the Bells, my clients would lease from the company that offered the lowest prices, in response to bid solicitations. Like other business customers, the smaller telecom companies worried that after the merger, the cost of leased circuits would rise substantially because of diminished competition.

According to many published reports, stiff competition in the telecom industry had produced declining prices for small and midsize businesses. Industry analysts expected the acquisitions to reverse that trend. "We expect competition in the SME [small and medium-size business] market to slow down," predicted one prominent analyst. "Pricing is likely to stabilize and possibly rise over time." Industry reports anticipated that after the mergers, pricing would become "better"—meaning higher—for SBC and Verizon.

The effect of the mergers on individuals was less predictable. Increases in consumer prices for telephone and Internet services might be restrained in some localities after the mergers by competition from wireless providers and cable companies that were beginning to enter the consumer telecom market. Some individual consumers might end up with a choice between the local cable operator and SBC or Verizon, depending on the area, for home and personal telecom needs.

Potential cable and wireless suppliers provided little solace to small and medium-size businesses. Cable companies offered few business services and were unlikely to check price increases by the merged companies for dedicated, secure, high-bandwidth business lines. Cell phones could not be used to transmit large amounts of data easily, either.

At any other time in antitrust enforcement history, I would have urged the Antitrust Division to simply block the deals, given the elimination of actual and potential competition both in long-distance and local markets, and the likelihood of significant price increases. But this was the Bush administration after the *Oracle* decision, and what was once "unthinkable" for antitrust enforcement had become "likely" and even "desirable" in some circles.

The best my clients could hope for was a forced divestiture of all overlapping facilities. SBC connected virtually all the buildings in its local operating areas with its own lines. AT&T, in its efforts to compete with SBC, connected some of those same buildings with the facilities it owned. After the acquisition with AT&T, SBC had little use for two overlapping networks that connected the same buildings in each local area. Verizon and MCI had the same kinds of overlaps.

All of the lines and switches of the acquired companies (AT&T and MCI) that overlapped with the existing assets of SBC and Verizon should be sold in bulk, I reasoned. The purchaser might emerge with a footprint in many local areas sufficient to offer postmerger price competition for the dedicated business circuits my clients cared about. Just two years earlier the Bush administration provided a precedent for this approach by demanding the sale of all overlapping assets as a condition for clearing a much smaller telephone merger.

My hopes were quickly extinguished. The government refused to acknowledge the precedent. In fact, once SBC and Verizon announced the acquisitions, the government began what looked like a perfunctory clearance review. My clients all maintained extensive databases of bids they received from the Bells, AT&T, MCI, and other companies to supply business circuits around the country. Analysis of the databases might explain the competitive conditions in the industry and, as in the Oracle case, predict the pricing effects of the acquisitions. Yet the government did not even ask for copies of the data.

At my urging, the clients hired ERS, an economic consulting firm that helped prepare Preston McAfee's testimony in the Oracle trial, to analyze the data. After weeks of detailed examination at a cost of many hundreds of thousands of dollars, the analysis revealed that three competing bidders produced lower prices to purchasers of business circuits than two, and four bidders even lower prices than three—not exactly a startling conclusion, but something, I thought, the government would be hard-pressed to ignore.

AT&T and MCI were the cheapest and most pervasive suppliers of business circuits in the client databases. Their aggressive bidding produced low prices regardless of the number of competing suppliers in a deal. Even the Bells responded to competition from AT&T and MCI by lowering their own prices for business circuits. Statistical analysis of the data showed likely price increases of 20 to 500 percent after the mergers, depending on the geographic area and the type of circuit. The empirical analysis by ERS strongly supported the predictions of widespread price increases published by many industry analysts.

I pressed the government to subpoena my clients' data and the economic analysis. After a couple of telephone conferences during the summer to discuss the ERS study, division lawyers and economists, along with outside experts retained by the Justice Department, began to audit the ERS results. I expected the government to do a thorough job, as befitting deals of such magnitude. The merging companies repeatedly represented to the press, the public, and the investment community that the deals were unlikely to close before the first half of 2006, so the government had adequate time. In addition, Tom Barnett had not yet been confirmed to lead the Antitrust Division. Usually, the Division waited to make final determinations on large acquisitions until it had a confirmed leader.

Suddenly, without explanation, the Justice Department rushed to judgment. The Division lawyers abruptly terminated their audit before even a single company's data had been fully reviewed, and instructed me to submit a white paper promptly if I wanted it considered. I quickly prepared a paper and asked for a meeting between the Division's front office and the CEOs of several of my clients. Because of scheduling conflicts, the Division lawyers said, the only time Tom Barnett could meet was 4 p.m. the Friday before Columbus Day weekend. Despite the inconvenience, I had CEOs and other high executives from four substantial companies sitting beside me on October 7, as I looked across the Antitrust Division's conference table at Barnett.

By the day of the meeting, the press was reporting that the deals were tracked for quick approval with only minor conditions. Reuters reported the antitrust review "coming out far better for the carriers than even the carriers anticipated." The government completely ignored the overall effect of eliminating two of the largest and most aggressive competitors from the market. A complete divestiture of all overlapping assets was not even under consideration. Instead, the merging companies would be required to sell certain lines, known as "last mile" connections, between their networks and specific buildings.

According to the press, the government's proposed remedy addressed just those buildings where a merging Bell company (SBC or Verizon) and a competitor eliminated by the mergers (AT&T or MCI) provided the only last-mile connections. If the merger created a single owner for both last-mile lines, what the lawyers called "2-to-1 building," one of the lines had to be sold off to a competitor, so the building would still have two line suppliers after the mergers.

No divestiture of any kind was required for the thousands of buildings with three or four (or more) pre-merger line suppliers, even where the mergers eliminated one of the buildings' suppliers—"3-to-2" and "4-to-3" buildings. Eliminating one of three or four competing suppliers surely meant higher prices for customers in the affected buildings (as the ERS study indicated), yet the government required no line divestitures to maintain the level of pre-merger competition.

As we sat down at the meeting, I told Barnett that the rumored remedy would be ineffective to prevent significant price increases.

"Would you choose no remedy at all over the one you've heard about?" Barnett asked with a slight grin.

I sat dumbstruck. Barnett was offering a remedy that prevented only a very few of the anticipated postmerger prices increases—take it or leave it. "Now wait a minute," I stammered.

"I thought so," he interjected, his grin broadening. Barnett thought he had caught me admitting that the proposed remedy produced at least some customer benefit. Clearly, something was better than nothing, apparently the standard for Bush administration antitrust enforcement.

"How can you give me a choice between an ineffective remedy and no remedy at all?" I argued.

One of the company executives had seen all he needed to evaluate the current state of antitrust enforcement. He interrupted me, addressing Barnett directly. "If all you are going to do is deal with the situations where two building suppliers before the mergers go down to one after the mergers, just don't do anything," my client said firmly. "Some gullible people might believe you're actually accomplishing something by doing that, but we all know you're really not. So, just don't do anything."

Barnett looked down at the table and the meeting ended quickly.

Three weeks later, with the deals still awaiting clearance, the *Wall Street Journal* ran an editorial criticizing Barnett for "sitting on the proposed

SBC/AT&T and Verizon/MCI mergers" and for requiring Oracle to submit to an antitrust review of its recently announced acquisition of Siebel Systems. The *Journal* later revealed that Oracle actually lobbied lawmakers against Barnett's nomination. The editorial ended by noting that "Mr. Barnett's nomination is pending before the Senate," but "he belongs in another job."

The day after the editorial ran, the Department of Justice announced the approval of the telecom mergers with only the minor divestitures Barnett talked about in the meeting. The Division's press release hailed the government's action, claiming that the divestitures would preserve competition for business telecommunication services. "The Division thoroughly investigated . . . all areas in which the merging firms compete," said the release, "and evaluated all overlaps between the merging parties." The transactions "will likely benefit consumers," the release continued, "due in part to 'exceptionally large merger-specific efficiencies.'"

During the campaign to convince the Antitrust Division to clear their deals, SBC and Verizon touted the money they would save—the companies called these savings "efficiencies"—by combining their own local services with the long-distance operations of the companies they were acquiring. They made little attempt to show that the savings would get passed on to consumers in the form of lower prices, as the Guidelines required. Presumably, they intended to pocket the increased profits.

Bill Baxter overrode these nominal "efficiencies" in favor of competition when he broke up the national telephone monopoly in 1982. Barnett, on the other hand, used the "efficiencies" to justify his ineffective remedy.

I can't say I was surprised. The legal press reported that SBC and Verizon had hired hundreds of lawyers, probably more than a thousand, to work for approval of the mergers. The division was badly outgunned and perhaps even intimidated by the show of force. After the *Oracle* decision, I'm not sure the division had the wherewithal to take on two big companies, even if Barnett wanted to challenge the mergers. Two weeks later, the division cleared Oracle's purchase of Siebel Systems without any conditions. Barnett's confirmation still remained in limbo.

A second *Wall Street Journal* editorial reported that Barnett's nomination had been placed on hold while two senators "asked Mr. Bush to reconsider the appointment on grounds [of] Mr. Barnett's activist antitrust bent." Only after the telecom mergers closed did the senators lift their hold, permitting Barnett's confirmation.

Because the Antitrust Division's clearance of the mergers required divestitures—however modest—the government had to comply with the Tunney Act. The government filed complaints along with proposed settlements and published the settlements for public comment, as the Tunney Act required. According to the government's complaints, each building in the nation comprised a separate antitrust market. The complaints alleged competitive injury from the two mergers, but limited relief to 2-to-1 buildings.

The Antitrust Division managed to reprise in a single case two of its most infamous merger enforcement debacles. Despite the scathing criticism of the West-Thomson merger review, the government again focused on small overlaps, obscuring the overall anticompetitive effect of the gigantic mergers. And the division adopted the very position it resisted in Vaughn Walker's court. It provided remedial relief only for "mergers to monopoly," refusing to even recognize harm from lesser reductions in competition (a reduction in competitors from three to two, for example).

———

Judge Emmet Sullivan drew the Tunney Act review assignments. President Reagan originally appointed Sullivan to the District of Columbia local court bench and the first President Bush promoted him to a higher judicial position on that court. President Clinton elevated Sullivan to the federal bench in 1994.

Although short on antitrust experience, Sullivan had repeatedly demonstrated a willingness to take on tough political issues. In a suit by environmental groups alleging the undue influence of energy companies on government policy, Sullivan ordered the production of Vice President Dick Cheney's energy task force records over White House objections. Sullivan ruled unconstitutional a federal law, championed by conservatives, that prohibited District of Columbia residents from voting on a ballot initiative to legalize marijuana for medical purposes. And he upheld a District of Columbia law banning hazardous rail shipments through the city.

In the Tunney Act review, Sullivan faced an important antitrust issue of first impression. The federal appellate court that reversed Judge Stanley Sporkin's *Microsoft* decision and threw Sporkin off the case had limited Tunney Act review to the question of whether the remedies sought by the Antitrust Division are "so inconsonant with the allegations charged [in the complaint] as to fall outside the reaches of the public interest." According to that decision, only if the proposed settlement would "make a mockery of the judicial function" is the district court permitted to reject it. In plain English, the proposed remedy had to be so ridiculous that it was offensive before a court could reject it.

The court of appeals' *Microsoft* decision all but eliminated the Tunney Act as a tool for effective antitrust enforcement. After the decision, the Antitrust Division routinely permitted merging companies to close transactions before judicial review under the Tunney Act was completed. Unwilling to try to unscramble merged assets, judges came to view Tunney Act proceedings as a purely ministerial exercise.

When the "mockery of the judicial function" standard was subsequently invoked by the court of appeals to reject Robert Bork's challenge to the Bush administration's settlement with Microsoft, Herb Kohl, the Democratic senator from Wisconsin, spearheaded bipartisan legislation to overrule the "mockery" language and restore more meaningful judicial review of antitrust consent decrees. The Antitrust Division opposed Kohl's initiative, as did the Antitrust Section of the ABA.

A compromise version of Kohl's original proposal was eventually enacted into law. It specifically rejected the "mockery" language from the decisions and set out a list of factors courts are required to consider when evaluating antitrust settlements, including the effect of the settlement under review on "competition in the relevant markets." Kohl explained the provisions of his Tunney Act amendment in a speech on the Senate floor. The Antitrust Division ignored Kohl's amendment and continued to permit merging parties to close transactions prior to court review.

The telecom mergers represented the first judicial test of Kohl's Tunney Act amendments. Judge Sullivan granted my petition to appear as a "friend of the court," on behalf of the smaller telecom companies, to challenge the adequacy of the proposed remedy. Citing Senator Kohl's speech on the

Senate floor, I argued that the 2-to-1 divestiture remedy proposed by the government should be evaluated for adequacy under traditional antitrust principles—meaning that it actually had to fix the competition problems caused by the mergers—rather than under the overly deferential *Microsoft* test.

Ed Whitacre, SBC's CEO, wasted no time exploiting his new market position. Ten days after the Antitrust Division cleared the AT&T acquisition, Whitacre told *BusinessWeek* that Google, Microsoft, and other Web sites were using his "pipes"—SBC's circuits—"for free." He wanted to start charging Web sites, he said, for the Internet traffic that ran over SBC's fiber cables, presumably on top of the fees that users already paid SBC and other carriers for their Internet connections. Whitacre wanted to charge twice for the same service, one charge to the supplier, one to the consumer. Verizon's CEO made similar statements, but in somewhat more conciliatory tones.

An Amazon executive accused Whitacre of trying to "extort fees from Internet companies because there is nowhere else for their [SBC's] customers to go."

"They have market power," added the Amazon executive. "If not monopoly then duopoly—and there are no other choices for consumers."

Web companies, worried by the prospect of dominant telecom providers restricting the growth of Internet traffic, banded together to ask Congress for "net neutrality" legislation—laws that would make it illegal for the telecom companies to discriminate against popular Web sites and services in favor of the telecom companies' own Internet offerings. A competitive market with a wide array of telecom competitors lessens the likelihood that any single supplier could acquire sufficient market power to make discrimination against popular Web sites an attractive business proposition. But lacking competitive alternatives after years of telecom industry consolidation, the Web companies had little choice but to call for government regulation.

In 1998, as conservative Utah senator Orrin Hatch prepared for congressional hearings into Microsoft's behavior, he warned that the failure of antitrust enforcement would lead to an "Internet Commerce Commission."

"It seems far better to have antitrust enforcement today than heavy-handed regulation of the Internet tomorrow," he said. Seven years later, ineffective antitrust enforcement made "heavy-handed regulation of the Internet" a preferable alternative to unfettered market power.

Whitacre closed the acquisition of AT&T in December 2005, before the government's settlements with SBC and Verizon were even published for public comment. He left only the sale of the 2-to-1 circuits specified in the settlements for completion after Tunney Act review. Then Whitacre launched a $500 million corporate "rebranding" advertising campaign, taking as the name of his company, the "new" AT&T. Three months later, he completed the industry roll-up, announcing the acquisition of Bell-South, the operating company for the southern United States—all before the first Tunney Act hearing in Judge Sullivan's court on the original SBC-AT&T deal. The BellSouth acquisition also consolidated Whitacre's control over the Cingular cell phone company, the nation's top wireless provider.

"I don't think we'll have to give back one thing to gain approval of the BellSouth merger," Whitacre said, responding to an analyst's question about the conditions antitrust enforcers might demand as part of the approval process. "And we really did not on the AT&T merger; I think the same conditions exist here, I don't expect to give back anything."

Whitacre's aggressive comments reminded everyone just how important Sullivan's Tunney Act review had become. The "old" AT&T of 1982 monopolized telephone communications. At stake in the Tunney Act hearing was the new AT&T's control over the "pipes" used for high-speed Internet connections—the facilities used for the transmission of news, information, data, Internet telephony, music, streaming video, and almost everything else required for business, education, and entertainment in the new economy.

Two months after granting my motion to participate in the Tunney Act review, Sullivan summoned me back to Washington for the first argument on the government's settlements. I chastised the government for adopting a remedy addressed to a small number of buildings instead of dealing with the larger anticompetitive effects of the two mammoth mergers. "It's as if the government in looking at these mergers is confronted by an elephant," I told the judge. "Instead of standing back and considering this multi-ton beast, the government is instead focusing on the elephant's toenail."

I put up posters in the courtroom with excerpts from the Antitrust Division's press release. The release claimed that the mergers would produce efficiencies in the form of cost savings that would benefit consumers. Then I put up an excerpt from one of the government's briefs, filed after I questioned the efficiencies assertion in the press release.

In the brief, the government abandoned the position "that efficiencies would overcome the anticompetitive effects" of the mergers after announcements from both SBC and Verizon that they would use their newfound wealth to buy back company stock in order to drive up their share prices. So much for the benefits to consumers of lower telecom costs. The government gave up trying to prove that the mergers would help consumers and retreated to the position that the deals would cause no competitive injury beyond that remedied in the settlements.

To back up my arguments against the mergers, I submitted two briefs and the declaration of the former chief economist of the FCC, who summarized the findings of the ERS data review. The government, by contrast, submitted nothing that described how it had undertaken its analysis of competitive injury and remedy. "I know that Your Honor has been on the bench for many years," I said, highlighting the Antitrust Division's failure of proof, "but I daresay this is the first case in which the government says they deserve to win . . . without putting on any evidence."

Sullivan was not yet ready to deal with the Tunney Act issues. Something else was bothering him. Looking at the contending legal teams, he wondered out loud why only business interests challenged the settlements. No public interest groups asked to participate in the proceedings. "Public interest groups know how to find their way to the courthouse when they want to. . . . No one has asked for leave to participate . . . which I would have granted," the judge said.

"I think the public's absence is not due to notice, but due to their satisfaction with the mergers and with the resolution here," Verizon's lawyer told the judge. It was a palpable lie. Representatives of several public interest groups sat in the gallery, watching the proceedings and trying to decide whether to spend their scant resources on a Tunney Act challenge, long perceived as a futile endeavor.

After the hearing, lawyers on my team called several of the leading public interest groups. We read them the judge's question and Verizon's response. Unless you come forward, we told them, the judge will conclude the Verizon lawyer is telling the truth. A couple of the public interest groups immediately phoned the judge's chambers to criticize the settlements. Others sent the judge letters. Several filed petitions asking to participate in proceedings as friends of the court.

Two weeks later, the judge called all the lawyers back to his courtroom. "Right now, the eyes of the antitrust world are locked on Judge Emmet Sullivan," the *Legal Times* reported. The Antitrust Division conscripted Claude Scott, its most experienced litigator, for the hearing. I felt sorry for Scott. Once he tried mightily to protect the public interest from Oracle's avarice. Now his superiors had him trying to defend a preposterous settlement.

The government was going to have to do more than trot out Claude Scott to win over Judge Sullivan. "I'm giving the parties a chance to make their case," said the judge as he took the bench. "I can't do it on unverified pleadings. There must be a basis for what's asserted in the proposed consent decree," he went on. "Give me the materials that will enable me to discharge my judicial and statutory responsibilities in a manner that Congress intended," the judge told Scott. Sullivan also granted the motions of several public interest groups to participate in the proceedings.

In response to Judge Sullivan's demand for materials he could use to evaluate the settlement, the government produced a mound of documents from the merging companies and competitors, along with a declaration from a staff economist. The declaration used a cheap drafting trick to evade the big issues in the case. It simply ignored the competitive injury the mergers were likely to cause, except for the reduction of competition in 2-to-1 buildings. The declaration said that the complaints filed in court "predicted" harm for 2-to-1 buildings and the settlements remedied that "predicted" harm. The declaration made no mention of all of the other injury the mergers would likely cause—harm that went unremedied by the settlements.

Despite the effort at obfuscation, the declaration highlighted the conflict with the division's position in the Oracle case. In the telecom mergers, the government demanded only a remedy for "merger to monopoly"— 2-to-1 buildings. It recognized no other diminution of competition worthy of remedy.

For the next several months, salvos of briefs flew back and forth. Judge Sullivan remained silent. The subsequent acquisition of BellSouth loomed over the proceedings, not yet reviewed by either the Antitrust Division or the FCC. In late September, UBS, the worldwide financial services firm, published a research report predicting antitrust clearance for the BellSouth deal. "AT&T and its regulatory people have strong relationships within the administration," the report stated, "and will be able to prevail upon friends in the White House to move forward with [the BellSouth] deal that has similar characteristics to two others [MCI and SBC-AT&T] that were approved."

In October, the Antitrust Division stunned the antitrust bar by clearing the BellSouth acquisition without conditions of any kind, not even divestitures in 2-to-1 buildings. By clearing the deal without a settlement agreement, the Division avoided any judicial review. The Division's press releases tried to make excuses for the subterfuge. "Although the Division required divestitures of certain [last-mile circuits] before SBC acquired the former AT&T," read the press release, "applying the same criteria to this transaction led the Division to conclude the divestitures were unnecessary to preserve competition."

Critics assailed the Antitrust Division's decision. Few accepted the Division's explanation as anything other than a pretext to avoid hearings in Judge Sullivan's court. Bill Baxter must surely have turned over in his grave. The Justice Department abdicated antitrust oversight of the telecommunications industry, ceding merger review to the Federal Communications Commission.

Democrats on the commission promised a fight. "With the lights off at the Justice Department, it becomes all the more important for the F.C.C.

to ensure that consumer interests have a seat at the table," Democratic commissioner Michael J. Copps said in a statement. Powerful senators and congressmen sent letters to the FCC urging a careful review of the BellSouth deal. A *New York Times* editorial called for taking "a long, hard look at the deal."

After Thanksgiving, Judge Sullivan convened the final Tunney Act argument on the AT&T and MCI mergers. He started the hearing by observing that the government had closed its investigation of the BellSouth acquisition without even filing a complaint. Lacking jurisdiction over the deal, there was nothing he could do to stop it. Then he noted that although he had not completed his review of the earlier acquisitions, the name of the MCI Center in Washington had been changed to the Verizon Center. "Is that what Congress intended," he demanded of Claude Scott. "That it's just a done deal because the merging parties considered it to be a done deal?"

Scott did his best to change the subject. Verizon's lawyer, on the other hand, decided to tell the judge that merging parties should be able to close without waiting for court review, the Tunney Act notwithstanding.

"Do you want to rethink that argument?" the judge asked incredulously. "They shouldn't wait until the Court conducts its independent review? That's pretty presumptuous to say the least." If he didn't approve the settlement, would the name of the building revert to the "MCI Center"? the judge asked.

"No, no, the merger is closed," said Verizon's lawyer. "It's not going to be unscrambled by anything this Court does."

Emmet Sullivan is likely the most gracious judge I've ever appeared before. He tells people in the courtroom *not* to stand when he enters and leaves. He once spent twenty minutes rearranging the court's calendar so that I wouldn't have to cancel a long-put-off family vacation in order to appear at one of the hearings. When a less experienced and very nervous lawyer for our side began a halting presentation, Sullivan interrupted to soothe and encourage him.

Verizon's lawyer was too much, even for calm-countenanced Emmet Sullivan. The judge looked like he was going to bound over his desk down into the well of the court and teach the Verizon lawyer some respect.

"The merger is not finished," snapped the judge. "The merger has not been approved by this Court."

"The merger is closed as of January 6, 2006," Verizon's lawyer responded defiantly. He didn't know when to just say, "Yes, sir."

"Congress needs to go back to the drawing board and make clear that mergers shouldn't close . . . until they've been subject to review by an independent District Court," said the judge, venting, presumably, to the Senate staffers from the Judiciary Committee who sat in the gallery.

Once again, "yes, sir" would have been a good response. Instead, Verizon's lawyer said, "Congress has certainly not done that." Then he tried to continue, but the judge interrupted him.

"I'm going to do an independent evaluation of the material before me, I can assure you of that. . . . We'll see where the merger stands at that point." The government lawyers blanched.

I began my argument by reminding the judge of his question months earlier about the absence of public interest groups. "I'm proud to say, Your Honor, they're here today." I pointed to the other lawyers at my counsel table. "And I have the privilege in this section of speaking not just for the business interests, but for the public interest groups as well." I listed some of the organizations that joined the argument: the National Association of State Utility Consumer Advocates, the New Jersey Rate Counsel, and even the attorney general of the State of New York, whose office appeared in the proceedings to protect the interests of New York consumers. I explained that the consumer groups were concerned about the prices of last-mile connections because cell phone calls, Internet communications, and emergency 911 calls go across those circuits. The interests of businesses and consumers frequently coincide in promoting competition. The judge could see it himself as he surveyed the courtroom full of lawyers challenging the deals.

Then I turned to the effect of the mergers on customer prices. Paradoxically, the Antitrust Division did my side an enormous favor by permitting the deals to close before the Tunney Act process was completed. Judge Sullivan's review stretched on so long that the harmful price effects of the mergers became apparent. I had no need to rely any longer just on predictions of price increases based on statistical analysis of past bids. I could show that prices *actually* increased after the mergers. AT&T did its part to help.

About five weeks after the mergers closed, the chief financial officer of AT&T made the company's quarterly earnings announcement to the investment community. Customer prices in the industry had been falling, but the mergers reversed the trend. The CFO claimed, in a statement subject to the accuracy requirements of the securities laws, that as a result of the "integration" of AT&T and SBC, the new AT&T saw "positive indications of price stability"—"more stability in pricing" after the merger. The CEO of the new AT&T, Ed Whitacre, made the same point at a securities conference a week later. "Prices have stabilized in our judgment and even in some cases, believe it or not, there's some upside to pricing, which is a good thing."

I could even show specific examples of price increases. The FCC review of the SBC-AT&T deal resulted in an order blocking for a time the ability of the merged company to raise prices on some last-mile connections. But outside the FCC's jurisdiction, the merged company raised prices with abandon. I put into the record examples of price increases for last-mile connections in Ohio, Indiana, Missouri, Michigan, Texas, and other states. The price increases were not limited to the 2-to-1 buildings the government's remedy addressed. So, a divestiture remedy limited to 2-to-1 buildings was never going to be sufficient to prevent widespread customer injury from the mergers, I argued.

The government's proposed divestiture remedy was so limited that it affected only a grand total of seven hundred buildings in the entire country, leaving AT&T and Verizon free to raise prices elsewhere with impunity. The judge was taken aback at the low number. "There are 700 buildings in the entire country that are impacted [by the mergers]?" he asked Claude Scott, wondering how the anticompetitive effects of the mergers could possibly be so limited. Scott said the remedy was restricted to areas in which SBC and Verizon operated. The judge wouldn't let him off the hook. "So that's a fair statement. 700 buildings in the entire country?" he asked again. Scott had to agree.

Even in those seven hundred buildings, the proposed remedy would hardly prevent price increases. The company that ended up purchasing the

circuits divested by SBC and Verizon, almost certainly a much smaller firm, could not possibly replace the extensive networks of AT&T and MCI. Nor would the company that purchased the divested circuits necessarily continue the aggressive price competition of AT&T and MCI. Prices were bound to go up even in 2-to-1 buildings.

At the conclusion of the arguments Judge Sullivan took the cases under review. The FCC met just before the end of the year and approved the BellSouth acquisition. One of the Republican commissioners recused himself because of a conflict, so the two Democrats on the five-person commission, aided by the uproar created by Sullivan's hearings, had greater leverage. The commission extracted significant concessions from AT&T, including voluntary price freezes, some divestitures, and a commitment from the company to "net neutrality."

After all of the anticipation, Judge Sullivan released a disappointing opinion the following spring. He continued to follow the *Microsoft* decision. In judging the effectiveness of the remedy, he could not look past the harm pled in the complaint, he held, unless the complaint was so limited that it made a "mockery of judicial power." A settlement that fixed the anticompetitive effects of the mergers only in a single household might violate the *Microsoft* opinion's "mockery" rule, he said, but apparently the settlements before the court that claimed only to remedy the anticompetitive injury in about seven hundred buildings in the entire country did not.

The judge acknowledged that standard economic models predicted higher prices for buildings where suppliers decreased from four to three or from three to two, but he held those injuries beyond the scope of the offenses charged in the complaint. He recognized as "significant shortcomings of the proposed settlements" the inability of purchasers of divested circuits to replace the competition lost by the acquisitions of AT&T and MCI. Nevertheless, because these shortcomings "did not completely undermine the settlements," he held the consent decrees "within the reaches of the public interest," again embracing language from the *Microsoft* opinion.

Rejecting both my arguments and Senator Kohl's statements on the floor of the Senate, the judge ruled that the government's remedy need not follow "sound, established antitrust principles." In other words, it need not fix all the problems the mergers produced. Satisfying the minimal standards from the *Microsoft* opinion was good enough for government work. In the end, the judge simply could not bring himself to do what he appeared to know was right. He could not declare the division's merger enforcement policy a sham.

The judge approved the settlements and the specified circuits were sold off at rock-bottom prices, mostly because they were worthless as competitive assets. The merged companies got to keep just about all of their overlapping circuits. Competitors were denied the use of assets the merged companies did not even need to service customers. The judicial review ended "not with a bang, but with a whimper," wrote one commentator.

We thought briefly about appealing Judge Sullivan's decision but decided against it. The legal proceedings generated public pressure sufficient to get some valuable relief from the Federal Communications Commission in the BellSouth review. My clients were happy enough, the public interest groups less so. Despite Judge Sullivan's lengthy review, the public interest went unprotected. It was a sign of the times. Not even direct evidence of postmerger price increases was sufficient to thwart anticompetitive acquisitions.

These days, the nation's subscribers to high-speed Internet service have to pay more for less, the obvious result of lost competition. The average high-speed service in Japan is ten times faster than the average service in the United States and costs about half as much. Since 2001, as AT&T, Verizon, and the cable companies have tightened their grip over Internet pipes, the United States has fallen from fourth in the world to fifteenth place in household adoption of high-speed Internet. Warnings of dire consequences abound, as the United States falls further and further behind the rest of the developed world in high-speed Internet service. Millions of new jobs and billions of dollars of increased economic activity depend on reasonably priced access to high-speed Internet, estimates a coalition of political, civic, and business groups. Yet no one seems able to translate these concerns into sound antitrust enforcement policy.

The high prices, poor quality, and limited coverage brought on by telecom consolidation burden the broader business community. More people connected to the Internet translates to more customers for just about every type of business in America. Yet we naively tolerate a choke hold on a vital business conduit, limiting the nation's economic growth.

The dearth of competition in high-speed Internet circuits is producing all of the socioeconomic ills liberals used to worry about. Far fewer lower- and middle-class households can afford high-speed Internet than households with higher annual incomes. Millions of rural households go unserviced. The percentage of racial and ethnic minority households with high-speed subscriptions lags far behind non-Hispanic white households. High-speed Internet access could help alleviate the nation's economic, geographic, and cultural divides. Instead, the high cost and limited availability of high-speed Internet service exacerbates those problems.

Conclusion

Almost twenty-five years after Bill Baxter's confrontation with Congress, the Supreme Court, at the urging of the Bush administration, agreed to reconsider the 1911 precedent that flatly prohibited manufacturers from dictating the minimum prices retailers must charge. The Court took for review a case involving a small manufacturer of women's handbags, hardly a significant factor in the highly competitive market for women's fashion accessories. The manufacturer had created a distinctive line of tooled-leather products and sold the line through small boutiques at prices set by the manufacturer. When a mom-and-pop retailer started offering customers a 20 percent discount on the line, the manufacturer stopped supplying the store, and the store's owners brought suit for resale price maintenance. They won $4 million, after trebling, from a Texas jury.

The manufacturer hired former Bush solicitor general Theodore Olson to make its argument in the Supreme Court. He was famous for winning *Gore v. Bush*, the Supreme Court decision that assured George W. Bush the presidency.

Olson was no more than six sentences into his argument when the more liberal members of the Court began to barrage him with skeptical questions. Justice Breyer warned that abandoning the per se rule against resale price maintenance would increase consumer prices on everything from prescription drugs to blue jeans. Justice Stevens expressed concern that dealers would conspire among themselves to force manufacturers to raise retail prices. Justices Ginsburg and Souter suggested that a change of such significance should be made by Congress rather than by the Supreme Court.

Olson was on the verge of being overwhelmed when Justice Scalia stepped in. "Is the sole object of the Sherman Act to produce low prices?" Scalia asked rhetorically.

"No," said Olson, grateful for the help.

"I thought it was consumer welfare," Scalia suggested, nudging Olson back on track.

"Yes, it is," Olson quickly agreed.

"And I thought some consumers would prefer more service at a higher price," Scalia continued.

"Precisely," Olson replied.

"So the mere fact that it would increase prices doesn't prove anything," Scalia announced. "If, in fact, it's giving the consumer a choice of more services at a somewhat higher price, that would enhance consumer welfare, so long as there are competitive products at the lower price, wouldn't it?"

"That is absolutely correct," replied Olson, who then quickly sat down.

In June 2007, the Supreme Court announced its decision. A sharply divided Court, in a 5–4 decision, abandoned a century's worth of settled law and overruled the per se rule against resale price maintenance, adopting instead the rule of reason's case-by-case analysis of competitive injury. It was the Supreme Court's fourth decision within a single year to limit the reach of antitrust law and yet another in a series of decisions over the last several years to reject rules that had prohibited various types of marketing agreements between companies.

All but ignoring thirty-seven briefs from consumer groups, discount retailers, and states opposing any change in the law, the majority opinion relied on what it called "respectable authorities in the economics literature." According to the majority, this academic research suggests, under certain concededly "theoretical" market conditions, that resale price-fixing can benefit consumers by increasing product and service options. The majority's position was supported by friend-of-the-court briefs from the Bush administration, the American Petroleum Institute, and the cellular phone industry, among other producer interests.

Justice Breyer's dissenting opinion countered the majority's reasoning with pricing data originally gathered by the government. The data indicated that the Court's decision would raise retail bills by up to $1,000 on average for an American family of four every year, adding $300 billion to annual consumer costs. The theoretical scenarios of consumer benefit touted by the majority cannot reasonably offset this demonstrable harm, Breyer argued.

In a front-page article a year after the decision, the *Wall Street Journal* assessed anecdotally the effect of the change in price-setting rules on consumer markets. Retailers reported widespread use of resale price maintenance by manufacturers. Consumer advocates told the *Journal* about the impact of the new antitrust policy—higher prices, particularly for baby goods, consumer electronics, home furnishings, and pet food. Discounters predicted their own demise as a result of the Supreme Court's decision. Online retailers were especially aggrieved.

The story seemed to validate predictions of widespread consumer price increases. Nevertheless, it is hard to justify a rule that makes resale price maintenance automatically illegal in every case. The per se rule very nearly ruined Apple in 1983 by scuttling the company's mail order prohibition and overturning its entire distribution plan. Apple escaped liability for resale price maintenance only after Judge Pamela Rymer reviewed the entire mail order case record and ruled dealer price-fixing charges unfounded. The mail order prohibition left pricing discretion to the dealers, Rymer ruled. A less disciplined judge might well have exposed the company to a massive damages claim under the per se rule by passing the resale price maintenance claim to a jury.

Apple's distribution restriction helped to assure the viability of the company that went on to revolutionize desktop computing (with the Macintosh), the recording industry (with the iPod), and the consumer telecommunications industry (with the iPhone). Apple's attention to customer support in the retail stores it started opening in 2001 even forced Microsoft to provide customer service representatives of its own in large retailing chains. In the long run consumers benefited immeasurably from Apple's mail order restriction, but the policy could easily have been struck down on inception under an inflexible per se rule that prevents explanation and analysis.

Antitrust surely needs a mechanism to quickly and easily identify and condemn conduct that hurts consumers without disturbing more beneficial behavior. But the answer to antitrust's malaise lies in strengthening the rule of reason, not in extending per se illegality beyond obvious anticompetitive practices. Antitrust advocates demand per se condemnation of business practices that do not always damage consumers largely because Chicago School machinations have reduced the rule of reason to pabulum.

The welter of conflicting factors to be weighed under a rule of reason analysis makes proof of anticompetitive effects nearly impossible. Consequently, the defendant always wins under the rule of reason, making it an ineffective vehicle for antitrust enforcement. This is not what Bill Baxter intended. He opposed per se treatment for vertical restrictions but argued equally that "the rule of reason should never mean that all topics are open for discussion."

Shoring up the rule of reason requires the use of commonsensical presumptions. Reasoned judgments can be made in close cases by deciding in advance which side bears the burden of coming forward with convincing evidence at crucial stages of the inquiry. Which side do we presume is right unless persuaded otherwise?

Robert Bork's 1978 book called for the use of "tiebreakers" in close cases. Relying on the notion of self-correcting markets and the simple economics of perfect competition, Bork's rules always elected against government intervention if circumstances were the least bit debatable. We now know that many modern markets will not automatically fix competitive imbalances (market forces frequently exacerbate them) and that companies, if given the opportunity, will scheme against their competitors in ways that sometimes hurt consumers. The default positions, the "tiebreakers," of antitrust analysis need to be reversed; restrictive practices and agreements that impede competition need to be justified by their proponents to escape legal sanction.

A dominant company whose business practices tend to exclude

competitors from the market (or even significantly to limit them by, for example, raising their costs) needs to prove the absence of consumer injury or an offsetting benefit in order to avoid liability. Companies with lesser market power need to prove, rather than merely to assert, an abundance of consumer choices to defend restrictions, including distribution restraints, against antitrust challenge. Mergers that remove aggressive and disruptive competitors ("mavericks") from the market, facilitate collusion (either tacit or actual), or raise the likelihood of unilateral price increases by the merged company warrant approval only on the strongest showings of consumer benefit. Patent schemes that exact tribute rather than foster innovation should be presumed unlawful and attacked under the antitrust laws. Agreements, transactions, and practices should always be evaluated in light of likely effects on innovation, as well as on price and output. In close cases, antitrust policy should default to protecting competition.

The Supreme Court has refused to simplify rule of reason analysis by adopting sensible presumptions to protect against competitive injury. Most recently, in 1999, the Court reversed an FTC decision that outlawed trade association restraints on advertising by dentists, holding that both the commission and the intermediate court of appeals inappropriately applied a simplified rule of reason analysis to find liability, rather than using a more fulsome evaluation that might never have produced that result. The Court implied in a footnote that even practices as pernicious as restrictions on competition among competitors should not be presumed unlawful in a rule of reason analysis absent empirical evidence of actual anticompetitive effects. The Court simply refused to mitigate the considerable burden of proving illegality under a rule of reason analysis. Having defanged the rule of reason in 1999, conservatives on the Court gladly chose in 2007 to apply their "defendant always wins" standard to resale price maintenance cases.

Two other 2007 Supreme Court decisions beat out the cadence to antitrust's death march. In one case, the Court limited a fifty-year-old precedent by making it far more difficult for private plaintiffs to bring conspiracy cases. The plaintiffs in the case claimed that the Baby Bells illegally agreed not to compete with one another and to prevent market entry by smaller competitors. The Court threw out the complaint before any formal fact gathering because the plaintiff had no evidence (or, at least, asserted no facts in the complaint) showing a conspiratorial agreement, beyond similar conduct by the Bells, which the Court said each alleged conspirator might have logically undertaken on its own, without an illegal conspiracy. Despite the acknowledged harm that competitor conspiracies cause, consumers now need the kind of evidence they used to get from the discovery process just to initiate lawsuits against illegal conspiracies.

In the second case, the Supreme Court set the stage for severely limiting the scope of antitrust enforcement. The Court immunized from antitrust attack securities underwriting practices that SEC rules specifically disapprove. Even absent an actual conflict between antitrust enforcement and SEC regulation, the Court held, the hypothetical possibility that antitrust enforcement might tend to interfere with the SEC's regulatory scheme justified dismissal of every possible antitrust challenge to the regulated conduct at issue in the case. The opinion raises the prospect of excluding antitrust enforcement from any industry subject to government regulation, however ineffective or piecemeal the oversight.

Hospital mergers promised to blunt rising health care costs by eliminating expensive duplication of services. Instead, the resulting industry consolidation spawned enormous hospital networks that forced price increases on private health care insurers and institutional purchasers of health care.

The antitrust enforcement agencies tried to turn the industry back to competition by bringing suits to enjoin prospective mergers that would inevitably raise prices. The agencies were rebuffed by the courts, case after case, year after year, decade after decade. Eventually the FTC stopped even trying to block hospital mergers, no matter how likely a postmerger increase in prices.

Taking a new tack, the commission filed an administrative case (inside the FTC rather than in the courts) in 2004 against the long-since-completed merger of two hospitals in the north Chicago suburbs, a deal that went unchallenged when it closed four years earlier. After years of litigation, the commission produced a record from internal company documents showing that senior officials at the merging hospitals anticipated the deal would give them greater leverage to raise prices, that the merged firm in fact raised prices substantially after completion of the transaction, and that the same officials attributed the price increases at least in part to the merger. But concerned about the costs and difficulties of unwinding a deal completed more than seven years earlier, the commission demanded nothing more than that the merged hospitals establish independent committees to permit those paying for hospital services to negotiate rates separately with each hospital.

The prevalence of anticompetitive hospital mergers came to symbolize antitrust's futility. In the spring of 2008, the largest hospital chain in northern Virginia announced the acquisition of its only significant competitor, a deal that would have given it control of over 73 percent of the licensed hospital beds in the area. The acquiring hospital conceded that it might well raise rates at the acquired hospital but claimed the deal would also improve the quality of care.

The commission's administrative complaint challenging the deal elicited little more than giggles from the acquiring hospital. "The FTC's challenge is not the final word on the proposed merger," read the hospital's statement. The commission had lost seven straight court challenges to hospital mergers dating back to 1990. "Most hospital CEOs are aware of the inability of the FTC to really have an influence," a Johns Hopkins professor told the *Washington Post*.

Even during the Bush administration, the FTC's Republican leadership frequently put practical enforcement benefits ahead of ideological misgivings. Additional personnel changes near the end of the administration left more traditional antitrust enforcers in charge of commission policy. This time, instead of playing dead, the commissioners decided to play hardball. They convinced the Republican attorney general of Virginia to join their lawsuit in federal court to block the deal. They changed their internal procedures to expedite an administrative trial of the case. And they argued in court that the FTC Act requires only a minimal showing to warrant a court injunction. When the judge signaled his support for the FTC's position, the hospitals abandoned the deal.

The commission scored an even bigger win a couple of months later. Whole Foods, the nation's largest organic grocery store chain, had announced the acquisition of its largest competitor, Wild Oats, in early 2007.

An FTC investigation turned up internal Whole Foods e-mails in which its CEO claimed the acquisition would "avoid nasty price wars" and prevent mainstream supermarkets from competing in the organic grocery business. Nevertheless, a federal judge took the word of the company's paid economic expert over that of its CEO and denied the FTC's request for an injunction, reasoning that competition from mainstream supermarkets would constrain the merged company's ability to raise price.

A higher court refused to stop the transaction until a formal appeal could be heard, and the parties closed the deal. Whole Foods began to take over some Wild Oats locations and close down or sell off others. Undaunted, the FTC pressed its appeal on the merits of the case and, a year after the deal closed, eked out a narrow victory. By a 2–1 margin the appellate court decided the trial judge used the wrong legal standard to decide the case and instructed him to reevaluate his decision. The FTC started challenging anticompetitive mergers more aggressively.

Later in 2008, the commission pointedly refused to endorse an Antitrust Division report on the legal standards for judging dominant firm behavior. The Division's report adopted just about every Chicago School argument for limiting antitrust enforcement, but the FTC would have none of it. In a caustic evaluation of the report, a bipartisan majority of FTC commissioners accused the Division of showing greater concern for the welfare of monopolists than the welfare of consumers. The Division "would place a thumb on the scales in favor of firms with monopoly or near-monopoly power," wrote the commissioners. They vowed to "fill any Sherman Act enforcement void" that the Division's policies might create.

The faint glimmer of hope from these developments does not portend the immediate ebbing of Chicago School influence. Changing the direction of antitrust policy requires more than flipping a switch, or even winning an election. There is much to unwind. Poorly reasoned judicial decisions nevertheless carry precedential authority. Chicago School ideologues continue to populate the federal bench.

Some new scholarship will be required. Greater attention to antitrust in the nation's law schools and among the country's intellectual elite would be helpful. As antitrust doctrine came to rely increasingly on economic analysis, the tools, processes, and goals of antitrust enforcement became less accessible to lay people, business leaders, elected officials, and even government policy makers. The circle of those debating the formulation of antitrust policy must be widened beyond the small number of self-interested economists and lawyers currently involved.

The litigation capabilities of the enforcement agencies, particularly the Antitrust Division, need to be rebuilt. "Do you have any idea how long that takes?" a former Antitrust Division litigator asked me, more to make a point than to elicit an answer. Training a new generation of litigators from scratch will take many years, five at a minimum for each cohort of new lawyers. Hiring litigators with even more experience who can lead a trial team means finding people willing to work in difficult conditions for a fraction of what they could make in the private sector. A serious commitment to antitrust enforcement really necessitates establishing a compensation system to make it easier for talented people to spend their careers in public service.

The nation faces unprecedented economic challenges. Our history has shown that even in difficult economic times the government needs to be proactive not only in underwriting investment in new technologies but also in restraining anticompetitive business conduct. To maintain the country's high standard of living in the coming decades, antitrust policy must renew its commitment to competition, the font of economic growth. Competition engenders innovation, and innovation will keep our country ahead in world markets. On that point, there are grounds for optimism. It is increasingly obvious to important people that the Chicago School approach is not working well. The consequences of laissez-faire are no longer blithely accepted. The time has come to move past Chicago.

Acknowledgments

Although this book is written in my voice, I could never have litigated any of the big cases I describe without the help of others. I always worked with a team of talented lawyers and paralegals, and frequently with a team of top-flight economists, as well. The general counsels of my various clients and others in the companies' legal departments also played key roles in the cases. From time to time in the manuscript, I am able to recognize the contributions of other lawyers to the outcomes I report. But I can't give adequate recognition to the scores, perhaps hundreds, of other lawyers whose hard work contributed to the case law results and the development of the legal doctrines described in this book.

I have wanted to write this book for a number of years, before it became fashionable (once again) to call for a greater role for the government in the free market economy. I began by retrieving my old case files. Fenwick & West chair Gordon Davidson and records supervisor Kathy Zubrod helped me to secure the court transcripts and public filings in the Apple mail order case and several of the other early cases I describe. Wilson Sonsini Goodrich & Rosati general counsel Don Bradley and practice support directors Mary Ryan and Tanya Miramontes helped me to retrieve portions of my records from the Lotus case, the Microsoft litigation, and several of the smaller cases described in the book.

Stanford Law School dean Larry Kramer and head librarian Paul Lomio gave me the run of the Stanford University libraries for my legal and economic research. Without the untiring assistance of reference librarian

Sonia Moss, I might still be working on the manuscript. Sonia always found what I gave up on finding, devoting time, energy, and, most important, expertise to my efforts.

I interviewed many people—Silicon Valley venture capitalists, journalists, former Antitrust Division employees—in the course of my research. Most requested anonymity for some or all of what they told me. I honored all such requests but nevertheless wish to acknowledge the countless hours of access and cooperation that were provided to me.

Barry Carr and John Ferrell, cofounders of Carr & Ferrell, along with firm administrator Sarah Ferguson, permitted me to conscript one of the firm's best conference rooms for two years while I reviewed all of my materials and wrote my manuscript. Without the support and encouragement of Barry, John, Sarah, and the other members and employees of the firm, I could never have completed the book. Dale Withers typed all the drafts and revisions of the manuscript, and cite checked most of it, cheerfully working evenings and weekends whenever necessary. She unfailingly met every unreasonable deadline I imposed on her.

Law professor Jonathan Baker, economist Michael Williams, and telecom expert Thomas Cohen read portions of the manuscript and provided helpful commentary and discussion. Any remaining errors are solely the responsibility of the author.

My agent Wendy Strothman always provided wise counsel and direction. The team at Portfolio, publisher Adrian Zackheim, editorial director Jeffrey Krames, assistant editor Jillian Gray, and marketing whiz Maureen Cole made extraordinary efforts to aid the publication of my book. They frequently spent as much time calming the angst of a nervous author as ably editing my manuscript, or so it must have seemed to them.

My daughter Jenna, son Ben, and wife Kathy provided the love and encouragement to keep me going during the many frustrating months of work. I never had the courage to admit to Jeffrey, my editor—as he marveled at how a lawyer could produce a coherent manuscript—that all of my work was vetted by Kathy, who actually made my writing readable.

Notes

INTRODUCTION

Page

1. **$1 trillion** "Paulson: We can't wait for regulatory reform." MSNBC Web site, 21 Sept. 2008.
1. **"toxic assets"** "Bush seeks $700 billion for bailout." MSNBC Web site, 20 Sept. 2008.
1. **Greenspan speeches** Federal Reserve Board Web site, 18 Sept. 2000, 8 Apr., 2005, 10 May 2001.
2. **"overdosed"** "Berkshire vice chairman: 'Stupid things' led to financial crisis." *San Jose Business Journal*, 5 May 2008.
2. **police themselves** "FDA was aware of dangers to food." *Washington Post*, 23 Apr. 2007: A1.
2. **resources** "Congressional Report Faults FDA Inaction." Consumer Affairs Web site, 13 June 2008.
2. **voluntarily** Marion C. Blakey speech. Federal Aviation Administration Web site, 11 Sept. 2007.
2. **Bush FAA quote** "Bush on travel woes: 'We've got a problem.'" MSNBC Web site, 27 Sept. 2007.
2. **Bush free enterprise quote** White House press release, 19 Sept. 2008.
2. **Great Depression** "Bush seeks $700 billion for bailout." MSNBC Web site, 20 Sept. 2008.
4. **"system of belief"** Demsetz (1974), 162.

CHAPTER 1

9. **average manufacturing plant** Jenks (1917) (based on census data).
9. **railroad defaults** Fox and Sullivan (1987), 939 n. 10.

10. **oil discovery; attributes** Chernow (1998), 43–75, 251, 286; Baylor, Review of *Titan*, EH.Net. Economic History Services Web site, 11 July 2001.

11. **Lloyd background; article** Henry Demarest Lloyd, "The Story of a Great Monopoly," *Atlantic Monthly* (Mar. 1881); 317–34; Caro Lloyd (1912); Thorelli (1955), 134.

11. **editions and reprints** Caro Lloyd (1912), 61–62; Thorelli (1955), 134.

12. **financial success** Chernow (1998), 224–29.

12. **Lloyd collusion article** Henry Demarest Lloyd, "The Lords of Industry." *North Am. Rev.* 331 (June 1884): 535–53.

13. **Americans conscripted** Hofstadter (1966), 229–31.

14. **Sherman Act** 26 Stat. 209 (1890), codified as amended at 15 U.S.C.§§ 1–7.

14. **early cases** Posner (2001b), 35–36; Bork (1978), 21–30; *United States v. Trans-Missouri Freight Assn.*, 166 U.S. 290 (1897); *United States v. Joint Traffic Assn.*, 171 U.S. 505 (1898); *United States v. Addyston Pipe & Steel Co.*, 175 U.S. 211 (1899).

14. **"For many years"** Chernow (1988), 298.

15. **most influential** Miller (1992), 335.

15. **"hard dealing," etc.** Tarbell (1904), vol 2, 287.

15. **"crush men"** "The Rockefellers, " PBS Web site.

15. **"hopelessness," etc.** Ibid.

15. **"most important"** "Ida Tarbell: Life and Works," Allegheny College Web site.

16. *McClure's* **readers** Chernow (1998), 449.

17. **"leaves the Standard"** Quote from government report earlier in the year. Jones (1922), 80.

18. *Harper's* **quote** Brian Trumbore, "Standard Oil—Part III." <http://www.buyandhold.com/bh/en/education/history/2000/standard_oil.3.html>

18. **court decision** *Standard Oil Co. v. United States*, 221 U.S. 1 (1911).

19. **"succession of lawsuits"** Appendix A, "The Trusts, The People and the Square Deal," *Outlook*, Nov. 1911, reprinted in Roosevelt (1911), 565–67.

20. **Breyer book** Breyer (1982).

20. **"helplessness"** Tarbell (1904), vol. 2, 282–83.

21. **Clayton Act** 38 Stat. 730 (1914), codified as amended at 15 U.S.C. §§ 12–27.

21. **FTC Act** 38 Stat. 717 (1914), codified as amended at 15 U.S.C. §§ 41–58 (2000).

21. **conduct; structure** Breyer (1982), 157.

21. **AT&T settlement** Link (1954), 75–77.

22. **prosecutors . . . case-by-case** Waller (2004), 579–80.

23. **best students** Ibid., 582–83.

23. **validated antitrust enforcement** Baker (2006), 501 n. 69 (gathering sources).

24. *Alcoa* **decision** *U.S. v. Aluminum Co. of America*, 148 F. 2d 416 (2d Cir. 1945).

24. **oligopolies** Baker (2002) 64, 71 n. 21 (gathering sources).

24. **60 percent** J. R. Williamson (1994), Preface.

24. **task force report** White House Task Force Report on Antitrust Policy, *Antitrust & Trade Regulation Report* (BNA), 411, Special Supplement II (27 May 1969).

24. **price cutting** *Utah Pie Co. v. Continental Baking Co.*, 386 U.S. 685 (1967).

24. **exclusive territories** *United States v. Arnold, Schwinn & Co.*, 388 U.S. 365 (1967).

25. **Mergers** *United States v. Von's Grocery Co.*, 384 U.S. 270 (1966).

25. **"Vertical" mergers** *Brown Shoe Co. v. United States*, 370 U.S. 294 (1962).

25. **monopolization cases** Baker (2002), 64.

25. **barrier to entry** Demsetz (1974), 182–83.

26. **never been attempted** O. E. Williamson (2003), 64.

26. **flawed models** Bailey, Elmendorf, and Litan (2008).

28. Economics explanation: Areeda (1983); Bork (1978), 92–104; Hovenkamp (2005), 16–20; Posner (2001b), 287–308.

28. **Williamson analysis** Heyer (2006), 4; Hovenkamp (2005), 26–29.

29. **tenfold** O. E. Williamson (2003), 64.

29. **surprised** Ibid.

29. **Williamson publications** O. E. Williamson (1968 and 1977).

29. **legitimate goal** Bork (1978), 90–91.

30. **looking to economics** Bork (1985), 116–133.

30. **"mood"** Bork (1978), 191.

30. **"simple ideas"** Bork (1985), 22.

30. **Balancing** Bork (1978), 108–9.

30. **Bork arguments** Ibid., 108, 179, 196, 310–11.

31. **"efficient structure"** McGee (1974).

31. **Bork quotes** Bork (1978), New Introduction x, 422.

32. **Bork on Williamson** Hovenkamp (2005), 26–29; Williamson (1968), 27.

32. **case studies** Baker and Shapiro (2008), 256; Kaplow and Shapiro (2007), 1168.

32. **Bork counted** Salop (2005), 12–13.

32. **"If consumers"** Fox and Sullivan (1987), 947.

32. **he also ignored** Lande (1982), 83–93.

CHAPTER 2

33. **"frostily cerebral"** *American Lawyer* (Apr. 1992): 50, 54.

34. **"doesn't happen"** *Fortune* (5 Oct. 1981): 180, 182.

34. **"sole goal"** *Wall Street Journal*, 4 March 1982: 28.

35. **"Antitrust policy"** Baxter (1985), 16.

35. **"shake some people"** *Wall Street Journal*, 8 July 1981: 1, 21.

35. **"lasted longer"** Rowe (1984), 1535.

36. **divestitures** *Washington Post*, 7 Aug. 1981: E1, E3.

36. **"inadvertently created"** Breyer (1982), 311.

36. **"detailed analysis"** Ibid., 314.

37. **"not going to sign"** *Washington Post*, 10 Apr. 1981: E1.

37. **"Divestiture"** Baxter confirmation hearings, 49.

37. **"command and control"** *Wall Street Journal*, 10 Apr. 1981: 2.

38. **"nuclear attack force"** Ibid.

38. **Baxter quotes** *Washington Post,* 10 April 1981: E1.

38. **Defense report** *Washington Post*, 13 Aug. 1981: D12.

39. **Reagan's remarks** Schmalensee (1999), 1326.

39. **"break up AT&T"** *Washington Post*, 18 Aug. 1981: D7.

39. **"lawyers without"** *Washington Post*, 20 June 1981: D7.

39. **"embarrassed"** *Washington Post*, 1 Nov. 1981: H7.

39. **"position of the United States"** *Washington Post*, 14 Aug. 1981: D7, D8.

40. **"irrational"** *Washington Post*, 3 Nov. 1981: D6.

40. **"basic rule"** Hovenkamp (2001), 273.

41. **"substantial economies"** *Washington Post*, 13 Aug. 1981: D14.

41. **"surrender"** *Wall Street Journal*, 11 Jan. 1982: 1.

41. **"exactly"** Ibid.

41. **"havoc"** *Antitrust & Trade Regulation Report*, 42 (11 Feb. 1982): 315.

41. **"largely invisible"** *Washington Post*, 1 Jan. 1984: D1.

42. **Baldrige reported** *New York Times*, 8 Apr. 1982: D1.

42. **price-fixing investigation** *Antitrust & Trade Regulation Report* 43 (29 July 1982): 270.

43. **Intel market exit** Burgelman (1994).

43. **conversation** *Wall Street Journal*, 25 Feb. 1983: 29.

43. **CEO quotes** Ibid.

44. **no support** *Wall Street Journal*, 28 Feb. 1983: 6.

44. **"novel"** *Wall Street Journal*, 25 Feb. 1983: 29.

44. **shun "novel theories"** *Wall Street Journal*, 20 Mar. 1981: 4.

44. **"sufficiently reprehensible"** Applebaum et al. (1981), 163.

44. **"fully vindicated"** *Washington Post*, 14 Sept. 1983: A13.

45. **"good corporate citizen"** *Washington Post*, 21 Mar. 1982: F1.

45. **"smothered"** *Wall Street Journal*, 5 Feb. 1982: 12.

45. **"very valuable things"** *Wall Street Journal*, 8 July 1981: 1.

46. **"benign indifference"** *Washington Post*, 28 Oct. 1981: D9.

46. **70 percent** *Wall Street Journal*, 8 July 1981: 1, 21.

46. **"wacko," etc.** *Wall Street Journal*, 4 March 1982: 28.

46. **95 percent** *Wall Street Journal*, 8 July 1981: 1.

46. **"intrude ourselves"** *Antitrust & Trade Regulation Report* 4 (30 July 1981): AA–3.

47. **"abandon"** *Antitrust & Trade Regulation Report* 42 (4 Mar. 1928): 470.

47. **Metzenbaum and Baxter** *Washington Post*, 28 Oct. 1981: D9.

CHAPTER 3

51. **Vise article** *Washington Post*, 13 Aug. 1982: A1, A26.

52. **"faithfully execute"** *Congressional Record,* 17 Aug. 1982: E3929.

52. **"most unusual"** *Washington Post*, 13 Aug. 1982: A26.

52. **Wozniak background** Freiberger and Swaine (1984), 263–70.

53. **Silicon Valley name** *San Francisco Chronicle*, 27 Dec. 1999: D1.

53. **Newton quote** Letter to Robert Hooke, 5 Feb. 1676.

54. **radio communication** *San Francisco Chronicle*, 30 Sept. 2007: A1, A15.

54. **Moffett Field** *San Francisco Chronicle*, 27 Dec. 1999: D1.

55. **1945 study** Computer Science and Telecommunications Board (1999), 30–33.

55. **70 percent** National Research Council of the National Academics (2003), 20.

55. **permitting universities** Scherer (2007), 14–20.

56. **all failed** Freiberger and Swaine (1984), 269.

56. **Wozniak showed his plans** Ibid.

56. **"young technologists"** Wilson (1986), 31.

57. **Johnson's efforts** Wilson (1986), 22.

57. **largest source** Wilson (1986), 22; Halloran (2008), 3A–05, 2007 Supp.

58. **start-ups** Kristi Craig, "The SBIC Program," Symposium on Mezzanine & Middle Market Finance 107, 15 May 2007, 4; Harry E. Haskins, e-mail to author, 31 Oct. 2007.

58. **academic study** Saxenian (1994), 32–57.

58. **"People say"** *Salon Magazine* Web site, 17 Apr. 1997.

58. **Government funding** National Research Council of the National Academies (2003), 13–22.

60. **since Ford** Linzmayer (2004), 59.

60. **Carter instructed** Background on company, sales program, etc., from Declarations of Gene P. Carter, 12 Dec. 1982 and 19 Oct. 1982, filed in *O.S.C. v. Apple Computer*.

61. **Dealer complaints** Dealer complaints, Apple response, competitors from Declarations of Armas Clifford Markkula, Jr., 19 Oct. 1982 and 13 Dec. 1981, filed in *O.S.C. v. Apple Computer*.

62. **Ravel quote** Marilyn Chase, *Wall Street Journal*, 4 Dec. 1981, 37.

62. **Ravel letter** Francis Ravel, Letter to A. C. Markkula, Jr., 5 Oct. 1981.

64. **1911 case** *Dr. Miles Medical Co. v. John D. Park & Sons Co.*, 220 U.S. 373 (1911).

65. **"too little"** *White Motor Co. v. United States*, 342 U.S. 253 (1963).

65. **about-face** *United States v. Arnold, Schwinn & Co.*, 388 U.S. 365 (1967).

65. **another U-turn** *Continental T.V., Inc. v. GTE Sylvania Inc.*, 433 U.S. 36 (1977).

66. **Baxter was looking** *Antitrust & Trade Regulation Report* 42 (4 Mar. 1982): 440.

68. **later decision** *United States v. E. I. DuPont de Nemours & Co.*, 351 U.S. 377, 391 (1956).

68. **economists' formulations** Lawrence J. White, "Market Power and Market Definition in Monopolization Cases: A Paradigm is Missing." DOJ/FTC Hearings on Single Firm Conduct, 7 Mar. 2007 <www.justice.gov/atr/public/hearings/single_firm/docs/222011.htm>

68. **consumer choices** *FTC v. Indiana Federation of Dentists*, 476 U.S. 447 (1986).

69. **Telser article** Telser (1960).

69. **Jobs quote** *Wall Street Journal*, 4 Dec. 1981: 37.

70. **Quotes from hearing** Reporter's Transcript of Proceedings, *O.S.C. Corp. v. Apple Computer, Inc.*, 21 Dec. 1981.

CHAPTER 4

73. **committee colloquy** *Joint Hearing on Federal Antitrust Enforcement and Small Business Hearings*, 97th Cong., 2nd Sess., 9 Sept. 1982. Washington, D.C.: GPD, 1982.

75. **real world** Scherer (1983), 694.

75. **more efficiently** Pitofsky (1983), 1493.

76. **very same Apple computers** *O.S.C. vs. Apple Computer*, Markkula Decl., 13 Dec. 1981, 19.

76. **Ravel testimony** *O.S.C. vs. Apple Computer*, Ravel Dep. Tr. vol. III, p. 116.

76. **Rymer background** Bill Girdner, "Profile," *Los Angeles Daily Journal* (6 Dec. 1983): 1.

77. **oral argument** Transcript of Proceedings, *O.S.C. v. Apple Computer*, 28 Nov. 1983.

78. **"limited potential"** *State Oil Co. v. Kahn*, 522 U.S. 3, 10 (1997).

79. **"estimates," etc.** Areeda (1983), 533.

80. **Bork contended** Bork (1978), 288–98.

80. **careful analysis** Scherer (1983), 697–700.

80. **"malt beverage industry"** *Antitrust & Trade Regulation Report* 45 (10 Nov. 1983): 753.

81. **"structured judicial inquiry"** Barnett (1982), 33.

81. **Baxter argued** *Antitrust & Trade Regulation Report* 45 (15 Dec. 1983): 965–67.

81. **bank example** Baxter (1983c), 749.

82. **consumer prices rise** Subcommittee on Antitrust and Monopoly of the Senate Judiciary Committee Hearings on S. 48. 94th Cong., 1st Sess., 174 (1975).

82. **passing cost savings** Scherer (1983), 701.

83. **curbing the retail competition** Pitofsky (1983), 1492.

83. **Pitofsky quote** Ibid., 1487, 1489.

83. **Rudman rider** *Washington Post*, 1 Dec. 1983: F1.

83. **"striking success"** *Wall Street Journal*, 5 Jan. 1984: 1.

83. **"Rockefeller would have . . ."** *The Economist*, 10 Dec. 1983: 65.

84. **"Baxter effect"** *The Economist*, 10 Dec. 1983: 65.

84. **Court established** *Monsanto Co. v. Spray-Rite Service Corp.*, 465 U.S. 752 (1984).

84. **Court's opinion** *Business Electronics Corp. v. Sharp Elec. Corp.*, 485 U.S. 717 (1988).

86. **strategy requires** Dixit and Nalebuff (1991), 33.

87. **"Welcome, IBM"** Freiberger and Swaine (1984), 349.

88. **Williamson spoke** Williamson (1983).

88. **Baxter's response** Baxter (1983b), 320.

88. **"The Limits of Antitrust"** Easterbrook (1984a).

88. **"no economic sense"** *Matsushita Elec. Co. v. Zenith Radio Corp.*, 475 U.S. 574, 587 (1986).

89. **"unambiguous facts"** Hovenkamp (2005), 48.

90. **"quality competition"** Schumpeter (1942), 84.

90. **Areeda quote** Areeda (1983), 534.

CHAPTER 5

93. **"confidence and security"** John Greenwald, *Time*, 7 Nov. 1983.

93. **cycles reinforced** Zachary (1994), 27.

94. **other markets** Shapiro and Varian (1999), 207–18.

95. **journal article** David (1985).

96. **mathematical models** Katz and Shapiro (1985); Farrell and Saloner (1986).

96. **economists attacked** Liebowitz and Margolis (1990).

96. **Consumers wanted** *Time*, 7 Nov. 1983.

96. **Three hundred** Freiberger and Swaine (1984), 350.

96. **"Many buyers"** Thomas Hayes, *New York Times*, 24 Oct. 1983.

96. **IBM PC architecture** Freiberger and Swaine (1984), 336.

97. **BIOS** *Wall Street Journal*, 3 Feb. 1984: 1.

98. **"hot buttons"** *New York Times*, 24 Oct. 1983.

98. **"had to be"** Isadore Barmash, *New York Times*, 10 June 1983.

98. **"Eagle seems"** *New York Times*, 24 Oct. 1983.

98. **"We have more"** *Time*, 7 Nov. 1983.

99. **Joseph Schumpeter** Schumpeter (1942), 85.

100. **different calculus** Peter S. Menell and Dennis S. Karjala, Supreme Court Amicus Brief, *Lotus v. Borland*, Dec. 1995, 11–20.

101. **Jefferson quotes** Letter to Isaac McPherson (13 Aug. 1813), *Writings of Thomas Jefferson* 13: 326–38.

101. **report** Report of Register of Copyrights, 87th Cong., 1st Sess. (1961).

101. **new copyright statute** Act of Oct. 19, 1976, Pub. L. 94-553, 90 Stat. 2541 (codified at 17 U.S.C. §§ 101 et seq.).

102. **Congress attached** Act of Dec. 12, 1980, Pub. L. 96-517, 94 Stat. 3015, 3028 (codified at 17 U.S. C. § 101).

104. **every significant** Zachary (1994), 27.

105. **headline** *Washington Post*, 13 Dec. 2004. Online.

CHAPTER 6

107. **"legal step"** *Boston Globe*, 20 Aug. 1993: 61.

107. **"unusual twist"** *Wall Street Journal*, 20 Aug. 1993: B4.

108. **patent lawyer** Linzmayer (2004), 14.

108. **Business executives** Ibid., 15.

109. **Kapor selected** Affidavit of Mitchell D. Kapor in *Lotus v. Paperback*, Nov. 27, 1989.

110. *Herald* **editorial** *Boston Herald*, 3 Apr. 1993: O16.

110. *Paperback* **opinion** *Lotus vs. Paperback*, 740 F. Supp. 37 (D. Mass. 1990).

111. **Kapor quote** *Computers & Intellectual Property Hearings*, 101st Cong., 2nd Sess., 243 (1990).

111. **illegal immigrant** G. Pascal Zachary, *Wall Street Journal*, 21 Dec. 1990.

111. **"Worst business plan"** *Wall Street Journal*, 2 June 1994: A1.

111. **name he bartered** *Wall Street Journal*, 30 Apr. 1998: 1.

112. **Lotus adopted** Examples in Borland brief, Trial Docket 141 at 53.

112. **200,000 copies** *Wall Street Journal*, 11 June 1990: B6F.

112. **"entrenched rival"** *Wall Street Journal*, 2 June 1994: A1.

113. **Saxenian study** *San Francisco Chronicle*, 27 Dec. 1999: D1.

114. **French roué** *New York Times*, 28 July 1997: D-1.

114. **"for a tour"** Zachary, *Wall Street Journal*, 21 Dec. 1990.

114. **Borland quotes** *Wall Street Journal*, 3 Aug. 1992: B1.
115. **"better chance"** *Boston Globe*, 2 Oct. 1991: b2.
115. **"some friends"** *Wall Street Journal*, 4 Oct. 1991: B2.
115. **March 1992 opinion** 78 F. Supp. 78 (D. Mass., 1992).
116. **"rich boy"** *Wall Street Journal*, 16 Sept. 1992: C1.
116. **"held its own"** *Wall Street Journal*, 25 Mar. 1992: B3.
116. **second long opinion** 799 F. Supp. 203 (D. Mass. 1992).
117. **"debatable"** *Lotus v. Borland*, Transcript, 16 Oct. 1992: 20.
118. **Keeton ruled** 831 F. Supp. 202 (D. Mass., 1993).
118. **bewildering opinion** 831 F. Supp. 223 (D. Mass., 1993).
118. **"cashectomy"** *Wall Street Journal*, 13 Aug. 1993: B3.
119. **"never entered"** *Lotus v. Borland*, Transcript, 15 Aug. 1993: 23–24.
119. **"At some point"** *Lotus v. Borland*, Transcript, 19 Aug. 1993: 19.

CHAPTER 7

121. **law journal article** Breyer (1970).
121. **congressional symposium** Proceedings of the Congressional Copyright and Technology Symposium, 99th Cong., 1st Sess., Feb. 4, 1984: 97–102.
121. **Boudin background** David Margolick, *New York Times*, 24 Apr. 1992. Online.
123. **"We want"** Transcription of tape of oral argument, 6 Apr. 1994: 19.
124. Court colloquy: Notes of Oral Argument, 6 Oct. 1994: 13–14.
124. **"all of his energy"** *Wall Street Journal*, 2 Jun. 1994: A1.
124. **Rumors** *Boston Globe*, 25 Feb. 1995: 67.
125. **"growing risk"** *Lotus v. Borland*, Order, 3 Mar. 1995.
125. **"stunning decision"** *Boston Globe*, 10 Mar. 1995: 73.
125. **majority opinion** 49 F. 3d 807 (1st Cir. 1995).
125. **concurring opinion** 49 F. 3d. 819–822.
125. **"Does everybody"** *Lotus v. Borland*, Transcript, 10 Mar. 1995.
126. **CD-ROM** *Washington Post*, 8 Jan. 1996: A15.
129. **almost everything** *Washington Post*, 7 Jan. 1996: C7.
130. **shortage of parts** *Washington Post*, 9 Jan. 1996: B1.
132. **argument quotes** *Lotus v. Borland*, Transcript, 8 Jan. 1996.
134. ***Sony* decision** *Sony v. Universal*, 464 U.S. 417 (1984).
135. **"dark ages"** *Washington Post*, 17 Jan. 1996: A3.
135. **"no answer"** Ibid.
136. **"big win"** Ibid., B8.
137. **"recent *amicus*"** *National Law Journal*, 1 Apr. 1996: A14.
138. **"a little disturbing"** Ibid.
138. **Center's opposition** *Legal News*, 76:4 (24 July 2007): 2057.
138. **cover story** *New York Times Magazine*, 16 Mar. 2008: 38–71.

CHAPTER 8

139. **"lead more"** *Wall Street Journal*, 10 Mar. 1995: A3.
139. **"like mad"** *New York Times*, 8 Jan. 1996: 38.
140. **IBM meeting** *Forbes ASAP*, 24 June 2002.
141. **direct reward** Baxter (1966) 273.
141. **Supreme Court** Ibid., n. 12.
142. **shortcomings** Ibid., 274–75.
142. **excise tax** Ibid., 274.
143. **congressional hearings** Scherer (2007), 12.
143. **Supreme Court** *Diamond v. Chakrabarty*, 447 U.S. 303 (1980).
143. **CAFC capped** *State Street Bank and Trust Co. v. Signature Financial Group, Inc.*, 149 F. 3d 1368 (Fed. Cir. 1998).
144. **press releases** United States Patent and Trademark Office Web site.
144. **Trade associations** Intellectual Property Owners Association Web site.
144. **$1 billion** <http://www.inventionstatistics.com/Licensing_Royalty_Revenues.html>
145. **economic studies** Scherer (2007), 27–30.
146. **respectability** Ibid., 42–45.
146. **commission's report** Federal Trade Comission, To Promote Innovation: The Proper Balance of Competition and Patent Law and Policy, October 2003.
147. **most important** *KSR International Co. v. Teleflex Inc.*, 550 U.S. —, 127 S. Ct. 1727 (2007).
147. **rolling back** *In re Bilski* (2008).
148. **book** J. Edstrom and M. Eller, *Barbarians Led by Bill Gates* (New York: Holt, 1998), 77.
148. **"vig"** David Bank, *Wall Street Journal*, 8 Jun. 1997.
148. **wallet online** <http://battlemedia.com/archives/002072.php>
149. **$1.5 billion** *Wall Street Journal*, 17 Sept. 2008: A1, A21.
149. **Patent Defense Fund** *Fortune*, 2–6 Jun. 2006.
149. **buying patents** *Puget Sound Business Journal*, 4 July 2008.
149. **twenty thousand** *Wall Street Journal*, 17 Sept. 2008: A1.
149. **business plan** *Puget Sound Business Journal*, 4 July 2008; *Fortune*, 26 June 2006.
149. **signing up technologists** Peter Moon, ITWorld Web site, 11 July 2007.
149. **"not going to make"** Michael Kanellos, CNET Web site, 20 Oct. 2006.
149. **Myhrvold explained** *Fortune*, 26 June 2006.
150. **"smokescreen"** Ibid.
150. **$2.5 billion** *Wall Street Journal*, 17 Sept. 2008, A21.
150. **told *Newsweek*** *Newsweek* Web site, 17 Oct. 2007.
150. **highly successful** Jon Leibowitz speech, 24 Apr. 2006. FTC Web site.
151. **court sided** *FTC v. Schering-Plough Corp.*, 402 F. 3d 1056 (11th Cir. 2005).
151. **declined** 126 S. Ct. 2929 (2006).
151. **threw out** 466 F. 3d 187 (2d Cir. 2006).
152. **Once again** 127 S. Ct. 3001 (2007).
152. **far more common** *Washington Post*, 25 Apr. 2006: A12.

152. **"no one expected"** John George, *Philadelphia Business Journal*, 17 Mar. 2006.

152. **Arnold brought** Scherer (2007), 3–4.

153. **editorial page railed** Ibid., 5.

153. **economic studies** Ibid., 6.

CHAPTER 9

157. **quotes** Department of Justice Transcript, 16 July 1994.

159. **"IBM-compatible"** Morris and Ferguson (1993), 92.

160. **rewrite completely** Manes and Andrews (1993), 287, 347.

160. **"church and state"** *BusinessWeek*, 21 Nov. 1983: 114.

160. **industry press** *Byte*, 1 Feb. 1991: 20, 36.

161. **never claimed** *InfoWorld*, 30 Dec. 1991: 107.

161. **application markets** Wallace and Erickson (1992), 398.

161. **commissioners yelling** Mark Lewyn, *National Review*, 24 Jan. 1994. Online.

161. **told *BusinessWeek*** *BusinessWeek*, 24 Feb. 1992. Online.

161. **he called** *National Review*, 24 Jan. 1994.

162. **few antitrust credentials** *Washington Post*, 29 Aug. 1993: H1.

162. **she groused** *California Lawyer* (May 1995): 46.

162. **"killed myself"** Ibid.

162. **"Hmph"** *Wall Street Journal*, 28 Oct. 1993: A1.

163. **"demonstrative and aggressive"** *Wired*, Apr. 1994.

163. **"fiery personality"** *New York Times*, 16 Feb. 1995: D6.

163. **"keyed-up"** *California Lawyer* (May 1995): 146.

163. **"most seasoned"** *New York Times*, quoted in *Wired*, Apr. 1994.

163. **"asphyxiation"** *California Lawyer* (May 1995): 45.

164. **"ambitious"** *Washington Post*, 19 Apr. 1994: C1.

164. **"fired up"** *Wall Street Journal*, 20 Oct. 1994: A1.

164. **"fountain of activity"** Robert Hershey, *New York Times*, 25 July 1994.

164. **"antitrust cops"** *Wall Street Journal*, 28 Oct. 1993: A1.

164. **"raised expectations"** *Washington Post*, 29 Aug. 1993: H1.

164. **"few people"** *Wall Street Journal*, 28 Oct. 1993: A1.

164. **"really big"** *Wall Street Journal*, 20 Oct. 1994: A1.

164. **get publicity** *National Review*, 24 Jan. 1994.

164. **"Nowhere"** *Washington Post*, 9 Aug. 1993: F16.

165. **"handing awards"** *Washington Post*, 20 Dec. 1993: F19.

165. **"100 percent results"** 16 July 1994 transcript.

165. **"major victory"** *San Jose Mercury News*, 18 July 1994: 1A.

165. **"stifling rivals"** *Wall Street Journal*, 18 July 1994: A1.

165. **"Nothing"** *Washington Post*, 18 July 1994: A1.

165. **"battle for the desktop"** *South China Morning Post*, 20 Sept. 1994: 1.

166. ***BusinessWeek* reported** *BusinessWeek*, 19 Dec. 1994: 35.

166. **largest transaction** Michele Flores, *Seattle Times*, 14 Oct. 1994.

166. Intuit details: Taylor and Schroeder (2003); *San Francisco Examiner*, 4 Dec. 1994: B5, B14.
167. **"Luke Skywalker"** *PC Newsletter*, 17 Oct. 1994: 2.
167. **"hopelessness"** *Fortune*, 20 Mar. 1995: 86.
168. **apparently concluded** Casey Corr, *Seattle Times*, 14 Oct. 1994.
171. ***Times* claimed** *New York Times*, 14 Nov. 1994: D3.
171. **"Visualize"** *InfoWorld*, 24 Oct. 1994: 1, 140.
171. **toll taker** *Wall Street Journal*, 17 Oct. 1994: A2.
171. **"unusual economic theories"** *Wall Street Journal*, 22 Nov. 1994: B6.
171. **"so speculative"** *New York Times*, 25 Nov. 1994: C5.
171. **"economic theory"** *Wall Street Journal*, 22 Nov. 1994: B6.

CHAPTER 10

172. **"snow days"** *Washington Post*, 10 Jan. 1995: D1.
173. **"whole empire"** *New York Times*, 18 July 1994: D1.
175. ***Post* headline** *Washington Post*, 12 Jan. 1995: D1.
175. **"secret cabal"** *Computerworld*, 28 Nov. 1994: 1.
175. **"mumbo jumbo"** Microsoft memorandum, 18 Jan. 1995: 17.
175. **"little disagreement"** Arrow Declaration, 17 Jan. 1995: 7.
176. **turned away** *Wall Street Journal*, 23 Jan. 1995: B6.
177. **argument quotes** *U.S. v. Microsoft*, Transcript, 20 Jan. 1995.
179. **"blunt ruling"** *New York Times*, 15 Feb. 1995: A1.
179. **"humiliation"** *Washington Post*, 17 Feb. 1995: B3.
179. **"considerable embarrassment"** *New York Times*, 15 Feb. 1995: A1.
179. **"stinging rebuke"** *Wall Street Journal*, 15 Feb. 1995: A3.
179. **opinion quotes** 159 F. R. D. 318 (D.D.C. 1995).
180. **"defeat and compromise"** *California Lawyer* (May 1995): 42.
180. **"theoretical legacy"** Ibid., 90.
181. **millions of dollars** Amy Borrus, *BusinessWeek*, 11 Feb. 2002.
181. ***Post* stated** *Washington Post*, 28 April 1995: A1.
181. **executives maintained** *Washington Post*, 21 May 1995: A1.
181. **press release** Department of Justice, 27 April 1995.
182. **deputy was quoted** *Washington Post*, 21 May 1995: A1.
182. **Several analysts** Casey Corr, *Seattle Times*, 21 May 1995.
183. **swells of cheering** *Washington Post*, 21 May 1995: A1.
184. **court of appeals ruled** 56 F. 3d 1448 (D.C. Cir. 1995).

CHAPTER 11

186. **Clark background** Lewis (2000); Larry Kanter, *Salon*, 24 Nov. 1999, online; Clark (1999).
187. **"sense of sight"** Lewis (2000), 37.

188. **developers explained** Keenan Mayo and Peter Newcomb, *Vanity Fair* (July 2008). Online.

189. **Gore said** Keith Perine, *Industry Standard*, 23 Oct. 2000. Online.

190. **"Don Corleone"** *Wall Street Journal*, 24 Apr. 1998: 1.

192. **"trial of the century"** Brinkley and Lohr (2001). Dust jacket.

192. **weeks later** Clark (1999), 238.

194. *Larry King Live* Transcript, 21 Aug. 1995. CNN Web site.

194. **"faded into the background"** *San Jose Mercury News*, 20 Apr. 1996.

194. **"deep freeze"** Michele Flores, *Seattle Times*, 20 Apr. 1996. Online.

195. **"potential to injure"** Easterbrook (1992), 130–31.

198. **"Irresponsible allegations"** *San Jose Mercury News*, 23 Aug. 1996: 1C.

198. **"hysterical response"** *Washington Post*, 21 Aug. 1996: F3.

198. **"wild and untrue"** *San Jose Mercury News*, 22 Aug. 1996: 1A.

198. **"collect dust"** Ibid.

198. **"future away"** C/NET news, 10 May 1996. Online.

198. **"*de facto* platform"** Bill Gates, "The Internet as PC" at 2. Microsoft Web site.

199. **raising their costs** Krattenmaker and Salop (1986).

199. **Supreme Court case** *Loraine Journal Co. v. United States*, 342 U.S. 143 (1951).

199. **"entirely correct"** Bork (1978), 345.

200. **outran received economic theory** Timothy Bresnahan, "Network Effects and Microsoft" (undated draft), 22 n. 39, 24–28, Bresnahan Web site.

200. **book explained** Bork (1978), 373.

201. **gain a benefit** Ibid., 375–81.

201. **"cacophony"** Easterbrook (1992), 121.

202. **Reviewers praised** *United States v. Microsoft*, 84 F. Supp. 2d at 44.

202. **"cripple Windows 95"** *United States v. Microsoft*, 84 F. Supp. 2d at 50.

203. **officials gave** Netscape internal memorandum.

203. **"quiet life"** John R. Hicks, "Annual Survey of Economic Theory: The Theory of Monopoly," *Econometrica* 3 (1980): 1–20 at 8.

204. **"vig"** *Wall Street Journal*, 5 June 1997: B1.

205. **"plays dead"** *Washington Post*, 24 Mar. 1998: C1.

205. *Times* editorial *New York Times*, 11 July 1997. Online.

205. **continue to support** *San Jose Mercury News*, 15 July 1997: 1C.

205. **"end of the rope"** *San Jose Mercury News*, 30 July 1997: 1C.

205. **"out of business"** *Wired* (Aug. 1997): 109, 112.

CHAPTER 12

208. **"Not very good"** *Financial Times*, 10 June 1996: 15.

208. **"rarely successful"** *Matsushita v. Zenith Radio Corp.*, 475 U.S. 574, 589 (1986).

208. **empirical case studies** Bolton, Brodley, and Riordan (2000), 244–45.

209. *BusinessWeek* Available online at <http://www.businessweek.com/1997/34/internal.htm>

210. **"educational background"** Herendeen transcript, 27 Aug. 1997.

210. **Mike McCue** McCue Transcript, 25 August 1997.

212. **Reno said** *San Jose Mercury News*, 21 Oct. 1997: 1A.

213. **"to heck with"** *Seattle Times*, 24 Feb. 2003. Online.

213. **"Microsoft's trajectory"** *San Jose Mercury News*, 26 Oct. 1997: 1A.

213. **"quickly and seriously"** Rubinfeld (1998), 869.

213. **"huge disaster"** *San Jose Mercury News*, 19 Jan. 1998: 1E.

213. *Journal* **reported** *Wall Street Journal*, 5 Feb. 1998: 1.

214. **Rubinfeld debunked** Rubinfeld (2004), 497.

215. **$3 million** Heilemann (2001), 88.

215. **"no prayer"** Clark quotes from contemporaneous notes.

216. **Easterbrook quotes** Easterbrook (1984a), 5.

218. **several pages** Carlton and Perloff (1990), 510–20.

219. **final version** Carlton and Waldman (2002).

219. **less technical readers** Carlton (2000).

219. **"court to enjoin"** Easterbrook (2003), 253.

219. **"jolting experience"** *United States v. Microsoft*, Government trial exhibit 684.

219. **"OEMs suffer"** *United States v. Microsoft*, 84 F. Supp. 2d at 51.

220. **blunt query** *United States v. Microsoft*, Government trial exhibit 38.

220. **"supplier of choice"** *United States v. Microsoft*, Government trial exhibit 309.

220. **attempt to settle** Heilemann (2001), 101.

220. **"socialist doodler"** Stephen Labaton, *New York Times*, 22 Dec. 1997.

221. **Bork press conference** <http://lists.essential.org/1998/am-info/msg01714.html>

221. **"fat consulting fees"** Robert A. Levy, Cato Web site, 16 July 1998.

221. *Slate* **posts** 11 Dec. 1998 (Kinsley); 30 Dec. 1998 (Bork).

222. **op-ed** *Wall Street Journal*, 22 May 1998: 1.

222. **"Theory and spin"** John Markoff, *New York Times*, 21 Oct. 1998. Online.

224. **"contradictory statements"** Auletta (2001), 184.

225. **Easterbrook quotes** Easterbrook (1984d), 11, 5, 2; Easterbrook (1992), 121, 131; Easterbrook (2002), 345.

226. *Times* **headline** Brinkley and Lohr (2001), 264.

227. **"the Netscape document"** Ibid., 327.

227. *Times* **editorial** 24 Sept. 2000. Online.

228. **Baxter remedy** *BusinessWeek*, 11 Nov. 1999. Online.

228. **Rubinfeld told** Heilemann 231.

228. **"great antitrust cases"** Auletta (2001), 45.

228. **"to set rules"** Brinkley and Lohr (2001), xiii.

CHAPTER 13

231. **"social mixer"** Bork (1978), 232.

231. **Posner wrote** Posner (2001a), 933.

233. **Wood noted** 221 F. 3d 928, 937 (7th Cir. 2000).

234. **"perennial gale"** Schumpeter (1942), 83–85, 99–106.

234. **appellate court upheld** 253 F. 3d 34 (D. C. Cir. 2001).

235. **86 percent** Rubinfeld (2004), 488 n. 11.

236. **that excluded rivals** Melamed and Rubinfeld (2007), 307.

236. **"Misguided conservatives"** Cato Web site, 5 Jan. 2000.

236. **less stringent** Lawrence Lessig, *New York Times*, 9 Nov. 2001: 27.

237. **editorial** *BusinessWeek*, 19 Nov. 2001: 157.

237. **"unsettling settlement"** *The Economist*, 10 Nov. 2001.

237. **"scandalous tax"** *Antitrust* (Fall 2001): 70.

237. **eye-popping** Brief, 12 Jan. 2001: 11.

238. **"power grab"** *New Atlantis*, 1 (Spring 2003): 125–27.

238. **enjoined VISA** *United States v. VISA and MasterCard*, 344 F. 3d 229 (2d Cir. 2003).

238. **artificial teeth** *United States v. Dentsply, Int'l*, 399 F. 3d 181 (3d Cir. 2005).

239. **2003 article** Easterbrook (2003), 349, 351, 357, 346, 347.

240. **decried** Schumpeter (1942), 840.

241. **five years** *BBC News*, 19 Oct. 2006.

241. **underwriting the Firefox browser** Gonsalves, *Information Week*, 7 Mar. 2006. On-line.

241. **Microsoft accelerated** Weber, *BBC News*, 10 May 2005.

241. **real threat** Sakar, theStreet.com, 5 Sept. 2008; Dignan, blogs, ZDNet, 2 Sept. 2008.

243. **Supreme Court decision** *Verizon Communications, Inc. v. Law Offices of Curtis V. Trinko*, 540 U.S. 398 (2004).

243. **reverse the calculus** Skitol, *Antitrust Source* Web site, May 2004: 5.

244. **encourages innovation** Baker (2007) (gathering cites); Rubinfeld and Hoven (2001), 74–82.

245. **"multiple commercial visions"** Greenstein, *IEEE Micro* (Mar.–Apr. 2002): 4.

245. **enforcement can be directed** Baker (2007), 589.

245. **Baxter once described** *Washington Post*, 7 Feb. 1982: G1, G3.

245. **practitioner wrote** Skitol, *Antitrust Source* Web site, May 2004: 6.

245. **Richard Posner** Skitol, *Antitrust Source* Web site, Apr. 2007: 9–10.

246. **largely intact** Bringhurst (1979), 157.

246. **permitting local companies** Singer (2000), 4–5, 208–9, 220–21.

247. **"another dime"** Ibid., 220.

247. **used the specifications** *IEEE Annals of the History of Computing* (2002): 62.

247. **written by customers** *IEEE Annals* (2002): 14, 41; (1994) 65.

248. **"vital condition"** *IEEE Annals* (2002): 64–71.

248. **as a public facility** Bank (2001), 147.

248. **"a muddled mess"** Ibid., 130.

249. **"Stay vigilant"** *The Economist,* 20 Sept. 2007.

249. **"deny[ing]"** Goodin, CNET Web site, 2 Nov. 1998.

249. **"all-out attack"** O'Reilly, *Salon* Web site, 16 Nov. 1999.

250. **proprietary extensions** 84 F. Supp. 3d at 67, 89.

250. **Consumers complain** Edlin, *Bepress*, Dec. 2007.

251. **"Everybody should . . ."** *BWOnline*, 18 Nov. 2002.

251. **"I split"** *BusinessWeek* Web site, 25 Aug. 2003.

252. **"violating the law"** "Answers from Oracle's Larry Ellison," FT.com, 14 Dec. 2001.

252. **"that dominant player"** Ellison, Black Rock conference, 15 July 2003.

CHAPTER 14

255. *Recorder* Scheer, *The Recorder*, 23 Feb. 1996: 2.

258. **Supreme Court explained** *U.S. v. Philadelphia Nat'l Bank*, 374 U.S. 321 (1963).

258. **8 percent** *U.S. v. Von's Grocery Co.*, 384 U.S. 270 (1966).

258. **"always wins"** 384 U.S. at 301.

259. **informal, anecdotal** "Remarks of Charles James," 10 June 2002.

260. **Baxter grounded** White (2006), 2.

262. **"non-operational"** Werden (2003), 253 n. 3.

262. **If entry** Baker and Shapiro (2008), 238.

263. **new competitor *could*** Baker (2003b), 196–98, 200.

264. **price increases** Werden and Froeb (1998); Baker and Shapiro (2008), 253–255.

264. **Baker replied** Baker (2003c).

264. **greater receptiveness** Kolasky and Dick (2003), 225.

265. **overstated** Baker and Shapiro (2008), 256; Kaplow and Shapiro (2007), 1155.

265. **"innovation markets"** Gilbert and Sunshine (1995).

265. **conservatives dismissed** Carlton, Testimony before FTC, 25 Oct. 1995.

265. **case-by-case** Katz and Shelanski (2007).

266. **"storytelling"** Kolasky and Dick (2003), 324.

269. **book title by book title** Morris, *American Lawyer* (Sept. 1996): 78.

269. **"treatise on torts"** Morris (2001), 78.

269. **"competing seedlings"** Ibid., 81.

269. **librarians publicly criticized** *Connecticut Law Tribune*, 4 Mar. 1996: 1.

269. **Arthur argued** Arthur (1990), 92.

CHAPTER 15

271. **enjoin LexisNexis** *West Publishing Co. v. Mead Data Central, Inc.*, 799 F. 2d 1219, 1227 (8th Cir. 1986), cert. denied, 479 U.S. 1070 (1987).

272. **hearing was convened** Hearings on H. R. 4426, 102nd Cong., 2nd Sess. 79 (1992).

272. **"BFD"** Morris, *American Lawyer* (Sept. 1996): 80.

273. **"overjoyed"** Morris (2001), 74.

274. **Congress rejected** Flynn and Bush (2003), 758.

274. **"knuckling under"** 119 Cong. Rec. S24598.

275. **The opinion** 56 F. 3d 1448 (D.C. Cir. 1995).

276. **he talked** All quotes from Transcript, 30 Sept. 1996.

277. **"with a smirk"** *Recorder*, 1 Oct. 1996: 1, 8.

278. **his opinion** 949 F. Supp. 907, 921, 922, 924.

279. **taken by surprise** All quotes from Transcript, 6 Feb. 1997.

280. **CNN released** Jackson, CNN Web site, 11 Apr. 1997.

280. *Time* **magazine followed** Novak and Weisskopf, *Time* Web site, 21 Apr. 1997.
280. *ABA Journal* Hansen, *ABA Journal* 83 (June 1997): 36.
280. **no questions** Hearings, 105th Cong., 1st Sess., 29 Apr. 1997.
281. **Robert Bork** Bork (1978), 221.
281. **teaches otherwise** Baker and Shapiro (2008), 253.
282. **fewer pages** Ryan, *The Bottom Line: Managing Library Finances* 14:1 (2001): 6–11.
282. **rate of inflation** *Legal Reference Services Quarterly* 17:1 (1 Jan. 1999): 13–22.
282. **"value added"** *San Francisco Daily Journal*, 21 Feb. 2002: 12.
282. *National Law Journal* McCollam, 25:43 (14 July 2003): S1.

CHAPTER 16

285. **Oracle's own bid data** Internal Oracle e-mail, Wohl to Ellison, 10 June 2003.
285. **after reflecting** *Financial Times*, 18 Dec. 2001.
286. *Daily Deal* Meyer, 10 July 2003.
286. **"going to deteriorate"** Black Rock Transcript, 15 July 2003.
286. **"all recognize"** Internal Oracle e-mail, Eklund, 16 June 2003.
287. **"wounded PSFT"** O'Neill e-mail.
287. **"hostage taking"** Jeff Mathews of RAM Partners.
287. **"all the disadvantages"** "The World's Most Competitive Man," CBS News Web site, 25 Feb. 2004.
290. **grandiose promises** Wilson (1986), 11.
290. **$4 million** Oracle company Web site, "1980s," May 2007: 28.
291. **"most important company"** CBS News Web site, 25 Feb. 2004.
291. **Valley lore** Wilson, *Forbes* Web site, 2 Apr. 2001.
291. **raise a football field** *San Francisco Chronicle*, 27 Mar. 2001: A1.
292. **"significant functional obsolescence"** Ibid.
292. **cutting six positions** Flinn, *Bloomberg*, 4 Apr. 2008.
292. **"unreasonably discriminatory"** Geralds Vnunet Web site, 15 Jun. 2001.
292. **share the limelight** Simmers, *Oakland Tribune*, 27 July 2003; Southwick (2003), 1, 7, 8.
293. **By one account** Southwick (2003), 16.
294. **they wanted to** Conway Oral History, 14. Computerworld Honors Program. Online.
295. **"launch on them"** *Wall Street Journal*, 9 June 2003: A1.
295. **"bullshit bid" etc.** Oracle presentation 16 June 2003; *San Francisco Chronicle* ("on hold"): A1, 10 June 2003; *Wall Street Journal* ("their heads"), 16 June 2003: B1.
296. **"bad behavior"** Pelline, *CNET*, 13 Dec. 2004.
296. **"going to happen"** *Wall Street Journal*, 11 Jun. 2003: B6.
296. **"and shoot it"** Pelline, *CNET*, 13 Dec. 2004.
297. **"Same playbook"** *Wall Street Journal*, 26 June 2003: B1.
298. **120 of them** Seiberg, *Daily Deal*, 11 Feb. 2004.
298. *Chronicle* **reported** *San Francisco Chronicle*, 20 June 2003: B1.

CHAPTER 17

302. **Nine resigned** Conway e-mail, 12 June 2003.

304. **one economist explained** Willig, "Unilateral Effects Analysis and Litigation Workshop," Federal Trade Commission, 12 Feb. 2008: 34.

306. **"final price"** *Wall Street Journal*, 5 Feb. 2004: A3.

306. **pressure on PeopleSoft** *Wall Street Journal*, 10 Feb. 2004.

306. **"stunned"** *Wall Street Journal*, 20 Feb. 2004: A12.

306. ***Journal* wrote** 23 Feb. 2004: A16.

306. **"only hope"** Vise, *Washington Post*, 24 Feb. 2004.

308. **"personal liberty"** Chorney, *The Recorder*, 31 Aug. 2004.

308. **"erratic"** *Recorder*, 21 Apr. 1998: 12.

308. **most reversed** *Recorder*, 16 Apr. 2001: 1.

308. **"cronyism"** *Reilly v. Hearst Corp.*, 107 F. Supp. 2d 1192, 1211 (N. D. Cal. 2000).

308. **"ask questions"** *Recorder*, 31 Aug. 2004.

308. **rebuffing Klein** "Walker refuses . . ." Business Wire, 15 Aug. 2000.

309. **"severe penalty"** PeopleSoft—planet Web site, posted 29 Sept. 2004. Statement at *Wall Street Journal*'s D Conference.

311. **"informant information"** *United States v. Oracle*, Transcript, 19 Mar. 2004: 16–17.

312. **Walker quotes** Transcript, 16 Apr. 2004: 42 ("national security case"); 5 ("legitimate interests"); 6 ("confidential information").

312. **"can be overridden"** *Foltz v. State Farm Ins.*, 331 F. 3d 1122, 1135 (9th Cir. 2003).

313. **Oracle trumpeted** Seiberg, *Daily Deal*, 23 Apr. 2004.

315. **government lawyers demanded** *United States v. Oracle*, Transcript, 10 Mar. 2004: 44–49.

315. **two economists asked** Katz and Shelanski (2007), n. 90.

315. **"no end"** *Daily Deal*, 23 Apr. 2004.

315. **convinced many observers** Flynn, *New York Times*, 15 May 2004.

316. **read the headline** *Wall Street Journal*, 7 June 2004: B1.

316. **"come down"** Dunlap, *InformationWeek*, 29 June 2004.

317. **judge interrupted** *United States v. Oracle*, Quotes from Transcript, 7 June 2004.

318. **Walker challenged** *United States v. Oracle*, Transcript, 7 June 2004.

319. **Scott announced** *United States v. Oracle*, Transcript, 8 June 2004.

320. **"In what way . . ."** *United States v. Oracle*, Transcript, 9 June 2004.

321. **asked rhetorically** *United States v. Oracle*, Transcript, 10 June 2004.

321. **"Walker's threats"** Boslet, *Wall Street Journal*, 11 June 2004.

321. **"chilling effect"** Liedtke, *USA Today*, 10 June 2004.

322. **"Scared the hell"** *United States v. Oracle*, Transcript, 10 June 2004.

CHAPTER 18

325. **next day's lead** *San Francisco Chronicle*, 19 June 2004: C1.

327. **lawyer promised** *United States v. Oracle*, Transcript, 10 Mar. 2004: 44.

329. **Ellison's cross-examination** *United States v. Oracle*, Transcript, 30 June 2004.

331. **"gave you his answer"** *United States v. Oracle*, Transcript, 20 July 2004: 4644.

331. **"elephant"** *San Francisco Chronicle*, 28 July 2004: C1.

332. **164-page opinion** *United States v. Oracle*, 331 F. Supp. 2d 198 (N. D. Cal. 2004).

333. **"dominant position"** 331 F. Supp. at 1118, 1123.

333. **SAP already bid** 331 F. Supp. at 1168.

333. **direct evidence** 331 F. Supp. at 1168–70.

333. **Economists blasted** *Antitrust* 19:2 (Spring 2005): 15.

334. **"incredible"** 331 F. Supp. at 1144.

334. **"discounted"** 331 F. Supp. at 1151.

334. **"bad day"** Dunlap, *InformationWeek*, 28 June 2004.

334. **difficult financial shape** Minnesota Public Radio Web site, 22 Sept. 2003.

334. **first customer** Barret, *Forbes* Web site, 10 Mar. 2008.

334. **first large enterprise** Weier, *InformationWeek* Web site, 5 May 2008.

335. **"largely unhelpful"** 331 F. Supp. 2d at 1130–31.

335. *could* 331 F. Supp. 2d at 1131, 1156.

335. **Phillips report** "PeopleSoft," *Morgan Stanley Research Note*, 26 Apr. 2002: 3.

336. **accurately reflected** *United States v. Oracle*, Transcript, 18 June 2004.

336. **"for spice"** 331 F. Supp. 2d at 1125.

336. **Emerson Electric** *United States v. Oracle*, Transcript, 14 June 2004.

337. **Verizon vice president** *United States v. Oracle*, Transcript, 9 June 2004: 609–13.

337. **rejected Professor Elzinga's** 331 F. Supp. 2d at 1158 ("sketchy"), 1173 ("inarticulable").

337. **rejected McAfee's** 331 F. Supp. 2d at 1168–69.

337. **SAP's discount forms** *United States v. Oracle*, Transcript, 23 June 2004.

338. **"policy smackdown"** *Wall Street Journal*, 13 Sept. 2004: A20.

338. **"in droves"** *Wall Street Journal*, 4 Oct. 2004: A3.

338. **rest of the world** Cooper, CNET Web site, 1 Oct. 2004.

339. **five thousand** Lai, *East Bay Business Times*, 14 Jan. 2005.

339. **"transitional status"** Lai, *East Bay Business Times*, 26 Jan. 2005.

339. **Duffield fund** *East Bay Times*, 1 Apr. 2005, 12 August 2005; Cassidy, *San Jose Mercury News*, 1 Nov. 2005; AMR Research Web site, 14 Feb. 2007.

340. **Ellison was motivated** Babcock, *InformationWeek*, 3 Oct. 2005.

341. **observed** *CIO* Wailgum, *CIO*, 12 Mar. 2008.

341. **15 to 20 percent** Whiting, *ChannelWeb*, 25 Jun. 2008.

341. **"starting to leverage"** *InformationWeek*, 26 June 2008.

341. **headline** McLure, *Legal Times*, 12 Jan. 2007.

CHAPTER 19

343. **Lawmakers envisioned** Landler, *New York Times*, 19 June 1997.

344. **"What you'll see"** Landler, *New York Times*, 3 Apr. 1996.

344. **"logical to think"** Ibid.

344. **"effort to sway"** *New York Times*, 6 June 1997.

344. **"unthinkable"** Hundt speech, FTC Web site, 19 June 1997.

345. **McCain quote** Mills, *Washington Post*, 12 May 1998: A1.

346. **Whitacre told** Ibid.

346. **$1 billion** Barbach, "AT&T Wireless–Cingular: Revealing a Lack of Regulatory Progress," *Pipeline*, May 2004.

346. **every month** Goldman, "Voices for Choices Wins Time," ISP-Planet, 13 June 2003.

346. **"As long as"** Hoexter, Press Release, Michigan Alliance for Competitive Telecommunications, 22 June 2002.

346. **"little guy"** Cauley, *USA Today*, 6 Mar. 2005.

347. **"telephone monopolies"** Polyakova, *Communications Daily*, 13 Oct. 2004.

347. **"bit of irony"** McCormack, Bear Stearns Equity Research, June 2005.

347. *Journal* **greeted** *Wall Street Journal*, "Antitrust Wars," 11 May 2005.

348. **"SME"** McCormack, Bear Stearns Equity Research, June 2005.

348. **"better"** UBS Investment Research, 3 Jan. 2006.

350. **repeatedly represented** King, *Kansas City Star*, 1 Feb. 2005.

350. **Division waited** Pappalardo, *Network World*, 1 Aug. 2005.

350. **Reuters reported** Kaplan, Reuters, 30 Sept. 2005.

351. *Journal* **ran** *Wall Street Journal*, "Antitrust Busters," 26 Oct. 2005.

352. *Journal* **later revealed** *Wall Street Journal*, 14 Feb. 2006.

352. **Division's press release** Department of Justice, 27 Oct. 2005.

352. **hundreds of lawyers** Stahler, *Crain's Chicago Business*, 16 May 2005 and 25 May 2005; McLure, *Legal Times*, 31 Oct. 2005.

352. **second editorial** *Wall Street Journal*, "Antitrust Anxiety," 16 Dec. 2005.

354. **"so inconsonant"** 56 F. 3d at 1461–62.

355. **"for free"** O'Connell, *BusinessWeek* Web site, 7 Nov. 2005.

355. **conciliatory tones** Kapustka, *InformationWeek*, 5 Jan. 2006.

355. **"extort fees"** Mohammed, *Washington Post*, 4 Nov. 2005.

356. **"heavy-handed"** Luening, CNET, 2 Jan. 2002; Lohr, *New York Times*, 9 Feb. 1998.

356. **"give back"** Transcript, Bernstein Strategic Decisions Conference, 31 May 2006.

357. **first argument quotes** *U.S. v. SBC and Verizon*, Transcript, 12 July 2006.

358. **"antitrust world"** Garam Falvi, *Legal Times*, 24 July 2006.

358. **"giving the parties"** *U.S. v. SBC and Verizon*, Transcript, 25 July 2006.

359. **UBS report** *Tell Me Daily*, UBS Research, 29 Sept. 2006: 2.

359. **Division's press release** Department of Justice, 11 Oct. 2006.

359. **"lights off"** Benton, *New York Times*, 12 Oct. 2006.

360. *Times* **editorial** *New York Times*, "Growing Free-for-All," 13 Oct. 2006.

360. **final argument quotes** *U.S. v. SBC and Verizon*, Transcript, 30 Nov. 2006.

363. **Sullivan opinion** *U.S. v. SBC and Verizon*, 489 F. Supp. 2d 1 (D. D.C. 2007).

364. **"with a whimper"** Sokler, Mintz Levine Communications Advisory, 9 Apr. 2007.

364. **high-speed Internet facts** InternetforEveryone.org Web site.

CONCLUSION

367. **oral argument quotes** *Leegin v. Kay's Kloset*, Transcript, 26 Mar. 2007.

367. **announced its decision** *Leegin v. Kay's Kloset*,—U. S.—, 127 S. Ct. 2705 (2007).

367. **series of decisions** Labaton, *New York Times*, 28 June 2007.

368. **front-page article** Pereiro, *Wall Street Journal*, 18 Aug. 2008.

368. **Apple's attention** "Microsoft Gurus . . ." MSN Web site, 5 Sept. 2008.

369. **"open for discussion"** Applebaum et al. (1981), 169.

369. **"tiebreakers"** Bork (1978), 133.

370. **Court reversed** *California Dental Ass'n v. FTC*, 526 U.S. 756 (1999).

370. **Two other** Bell Atlantic v. Twombly,—U.S.—, 127 S. Ct. 1995 (2007); *Credit Suisse v. Billing,*—U. S.—, 127 S. Ct. 2383 (2007).

372. **"not the final word"** Mack, *Washington Post*, 10 May 2008: B5.

372. **"Most hospital CEOs"** Francis, *Washington Post*, 12 May 2008: B2.

373. **appellate court** *FTC v. Whole Foods*, Slip Opinion (July 29, 2008).

373. **"enforcement void"** "Statement of Commission Harbour, Leibowitz and Rosch," FTC Web site, 8 Sept. 2008.

Selected Bibliography

Applebaum, Harvey M., et al. "Interview with William F. Baxter, Assistant Attorney General, Antitrust Division." *Antitrust Law Journal* 50 (1981): 151–71.

Areeda, Phillip. "Introduction to Antitrust Economics." *Antitrust Law Journal* 52 (1983): 523–37.

Arthur, W. Brian. "Positive Feedbacks in the Economy." *Scientific American* (Feb. 1990): 92–99.

Auletta, Ken. *World War 3.0*. New York: Random House, 2001.

Baily, Martin H., Douglas W. Elmendorf, and Robert E. L. Litan. "The Great Credit Squeeze: How It Happened, How to Prevent Another." Brookings Institution, 2008.

Baker, Jonathan B. "A Preface to Post-Chicago Antitrust." In *Post-Chicago Developments in Antitrust Law*, ed. Antonio Cucinotta, Robert Pardolesi, and Roger Van den Bergh, 60–75. Northampton, Mass.: Edward Elgar, 2002.

———. "Beyond Schumpeter v. Arrow: How Antitrust Fosters Innovation." *Antitrust Law Journal* 74 (2007): 575–602.

———. "The Case for Antitrust Enforcement." *Journal of Economic Perspectives* 17:4 (2003a): 27-50.

———. "Competition Policy as a Political Bargain." *Antitrust Law Journal* 73 (2006): 483–530.

———. "Developments in Antitrust Economics." *Journal of Economic Perspectives* 13:1 (1999): 181–94.

———. "Market Concentration in the Antitrust Analysis of Horizontal Mergers." In *Antitrust Law & Economics*, ed. Keith Hylton. (forthcoming, 2009).

———. "Recent Developments in Economics That Challenge Chicago School Views." *Antitrust Law Journal* 58 (1980): 645–55.

———. "Responding to Developments in Economics and the Courts: Entry in the Merger Guidelines." *Antitrust Law Journal* 71 (2003b): 189–206.

———. "Why Did the Antitrust Agencies Embrace Unilateral Effects?" *George Mason Law Review* 12:1 (Fall 2003c): 31–37.

Baker, Jonathan B., and Carl Shapiro. "Reinvigorating Horizontal Merger Enforcement." In

How the Chicago School Overshot the Mark, ed. Robert Pitofsky, 235–88. Oxford: Oxford University Press, 2008.

Bank, David. *Breaking Windows: How Bill Gates Fumbled the Future of Microsoft*. New York: Free Press, 2001.

Barnett, E. William, et al. "Interview with William F. Baxter, Assistant Attorney General, Antitrust Division." *Antitrust Law Journal* 52 (1983): 23–42.

———. "Interview with William F. Baxter, Assistant Attorney General, Antitrust Division." *Antitrust Law Journal* 51 (1982): 23–40.

Baxter, William F. "Antitrust: A Policy in Search of Itself." *Antitrust Law Journal* 54 (1985): 15–20.

———. "Conditions Creating Antitrust Concern with Vertical Integration by Regulated Industries." *Antitrust Law Journal* 52 (1983a): 243–47.

———. "Legal Restrictions on Exploitation of Patent Monopoly: An Economic Analysis." *Yale Law Journal* 76:2 (Dec. 1966): 267–370.

———. "Reflections upon Professor Williamson's Comments." *St. Louis University Law Journal* 27 (1983b): 315–20.

———. "Vertical Practices—Half Slave, Half Free." *Antitrust Law Journal* 52 (1983c): 743–54.

———. "The Viability of Vertical Restraints Doctrine." *California Law Review* 75 (1987): 933–50.

Baxter Antitrust Class Lecture Notes. Stanford Law Review Note Pool, Spring 1974; Fall 1974; Fall 1980.

Bolton, Patrick, Joseph F. Brodley, and Michael H. Riordan. "Predatory Pricing: Strategic Theory and Legal Policy." *Georgetown Law Journal* 88 (2000): 239–330.

Bork, Robert H. *The Antitrust Paradox: A Policy at War with Itself*. New York: Free Press, 1978. New introduction and epilogue, 1993.

———. "The Role of Courts in Applying Economics." *Antitrust Law Journal* 54 (1985): 21–26.

Bowman, Ward S. "The Prerequisites and Effects of Resale Price Maintenance." *University of Chicago Law Review* 22 (1955): 825–43.

Brands, H. W. *The Reckless Decade: America in the 1890s*. Chicago: University of Chicago Press, 2002.

Breyer, Stephen. *Regulation and Its Reform*. Cambridge, Mass.: Harvard University Press, 1982.

———. "The Uneasy Case for Copyright: A Study of Copyright in Books, Photocopies, and Computer Programs." *Harvard Law Review* 84:2 (1970): 283–351.

Bringhurst, Bruce. *Antitrust and the Oil Monopoly: The Standard Oil Cases, 1890–1911*. Westport, Conn.: Greenwood Press, 1979.

Brinkley, Joe, and Steve Lohr. *U.S. v. Microsoft: The Inside Story of the Landmark Case*. New York: McGraw-Hill, 2001.

Burgelman, Robert A. "Fading Memories: A Process Theory of Strategic Business Exit." *Administrative Science Quarterly* 39 (1994): 24–56.

Carlton, Dennis W. "The Lessons from Microsoft." *Business Economics* 36:1 (Jan. 2000), 47–53.

Carlton, Dennis W., and Jeffrey M. Perloff. *Modern Industrial Organization.* Glenview, Ill.: Little, Brown, 1990.

Carlton, Dennis W., and Michael Waldman. "The Strategic Use of Trying to Preserve and Create Market Power in Evolving Industries." *RAND Journal of Economics* 33:2 (Summer 2002): 194–220.

Chernow, Ron. *Titan: The Life of John D. Rockefeller, Sr.* New York: Random House, 1998.

Clark, Jim, with Owen Edwards. *Netscape Time.* New York: St. Martin's Press, 1999.

Computer Science and Telecommunications Board, National Research Council. *Funding a Revolution: Government Support for Computing Research.* Washington, D.C.: National Academy Press, 1999.

Cross, Dennis. "To Doric Simplicity and Back: The Ups and Downs of Vertical Price Restraints." *Antitrust* (Spring 2007): 59–60.

Cusumano, Michael A., and David B. Yoffie. *Competing on Internet Time.* New York: Free Press, 1998.

David, Paul A. "Clio and the Economics of QWERTY." *American Economic Review* 75:2 (1985), 332–37.

Demsetz, Harold. "Two Systems of Belief About Monopoly." In *Industrial Concentration: The New Learning,* ed. Harvey J. Goldschmid, H. Michael Mann, and J. Fred Weston, 164–84. Boston: Little, Brown, 1974.

Dixit, Avinash K., and Barry J. Nalebuff. *Thinking Strategically: The Competitive Edge in Business, Politics, and Everyday Life.* New York: Norton, 1991.

Easterbrook, Frank H. "Ignorance and Antitrust." In *Antitrust, Innovation, and Competitiveness,* ed. Thomas Jorde and David Teece, 119–136. New York: Oxford University Press, 1992.

———. "The Limits of Antitrust." *Texas Law Review* 63:1 (1984a): 1–40.

———. "Predatory Strategies and Counterstrategies." *University of Chicago Law Review* 48 (1981): 203–337.

———. "Vertical Arrangements and the Rule of Reason." *Antitrust Law Journal* 53 (1984b): 135–73.

———. "When Is It Worthwhile to Use Courts to Search for Exclusionary Conduct?" *Columbia Business Law Review* 2 (2003): 345–58.

Farrell, Joseph, and Garth Saloner. "Installed Base and Compatibility: Innovation, Product Preannouncements, and Predation." *American Economic Review* 76:5 (1986): 940–55.

Feinstein, Deborah L. "Recent Trends in U.S. Merger Enforcement: Down But Not Out." *Antitrust* (Spring 2007): 74–81.

Flynn, John J., and Darren Bush. "The Misuse Abuse of the Tunney Act: The Adverse Consequences of the 'Microsoft Fallacies.'" *Loyola University Chicago Law Journal* 34 (2003): 749–814.

Fox, Eleanor M. "The Battle for the Soul of Antitrust." *University of California Law Review* 75 (1987): 917–23.

Fox, Eleanor M., and Lawrence A. Sullivan. "Antitrust—Retrospective and Prospective." *New York University Law Review* 62 (1987): 936–88.

Freiberger, Paul, and Michael Swaine. *Fire in the Valley: The Making of the Personal Computer,* 2d ed. New York: McGraw-Hill, 1984.

Gilbert, Richard J., and Steven C. Sunshine. "Incorporating Dynamic Efficiency Concerns in Merger Analysis: The Use of Innovation Markets." *Antitrust Law Journal* 63 (1995): 509–601.

Halloran, Michael J. *Venture Capital & Public Offering Negotiation.* New York: Aspen (update 2008).

Heilemann, John. *Pride Before the Fall.* New York: HarperCollins, 2001.

Heyer, Kenneth. "Welfare Standards and Merger Analysis: Why Not the Best." *Competition Policy International* 2:2 (Autumn 2006).

Hofstadter, Richard. *The Age of Reform: From Bryan to F.D.R.* New York: Alfred A. Knopf, 1966.

Hovenkamp, Herbert. *The Antitrust Enterprise: Principle and Execution.* Cambridge, Mass.: Harvard University Press, 2005.

———. "Post-Chicago Antitrust: A Review and Critique." *Columbia Business Law Review* 2 (2001): 257–337.

———. "The Reckoning of Post-Chicago Antitrust." In *Post-Chicago Developments in Antitrust Law,* ed. Antonio Cucinotta, Robert Pardolesi, and Roger Van den Bergh, 1–33. Northampton, Mass.: Edward Elgar, 2002.

Jenks, Jeremiah Whipple, and Walter E. Clark. *The Trust Problem,* rev. ed. New York: Doubleday, 1917.

Jones, Elliot. *The Trust Problem in the United States.* New York: Macmillan, 1922.

Kaplow, Louis, and Carl Shapiro. "Antitrust." In *Handbook of Law and Economics,* Vol. 2, ed. A. Mitchell Polinsky and Steven Shavell, 1073–226. Amsterdam: North Holland (2007).

Katz, Michael L., and Carl Shapiro. "Network Externalities, Competition and Compatibility." *American Economic Review* 75:3 (1985): 424–40.

Katz, Michael, and Howard Shelanski. "Mergers and Innovation." *Antitrust Law Journal* 74 (2007).

———. "'Schumpeterian' Competition and Antitrust Policy in High Tech Markets." *Competition* 14:2 (2005): 47–60.

Kolasky, William J., and Andrew R. Dick. "The Merger Guidelines and the Integration of Efficiencies into Antitrust Review of Horizontal Mergers." *Antitrust Law Journal* 71 (2003): 207–51.

Koracic, William E., and Carl Shapiro. "Antitrust Policy: A Century of Economic and Legal Thinking." *Journal of Economic Perspectives* 14:1 (2000): 43–60.

Krattenmaker, Thomas, and Steven Salop. "Anticompetitive Exclusion: Raising Rivals' Costs to Achieve Power over Price." *Yale Law Review* 96:2 (Dec. 1986): 209–93.

Lande, Robert H. "Chicago's False Foundation: Wealth Transfer (Not Just Efficiency) Should Guide Antitrust." *Antitrust Law Journal* 58 (1989): 631–59.

———. "Proving the Obvious: The Antitrust Laws Were Passed to Protect Consumers (Not Just to Increase Efficiency)." *Hastings Law Journal* 50 (1999): 959–68.

———. "Wealth Transfers as the Original and Primary Concern of Antitrust: The Efficiency Interpretation Challenged." *Hastings Law Journal* 65 (1982): 65–150.

Lécuyer, Christophe. *Making Silicon Valley: Innovation and the Growth of High Tech, 1930–1970.* Cambridge, Mass.: MIT Press, 2007.

Lessig, Lawrence. *The Future of Ideas.* New York: Random House, 2001.

Leuchtenburg, William E. *Franklin D. Roosevelt and the New Order.* New York: Harper & Row, 1963.

Lewis, Michael. *The New New Thing.* New York: Norton, 2000.

Liebowitz, S. J., and Stephen Margolis. "The Fable of the Keys." *Journal of Law & Economics* 30:1 (1990): 1–26.

Link, Arthur S. *Woodrow Wilson and the Progressive Era.* New York: Harper & Row, 1954.

Linzmayer, Owen W. *Apple Confidential 2.0: The Definitive History of the World's Most Colorful Company.* San Francisco: No Starch Press, 2004.

Lloyd, Caro. *Henry Demarest Lloyd, 1847–1903: A Biography.* New York: Knickerbocker Press, 1912.

Lloyd, Henry Demarest. *Wealth Against Commonwealth.* New York: Harper, 1894.

Manes, Stephen, and Paul Andrews. *Gates: How Microsoft's Mogul Reinvented an Industry—and Made Himself the Richest Man in America.* New York: Touchstone, 1993.

McGee, John S. "Commentary." In *Industrial Concentration: The New Learning,* ed. Harvey J. Goldschmid, H. Michael Mann, and J. Fred Weston, 101–4. Boston: Little, Brown, 1974.

Melamed, Douglas A., and Daniel L. Rubinfeld. "*U.S. v. Microsoft*: Lessons Learned and Issues Raised." In *Antitrust Stories,* ed. Eleanor Fox and Daniel M. Crane, 287–310. Foundation Press, 2007.

Miller, Nathan. *Theodore Roosevelt: A Life.* New York: William Morrow, 1992.

Millstein, Ira M. "Economics: Use and Misuse." *Antitrust Law Journal* 52 (1983): 539–50.

Morris, Charles R., and Charles A. Ferguson. "How Architecture Wins Technology Wars." *Harvard Business Review* (Mar.–Apr. 1993): 86–96.

Morris, Edmund. *Theodore Rex.* New York: Random House, 2001.

National Research Council of the National Academies. *Innovation in Information Technology.* Washington, D.C.: National Academies Press, 2003.

Panel Discussion: "Counseling Your Client on Horizontal and Vertical Restraints." *Antitrust Law Journal* 55 (1986): 293–318.

Pitofsky, Robert. "Are Retailers Who Offer Discounts Really 'Knaves'?: The Coming Challenge to the *Dr. Miles* Rule." *Antitrust* (Spring 2007): 61–65.

———. "In Defense of Discounters: The No-Frills Case for a *Per Se* Rule Against Vertical Discounting." *Georgetown Law Journal* 71 (1983): 1487–95.

———. "The Political Content of Antitrust." *University of Pennsylvania Law Review* 127 (1979): 1051–75.

Posner, Richard A. "Antitrust in the New Economy." *Antitrust Law Journal* 68 (2001a): 925–43.

———. *Antitrust Law,* 2d ed. Chicago: University of Chicago Press, 2001b.

———. "The Next Step in Antitrust Treatment of Restricted Distribution: Per Se Legality." *University of Chicago Law Review* 48 (1981): 6–26.

President's Information Technology Advisory Committee. *Computational Science: Ensuring America's Competitiveness—Report to the President,* 2005.

Roosevelt, Theodore. *An Autobiography.* New York: Charles Scribner's Sons, 1913.

Rowe, Frederick M. "Antitrust in Transition: A Policy in Search of Itself." *Antitrust Law Journal* 54 (1985): 5–14.

———. "The Decline of Antitrust and the Delusions of Models." *Georgetown Law Journal* 72 (1984): 1511–70.

Rubinfeld, Daniel L. "Antitrust Enforcement in Dynamic Network Industries." *Antitrust Bulletin* (Fall/Winter 1998): 849–82.

———. "Maintenance of Monopoly: U.S. v. Microsoft (2001)." In *The Antitrust Revolution: Economics, Competition, and Policy*, ed. John F. Kwoka, Jr., and Lawrence J. White, 476–501. New York: Oxford University Press (2004).

Rubinfeld, Daniel L., and John Hoven. "Innovation and Antitrust Enforcement." In *Dynamic Competition and Public Policy: Technology, Innovation, and Antitrust Issues*, ed. Jerry Ellig, 65–94. Cambridge, UK, and New York: Cambridge University Press, 2001.

Salop, Steven C. "Question: What Is the Real and Proper Antitrust Welfare Standard?" Statement to the Antitrust Modernization Commission, Nov. 4, 2005.

Saxenian, AnnaLee. *The New Argonauts: Regional Advantage in a Global Economy*. Cambridge, Mass.: Harvard University Press, 2006.

———. *Regional Advantage: Culture and Competition in Silicon Valley and Route 128*. Cambridge, Mass.: Harvard University Press, 1994.

Scherer, F. M. "Conservative Economics and Antitrust." In *How the Chicago School Overshot the Mark*, ed. Robert Pitofsky, 30–39. Oxford, UK: Oxford University Press, 2008a.

———. "The Economics of Vertical Restraints." *Antitrust Law Journal* 52 (1983): 687–718.

———. "The Political Economy of Patent Policy Reform in the United States." Faculty Research Paper Working Series, Kennedy School of Government, RWP07-042 (2007) forthcoming in *Journal of Telecommunications and High Technology Law*.

———. "Technological Innovation and Monopolization." In *Issues in Competition Law and Policy*, ed. W. Dale Collins, 1033–68. Chicago: American Bar Association, 2008b.

Schmalensee, Richard. "Bill Baxter in the Antitrust Arena: An Economist's Appreciation." *Stanford Law Review* 51:5 (1999): 1317–32.

Schumpeter, Joseph A. *Capitalism, Socialism and Democracy*. New York: Harper & Bros., 1942.

———. *The Theory of Economic Development*. Cambridge, Mass.: Harvard University Press, 1934.

Shapiro, Carl, and Hal R. Varian. *Information Rules: A Strategic Guide to the Network Economy*. Boston: Harvard Business School Press, 1999.

Singer, Jonathan W. *Broken Trusts: The Texas Attorney General Versus the Oil Industry, 1889–1909*. College Station: Texas A & M Press, 2002.

Southwick, Karen. *Everyone Else Must Fail*. New York: Crown, 2003.

Steuer, Richard M. "The Turning Points in Distribution Law." *Antitrust Bulletin* 35:2 (1990): 467–536.

Stigler, George. "A Theory of Oligopoly." *Journal of Political Economy* 72 (1964): 44–61.

Tarbell, Ida M. *The History of the Standard Oil Company*. New York: McClure, 1904.

———. *The History of the Standard Oil Company: A Briefer Version*, ed. David M. Chalmers. New York: Dover, 2003.

Taylor, Suzanne, and Kathy Schroeder. *Inside Intuit*. Boston: Harvard Business School Press, 2003.

Telser, Lester. "Why Should Manufacturers Want Fair Trade?" *Journal of Law & Economics* 3 (Oct. 1960): 86–105.

Thorelli, Hans B. *The Federal Antitrust Policy*. Baltimore: Johns Hopkins Press, 1955.

Tindall, George Brown. *America: A Narrative History*. New York: Norton, 1984.

United States Senate. Committee on the Judiciary. Confirmation Hearing of William F. Baxter, 19 Mar. 1981. 97th Cong., 1st Sess. Washington, D.C.: Government Printing Office, 1981.

Wallace, James, and Jim Erickson. *Hard Drive: Bill Gates and the Making of the Microsoft Empire*. New York: Wiley, 1992.

Waller, Spencer Weber. "The Antitrust Legacy of Thurman Arnold." *St. Johns Law Review* 78 (2004): 569–613.

Werden, Gregory J. "The 1982 Merger Guidelines and the Ascent of the Hypothetical Monopolist Paradigm." *Antitrust Law Journal* 71 (2003): 253–75.

Werden, Gregory J., and Luke M. Froeb. "The Entry-Inducing Effects of Horizontal Mergers: An Exploratory Analysis." *Journal of Industrial Economics* 4 (Dec. 1998): 525–43.

Whinston, Michael D. *Lectures on Antitrust Economics*. London: MIT Press, 2006.

White, Lawrence J. "Horizontal Merger Antitrust Enforcement: Some Historical Perspectives, Some Current Observations." Presentation to Antitrust Modernization Commission, 10 Mar. 2006.

Williamson, James R. *Federal Antitrust Policy During the Kennedy-Johnson Years*. Westport, Conn.: Greenwood Press, 1994.

Williamson, Oliver E. "Antitrust Enforcement: Where It's Been, Where It's Going." *St. Louis University Law Journal* 27 (1983): 289–314.

———. "Economics and Antitrust Enforcement: Transition Years." *Antitrust* (Spring 2003): 61–65.

———. "Economies as an Antitrust Defense: The Welfare Tradeoffs." *American Economic Review* 58 (1968): 18.

———. "Economies as an Antitrust Defense Revisited." *University of Pennsylvania Law Review* 125.4 (1977): 699–736.

———. "The Merger Guidelines of the U.S. Department of Justice—In Perspective." United States Department of Justice Antitrust Division: Twentieth Anniversary of the 1982 Merger Guidelines, 6 June 2002.

Wilson, John W. *The New Venturers: Inside the High-Stakes World of Venture Capital*. Menlo Park, Calif.: Addison-Wesley, 1986.

Wilson, Mike. *The Difference Between God and Larry Ellison*. New York: Morrow, 1997.

Winerman, Marc. "The Origins of the FTC: Concentration, Cooperation, Control, and Competition." *Antitrust Law Journal* 71 (2003): 1–97.

Zachary, G. Pascal. *Showstopper: Breakneck Race to Create Windows NT and the Next Generation at Microsoft*. New York: Free Press, 1994.

Zittrain, Jonathan. *The Future of the Internet and How to Stop It*. New Haven, Conn.: Yale University Press, 2008.

Index